BRING ON THE EMPTY HORSES

Also by the Author

ONCE OVER LIGHTLY
THE MOON'S A BALLOON

David Niven

BRING ON
THE EMPTY HORSES

G. P. Putnam's Sons
New York

*With love to friends and acquaintances
who do not happen to be mentioned in these pages,
but who know, of course, that they, too,
are part of them*

Thirteenth Impression

COPYRIGHT © 1975 BY DAVID NIVEN

Niven, David, 1910–
    Bring on the empty horses.

    Includes index.
    1. Niven, David, 1910–   2. Moving picture actors and actresses—United States—Correspondence, reminiscences, etc.
3. Moving-picture industry—United States—Hollywood, Calif.
    I. Title.
PN2598.N5A29   791.43′028′0924 [B]   75-17524
ISBN 0-399-11542-0

PRINTED IN THE UNITED STATES OF AMERICA

Contents

Illustrations follow page 226

Introduction

*I*F at this moment you are in a bookstore leafing through these early pages and wondering if the whole thing is worth a sizable expenditure, may I suggest that you keep your back toward the salesman and read on because, coming up, is a brief description of what this book is all about.

To be an actor, it is essential to be an egomaniac; otherwise it just doesn't work. The supreme act of egomania is to sit down and write 130,000 words about oneself. That I have already done in *The Moon's a Balloon,* so you will be relieved to learn that this is *not* a book about David Niven . . . at least, it is not *meant* to be. Unfortunately, the actor's urge to take up a firm position at center stage is a strong one, and if, despite valiant efforts to remain in the wings, I have, on occasion, eased myself forward, I apologize.

This book is about Hollywood; not the whole mishmash, because that has been done a hundred times, and anyway, the canvas is too huge and quite beyond my mini-brushwork, so I have attempted to splash a little color on just one corner—the twenty-five years between 1935 and 1960.

I was there from "extra" on down (or up—it's for you to decide), and I was part of it, but I have made little effort to keep things in chronological order; provided the people and events coincided with the allotted time span, I have just described them as I saw them.

The period covered in this book is often hailed as the

Great Days of Hollywood. Perhaps they were, perhaps not, but, with those days gone forever, it is certainly not my intention to try to prove that they were superior to the Hollywood of today.

If now Hollywood is booming and full of talent, but controlled by conglomerates, lawyers, bankers, computers, and a handful of agents, then it was booming, filled with great personalities, but controlled by arrogant moguls, overcrowded and smelling of despotism, nepotism, and blacklists.

Hollywood was Lotus Land between 1935 and 1960 and bore little relationship to the rest of the world, but it was vastly exciting to be part of a thriving, thrusting "first growth" industry—the greatest form of mass entertainment so far invented—and if exaggeration became the norm, it was hard to recognize the fact, when a "great star" could confidently expect to receive 20,000 letters a week and newspapers all over the world daily set aside several pages for the news and gossip pumped out by the Hollywood self-adulation machines.

There was friendliness, generosity, excitement, sadness, success, despair, and no smog in that long-ago Hollywood, but, "high" on lotus, few of the inhabitants, when World War II shattered the calm, realized that all the old standards would be changed, including the public taste in canned entertainment, and like an out-of-condition heavyweight, Hollywood was ill prepared to cope with the second onslaught which followed quickly on the heels of the first—the sudden advent of television—and by burying its head in its arms and hoping that the enemy would go away, it very nearly went down for the count.

But before Hollywood was forced to shift gears, the moguls controlled the industry they had invented. They were master showmen; 200,000,000 people each week paid to see their product, and among the names in lights above their theaters were Garbo, Gable, Astaire, Cooper, Dietrich, Grant, Chaplin, Bogart, Garland, Hepburn, Flynn, and Davis. It was a fascinating canvas, there will never be another like it, and I hope, by trying to add a little firsthand light and shadow, that I have not spoiled it.

DAVID NIVEN

Kuala Lumpur, Malaysia

BRING ON THE EMPTY HORSES

1
The Playpen

$\mathcal{W}$HEN Gertrude Stein returned to New York after a short sojourn in Hollywood, somebody asked her, "What is it like—out there?"

To which, with little delay and the minimum of careful thought, the sage replied, "There *is* no 'there'—there."

To try to describe to the reader the self-styled "Glamor Capital of the World," it seems best to do so as it appeared just before the outbreak of World War II, because although this book describes some events between 1935 and 1960, that particular upheaval caused the number of inhabitants and automobiles in Los Angeles to double. Up until then there had been plenty of room and fresh air for everyone—one square mile for every four persons, to be precise—very little industry, the worst transportation system of any major U.S. city and clear blue skies without a hint of "smog"—not a word invented by a local wit, but borrowed from the city of Glasgow, where it had justifiably been in constant use since the turn of the century. The reader will find on page 26 a list of the actors and actresses who were that same year under contract to just one of the seven major studios, giving him an idea of the investment the moguls had in talent and the problems they must have had in keeping that talent gainfully employed.

There were four ways to approach Los Angeles from the East Coast: (1) by automobile, which took ten days of fast driving and entailed facing red dirt roads across large tracts of Arizona and New Mexico with no prospect of a motel at the end of the day; (2) by train, leaving New York on the 20th Century Limited at 6 P.M. and standing respectfully aside while famous movie stars smiled for the New York papers as they were escorted by railroad officials along a red carpet to their sleeping compartments; on arrival at Chicago the following morning, the sleeping cars were shunted around the marshaling yards and by noon were tacked on to the rear of the Santa Fe Chief (steam locomotives until 1939), which two days later puffed to a stop at the Union Station, Los Angeles, where the famous movie stars perched on piles of matching baggage and smiled for the Los Angeles papers; (3) by plane, which was not for the fainthearted—a minimum of eighteen cramped and often nerve-racking hours flying in unpressurized and largely unheated twin-engined machines at low altitudes through sometimes appalling weather with the nasty possibility of thudding into either the Allegheny or Rocky mountains at one end of the trip—or (4), as I did it, by sea, an endless voyage of fluctuating comfort in a "dry" ship via Cuba and the Panama Canal.

The whole Los Angeles area was subject to frequent earth tremors, accounted for by an ill-advised proximity to the San Andreas Fault, and on the very day of my arrival in San Pedro I had noted from the deck of SS *President Pierce* that people at dockside beneath a swaying water tower were scurrying about looking nervously upward, wondering which way it would fall. It didn't, as it happened, and the next morning the Chamber of Commerce routinely reassured us that there had been no cause for alarm, but it was perhaps an early warning that I was heading for the breeding ground of stresses and strains.

The "film folk," I discovered, unwound at their favorite playgrounds, the beaches, the mountains at Arrowhead and Big Bear and the desert at Palm Springs—a tiny colony in the middle of Indian-owned land which boasted a main street and two hotels. Santa Anita Racecourse was also very popular with them, and there were various country clubs which dispensed golf, tennis, and an extraordinary degree of segregation. Not one had a black member, and several refused to have Jewish members, prompting the Jewish community to start their own country club and to take in no Gentiles. (They also found oil in satisfactory quantities beneath their fairways, which provided them with a splendid opportunity for nose thumbing.) But the topper was the prestigious Los Angeles Country Club which adamantly refused to have anything whatever to do with *anyone* in the motion-picture industry irrespective of race, creed, or color.

Greater Los Angeles, a city which grew more quickly than the city planners had planned, was not remarkable for its beauty, and it was necessary to disregard the largely temporary appearance of the buildings and the unsightly forests of poles and overhead wiring and concentrate on its truly remarkable setting, in the horseshoe of the San Gabriel Mountains, and on the sunsets.

In Hollywood itself, a place of dusty Baroque charm, one important thoroughfare, La Cienega Boulevard, with great subservience separated on either side of an oil derrick pumping slowly like a praying mantis, and in the scrub-covered hills above, underlining its claim to fame, was a forty-foot-high wooden sign: HOLLYWOODLAND.

Beverly Hills, another suburb, had gone against the haphazard planning of Greater Los Angeles, and when the Rodeo Land and Water Company decided to develop its gently sloping acreage, it had the great good taste and foresight to send for an expert from Kew Gardens, London, who planted a different species of tree for every street, and thereafter a fascinating variety of architecture proliferated beneath maples, magnolias, palms, corals, pines, sycamores, flowering eucalyptus, elms, olives, jacarandas, and oaks. A home in Beverly Hills was the status symbol of success in the prewar motion-picture industry, and the area boasted more private swimming pools and detectives to the square mile than anywhere else in the world.

Everything in Southern California seemed to me to be an enlargement—the bronzed and sun-bleached girls and boys of the beaches were representatives of a master race bred in freedom, sunshine, and clean air—but if the robins were the size of pigeons and the butterflies had the proportions of bombers, the diminutive honey-hunting hummingbirds brought things back into perspective as they whizzed merrily about with their tiny waistcoats of turquoise, vermilion, and gold flashing in the sunlight.

The relaxed villagelike atmosphere of Beverly Hills was very catching, and at the hub of the movie social wheel in the Brown Derby restaurant, the men wore loafers, open-neck shirts, and sports jackets, while the girls, lately liberated by Marlene Dietrich's earthshaking appearance in a man's suit, appeared enthusiastically in slacks, and the waitresses were pretty, would-be actresses in varying stages of disenchantment.

The two tennis clubs most highly regarded by the movie colony were the Beverly Hills and the Westside. The Beverly Hills was by far the better club, and the tennis there was of a much higher standard, with Fred Perry giving points and taking on all comers, but I myself joined the Westside because the committee had wisely decided that beautiful girls were a more digestible ingredient than perspiring professionals, and I will never forget a fancy dress party on the premises at which a young lawyer named Greg Bautzer arrived, on his face a grin so wide he looked like a Hammond organ and on his arm, aged seventeen, ridiculously beautiful, and dressed as Bopeep, Lana Turner.

The home of the phony phone call was the over-chlorinated pool of the Beverly Hills Hotel, around which little-known agents reclined, red-eyed and sweaty, waiting for the loudspeaker to relay messages which they themselves had carefully arranged to be broadcast: "Mr. Bleepburger, please be good enough to call Mr. Darryl Zanuck and Miss Claudette Colbert when you have a moment—urgent."

Written-out gag writers were also present, keeping their ears open for any anecdote that could be twisted to their advantage. "Fun-nee! . . . Fun-nee!" They would nod sagely without a glimmer of a smile, then hasten away to make notes, and all the time the long-legged, high-bosomed, tight-assed girls in swimsuits and high heels hopefully ebbed and flowed around the recumbent denizens of the water hole.

In the late thirties the twice-weekly program presented by most theaters consisted of a newsreel, a cartoon, a short, the second feature, and the first feature. The whole show lasted for a bum-numbing four hours, but as a result, Hollywood was booming, with Metro-Goldwyn-Mayer, one of the seven major studios, boasting that it alone turned out one feature film each week.

Edmund Lowe was famous for many films, but chiefly for the ones he made in partnership with Victor McLaglen, and he and his secretary befriended me soon after my arrival in Hollywood because she decided that I looked like her employer. She had noticed this resemblance because I had been standing outside the main gate of Paramount Studios watching for the stars in their fancy automobiles and had stood out, apparently, from the curious throng of sightseers and out-of-work extras, because in my mouth had been a large cork. This cork and the likeness to Edmund Lowe had so intrigued the lady that she had ordered the chauffeur to return and bring me before her master. Eddie Lowe was a friendly, smiling man; he explained that he was looking for a double and asked me if I would be interested in the job. I thanked him and told him that I was hoping to become an actor myself and did not mention that I thought he looked like my father.

"Why the cork?" he asked. I explained that E. E. Clive, an elderly character actor from the theater who had cornered the film market in butler and judge roles, had lately given me a valuable hint on how to increase the resonance of my voice which he had decided was negligible.

"Get a long cork, my boy," he had ordered, "out of a hock bottle preferably—though I doubt if many people drink hock in this backwater—shove it lengthwise between your teeth, and when you have nothing better to do, repeat the Lord's Prayer half a dozen times. It'll work wonders."

Eddie Lowe taught me much about Hollywood in the weeks to come, tried valiantly but unsuccessfully to arouse the interest of his producer friends in my stagnant career, and personally gave me a conducted tour of one Dream Factory in which he worked. He drove me around the cozily named back lot—a 200-acre spread upon which stood the permanent sets, including New York streets (some smart, some brownstone), New England, French, and Spanish villages, medieval castles, a railroad station complete with rolling stock, lakes with wave-making machines and rustic bridges, a university campus, an airliner, a section of jungle and another of pine forest, a Mississippi steamboat, a three-masted schooner, native canoes, a submarine, a stretch of desert with ruined fort and, in case anything was missing, several acres of carefully dismantled, docketed and stored streets, villages, cathedrals, mud huts, dance halls, skating rinks, ball parks, theaters, vineyards, slums, Southern plantations, and Oriental palaces.

Lowe also took me to the studio's Western ranch: several hundred acres of rolling hills in the San Fernando Valley upon which stood the permanent townships and Indian habitations. Huge tracts of make-believe were necessary to Hollywood because air travel was in its infancy, and if, for instance, a film were set in Venice, canals, churches, palazzi, gondolas, and bridges would soon be conjured up locally. Small wonder, then, that *Gone with the Wind* was filmed in Culver City, *Mutiny on the Bounty* just off Catalina Island, *The Charge of the Light Brigade* in the San Fernando Valley, *The Hunchback of Notre Dame* adjacent to Vine Street, *The Ten Commandments* behind the Western Costume Company, *The Adventures of Marco Polo* a hundred yards from the city gasometer, and Scrooge's breath in *A Christmas Carol* imaginatively photographed in a vast refrigerator near the Ambassador Hotel. Under Eddie Lowe's sponsorship I spent days wandering about the back lot and also the main studio at the heart of the Dream Factory, where for some reason the buildings, parking lot and streets were uniformly white or pale yellow, thus extracting the maximum amount of glare from the cloudless California sky, and where the whole place resembled a mixture of the business district of a thriving small town and the maintenance area of a busy airport. Twenty or thirty towering, hangarlike sound stages clustered together dominated the center, surrounded by the fire department, the generator turbines, the electrical grid, the transportation, construction, carpenter and plasterer departments, camera and electrical stores, wardrobe departments, legal departments, acres of dismantled sets and furniture repositories, tailoring and dressmaking shops, and ever-widening circles of photographic studios, painters' stores, cutting rooms, makeup, hairdressing, and sound departments, projection rooms and theaters, rehearsal halls, orchestra recording theaters, accommodation for set designers and set dressers, the story department, accounting offices, publicity offices, casting offices, fan mail departments, greenhouses, restaurants, a hospital, a gymnasium, and a shoeshine parlor.

An outer circle was rather stately by comparison, and green lawns softened the overpowering glare of the buildings, the barnlike dressing rooms allotted to the swarming extras and the double-decker rabbit warrens which housed the small-part actors. Shaded by trees, connected by paths, and surrounded by flowering shrubs, the bungalow dressing rooms of the stars gave an outward impression of an enclave of peace and tranquillity, but inside, as I was to learn, their walls bore the scars of countless exhibitions of temperament, noisy moments of triumph, and far too many lonely heartbreaks.

I was also to learn that writers got drunk, actors became paranoid, actresses pregnant, and directors uncontrollable. Crises were a way of life in the Dream Factories, but by some extraordinary mixture of efficiency, compromising, exuberance, gambling, shrewdness, experience, strong-arm tactics, psychology, blackmail, kindness, integrity, good luck, and a firm belief that "the show must go on," the pictures came rolling off the end of the production lines.

The star system was the logical answer to the first question asked by investors when it was hinted that they might put money into a film or by moviegoers when it was suggested that they should buy tickets to see the finished product.

"Who's in it?" they would cry.

The studios expended immense sums providing attractive answers to this question by signing established stars to long-term contracts and by discovering and developing young unknowns to take their places later. Once a studio was convinced that performers had "caught on" with the public, great care was taken to maintain their popularity by presenting them only in roles and vehicles in which their special talents and attractions would be displayed to the maximum advantage. On the other hand, when a studio became disenchanted and convinced that a star's popularity was waning, a wide variety of maneuvers were employed to bring their mutual contract to a speedy conclusion. The easiest way, of course, was to mobilize the forces of the actor's own congenital insecurity and give him an inferior part to play. The actor would fluff up his feathers of hurt pride and "refuse to be seen in such a crappy role." The studio then, piously referring to the wording of the long-term agreement between the actor and itself, would suspend the actor's contract for the duration of the picture and instruct its publicity department to leak the news to the world that their hero was a man who refused to honor his obligations. Certainly if an actor refused to perform, he could not expect to be paid, but the monstrous thing was that even if the studio handed an actor a bad part *truly* believing it to be a good one, and he turned it down, not only was he suspended for the duration of the filming of the picture (probably at least four months), but he was also suspended for an additional 50 percent of that time *as a punishment* . . . and the entire period of six months was added to the end of the contract.

Some of us gave twelve or fourteen sulfurous years of our short actor's lives working off a seven-year contract which had originally been conceived in mutual admiration and respect.

After one important actress had the guts to take her case against Warner Brothers all the way to the Supreme Court, a ruling was handed down that no contract with an employee could be extended without the employee's consent, and every contract actor in Hollywood blessed Olivia de Havilland . . . but after her courageous stand, she was seldom offered a role in a Hollywood picture. There were, of course, iniquities on both sides—the moguls were not the only villains and many stars behaved abominably to those who had discovered them and given them the keys to the local kingdom—but the classic use of a contract as a one-sided weapon has to be this:

An actor made a great hit in a Broadway play and celebrated the fact by having a not too well-camouflaged affair with the wife of a Hollywood producer. One day a representative of the producer's studio appeared in the actor's dressing room at the Shubert Theater and offered him a very lucrative seven-year Hollywood contract. The actor, overjoyed, packed up, kissed good-bye to New York audiences, and prepared to become the darling of the world. On arrival in Hollywood he was accorded the "A" treatment, press interviews, publicity layouts, et cetera; then the boom dropped. One day he was called to the makeup department at 6:30 A.M. to be prepared for "photographic tests" at 8 A.M. In a high state of excitement he arose at 4 A.M. and drove to the studio. For seven years, thereafter, he was called six days a week to the studio. If he did not show up, his contract was prolonged, if he did, he was paid handsomely, but he never appeared in front of a camera, and when he was last heard of, though he was a moderately successful and devoutly alcoholic real estate salesman in Canoga Park, his actor's heart had been broken.

Twenty-five years before Hollywood turned its first camera, the writer G. K. Chesterton wrote: "Journalism largely consists of saying, 'Lord Jones Dead!' to people who never knew that Lord Jones was alive." When a film was completed, the next trick was to sell it to the public, and studios allocated millions of dollars to their publicity departments to this end.

In the earliest days circus-type ballyhoo had been employed, and the first recorded press agent, Harry Reichenbach, was in fact lured away to the "moving pictures" from Barnum and Bailey's Circus. The first film he was hired to publicize was *The Return of Tarzan*. His method was effective. He booked into a smart New York hotel just across from the theater where the picture was opening, and a wooden crate was delivered to his room. He then called room service and ordered fifteen pounds of raw meat to be served for his luncheon. The waiter on arrival let out a piercing yell and dropped the meat—wearing a napkin, a large lion was sitting at the table. The waiter sued Reichenbach, and the headlines blossomed.

Francis X. Bushman was nervous about the possible nonrenewal of his contract, so he hired Reichenbach to impress his studio by underlining his popularity.

Reichenbach made Bushman walk with him from Grand Central Station all across New York City to the studio office. By the time he arrived the easily identifiable figure of Bushman was being followed by enthusiastic thousands, traffic was jammed, and the studio heads witnessed a most impressive chaos from their windows. What they had not noticed was Reichenbach walking immediately behind Bushman and dribbling several hundred dollars' worth of nickels and dimes through a hole in his overcoat pocket.

As movies became more sophisticated, the efforts of the publicity departments did not always keep pace, and Gloria Swanson at Paramount was photographed being transported from her dressing room to the sound stage in a sedan chair, but finally highly intelligent men took charge, among them Howard Dietz and Howard Strickling at MGM, Charlie Einfeld at Warner's, Harry Brand at Twentieth Century-Fox, Russell Birdwell with David Selznick, and Jock Lawrence with Samuel Goldwyn.

Publicity departments went through their most difficult period when the studio heads decided that their stars should represent the sum total of all the virtues: They should not drink, swear, or, above all, copulate, and they must be presented to the public as the All-American Boy or the Girl Next Door. Self-inflicted dents in the facades of these paragons had, therefore, to be papered over without delay, so close contacts were forged with the police departments of Los Angeles, Beverly Hills, and the San Fernando Valley, and over the years only a thin trickle of the normal output of nightclub brawls, drunk drivings, scandals, accidents, assaults, attempted suicides, and rapes were reported in the press.

The policy of the studios was to sell their pictures on the names of their stars; they had a vested interest in their performers, and it was to their advantage to build them up. If they did so successfully, their investment was returned with interest, but the contracts of the actors were long, and the work of the publicity departments was painstaking; it was a case of piling up grains of publicity sand until they became mountains, and at the end of it the public might say, "Joe

Doakes beats his wife," or "he drinks his bath water," but it did not ask, *"Who* is Joe Doakes?"

For each production a unit publicist was ordered to remain on the set from the first day of shooting in case anything newsworthy took place; in addition, in the main office, were specialists for the trade papers, general news specialists, magazine specialists, radio specialists, and legmen whose only job was to service the top columnists throughout the country, and all the while the still photographers dutifully pumped out reams of cheesecake, home layouts, and fashion layouts. Publicity campaigns for personalities and individual pictures were not always mounted with the meticulous planning of D day, and occasionally they misfired.

Mae West, at the height of her popularity, started a picture at Paramount titled *It Ain't No Sin.* One hundred and fifty parrots were bought and placed in intensive training to learn to imitate her sexy drawl and to repeat endlessly, "It ain't no sin," the objective being to park the unfortunate birds in theater lobbies and public places to coincide with the openings of the picture.

All went well, and at last the proud trainers reported that their troops were ready for action, but on the same day the Hays Office (charged with keeping clean Hollywood's public image) announced that the title of the picture must be changed because *It Ain't No Sin* was too "suggestive." The parrots were then given a crash course in saying, "I'm no angel." As a result, the theater lobbies and public places reverberated with frustrated whistles and rude noises, and the dejected birds were sent home in disgrace.

Warner's, with misguided zeal, tried to show its top "tough guy," Edward G. Robinson, out of character and persuaded the iron man to be photographed in a bubble bath, but it quickly had to mount a second campaign to nullify the first because whispers became widespread that Eddie Robinson was a "fairy."

Walt Disney's publicity department had its problems too. For the opening of *Pinocchio* in New York it was decided to hire eleven midgets, dress them in *Pinocchio* costumes, and have them gambol about on top of the theater marquee on opening day.

Food and light refreshments, in the shape of a couple of quarts of liquor, were passed up to the marquee top at lunchtime, and by three o'clock in the afternoon a happy crowd in Times Square was treated to the spectacle of eleven stark naked midgets belching loudly and enjoying a crap game on the marquee. Police with ladders removed the players in pillowcases.

Starting with Clara Bow as the "It Girl," individual girls were built up with catchy titles. Jean Harlow became the "Platinum Blonde" and Betty Grable the "Pinup Girl." Finally, lovely redheaded Ann Sheridan at a highly publicized dinner party paid for by the Warner Brothers publicity department was voted by the "Ten Most Eligible Bachelors in Hollywood" as the "Oomph Girl." (The "Most Eligible Bachelors," it is perhaps worth noting, were purely a Warner Brothers selection and included Edmund Goulding, Errol Flynn, myself, and seven others who just "happened" to be making pictures, of all places, at Warner Brothers—a good "double play.")

As press and public became less gullible and more cynical, the publicity gimmicks gave way to publicity junkets, although a few diehards still tried stunts. Jayne Mansfield got a certain amount of mileage out of wearing her pink nightie in her pink heart-shaped bed inside her pink house with her pink Cadillac standing outside, but nobody believed a word of her being shipwrecked on the pink sand of a tropical island in the Caribbean despite the fact that when she showed up, she was covered in pink sand fly bites.

Warner's splurged on a five-day junket to publicize *The Santa Fe Trail*, and reporters eagerly accepted invitations to congregate in Santa Fe, New Mexico. The studio, wary of Errol Flynn's capacity as a roisterer, assigned three men working twenty-four hours a day in shifts to keep him sober and in his own bed, but Errol outdrank and outmaneuvered the three men, and the junket lasted twice as long as planned.

One junket to Mexico City to publicize *Viva Villa* ended with strained relations between the two countries when one of the American stars of the film high up in his hotel room became tired of the noisy adulation of the vast crowd below and decided to dampen down their ardor by relieving himself upon them from the balcony.

A quite extraordinary rapport existed between many stars and the publicity chiefs of their studios—the sort of understanding that soldiers develop for one another when experiences have been shared—and many stars, who had been nursed through marriages, divorces, disasters, scandals, tremendous triumphs, and dreadful deflations, found themselves disproportionately dependent on the counsels of these men. A risky situation, when one considered the number of cupboards that were clanking with skeletons, and, with puritanism rampant across the country, how fatal to careers it could have been if there had been a misuse of the keys, but there was a flamboyant honor among the publicity men, and I never heard of one of them breaking his vows of silence.

Hollywood was a village, and the studios were the families. Everyone knew everyone else's business, weaknesses, kinky leanings, and good points. We were all in the same boat, involved in the early years of a terribly exciting experiment; it was an international community, and there was the maximum of camaraderie and the minimum of bitchiness. At all studios, employees from the most glamorous stars to the lowliest riveters on the heavy construction gangs felt that they were members of a team, gloried in the success of their "hit" pictures, and occasionally indulged in college humor at the expense of their rivals. "In case of an AIR RAID"—they chalked up on the main entrance at Paramount—"go directly to RKO . . . *they* haven't had a hit in years."

Hollywood was hardly a nursery for intellectuals, it was a hotbed of false values, it harbored an unattractive percentage of small-time crooks and con artists, and the chances of being successful there were minimal, but it was fascinating, and IF YOU WERE LUCKY, it was fun. And anyway, it was better than working.

Work consists of whatever a body is *obliged* to do . . .
Play consists of whatever a body is *not* obliged to do.
—MARK TWAIN,
The Adventures of Tom Sawyer

All the major studios kept stables of famous stars. The following is a partial list of those under contract to just one of them from 1939 to 1940:

Metro-Goldwyn-Mayer

June Allyson
Ethel Barrymore
John Barrymore
Lionel Barrymore
Wallace Beery
Ingrid Bergman
Louis Calhern
Joan Crawford
Melvyn Douglas
Marie Dressler
Nelson Eddy
W. C. Fields
Clark Gable
Greta Garbo
Ava Gardner
Judy Garland
Greer Garson
Van Johnson
Gene Kelly
Hedy Lamarr
Charles Laughton
Myrna Loy
Jeannette MacDonald

The Marx Brothers
Robert Montgomery
Frank Morgan
George Murphy
Walter Pidgeon
Eleanor Powell
William Powell
Luise Rainer
Debbie Reynolds
Mickey Rooney
Norma Shearer
James Stewart
Lewis Stone
Elizabeth Taylor
Robert Taylor
Franchot Tone
Spencer Tracy
Sophie Tucker
Lana Turner
Johnny Weissmuller
Esther Williams
Robert Young

2
The King

A blond sunburned fuzz covered his muscular forearms, and his potbelly hung over the top of his pants. Gross, pig-eyed and rude, Chet Liebert was a loathsome human being but he had one great asset—a 45-foot spearfishing boat named *König*. He also had an undeniable talent in his chosen profession, and by the other charter boat skippers working out of Balboa, California, he was grudgingly acknowledged to be the most successful. They had no option but to bestow this accolade on him because every year he caught more broadbill and marlin swordfish than they did.

He kept his huge frame topped up with beer, swore endlessly in a heavy Dutch accent and never by any chance gave credit where credit was due. In an effort to keep deckhands, he paid generously, and this attracted me to him like a moth to a flame. As a $2.50 a day Hollywood extra, who worked only spasmodically, I was in no position to be choosy, so I swallowed the heavy insults and eagerly grabbed the $6 a day he gave me for ten hours of dangerous, dirty, and backbreaking work as a deckhand, spotter, spearman, hauler, gutter, and swabber.

When we were out spearing the giant broadbill swordfish for sale in the market, I took those six bucks, but I also gratefully pocketed the generous tips that were slipped into my hand when *König* was chartered by private individuals in the more exciting and less exacting pursuit with rod and reel of the blue and white marlin.

"Okay, so you're late," said Liebert when I showed up for work at five o'clock one morning. "Get her cleaned up from top to bottom, gut a dozen flying fish, and check two sets of gear and the teasers—make sure the head is spotless too, goddammit, because we've a charter today and the guy is bringing a broad with him. They'll be here at six thirty, and they'll need breakfast, so see that the coffee's ready, and stand by with ham and eggs and all the crap. They're picture people," he added, "so keep your goddamned trap shut about being a lousy phony actor, and get on with the job."

Liebert had a sneaking regard for me, I suspected, because on the very first day I had worked for him, he had slipped on the wet, pitching, gut-slick flooring and had misjudged the gaffing of a 200-pound marlin which an exhausted oil executive had finally brought alongside after a slashing, fighting, plunging three-hour battle. The giant fish with its last gasp had managed to spew out the hook and, with the gaff not planted, was free and sliding down tailfirst into the dark-blue water. In a moment of madness, I had grabbed the disappearing sword with my left hand, removing most of the skin off my palm, and with my right, I had punched the poor brute in its large saucer eyeball, thereby paralyzing it for the split second which Liebert needed to sink the gaff.

Not a word was said, but there had been a tiny flicker of recognition in the puffy red pig eyes of my employer.

By six o'clock on a still and cloudless morning *König*, as ordered, was swabbed down, mopped, dried, and polished, and by the time a large open Packard turned onto the quay, the aroma of good coffee was rising from the galley.

"Okay, now go over and fetch their gear, and don't get movie-struck," he added.

When I approached the Packard, I saw what he meant— the girl was blond and willowy with a fresh, open, fun-loving face. She wore a blue reefer jacket and red slacks, and her yachting cap was tilted at a rather exotic angle over her right eye. I don't think I noticed what the large, muscular man was wearing—he was opening the trunk of the car, and his back was toward me—but when he turned around, smiled, and said, "Hi, it looks like a good day," I nearly fell into the harbor. The man was Clark Gable.

I relieved him of rods, various professional-looking tackle boxes, a large ice bucket, a bottle of scotch, and watched him stride purposefully toward *König;* the blonde held onto his arm.

"Okay, Chet, bait 'em up and let's go," he yelled happily as he leaped aboard.

We had a lucky day. Gable landed two big blue marlin and was once broken after an hour's struggle with a gigantic, leaping mako shark. We also found a school of hungry yellow tail tuna which were striking at everything in sight, and even the blonde amid shrieks of excitement landed a couple of twenty-pounders. She also became rather maudlin toward late afternoon when she hooked a dolphin on a white feather lure and decided that it was the soul of a dead sailor . . . the whiskey bottle was almost empty by then. She pawed Gable a great deal.

The deckhand was working at full throttle throughout the day, and when not perched uncomfortably in the crosstrees of the mast looking for fins or telltale swirls, I was baiting hooks, gutting and cleaning the catch, making sandwiches, or mixing drinks.

When Gable heard my voice, he immediately pinpointed my accent and voiced a mild curiosity as to why I was there and doing what I was doing.

Liebert gave me a long, hard look as I prepared to answer, but suddenly, the first blue marlin hit, and forty-five minutes later, when he triumphantly unstrapped his shoulder harness, Gable's curiosity had vanished.

Six months later, in the spring of 1935, I landed something myself, a small contract with Samuel Goldwyn, the doors of Hollywood began to open, and I met Gable again. The iron man from Cadiz, Ohio, was looking rather trapped in white tie and tails, but the occasion demanded his discomfort. It was the Academy Awards presentation dinner—the annual handing out of the early Oscars.

The year before he had won one himself for his performance in *It Happened One Night,* and his acceptance speech was the shortest on record, two words—"Thank you!" That night Hollywood history had been made. Gable had been lent by MGM to the despised Harry Cohn and his struggling company, Columbia, as a punishment for intransigence in turning down too many mediocre scripts. Claudette Colbert was being similarly chastised for the same reason by her studio—Paramount—but between them they had outsmarted their bosses and persuaded the brilliant director Frank Capra to direct the picture for which Cohn had borrowed them. As a result, Claudette, Capra, and Gable all collected golden statuettes, the picture was voted Best Picture of the Year, and Columbia Pictures entered the big league.

Now, a year later, the Academy Awards had come around again, and Hollywood—still very much a village—was honoring its own with its strange tribal rites. Gable did not win this time, though his picture *Mutiny on the Bounty* came out on top. Excitement ran high among the 200 tribesmen and women who filled the private banqueting room downstairs at the Ambassador Hotel. A demure Bette Davis was proclaimed the winner for her performance in *Dangerous,* and Victor McLaglen (who, to everybody's delight, belched loudly when receiving his prize) was voted Best Actor for his portrayal in *The Informer.*

It was a vintage year, and the competition for votes must have been fierce because among other classic offerings that night were Gary Cooper in *The Bengal Lancers,* Fred Astaire in *Top Hat,* W. C. Fields in *David Copperfield,* and Garbo in *Anna Karenina.*

Less successful in all departments had been the Warner Brothers entry—*A Midsummer Night's Dream* with James Cagney as Bottom and Mickey Rooney as Puck. For the premiere in Beverly Hills, an elaborate program had been presented to each member of the audience, embossed on the cover of which were four golden plaques, each containing a well-known profile: the three Warner brothers and William Shakespeare.

Gable was seated at another table with a party from his studio—Irving Thalberg, the producer of *Mutiny on the Bounty;* Thalberg's wife, Norma Shearer; Jean Harlow; William Powell; Joan Crawford; and others. Ria, Gable's second wife, was also there, and I looked at her with interest. Several years older than her husband, she looked very calm and distinguished, and Gable was smiling across the table at her in the conspiratorial way happily married couples signal mutual boredom at dull parties. I was remembering with pleasure the unaffected charm and friendliness Gable had dispensed aboard *König* when, suddenly, he glanced directly at me. For a moment he looked puzzled; then my face must have clicked into place because he waved, smiled a friendly smile, and mimed the hooking of a big fish. I nodded and waved back, and after the presentations were over, he came to Goldwyn's table and shook my hand.

"Good to see you again," he said. "What are you doing here, trying to get Sam to go tuna fishing?"

I felt embarrassed at first telling it to the "King," as he was known throughout Hollywood, but bathed in the warmth of the great man's personality, I relaxed and explained that I had changed my job and had lately landed a contract with Goldwyn.

"Well, that's just *great,*" he exploded. "Lots of luck, kid, and don't forget—the first thirty years are the hardest!" Then he added quite seriously, "And don't give up fishing—you'll find it's a great help sometimes."

When he had made the rounds of our table, followed everywhere by looks of great affection, he spoke to me once more. "I'm moving over to the Goldwyn lot for the next one, so I'll hope to see you around. We can forget about making pictures for a while and yak about steelhead—is that a deal?"

"Fine," I said, delighted at the prospect of seeing him again and not unaware of the soaring of my personal stock among my high-powered dinner companions.

Several weeks later Goldwyn gave me my first speaking part: the roll of a sailor in *Barbary Coast*—it consisted of one line. Thrown out of the window of a waterfront brothel in San Francisco and sailing past the madam, I was called upon to say, "Orl right—I'm goin'!" Then as I lay facedown in several inches of mud, the two stars of the picture, Miriam Hopkins and Joel McCrea, accompanied by several donkeys and a posse of vigilantes, walked over the top of me.

Gable was by now working at the Goldwyn Studio making *The Call of the Wild,* and on the morning of my big moment he, the greatest star in the Hollywood firmament, took the time and the trouble to walk over to the back lot to wish good luck to an unknown beginner. He also insisted on stills being taken of the two of us, and the Goldwyn publicity department gleefully grabbed the golden opportunity to rub off a little of the "King's" glamor onto their nameless charge.

Several times I visited Gable while *The Call of the Wild* was being made, and I soon discovered that he had many other things to talk about besides fishing and hunting.

Certainly, more than anything, he enjoyed the great outdoors, and just as surely he felt uncomfortable at formal parties and despised the Hollywood hostesses and their "success lists."

"They only invite me because at the moment I'm on top of the heap," he said, "but when I fall on my ass, they'll just move someone else up a notch, and I'll go down to the bottom of the pile."

One January day we did more than talk about the big fighting seagoing rainbow trout of Oregon. His excited voice came over the telephone. "Hey! Let's go! . . . I've just been talking to some pals who have a fishing camp on the Rogue—the steelhead are running!"

"I don't have a rod," I said feebly.

"Forget it," said Clark. "I've got everything—I'll pick you up at midday, we'll spend the night in Frisco and be at Grants Pass by tomorrow afternoon."

He was a fast and dedicated driver, and he made it clear that he could do without the small talk because it ruined his concentration. This was perfectly all right with me, and I sat back and reveled in the glories of two-thirds of California.

At Grants Pass, where we stayed overnight at the fishing lodge, we were joined in the cold dark of the following morning by the guide, who came with his wife to fetch us. A squat, unsmiling, flaccid-faced Indian who smelled heavily of spirits, he was, according to Clark, the best man on the river. He was also the worst driver in the neighborhood and in the semigloom of that freezing winter dawn, his dilapidated Chevy, unbalanced by trailing a heavy fishing skiff behind it, swung terrifyingly around icy mountain bends. Clark watched me averting my eyes from the roaring river several hundred feet below, noted my tight smiles and high-pitched polite conversation, and correctly diagnosed my condition as one of abject terror.

"Don't worry," he said. "He'll make up for it when he gets on the river, and his wife, thank God, drives us back." He indicated the almost totally round and equally smelly lady who was huddled, unspeaking and blanketed, beside her erratic husband.

As the sky began to lighten, we slithered down a winding track and came to rest on a sandy beach between towering gray pine-topped cliffs. There we manhandled the skiff into the water, loaded it, and watched as the spherical wife took her husband's place behind the wheel and disappeared in a barrage of flying gravel up the almost perpendicular hillside, to meet us at dusk miles downriver.

Gable was wearing a heavy checkered mackinaw and his "lucky" long peaked cap. He had not bothered to shave, and a heavy black stubble was discernible in the growing light. It was bitterly cold.

"What are you giving us for breakfast, Chuck?" he asked the Indian.

"Small trout fried in butter," said the unsmiling one, "but you've got to catch 'em before I can cook 'em, don't you?"

"Sure thing, Happy." Gable grinned. "Let's get going."

The river was broad and sluggish where we put in, but the Indian knew the likely pools, and using a wet fly, we soon had half a dozen beautiful brook trout about eight inches long.

We pulled over to a sandbank, and while Gable and I collected dry driftwood, the guide, with a few quick flashes of his hunting knife, cleaned our catch.

On the east ridge high above us, the sun was backlighting the snow-covered firs. They looked as though they were on fire, but down on the sandbank it was still well below zero, and we huddled gratefully around the fire, sniffing the coffee and watching the deft movements of the Indian. A family of deer, seven of them, came down to drink at the riverbank opposite, a pastoral scene that was rudely shattered when an eagle flashed out of the sky and picked up a large rattlesnake from the rocks beside them. With his prey in his talons the great bird spiraled upward, gaining height till up near the ridge the sun caught them, and for a long time we could see the writhing silver underbelly of the reptile flashing out distress signals.

Clark was a true sport fisherman. He was uninterested in catching his limit of "meat," a comparatively easy achievement during the winter run when the silvery twenty-pound trout, slashed with vivid scarlet streaks at their sides after years away in the big ocean, were making their way in thousands far up the river to spawn in the selfsame gravel whence they had come. After a big January rain the barriers of flotsam had been washed from the river, the snow melt from the mountains had augmented the torrent, and the rapids between the pools were a roaring, rocketing menace.

The big pools were full of fish, and the air was so cold we had to dip our rods constantly in the water to free the guides of ice—it was very exciting. The fish were taking single salmon eggs washed free from the high spawning grounds, but Clark spurned the conventional use of these, and we cast with brightly colored salmon flies—a much trickier operation. Clark had two rods, a beautiful English Hardy, which he lent me, and a dream of a Cross, which he used with great effect himself.

You learn a lot about a man in four days of strenuous fishing and four nights of medium to heavy drinking. There was not a phony bone in Gable's body.

Around the log fire or drifting down calm broad reaches between the tumbling rock-strewn rapids of the aptly named Rogue, he would talk frankly and unemotionally about Hollywood and the people who controlled it.

The curvaceous blonde comedienne Thelma Todd had just been found dead in her garage near Santa Monica, found dead in the most mysterious circumstances, and for days the newspapers had hinted darkly at foul play and gangster connections.

"Thelma didn't read the small print," said Clark.

"The small print?" I queried.

"Yes. We all have a contract with the public—in us they see themselves or what they would like to be. On the screen and in our private lives, we are the standards by which they mea-

sure their own ideals of everything—sex, guts, humor, stupidity, cowardice, crumminess—you name it. They love to
put us on a pedestal and worship us and form fan clubs and
write thousands of letters telling us how great we are. But
they've read the small print, and most of *us* haven't—they expect us to pay the price for it all . . . we have to get it in the
end! So, when we get knocked off by gangsters, like Thelma
did, or get hooked on booze or dope or get ourselves thrown
out of the business because of scandals or because we just get
old, that's the payoff and the public feels satisfied. Yeah, it's a
good idea to read that small print."

Clark had a moderate opinion of studio heads.

"They're bastards," he said flatly. "They encourage people
to be larger than life, they'll give 'em anything, take any crap
from them provided they'll interest the public and the public
pays to see them, but the moment they slip—oh, brother!
Look at the kids on our lot at Metro now, Garland, Taylor,
Gardner, Rooney, great kids, all of 'em, and loaded with talent, but they'll probably ruin 'em all. Right now they can do
anything they like, show up late, keep everyone waiting, go
home when they want to, but God help them if the public
stops coming—they'll pull the rug out from under 'em all
over town."

I asked him how it felt to be in the number one spot in the
whole industry.

"Well"—he laughed—"as sure as hell there's only one
place I can go from where they've got me now! So I just go
along with Tracy's formula and hope for the best."

"Tracy's formula?"

"Sure. Get there on time, know the jokes, say them the best
way you can, take the money, and go home at six o'clock."

Gable talked about Hollywood and everything connected
with it, but he remained completely unimpressed by it. He
certainly never took his success for granted.

"Look," he said, "so they call me the goddamn 'King' at the
moment, but there are dozens of people warming up in the
wings, and anyway I'm just out in front of a team, that's all.
Metro has half a dozen people, top writers, whose only job is
to find the best possible properties for me, things that I fit
into with the least risk of falling on my ass . . . that way I re-

main valuable to them, and everyone's happy—for the moment.

"Don't ever let them kick you around," he warned. "They squeeze people dry and then drop them. When you start to fade, they put you into skid pictures so you'll turn them down and they can put you on suspension and get you off the payroll. Be tough with them if you get up there, because it's the only language they understand, and that's the only place where you can use it. Remember you're dealing with people who believe than a two-thousand-dollar-a-week writer is guaranteed to turn out better stuff than a guy who is only asking seven fifty.

"Most executives at the big studios have no guts. They're so busy holding onto their jobs they never stick their necks out. Know how Lubitsch found out the other day that he was no longer head of Paramount? From his goddamn masseur, for chrissake! This guy had been rubbing down the studio brass, and they all told him what was happening, but nobody had the guts to tell Ernst to his face that he was through."

Next to fishing and hunting, Clark loved to play golf, and we played a great deal together. He was a splendid sight at Pebble Beach, his favorite course. He didn't walk between shots—he strode. He had a fearsome slice, which he never completely corrected, so we bent the rules slightly so that he could continue to play when his ball had drifted out of bounds onto the beach, and roars of laughter would rise from below as he hacked happily away among the seaweed, the crabs, and the small pools.

He was a doughty opponent, but he lacked concentration, and in an important foursome match I gleefully saw him falter because my partner was Group Captain Douglas Bader, the legless RAF fighter pilot.

Douglas visited me in California soon after World War II. He had come out to tour the hospitals and encourage hundreds of double amputees who were wondering what the future could possibly hold for them.

He did untold good recounting to them his own story of being shot down and bailing out over France, where he buckled one of his artificial limbs. The German commandant of the prison camp in which he soon found himself was so impressed by Bader that it was agreed at a prearranged time one Spitfire could fly over the camp and drop him a new leg. When the leg arrived, Bader thanked the commandant, put it on, and that night escaped.

At dawn he was recaptured, hobbling gamely along ten miles from the camp. Thereafter both his legs were taken away from him at night and locked up in the guardroom.

Playing golf against the legless Bader, as Gable soon discovered, was a hazardous undertaking, and knowing of Clark's feeble concentration, I was quietly confident of the outcome.

Bader's first ploy manifested itself on the second tee. Just as Clark was about to drive, Bader, with a noise like a machine gun, knocked the ashes out of his pipe against his artificial thigh. On the fifth green he winked at me and tightened a little wheel in his knee; then by moving very slightly just as Clark pulled back the head of his putter he produced a high, penetrating mouse squeak. Thereafter a jittery Gable and his unnerved partner never felt completely secure, and Bader and I coasted to an easy victory.

Gable never spoke much about his wives; he felt no urge to unburden his domestic problems on his friends, and he was strangely fatalistic when his marriages broke up, which they did with great regularity. In fact, he was strangely fatalistic about everything. He never went out of his way to make men friends. He reckoned that he was what he was, people could take him or leave him, and if they preferred to leave him, that was perfectly OK with him. Above all, unlike so many big stars, he felt absolutely no need to bolster his ego by surrounding himself with stooges and sycophants, so his circle of friends was small and independent.

It is difficult to paint a fascinating picture of a man whom nobody seemed to dislike. As David Selznick remarked during the filming of *Gone with the Wind,* "Oh, Gable has enemies all right—but they all like him!"

However, wherever there is competition there is jealousy, and where there is jealousy the knockers will knock. So in Hollywood people occasionally nudged each other and said, "Gable only likes older women."

It was the understatement of the century—Gable loved *all* women: older, younger, blondes, brunettes, and red-heads . . . he loved the lot.

True, his first wife, Josephine Dillon, happened to be twelve years his senior, and his second wife, Ria, five years more than that, but Carole Lombard, Sylvia Fairbanks, and Kay Williams, when they became numbers three, four and five, were all in the junior league.

It was said by the knockers that Josephine, who was a well-educated drama teacher, had "invented" Gable, and the same source of bitchery passed around the happy word that Ria had paid for him to have his teeth capped. Clark just laughed when he heard this. "My mom and dad invented me," he said, "and L. B. Mayer paid for my teeth."

Clark was not really stingy with money; he was "careful." With the whiskey bottle, however, he was always lavish, and for years I was amazed at the amount he could consume with no apparent effect.

Gable said that acting did not come naturally to him—"I worked like a son of a bitch to learn a few tricks, and I fight like a steer to avoid getting stuck with parts I can't play."

As an unsuccessful Broadway actor he made three safaris into the Hollywood jungle. If the first trip in 1924 was a flop (he worked only in small theatrical roles around Los Angeles or occasionally as an extra in the studios), the second was to-tal disaster—he didn't work at all. Back again on Broadway, he finally smelled success when the egomaniacal George M. Cohan cast him as the lead in *Gambling,* but after the open-ing in Philadelphia, the sweet smell changed rapidly to some-thing more unattractive. Cohan decided that he would like to play the part himself and fired Gable. Understandably short on self-confidence, Gable thereafter ricocheted off a succes-sion of short-term flops till one day he was offered a part in a Los Angeles stage production of *The Last Mile,* and his third and final safari began. He never agreed that his subsequent breakthrough into the Hollywood big time was the glamor-ous rocket-propelled affair claimed by the MGM publicity department and always gave credit for it to two people: Lio-nel Barrymore and Joan Crawford.

Barrymore got him a test for the native boy in *Bird of Para-*

dise. Barrymore directed the test himself, and according to Gable, "They curled my hair; then they stripped me and gave me a G-string; a propman stuck a knife in my G-string, which scared hell out of me in case his hand slipped; then he stuck a goddamn hibiscus behind my ear and told me to creep through the bushes."

Irving Thalberg, the boy wonder of MGM, saw the result and told Barrymore, "You can't put this man in a picture. Look at his ears . . . like a bat!"

Nevertheless, he was finally hired by MGM to play a milkman in a Constance Bennett picture, and a small contract followed, which brought in its wake the all-important contribution by Joan Crawford. She bullied and cajoled the studio till Gable was given a major part in *Dance, Fools, Dance*—a tough hard-boiled character. His success was instantaneous. The critics raved, and the movie audience found a new hero, and for what it's worth, both Crawford and Gable always vehemently denied that their friendship was anything but platonic.

I have hinted that Clark was a little close with a buck, but this was only in connection with things his honest Dutch-German blood persuaded him were extravagant or unnecessary. For instance, none of the many women in his life were ever seen festooned with goodies.

Divorce, however, was something else again. Gable never skimped on that, and to obtain his freedom from Josephine, Ria, and Sylvia, he, almost without arguing, was nearly wiped out financially three times in the process. Each time he was divorced, he issued the same hopeful statement: "I don't intend to marry again—ever" but each time he soon forgot what he had said.

One of the interim ladies to whom he was attached for a while observed, rather sourly, "Of course, Clark never really *married* anyone. A number of women married *him* . . . he just went along with the gag."

As I came to know him better, I became convinced that he would consider no marriage perfect without a son—he really longed to have a family.

In the mid-thirties there was a rather snooty success-conscious club in Hollywood named the Mayfair, whose members attended dinner dances in a small ballroom in the Beverly Wilshire Hotel. Norma Shearer, the reigning queen of MGM, and her brilliant, self-effacing husband, Irving Thalberg, arranged a foursome there one Saturday night and invited me to bring the delectable Merle Oberon.

Everyone at the club got dressed up to the nines; white tie and tails for the men, and the women were told most particularly to wear white. Everyone in the film business knew that a splash of red on the screen immediately drew all eyes, and the dress designers, in those early days of Technicolor, invariably swathed their leading ladies in crimson or vermilion. There was, therefore, a gasp of indignation when our party made its entrance and it was seen by the local vestal virgins that alone in the room, Norma Shearer was wearing a bright-red dress.

Gable that night was escorting the fascinating Carole Lombard, who was renowned for her uninhibited observations, but a second gasp went up when she asked in a loud voice, "Who the fuck does Norma think she is? The house madam?"

Carole and Clark made a highly attractive couple. Carole had everything that Clark wanted in a woman. Supreme blond good looks, a sense of humor, lovely wild bursts of laughter, his own brand of down-to-earthness and, most important, his love of wild country, hunting, fishing, and the same determination to separate her public life from her private one. They were soon openly living together, a situation made a little tricky by the fact that Clark was still married to Rhea.

Hollywood was going through a housecleaning phase at that time, and people shacking up together came in for some tart observations from various organizations, church groups, legions of decency, and so forth.

The number one fan magazine, *Photoplay,* brought this simmering criticism to a boil with an article entitled "Hollywood's Unmarried Husbands and Wives."

It is difficult to imagine in these permissive days that such a dreary piece of journalism could so easily have put the cat among the local pigeons, but the cluck-clucking of disapproval first heard in the Bible Belt of mid-America became a rising crescendo of threats to box-office receipts by the time it reached California, and the big studio brass soon hauled their emancipated stars onto the mat and bludgeoned them into reorganizing their nesting habits.

Clark and Carole, Constance Bennett and Gilbert Roland, George Raft and Virginia Pine, Robert Taylor and Barbara Stanwyck, Paulette Goddard and Charlie Chaplin were all mentioned in the article, and most of them bustled briskly off to their nearest priest, minister, or rabbi and toed the party line.

Ria Gable played a cool hand with good cards, and Clark paid a stiff price to become respectable, so stiff in fact that whenever thereafter he criticized Carole, she was apt to crack, "Well, what did you expect for a lousy half million, for chrissake—perfection?"

In 1936, far away in Czechoslovakia, an unknown actress named Hedy Kiesler was chased naked through a wood in a film called *Ecstasy* and became an overnight sensation when the film was displayed in the United States. She was quickly signed up by L. B. Mayer, and her last name changed. Far more important for his studio than the discovery of Hedy Lamarr was that of Margaret Mitchell, a schoolmistress, in Atlanta, Georgia, who had given up teaching and been on the knife-edge of starvation for five years because she felt she had a great story to tell. Now she had finally and painfully arrived at the last chapter of her epic; *Gone with the Wind* was about to be published, and L. B. Mayer's son-in-law, the brilliant, independent producer David O. Selznick, from right under his father-in-law's nose had snapped up the film rights for a measly $50,000.

So great was the impact of the novel on the American public that the casting of the roles of Rhett Butler and Scarlett O'Hara took on the proportions of a national pastime. There was never any doubt in anybody's mind as to who was the perfect Rhett—Clark Gable—but Scarlett remained an international question mark, and Selznick greatly enjoyed the ensuing publicity. This enjoyment was tempered by the fact that Clark was under contract to Mayer and Selznick was determined to have Gable without his overpowering relative's hot, sticky breath on the back of his neck all during production. Finally, after two years of infighting, a deal was made between Selznick and MGM whereby Gable would be lent to Selznick to play Rhett Butler, but MGM would have the right to distribute the result. Gable, the pawn in the game, never forgave L. B. Mayer for refusing him even the minutest financial participation in the project which brought his company millions.

Selznick utilized the long months of negotiations with MGM by making scores of tests for the part of Scarlett. There was hardly an actress, great or small, in Hollywood who did not covet the role, and Selznick, as I can testify, put most of their aspirations on film.

I was making *The Prisoner of Zenda* for him at the time, so whenever I had a day off, Selznick would comandeer me, stuff me into a Confederate uniform to play Ashley Wilkes with my back to the camera, while the female elite of Hollywood hacked its way through dozens of versions of Scarlett O'Hara. Every evening I would report to Gable on the prospects—none seemed very promising, but all were different. One very perky little number by the name of Judy Turner was among those tested at that time. She had a perfectly packed little body and a behind that signaled a most beguiling message of welcome when she walked, which undoubtedly was the reason why Charlie Richards, Selznick's casting director, ordered her to wear a swimsuit instead of a crinoline for her test.

She did not land the part of Scarlett, but Mervyn LeRoy saw the test and signed her up for his next picture, *They Won't Forget* —a prophetic title as it turned out because Judy (renamed Lana for the occasion) made an instantaneous impact on the public.

After *The Prisoner of Zenda* I moved back to the Samuel Goldwyn lot to make *Wuthering Heights* with Laurence Olivier and Merle Oberon, and it was there that Scarlett was finally found.

The utterly delicious and kittenlike Vivien Leigh had come out to Hollywood to be with Laurence Olivier during the shooting of *Wuthering Heights* —they were deeply and touchingly in love.

Myron Selznick, the top Hollywood agent and David's

brother, happened to visit the set one day when Vivien was there, and within minutes of meeting her, he put her firmly into a large black limousine and whisked her across town to be paraded before his brother. Her own personal magic struck twice that day, and by evening, much to the fury of countless local ladies, it was officially announced that the search for Scarlett O'Hara was over.

Mindful of *Photoplay,* David Selznick posted a heavy guard outside the modest little hideaway of Scarlett and Heathcliff.

Apart from a few almost clandestine games of golf, I saw little of Clark once Carole entered his life; they were completely happy in each other's company and needed no stimulation from outsiders. I tried to organize a couple of all-male fishing safaris, but Clark made no bones about the reason for sidestepping my invitations. "The trouble is," he said, "Carole thinks you're a pain in the ass." I must have looked a little crestfallen because he laughed and softened the blow by adding, "As a matter of fact, she thinks anyone is a pain in the ass who might be a better fisherman, a better shot, or a bigger boozer than she is. Don't forget this is my third time up at bat, and one lesson I have learned about wives is that the first thing they want to do is get rid of all their husband's friends. It'll soon pass, but I'm not going to fight it."

In September, 1939, they invited me out to the house for a farewell dinner. Clark and I sat in deep armchairs in the paneled den, and Carole sat on the floor at Clark's knee. We ate and drank, and the conversation was perhaps a trifle stilted because I was off to the war, and as none of us knew what the hell I was letting myself in for, we talked of other things. They were so happy and evidently had so much together that I wondered aloud if there could be anything else they had their eyes on. Carole looked up into Clark's face.

"I'll tell you what Pappy wants," she said quietly, "and I just hope to Christ I can give it to him. . . . He wants a kid."

"Yeah, that's right," said Clark, stroking her hair. "I'd give my right arm for a son."

There was a semi-embarrassed silence till Carole let out one of her famous yelps of laughter. "And he's sure as hell working on it!"

Shooting had just finished on *Gone with the Wind,* and

Clark said he was delighted with the result. He had nothing but praise for Vivien—"She's going to be the biggest thing in this business when they see the picture."

David Selznick he admired enormously, but Selznick's penchant for bombarding him daily with memos about his performance left him unmoved—"I never read the goddamn things." He said, "All you can do is put your trust in the director and try to give him what he wants. If you start horsing around trying to please everyone, you wind up a nothing."

Gable insisted that his only contribution to the success of the picture had been arson.

Before shooting had started, it had been necessary to pull down a big cluster of old standing sets at the Selznick Studios in order to make room for the building of Tara and parts of Atlanta. "Why not," he suggested to Selznick, "put a match to the whole damn lot of 'em one night and photograph it? It'll look like Atlanta going up in smoke."

Selznick was delighted with the idea, and with some fireproofed stunt men doubling for Rhett and Scarlett making their horse-drawn getaway from the burning town, that's exactly how flaming Atlanta came to the screen.

When I bade good-bye to them that night, Gable gave me a word of advice—"Stick to scotch if you want to be brave—gin only makes you piss"—and Carole gave me one of her silk stockings to remember her by and "to wrap round your neck if you get a sore throat."

Just before Christmas of that year, shivering and miserable with my regiment encamped on Salisbury Plain, I read of the highly publicized world premiere of *Gone with the Wind* in Atlanta. The picture was a smash and has rightly remained so to this day. Vivien Leigh and Victor Fleming, the director, won Academy Awards, and the film itself was voted Best Picture of the Year. Though an odds-on favorite, Clark did not win (the Oscar went instead to Robert Donat for *Goodbye, Mr. Chips*), and with a most uncharacteristic flurry of pique, Gable promptly gave his original Oscar to the small son of Carole's secretary, instructing him to prop open his bathroom door with it.

Margaret Mitchell, whose self-denial and near starvation

had bought her the five years necessary to write her masterpiece, was shortly after the premiere knocked down by a car
in Atlanta. She died of her injuries, and such was the ferocity
of the income tax laws that having been relieved of an iniquitous percentage of her earnings from book and movie sales,
most of which had accumulated during one year, she died
penniless.

During our last evening together Carole had talked a little
about Hitler. She really hated everything he stood for. Clark
had been more phlegmatic—for him it all seemed like a fam-
ine in China, something one read about in the papers before
one turned hurriedly to the sports page—but Carole was already arguing powerfully that the United States should get
into the war. Later her sense of patriotism increased a
thousandfold, and the day after Pearl Harbor she wired
President Roosevelt offering both her own and Gable's services in any way they could be useful. This hardly earthshaking but nevertheless helpful offer to a harassed chief of state
was duly filed in some government office, and later their help
was invited to go on a bond selling tour. Clark was stuck
finishing a picture, so Carole went alone.

The tour started in Salt Lake City and wound south
through Texas. The last stop was Fort Wayne, Indiana.

Carole booked a sleeper on the train for Los Angeles, but
at the last second, anxious to get home, she changed her
mind and caught a milk-run plane instead. Gable was delighted when she phoned him and made plans for her early
return. Carole loved gags, so Clark dreamed up a surefire
one. He borrowed a wax nude dummy from the studio, fixed
it up with a long blond wig, and carefully arranged it in a
suggestive pose in Carole's bed. Then he spruced up to go to
the airport. Carole's plane had already taken off from Las
Vegas, the last stop, about an hour before, and Clark was just
getting into his car when a call came from the studio police
department. Something had gone wrong with Carole's flight,
they said; they had no other details, but Eddie Mannix, one
of the vice-presidents of MGM and a close friend of Clark's,
was on his way out to the house; a plane had been chartered
to fly to Las Vegas.

A terrible chill settled on Clark. He waited for Mannix. On

the way to the chartered plane Mannix told him the latest news. Someone had seen an explosion in the sky thirty miles from Las Vegas, and another pilot had reported a fire burning fiercely on Table Rock Mountain. Carole's plane was still unreported two hours later, when Gable and Mannix reached Las Vegas and a search party with packhorses had been readied to make the ascent to the summit. Mannix talked Gable out of going with the searchers.

"It could be a false alarm, Clark," he said. "How will she feel if she arrives home and you're not there to meet her?"

Clark remained at the foot of the mountain, and Mannix went up with the climbers. After hours of toiling through deep snow the charred and smoking debris of the plane was found scattered over a large area. Mannix was able to identify Carole chiefly by a pair of earrings which he had helped Clark choose for her.

Clark did not delegate to anyone the making of the necessary heartbreaking arrangements. Ice-cold and monosyllabic, he supervised everything himself from the ordering of a hot meal for the exhausted search party on that dreadful night to the choosing of hymns for the funeral three days later. Then he went to the Rogue River, holed up at his favorite fishing camp, and for three weeks drank himself into a stupor.

MGM, with the soaring costs of an unfinished picture very much on their minds, dispatched mealymouthed emissaries to inquire as tactfully as possible when their star might be expected to report for work. Clark never saw them. He just roared through the locked door of his cabin, "I'll be back when I'm good and ready . . . now beat it."

Finally, he showed up unexpectedly at the Culver City lot. Outwardly he appeared unchanged. He kidded with old friends and dropped in to see acquaintances. Always on time, always knowing his lines and as always, the complete professional. Grief, like everything else, was very private to Clark.

The day his picture was finished he enlisted, asked to be trained as an air gunner and to be posted overseas.

By the summer of 1943 I had offset the misery of military life by the happiest of all acquisitions: a beautiful wife and a baby son. They lived in a thatched cottage two miles from Windsor Castle, and whenever I got leave, I rushed to join them. They had a few chickens and a vegetable garden to augment their joint rations of two eggs a month, two chops a week, and eight ounces of cooking fat every ten days. I was usually far away, leave was scarce, and communication with family almost nonexistent, but one summer evening I came home to find a large American Air Force officer sitting under *my* beech tree in *my* deck chair; on his knee was *my* little boy, and serving him from *my* last bottle of whiskey was *my* wife.

It was a great reunion. Clark was stationed in the Midlands, and from then on our cottage became his refuge from military life.

Gable had been dealt the cruelest of blows, but on the surface, at least, he was making the best of it. In his own deep misery he found it possible to rejoice over the great happiness that had come my way, and he became devoted to my little family, always showing up with unheard-of goodies such as concentrated orange juice and nylons from the bountiful American PX. He had had a difficult time, he told me, becoming an officer. Passing the written exam had been hell, but he had managed it, not by studying in the ordinary way . . . he had locked himself in the lavatory after lights out and, night after night, with his actor's mind, had memorized textbooks like scripts.

He found it rough being Clark Gable. He was caught between two extremes: those who fawned on him and those who automatically thought he ought to be chopped down. Whichever way it went, it was almost impossible for him to be just an ordinary guy—something he longed to be now more than ever.

For a year before I embarked, fumble-fingered with fear, for Normandy, we saw Clark frequently. The terrible wound of Carole's death seemed to be healing, but she was never far from him, and the very happiness of our little group would sometimes overwhelm him. Primmie found him one evening on an upturned wheelbarrow in the garden, his head in his hands, weeping uncontrollably. She held the huge bear of a man in her arms and comforted him.

Clark did several bombing missions over Germany as an

air gunner, and one flak-shredded plane he was in nearly disintegrated over the Ruhr. No false hero, he said he was scared stiff the whole time, but the one thing that really put the fear of God into him was the thought of having to bail out. Not so much was it the prospect of the actual descent and landing that unnerved him; it was the thought of what Hitler might do to him on arrival: "That son of a bitch'll put me in a cage and charge ten marks a look all over Germany."

With the end of the war in Europe in sight Clark was released from the service.

GABLE'S BACK AND GARSON'S GOT HIM screamed the billboards all over the world. Clark was being relaunched by MGM in a dreary potboiler with, as costar, someone not among his most favorite leading ladies.

He lived at his Encino ranch, the thirty-acre spread in the San Fernando Valley where he had so far spent his happiest days. Carole's room was a shrine, and nothing was allowed to be touched—her clothes, photographs, perfume bottles, all remained exactly as she had left them—but the sprawling white brick-and-frame house did not become a mini-monastery. Far from it—its steps were polished by the expectant arrival and disappointed departure of a steady stream of carbon copies of Carole Lombard: beautiful blond ladies of the utmost attraction and sophistication whom he entertained, "used," perhaps, and in several cases, sent away brokenhearted, actresses, society ladies from New York, cover girls and secretaries.

They all did their best to fill Carole's shoes. They laughed with him, drank with him, and even apprehensively donned blue jeans and safari jackets and went duck hunting with him, but when each in turn failed to measure up, Martin, his faithful majordomo, would lower the electrically controlled boom at the end of the driveway and Clark would seek lonely comfort in his favorite whiskey.

When I returned to Hollywood after the war, Clark seemed to be withdrawing more and more into his shell. I think the arrival of Primmie and myself, by now with a second little boy, six months old, provided him with a tiny port in his personal storm. At any rate, hardly a day went by when he did not drop in at the appalling Moorish prison of a house which we had rented in Beverly Hills, and as always, he arrived loaded with goodies for the children and played with them for hours, and as before, he found great peace and comfort in the calm serenity of Primmie.

We had been installed in the Moorish prison only six weeks when Clark called early one morning.

"Come on, kids," he said. "I've got it all fixed. We'll drive up to Pebble Beach and play golf for a few days. I've got a bungalow for you two at the country club, and I've got permission for us to fish in the reservoir up in the forest . . . that's elk country in there . . . maybe we'll show Primmie an old-fashioned California elk."

We took off, and Primmie's eyes were like saucers as we drove north through green rolling hills to Santa Barbara through the Alisal Ranch and San Luis Obispo, then along the coast road below W. R. Hearst's castle at San Simeon, through Big Sur, and along the high winding scenic route to Monterey with the tumultuous and incongruously named Pacific crashing against the rocks far below.

We played a lot of golf, stayed up much too late, caught very few fish, saw no elk, and laughed all the time. Clark was at his best, completely relaxed and reveling in showing Primmie such a spectacular section of his beloved California. During the weekend Primmie wrote to her father in England saying she had never been so happy in her life. Two days after we returned to Beverly Hills, as the result of an accident, she died.

I don't know how people can get through periods of great tragedy without friends to cushion and comfort them. To be alone in the world when disaster strikes must be an unbearable refinement of the torture, and I will forever bless those who helped me over the initial shock, but there comes a time when friends have to get on with their own lives and you have to face the problem alone—this is the worst part.

During that long period of utter despair Clark was endlessly thoughtful and helpful, and he checked up constantly to see if I was all right. Without my realizing it, he was drawing on his own awful experience to steer me through mine, and for the next eighteen months I saw a great deal of him, being one of the small handful whose voice on the intercom at the electrically controlled ranch gate was instantly greeted by Martin with "Why, drive right on up—Mr. Clark is right here."

Martin adored Clark and always had his best interests at heart, but sometimes his anxiety over his employer's well-being got the better of his judgment. Once I drove "right on up" with a particularly attractive companion who happened to be a happily married lady from San Francisco, and Martin decided that she was just his master's type, so he slipped an old-fashioned Mickey Finn into my drink and drove me home semiconscious.

Women adored Clark, but although he loved them and their beauty and gaiety, he was never a womanizer in the crude sense of the word.

"Hell," he said, "if I'd jumped on all the dames I'm supposed to have jumped on, I'd never have had time to go fishing."

If he ever discussed any of the aspiring beauties who visited the ranch, it was only in a generous, laughing, and flattering way—very unlike the broadsides he reserved for the new guard at MGM. L. B. Mayer, whom he had disliked but respected, had been replaced by others whom he disliked and despised. He also seemed to have lost interest in making pictures, a normal reaction among actors who had been away fighting a war; it seemed so childish for a fully grown man to put on makeup and spend the day playing charades.

He drank more than before and gained weight, which worried him. To counteract this tendency, he lapped down Dexedrine, which was supposed to make him lose his appetite. All it did, however, was make his head shake alarmingly.

I went away to Europe for six months to make a film, and when I returned, Clark seemed slightly perked up. He was even issuing occasionally from the ranch and being seen in public with a couple of his favorite dates, a sweet, gentle blond actress who lived near him in the Valley—Virginia Grey—and Anita Colby, a top cover girl from New York who was so beautiful she was known all over the United States as the Face.

He also seemed to take heart from the fact that, with great good luck, I myself, after two years, had again found great happiness and had remarried while in Europe. He approved mightily of Hjördis and was the first guest we invited to our house in Pacific Palisades. Hjördis decided to give a small dinner for half a dozen of my friends.

"We'll have a roast suckling pig," she announced as I was rushing out early in the morning in danger of being late for work.

This was a Scandinavian dish with which I was not too familiar, so when she inquired where she would be able to find such a thing, I mumbled through a mouthful of breakfast, "At the Mayfair market, I suppose," and headed for the car.

At that point Hjördis had a rather tentative grip on the English language, and nobody knows what she said that morning in the market. In any event, later in the day a van arrived at our house and deposited an entire hog of enormous proportions; dead, luckily. Our cook gaped at it apprehensively and suggested that instead of the traditional apple in its mouth, it would look better munching a melon; then she bravely set about cooking it in oven-sized sections, hoping, I suppose, to weld them together later like one of Henry Kaiser's Liberty ships.

"You all had better round up a few more friends," she advised Hjördis, "or this family'll be eatin' pig meat for five years."

Hjördis put out an SOS to her Swedish reserves. Viveca Lindfors, for one, leaped gallantly into the breach and rounded up a whole clutch of hungry Nordic pork lovers, plus her mother who had arrived that very morning for her first visit to the United States. "She doesn't speak a word of English," warned Viveca.

Gable showed up for the intimate dinner to find the house bursting at the seams with blue-eyed towheaded strangers, but he rose above it and did his best to make everyone happy.

"What do we do with the old broad?" he whispered to me, indicating Viveca's mother, who was sitting alone on a sofa.

"Slip her a belt of schnapps," I hissed, and hurried off to cope with some new arrivals.

It is possible that he gave the old lady a flower-vase full of the stuff because she became very uninhibited, suddenly burst loudly into song and, with skirts held high, went into a spirited dance.

Clark made no bones about it—he was longing to be married again—but when a man of fifty is looking around desperately hoping to fill a void, he is usually not seeing too clearly.

Sylvia Fairbanks, the widow of the inimitable Douglas, fascinated Clark from the moment he met her, and because of her ravishing blond beauty, her outspokenness, and her impeccable sense of humor, she seemed to him to be out of the same mold as Carole. There is no question—he rushed it. A few weeks after he had met Sylvia they called us from Santa Barbara in a haze of champagne (not his favorite drink incidentally).

"Guess what?" yelled Clark. "We've done it! We're married!"

As usual, Clark had kept his mouth shut about his love affairs, and it would have been grossly unfair, in the unlikely event that he had asked my advice, if I had by a single word tried to reverse the trend, but I had known both of them for many years, and I would certainly have marked them down as a high-risk combination.

Clark was a selfish man; Sylvia was a selfish woman . . . so far a standoff. Clark was a man's man, but Sylvia was a man's woman . . . a red light. Clark lived for the open air, blood sports, the big country, and large dogs. Sylvia was devoted to the great indoors, to her milky white skin, her flawless complexion, loathed the thought of animals being slaughtered, was happiest among the chattering chic of café society and owned a Chihuahua the size of a mouse named Minnie.

Possible friction points could perhaps have been welded into a great happiness by their mutual devotion to laughter had it not been for a further divergence: Clark was close with a buck, while Sylvia adored spending money.

Three weeks after they were married Clark was looking grim. Sylvia had blithely revamped Carole's room at the ranch and invited some smart friends from the East to come out and stay in it.

The King, with the expression of a man with a dead fish

for a tiepin, was occasionally seen carrying Minnie, and when he returned from Long Island and Nassau, whither Sylvia had dragged him to meet some of the "beautiful people" of the day, it was obvious that a gross miscalculation had been made. After seventeen months of marriage Sylvia, claiming she had been locked out of the ranch upon returning from a second and this time solitary trip East, retained the great criminal lawyer Jerry Geisler to take care of her side of the divorce proceedings, only to discover that Clark had no intention of being wiped out for a third time by the California laws on community property and had taken certain evasive action. He had arranged for his contract to be suspended by MGM and had created a legal residence in Nevada, whence he moved everything he owned except the walls and roof of the ranch.

True to form, Gable kept his mouth shut about how much this latest and shortest idyll had cost him, but once the settlement had been made, his sense of humor returned, and he took a certain delight in displaying to his friends his Christmas card from Sylvia: "THANKS A MILLION." Then he issued his customary statement—"I don't intend to marry again *ever* "—and took off for Africa to make *Mogambo* with Ava Gardner and Grace Kelly.

When he returned from Africa, he spent a few months touring around Europe in a sports car; the passenger seat was seldom empty. I was filming in England and Italy, so Hjördis and I were treated to previews of the selected passengers, and inevitably the ones in whom he seemed most interested were all outwardly Lombardesque. Suzanne Dadolle was a very beautiful and intelligent French girl to whom Clark seemed genuinely attached. They came to visit us on location on Lake Como, and it seemed possible that the odds might be shortening when he hid her in a cupboard in his bedroom at the Villa D'Este and she stepped out suddenly to present us with a bottle of champagne.

Admirably but maddeningly close with information about all his liaisons, Clark was a difficult man on whom to place a bet, but with Suzanne beside him, the tour of Europe was prolonged again and again, and I had seldom seen him happier. But it ended suddenly—he never said why.

Mogambo was released and was a big hit, the most successful picture Clark had made since MGM wanted him to sign a new long-term contract, but the King was tiring. He was sick of the studio, the people who were running it, and the petty politics in which they indulged. So after fifty-four pictures and twenty-three years, he left MGM, never to return. He was oddly vitriolic about the company that had found him and built him up. Of course, he too had had a sizable hand in his own success, but surprisingly for such a down-to-earth man he fell into the actor's trap of thinking he had done it all by himself, and nothing would ever persuade him to make another picture at the studio. MGM, in turn, fell into the usual studio trap—they thought they could "buy" him back, and the more vehemently he refused to return, the higher went their offers. They finally gave up when they learned of his instructions to his agent: "See how high you can get those sons of bitches to go; then tell 'em to take their money and their studio and shove it up their ass."

His choice of pictures after leaving MGM was not inspired; in his mid-fifties even the King was finding it difficult to land good roles. A realist, he tried not to look over his shoulder, but he knew only too well that the Young Pretenders were breathing down his neck. A long love affair with scotch was also beginning to show. He was becoming heavy and bloated, but above all, he was lonely, and his dream of a happy marriage and perhaps a son was fading rapidly. There was a discernible air of quiet desperation about him, but he kept his own counsel, retained his humor, and soldiered on.

The sun when least expected came out for Clark at the age of fifty-five. One day he ran across someone he had seen only a couple of times in the past ten years, Kay Williams. Kay was his type in looks, blond, beautiful, and with periwinkle-blue eyes, but she also possessed something which attracted him even more, something which Carole had had in abundance. She was gutsy; she didn't kowtow to anyone; she was prepared to give as good as she got.

She had a couple of other things too that he liked the look of as soon as he saw them—a little boy of four and a girl of three.

"The kids'll screw it up for Kay," sniffed one of Clark's ex-girlfriends to me. "The son of a bitch might go for her if she had dogs instead of children."

Kay had been divorced three times, was now in her mid-thirties, and had decided that her acting career would never amount to much, so she was ready with a wealth of experience to settle down and make the right man happy. His friends knew it was serious when Clark disappeared from view, the boom was lowered at the ranch, and he no longer showed up at gun clubs and golf courses. A year later the two of them surfaced to get married in northern California.

Kay was perfect for Clark, and she set out intelligently to make him happy and content. Instead of sweeping the memories of Carole under the rug, she encouraged them. She became a good shot and an excellent fisherwoman, played golf with him and, if she didn't actually go drink for drink with him, usually contrived to have a glass in her hand at the same time he did.

Although she never asked for anything for herself, she gently indicated his purse till he loosened the strings. He bought a sports Mercedes 300 XL and a piece of desert where he built a small house beside the sixth fairway of the Bermuda Dunes Golf Course, but even Kay was astonished when, on a Christmas shopping trip to New York, he suddenly steered her into Cartier's.

Jules Glaenzer, the ubiquitous head of the store, started washing his hands with invisible soap when he saw the prospective customers walk in through the Fifth Avenue entrance. He ushered them into a private room where the chairs had been polished by the bottoms of oil sheiks and maharajas and proceeded to display tray after fabulous tray. Gable began to sweat. Finally he got to his feet. "Er, I saw something down the street I like better," he said, and led a mystified Kay to Abercrombie and Fitch, where he bought her a shotgun. Soon after they were married, Kay became pregnant, and Clark was ecstatic with joy, but after eleven weeks, she lost the baby, and he doubted if his longing for a son could ever be fulfilled. Kay's two children adored Clark, and he was a redoubtable stepfather but—

Every picture was a job to Clark; the complete professional, he gave full value to the work at hand. He was always on time, always word-perfect, always prepared to do his utmost to give the director what he wanted. Engrossed as he was in his marriage, he did jobs as they came along, but his popularity remained enormous, and in spite of the rather mediocre material he selected, on the edge of sixty he seemed indestructible.

Early in 1960 he finished making *It Started in Naples*. The shooting of this nonsense had been mostly on the island of Capri, and bored by the smallness of the place and by the endless attentions of the paparazzi sent swarming over from the mainland by his leading lady's producer husband, he took heavily to the pasta and red vino. By the time he returned to the ranch he was thirty pounds overweight, but he couldn't have cared less and even talked blithely of retiring. Then one day a script arrived on his desk that really fascinated him. The screenplay of *The Misfits* had been written by America's number one playwright—Arthur Miller. John Huston was to direct, and for costars he would have the delectable and highly salable Marilyn Monroe and Montgomery Clift. The role was perfect for Gable, the best he had been offered in years, and in a high state of excitement he and Kay took off for the desert, where he promised himself he would get into top shape before shooting started. He played golf every day, watched his diet, and cut right down on the booze; the professional was getting down to his fighting weight for a special job. In July, 1960, he reported to the location near Reno, Nevada. He was the picture of health and vitality and looking forward eagerly to the start of the film. There was a delay. Monroe called from Los Angeles to say she was unwell and could not come up for several days. Shooting was postponed, but any annoyance or letdown that Clark might have felt was quickly eliminated when a radiant Kay arrived with the best possible news from her doctor: She was pregnant again. That was a lovely day for Clark. Everything at last seemed to be perfect, and it is unlikely that in his happiness he would have remembered the advice he had given to a young actor many years before: "Read the small print."

John Huston was not too happy with Arthur Miller's script—the first screenplay Miller had tackled incidentally—but the annoyances of rewrites and script conferences paled into insignificance with the arrival of Marilyn Monroe and Montgomery Clift. Marilyn had acquired a reputation for unprofessionalism and had a nasty habit of showing up late for work. She had become a mass of inhibitions, terrors, and indecisions, and the poor doomed girl was headed for a breakdown. Montgomery Clift a few months previously when leaving the hilltop home of Elizabeth Taylor and Michael Wilding had smashed through the guardrail on the twisting mountain road, and when he had been extricated from the wreck, many bones were broken and his face was terribly disfigured. Plastic surgery had done miracles, but the shock and the necessary pain-killing drugs had changed him terribly. Now he was subject to fits of the blackest depression, and he, too, frequently found it unbearable to show up on the set.

On the Reno location Miller kept rewriting the script and Huston kept rewriting the rewrites; then either Monroe or Clift would be hours late—sometimes they never turned up at all—and every day Clark was there on time ready to start work, and every day the sun climbed relentlessly in the cloudless sky. By eight o'clock it was 100 in the shade, by midday over 130, and every afternoon the hot desert wind covered everything and everybody with a thick alkali dust from the dried-up lake bed.

Out of pure boredom, Clark insisted on doing some stunts that would normally have been done by a double. Anything was better than sitting day after day in the baking desert just waiting, but roping a wild mustang in searing heat and being dragged along the desert floor at 30 mph behind a truck are not sensible pastimes for a man of sixty. Huston tried to dissuade him, and Kay was appalled when she nightly doctored his cuts and rope burns, but he persisted, and never once did he say a word against the others. He understood their problems and felt desperately sorry for Arthur Miller, who was married to Monroe and must have been bearing the brunt of all her difficulties behind the scenes.

At long last and weeks over schedule, the picture finished. Clark saw a rough cut, and although he hardly ever discussed his work, he told one and all that it was the best thing he had done since *Gone with the Wind* ; then he forgot about the past miserable months and sat back and waited contentedly but impatiently for the birth of his child.

Early one morning Kay woke to find Clark standing by the bed half dressed, his face chalky white. "I've a terrible pain," he said simply.

The doctor was called and immediately sent for an ambulance. It was a massive heart attack. Kay moved into the hospital with him, and he improved steadily over the next nine days.

On the tenth day he looked like a new man, relaxed and happy. Kay says that he asked her to stand sideways against the light so that he could see her silhouette. Laughing happily, he used the doctor's stethoscope to hear the heartbeat of the little boy he longed for so much but would never see. During the night he was struck down a second time.

In Clark's copy of *The Misfits,* Arthur Miller had written: "To the man who did not know how to hate."

3
Our Little Girl
(Part I)

$\mathcal{M}$ ISSIE was described by the newspapers as a "sex symbol" or a "love goddess" and by us at the studio as "the Boys' Erector Set."

Her face, which was snub-nosed and pretty, was saved from being unremarkable by a pair of huge gray eyes. It was topped by a cloud of golden hair and had the great good fortune to be strategically placed above the most beautiful body in Hollywood.

Most of her adult life Missie had been part of the Hollywood scene. One year out of an Arizona high school and still thinking a chocolate marshmallow sundae was a "big deal," she had been spotted by a studio talent scout and offered a solo number in a Busby Berkeley musical. She had immediately kissed good-bye to her mother and headed for California. A long-term Hollywood contract had followed, and the paucity of her acting talent had been minimized by her pretty face, her gray eyes, and her quite extraordinary shape. The studio publicity department had encountered little difficulty in hoisting her to the top of "The Girl Most Wanted" list, and through the years she had accumulated a large and appreciative following in moneymaking pictures which had tested the guidelines of the Legion of Decency to the limits.

Missie was not the cleverest girl in the school, but she was smart enough to realize that her beautiful body and her enthusiastic use of it should not be distributed as largess to all and sundry, and as a general rule, she bestowed her favors where they would reap the most bountiful harvest—among the producers, directors, writers, and cameramen, in that strict order of "billing."

It was a "nervous" night. The hot desert wind—the Santa Ana—was blowing, skins felt dry and itchy, tempers were short, and problems were magnified. Missie, encased in the lightest of cotton sheets, was lying naked on her back—not her most unfavorite position, let us remind ourselves—but this time she was alone, naked because she liked the feel of the voile sheets around her curves and on her back because Cary Grant had told her that sleeping in that position was the only way to avoid getting wrinkles. The music was far away, and it entered her sleeping brain through a tiny attic window far up in her skull; slowly it filtered down, growing implacably louder until she could identify the song—"You smile . . . and the angels sing."

Missie stirred petulantly and made a brushing movement of her arm, but the music did not go away, and she realized it was the new alarm clock which "He" had given her, tuned in to the twenty-four-hour "music station." She knew that if she reached out a hand and switched it off, it would relentlessly come on again every thirty seconds until she climbed out of bed and yanked it out of the wall. She groaned and lay for a while listening to the song. When it ended and the all-night disc jockey started his hearty early-morning patter, she rolled out of bed and pulled the plug out of its socket—4 A.M.

Missie's head felt like lead, and her mouth like the bottom of a parrot's cage. Why, oh, why, she asked herself, had she been so stupid? "One of my sleeping pills a night, *only*," her doctor, "Needle Ned," had prescribed, but she had doubled the dose last night because "He" had invited a group over for supper and cards, and although she had tiptoed away at ten o'clock, making movie-camera, hand-turning signals, she had still found herself wide awake at midnight with only four hours to go before another exhausting day's work.

She tottered into her yellow tiled bathroom and switched on her mirror lights, but she was not happy with what she saw. Her famous creamy white skin was, despite Cary's advice, creased upon her face, her famous cat's eyes were half closed and puffy, and the stretch marks on her abdomen caused by little Sharon looked like streaky bacon held up to the light. She was thirty years old and felt fifty, but she doggedly set about making herself presentable for the gatemen, the studio police, and the departing shifts of maintenance men who might see her as she was driving through the studio gates.

At four-thirty she glanced out her bathroom window. Alvin was already there, and he knew his business, so he sat patiently in the driveway with his side lights on to show he had arrived on schedule.

"Thank God for Manny," she thought. "At least I don't have to drive myself to work at this hour of the night."

It was still pitch black when Missie let herself out of the house. She had peeked into "His" room on the way down and had blown a kiss to his sleeping form—a vague mound in the middle of the bed. Downstairs it had smelled of stale cigar smoke and booze, so she had opened the drapes and windows, then she had covered her cream-colored jacket and slacks with a mink coat, tied a silk scarf under her chin, and let herself quietly out of her house.

"Mornin', Missie," said Alvin, touching the peak of his soft black cap. "Sleep well?"

"Not enough, Alvin," she replied as she settled herself in the backseat, switched on a reading light, and during the half-hour drive studied the scenes scheduled for the day's shooting and cursed herself for not having been strong enough to say—"The hell with your party . . . *I'm* going to bed."

"Mornin', Missie," said "Red," the gateman. "Lovely mornin'."

Missie got out of the car outside her dressing-room bungalow and sniffed the cool fragrance of the California dawn; far away an orange glow was beginning to silhouette the semicircle of mountains that held Los Angeles imprisoned in a half-clenched fist.

"Coffee's all ready, Miss Missie." Vergis beamed. Missie kissed the shiny black cheek. "Who's looking after the kids today, Vergis?" she asked.

"Oh! I have good neighbors down there in Watts; they all

take turns!" Vergis laughed a happy laugh as she poured the steaming Maxwell House.

At five thirty on the dot the makeup man appeared, lugging a huge leather-covered box containing all the bottles, brushes, pots, and pastes of his very considerable craft. He was as unemotional and methodical as a country policeman.

"Mornin', darling," he said, peering at her. "You look like hell—got your period?"

"No, thank God," said Missie. "Anyway, I get three days off when it comes—thanks to Manny . . . he got it added to the contract."

"Well, then get more sleep, for chrissakes," said Carl. "I don't want to lose *my* job! Like I said to Doris, the other morning, when she came in lookin' like that, 'Little Day— you've had a busy man!' . . . Eye drops first."

Missie lay back in her reclining chair and watched in the mirror while Carl transformed her from a pasty-faced dull-eyed woman of thirty into a vibrant, sparkling girl in her early twenties.

"Thank God the body's still good," muttered Carl, "but you'd better watch it, darling—those bastards in the front office have ice water for blood . . . they'll smile at you and tell you that you're 'their little girl,' but all you need is to get the blame for a couple of *their* big flops, and you'll be out on *your* cute little ass. . . . Hey! I nearly forgot. We have to put the scar on you today . . . just a tiny one on the right cheekbone." Carl applied fish skin, surgical spirit, liquid rubber, and Max Factor blood with great dexterity while Missie complained about her leading man's body odor.

"Honest, Carl . . . I can't stand it! It makes my eyes water! Can't you have a word with him?"

"Very difficult, darling," said Carl. "But I'll do my best. If we suggest he eat parsley all day long, he may get offended."

"I *dread* the love scenes." Missie sighed. "The poor boy's so nervous . . . that's probably the reason."

"Why don't you give him a piece?" said Carl. "He's obviously got the hots for you. That might do the trick . . . you know . . . relax the poor bastard?"

"Out! out! out!" came a high-pitched squeal from the dressing-room door, and clapping his hands, in swished

Frankie, the head hairstylist. "Verg, darling, move your beautiful black ass and get Mother a cup of coffee."

"Yes, ma'am." Vergis, not to be outdone, giggled.

"Out, wrecking crew, I say, and leave this old bag to me."

"It's all yours, Buddy." Carl grinned good-naturedly. "Our girl needs help today, Frankie, so fluff her up and pray for backlighting. . . . See you on the set, darling." He withdrew.

Frankie soon had a mouthful of hairpins and was working with professional mastery at incredible speed. He never drew breath.

"Saturday night is bath night for me, sweetheart. . . . Only two more days, and I'll be in the full black nightie with one of Hedy's wigs on. . . ."

Missie had heard it all before, and she knew that two evenings hence middle-aged Frankie would be sitting hopefully on a tacky stool in Ricky's dingy bar on the Sunset Strip, checking on the "studs" and "scores" through a tangerine twilight of smoke, fluttering his eyelashes at the bikeless motorcyclists in their shiny outfits and the horseless cowboys in their unaccustomed buckles and boots. She only half listened to the depressing "drag" talk and the boasts of "juice" and "joints," "Bennies" and conquests.

She changed the subject. "I didn't think much of the dailies last night," she said.

"Nor did Mother, sweetheart," Frankie replied. "Between them, that camera queen and Mrs. Director really gave you a fucking . . . you looked *ninety!*"

"I don't want to rush you," said a calm Texas voice from the entrance hall of her bungalow, "but we'll be ready to turn over at nine o'clock sharp . . . it's not quite eight-thirty now . . . we'll go on where we left off last night."

"Okay, Chuck," she called. "I'll be there. Which gives you about five minutes more, Frankie," added Missie. "How're we doing?"

"The pink net's just going on, sweetheart," said the hairstylist with a last flourish of the curling iron. "Tell Vergis to wash you tonight—it's getting awful dry."

"It's those damn arcs," said Missie. "Nobody's ever used so many as this guy . . . he's baking my scalp."

"He's a lousy cameraman," said Frankie helpfully. "Why

didn't you ask for Daniels or Stradling or Maté? You *know* what they do for girls."

"I did," said Missie, "and I also asked for Cukor or Franklin to direct because they're good for girls too . . . but they'd all been put on other pictures."

Missie's heart gave a little lurch as she said this. She knew she had made a big mistake, by evening it would be all over the lot that she was slipping.

Before she left her bungalow, Missie examined herself carefully in the long three-way mirror. Her morale rose, and she climbed into the backseat of Alvin's Cadillac. As the car wound through the studio streets to Stage 23, many workers waved a cheery greeting. Missie sighed and thought of those happy days when everyone at the studio had protected her and cosseted her and made it their business to approve or disapprove of her boyfriends and to watch with pride the development of her early-blooming figure.

Missie's portable dressing room, a large cubicle on wheels complete with dressing table, mirrors, a telephone and a comfortable couch, had, like her bungalow, been decorated to her taste. It had been towed to a quiet corner of the sound stage, conveniently close to the brightly lit activity where the day's shooting would soon take place.

Marie, from the wardrobe department, was waiting at the door. They kissed good morning.

"Afraid the costume weighs a ton, honey," she said, "and there's no way you can sit in it without creasing around the middle—I've asked Props for a slant board; he's gone to get one. Let's go, hon," she added. "The Creep's already looking at his watch."

The Creep was the nickname of the unpopular director. He was a brash but indecisive young man with a penchant for bullying those least able to defend themselves. The day before he had not endeared himself to the crew by standing two feet away from a quailing young actress and shouting, "No *good* . . . do it *again* . . . and this time, for chrissakes . . . *R E L A X!*"

"The Creep" had a couple of successful low-budget films to his credit and had been given the break of directing Missie's picture by its youthful producer, known behind *his* back as Coattails—a nephew of the studio head.

"Think positively," Missie told herself as she slipped out of her slacks and stood naked in the cubicle.

Marie ordered Missie to breathe in and hooked her into a Merry Widow which gave her a nineteen-inch waist, jutting bosoms, and acute discomfort. The basic hoop and petticoats came next, and at last the costume itself. Marie had been right—the weight was horrendous—but the result was spectacular, and Missie made a few pirouettes to watch the skirts swirl and fall.

"I hope my tits don't pop out," she said. "They're awful near the danger line."

"I'll keep an eye on them," said Marie.

"So will about fifty guys." Missie laughed.

A few last-minute dabs of powder by Carl, and sharp at nine o'clock, Missie walked out into the bright lights to start eight slogging, exhausting hours of nervous tension and high concentration.

Things went well for the first hour. "The Creep" was calmer and more inventive than usual, and the leading man appeared to have bathed in Knize 10, but the head of publicity cornered a resting Missie on her slant board.

"The front office have okayed some visitors today, darling," he said. "That dame from *Photoplay* wants to have lunch with you."

"No way," said Missie. "By the time I've gotten out of this dress I've less than half an hour before I have to get back into it again—all I do is grab a sandwich and call home—it's my only chance to talk to Sharon. She'll be asleep when I get back tonight."

The man sighed. He was used to rolling with the punches, and he got them from all sides, but he had a plan.

"Then there's the whole Ohio State football squad. They're playing at the Rose Bowl New Year's Day—they just want to come and look at you around three o'clock . . . they've elected you their mascot for the game . . . it'll mean a few pictures and autographs but tremendous coverage. How's about it?"

"Okay," she groaned, "but don't let me get trapped."

"A deal," he said. "I've turned down several others for to-day, the Boston *Globe,* the Des Moines *Register,* and the Washington *Star*—we can knock them off later. The president of the Foreign Press Association wants to come this morning—they're getting very important now, the foreign press. . . . He's a nice Swede and we might be able to swing an award from them later—that's getting more coverage every year. . . . Whaddya say, darling?"

"Not today, Eddie," begged Missie. "We've got a lot of awful tough scenes . . . maybe he could take me to lunch when the picture's over?"

"I'll tell you what I'll do, darling," said Eddie, looking away from her to lessen the impact. "I'll can the Swede . . . if you'll see Hedda."

"Hedda!" Missie almost screamed. "What the hell does *she* want? . . . You mean she's coming out to the studio? She *never* does that!"

"She does when she's on to a story, darling," said Eddie smoothly, "and I'm afraid she's on to 'Him.'"

"Oh, Jesus!" said Missie. "What time is she coming?"

"She's here already," said Eddie, "over on Stage Nine at the moment. Just string her along. . . . She can be a good friend too, you know, and it's better to have her on your team than playing against you."

"On the set, please," said a calm Texas voice.

Missie worked on doggedly, but she kept looking into the darkness behind the camera, dreading the sight of the icy supercolumnist. At last, in an interval for relighting, Missie was confronted.

"We don't have much time, my dear," said the spare, over-hatted Hedda, "so let's get down to business. . . . I hear that 'He' is living with you now. I know what he gets for breakfast, and I know he sometimes drives Sharon to school—a convent school, isn't it? . . . Do you think this is good for your image? . . . And what do you think will happen to your contract here if the Catholic Legion of Decency decides to ban your pictures?"

Missie's hand shook as she lit a cigarette.

"It's my private life, Hedda," she said defensively.

"Nonsense," said Hedda. "You *have* no private life—you sold that long ago for a contract, and you'll be getting twenty-five hundred a week if your option is taken up next month. You belong to the public, and a lot of people in the country still like people in the public eye to lead clean, decent lives and to rear their children in a clean decent home. They stomached your divorce because they'd loved you since you were a child, but they won't stand for 'Him' in your life . . . I'm warning you."

"Are you going to tell them, Hedda?" asked Missie in a quiet, little voice.

The columnist thought for a moment and gazed directly into the big gray eyes.

"No, my dear . . . not unless you force me to," she replied slowly, "but I'll tell you something that may make things easier for you: 'He's' a no-good son of a bitch . . . I've watched him for years . . . he always was, he always will be . . . he's a crook in business, which we all know, but . . . he's cheating on you already."

"Waiting on the set, Missie," said a calm Texas voice. "Dialogue off camera, please."

In a daze and with legs turned to jelly, Missie walked toward the camera. She glanced back and saw Eddie deferentially shepherding Hedda's regal figure toward the door: then she faced her nervous young leading man, standing in his Gold Rush outfit under the full glare of the lights. It was his close-up in a difficult emotional scene, and he needed all the help she could give him. She put everything she could into it. The boy thawed out and responded, and when it was over, he bounded up to her like a big puppy. "Gee, thanks loads! . . . You sure did help me! . . . It's so lonely out there, I've been dreading that close-up ever since we started the picture!"

Impulsively, he hugged her. Missie burst into tears, ran to her trailer, slammed the door, and reached for the telephone. Stifling her sobs, she spoke to her secretary. "Morning, Pat. Did Sharon get to school okay?"

"Oh, yes," answered the girl. "'He' took her—they only just made it—he had a tough time getting up, I guess!"

Missie took a calming breath.

"Is 'he' there now, Pat? I'd like a word with him."

"No, he just left for Lakeside . . . he has a golf game—said if you called to give you his love . . . he'll be back around six."

"OK, Pat, you come on out here then." She hung up.

A discreet knock, and the kindly face of Mac, the first assistant, peered around the door. Vergis was hovering behind.

"You okay, little girl? What's upset you? Anything I can do?" Missie dabbed her eyes and controlled herself.

"It was the scene, I guess . . . sorry, Mac . . . ask Carl to come and repair the damage, will you, please?"

"Sure, darling. Take your time; there's a lighting job coming up . . . call me if you need anything."

Carl went to work in silence—he knew better than to talk when temperament was on the boil whatever the cause—but the silence was broken by another knock on the door. Vergis opened it a few inches and relayed a whispered message.

"It's the man from the *Hollywood Reporter* . . . says to tell you they've reserved a full page for your Christmas ad again this year and to remind you the five hundred is deductible."

"Tell him to drop dead," said Missie, and she could feel hysteria rising within her.

The phone rang. It was her agent.

"I'll be out at the studio today, darling," said Manny. "I'll drop by and see you about five . . . okay?"

"It's a tough day, Manny," groaned Missie. "Can't it wait?"

"Won't take but a few minutes, darling . . . see you at five." He hung up.

"Ready on the set," came a calm Texas voice through the door.

Till noon the work was hard and mercifully needed the maximum of concentration, endless rehearsals that called for meticulous timing and the cooperation of two spaniels and three small children. The "child-actor mothers" were the usual mean-faced, grasping, jealous dragons, and the dog handler smelled of bourbon.

"Coattails," the producer, put in a brief appearance. He was full of concern.

"Missie, darling, I couldn't come before—I had a budget meeting—but they called to say you were not feeling well.

Are you better now? . . . The studio doctor should see you during the lunch break—for the insurance, you know. . . ."

Missie reassured him he would not fall behind by a minute on his precious schedule because of her, but the thoroughness of the studio spy system irked her.

Just before the one o'clock lunch break, Coattails' uncle, the head of the studio, paid one of his infrequent visits to the set. At the very sight of him, surrounded by his henchmen, the whole tempo of work quickened.

The young director, who had been leaving the intricacies of coping with the dog and the children to the experienced Mac, immediately assumed full and ostentatious command, and everyone was scurrying about, reeking of efficiency. The grapevine had alerted Frankie, and he arrived in time to fiddle unnecessarily with Missie's curls.

"The Big Wheel" came over, tall and immaculate in a light-gray suit. His high-domed forehead was brown, blotched with bright pink patches where his beloved desert sun had peeled off one layer of skin and been too quickly allowed to burn its tender replacement—the pink patches were permanent. His wife, who baked herself for hours every day at Palm Springs, had achieved the complexion of a heavily worked Western saddle.

He smiled at Missie through rimless spectacles, but the smile only displayed his perfectly capped teeth—it did not extend to his eyes. He put his arm around her.

"And how's our little girl today?" he asked . . . not pausing for an answer. "Everyone tells me the picture looks real great . . . and you're giving a *great* performance . . . wish I had time to see all the dailies, but with fourteen pictures in production right now—you're the least of my worries—you got any problems, darling?"

Missie maneuvered him out of range of the flapping elephant ears of his entourage.

"Joe's a great cameraman, I know, but he uses so much *light* . . . I look like a death's head!"

"Damn right he's a great cameraman," said the studio head through a quickly diminished smile. "Tracy and Bogart fall over themselves to get him."

"But I don't want to look like Tracy or Bogart," wailed

Missie. "I want to look like *me*. Couldn't he at least put a gauze over my key light?"

He patted her shoulder. "I'll have a word about it," he promised soothingly. "Leave it with me." He started away but turned back. "Oh, by the way, darling, I've sent for that agent of yours. He'll be in this afternoon . . . I want to have a little chat with him about our little girl's future . . . be good, darling, we all love you."

He shook a few hands on the set, listened to a few reports, checked the script girl's work sheet, and was gone.

Pat, the secretary, arrived just before the lunch break. She waited while Missie was released from the purgatory of her dress and then accompanied her in Alvin's limousine. Missie gazed absently out of the window as they threaded their way through the crowd headed for the commissaries, some seated in little gaily colored, awning-topped trolleys, but most on foot, and workmen carrying their lunch pails and radios headed for quiet corners behind buildings or for the vast acreage of the back lot. A multitude of extras in the varied costumes of fourteen different productions, the snooty dress extras in their white ties and tails with Kleenex stuffed inside their high collars for protection against makeup, and the girls with tissues in the tops of their dresses guarding the fabric from underarm stain. Glamor! thought Missie. The writers were headed for the writers' table in the private dining room, the directors would be huddled together at theirs, and the producers would be far removed in another enclave—all preferring the company of their peers in a rigidly class-conscious society. The stars in their allotted limousines were rolling toward their bungalows, and a few free souls were bustling off the lot for drinks and a snack across the street.

In her bungalow, while Vergis and Pat busied themselves in the kitchen, Missie spoke to Sharon, who had a free afternoon. The young clear voice cheered her.

"Mom, I'm going over to Virginia's for lunch and maybe stay till supper . . . a lot of the kids'll be there . . . we're going to play tennis and roller skate and stuff. . . . Work hard! Try and come home early so I can see you! . . . Bye now." She hung up with the single-mindedness of youth.

Missie dialed again and spoke to her cook.

"No, he's gone golfin'—went around eleven, I guess—Lakeside, I think he said."

She called the club, something she had never done before. Did she imagine an evasiveness about the secretary's voice at the other end?

"I got here late today, he's probably halfway around the course by now . . . I'll tell him you called when he gets in."

Missie picked dispiritedly at her low-calorie cottage cheese and pineapple while Pat sought to extract some decisions from her about Christmas.

"I reckon that including the staff at the house, the crew on the picture, and the usual studio list, you'll have to come up with around a hundred and thirty gifts," she said. "I'm mailing four hundred cards today and about a hundred telegrams on Christmas Eve. The stores stay open late starting next week. You'll want to pick up stuff yourself, won't you, for people like Manny and Louella and Hedda and, of course, family. . . . And don't forget Dan. . . ."

"No, don't forget *him* whatever happens," said a hearty voice from the doorway.

Missie jumped out of her chair and rushed to a large comfortable red-faced man in a loud sports jacket who was taking off a raincoat and removing from his head a homburg enveloped in a plastic covering.

"Radio said rain later on," he explained.

"Dan, darling," cried Missie, "do you want some food?"

"No, thanks, honey . . . I was on the lot, so I just dropped by to say hello. I'll take on a little scotch, though, if you have some."

"I'll fix it," said Pat. She liked Missie's business manager—he seemed honest and straightforward.

"Well, Dan, am I broke as usual?" Missie laughed. She was relieved to have something to wrench her mind away from Lakeside.

"Not quite, darling," said Dan. "But I'm afraid we've had a little setback: The government's come after you for sixty thousand bucks in back taxes from four years ago—they've turned down a claim for exemptions over the divorce settlement."

"Jesus," said Missie, "have we got it?"

"We can find it, honey," said Dan cautiously, "but we have
to watch all the outlays next year . . . no big entertaining,
no gambling on oil wells . . . no—"

"But all that's deductible, isn't it?" asked Missie.
". . . From taxes, I mean?"

"Honey," explained Dan gently, "lots of things are deductible—the ten percent of your earnings you pay to Manny, the
five percent to me, Pat's salary, your lawyer's fees, your business gifts, clothes, publicity, entertaining—all sorts of things
are deductible from tax, but you have to *pay* tax before you
can deduct from it, and you don't pay tax unless you have an
income . . . and actresses who don't work don't have in-
comes . . . and your contract comes up for renewal any day
now . . . so, like I said, we have to watch it."

Missie spoke slowly. "They're . . . not going . . . to
drop me, are they? . . . I mean, I've been here on this lot for
more than twelve years."

"You've plenty more years ahead of you yet, darling," said
Dan soothingly. "If not here, then someplace else, but the
studios are all cutting their overheads, and your option calls
for three years straight at a big raise. . . . Let's pray they
pick it up." He drained his glass and made his good-byes.
"Don't worry, honey," he said. "Just keep the positive
thoughts."

The phone rang. Missie picked it up eagerly.

"Just checking," said a calm Texas voice. "We'll be ready to
go right on the dot of two o'clock."

"Thanks, Chuck," she answered dully. "I'll be there."

As she got into Alvin's Cadillac, she said to her secretary,
"Finish your lunch in peace, Pat, dear, and before you go,
call the caddie shop at Lakeside and ask the pro what time he
reckons 'He' will be finished . . . don't make a big thing of
it."

The afternoon's work progressed normally, but it became
increasingly oppressive on Stage 23 as the big sun arcs ate up
the oxygen. Missie began to feel listless and edgy, and all the
time, as though a door had been left open somewhere, there
was a draft in her heart.

At last Pat reappeared, and Missie hurried across to her at
the earliest moment.

"The pro says he hasn't been at the club all day," said the secretary.

"I see," said Missie in a small voice.

The head of publicity materialized in the offstage gloom. "The boys are all set, darling . . . over by the big doors . . . it won't take but a moment." She followed him and spent the next half hour surrounded by forty grinning behemoths, gracefully accepting heavy-handed compliments, signing autographs, filling in silences by asking, "And where are *you* from?" and praying that nobody would answer, "From Phoenix, Arizona, ma'am—*your* hometown."

"We're all ready for you," came a welcome Texas voice. "The director would like to rehearse the barn dance sequence . . . the dancers are all in position."

By late afternoon Missie was drained, mentally and physically, but there was still an hour and a half to go before the witching hour. "Thank God for Manny," she thought. "At least he got me the six o'clock clause . . . they can't ask me to work after that. *Manny!* Oh, my God! I'd forgotten all about *him.*"

In a wave of near panic and with her mind feathering in different directions like a foxhound, she took a course of action she had never before taken—she called Frankie in the hairdressing department.

"I need your help, Frankie. I don't think I can get through the day I'm so exhausted. . . . Can you give me one of those little pills of yours to help me keep going?"

"Sure thing, darling," came the answer. "Mother will be right over, and I'll bring a spare for emergencies."

Whatever it was, the drug took almost instant effect. Missie soon felt clearheaded but slightly detached, and by five thirty when Manny arrived she was in a brightly gay mood.

Her agent was one of the most powerful in Hollywood, not physically—he was a little man despite his lifts, but he had muscle. He wore no spectacles, but there was a sheet of frosted glass between his eyeballs and his brain, and his face incompetently lifted, instead of youthfulness, gave an impression of drawn, lineless age. He invariably wore dark suits and tight white collars.

Manny had muscle in Hollywood because he handled some of the most illustrious names in the business, and he kept his stable valuable by poaching promising beginners from small agencies and pushing them into important pictures on the backs of his sought-after stars. As soon as he had concluded his business with Missie, he would be on his way to meet a young actor whose performance had caught his eye at a sneak preview in San Diego the night before.

Back in the bungalow, Manny waited while Missie made one more abortive call to her home; then he wasted no time.

"I've just come from talking to the Big Wheel," he said. "The studio is exercising its option—three years straight and the raise."

"Great! Wonderful! Yippee!" yelled Missie, jumping up and kissing him.

Manny held up a hand. "Not all *that* wonderful, darling," he said. "Your first picture under the new deal will be *The Green Shoot.*"

Missie burst out laughing. "Is he out of his mind or something? I may get away with twenty-four or -five, but I'd still be ten years too old for *that* part . . . the kid's *fourteen,* for God's sake!"

"Twelve," corrected Manny. "But that's not the part. They want you for the mother."

Missie felt an icy hand clench itself around her intestines.

"I think I'm going to throw up," she said.

"She's a very young mother," said Manny, flicking a dead eye in her direction, "thirty-one, to be exact, so it wouldn't mean graying up or anything like that . . . and it's one hell of a script."

"Maybe," retorted Missie, "but it's not one hell of a *part* . . . everyone in town's turned it down . . . it's the kid's picture . . . it *has* to be."

"There's another thing. The Big Wheel thought," said Manny softly, "he thought it would be just great publicity-wise and in every other way if Sharon played the kid."

"I *am* going to throw up," said Missie. "Over my dead body will Sharon ever become a child actress—I know what it's like."

"The Big Wheel just put it out as an idea—that's all," said

Manny. "He also said that he's worried because your fan mail has been falling off lately, and he mentioned that if it hadn't been for the pressure the studio was able to put on that Santa Monica judge, the more, er, spectacular parts of your divorce would have been on every front page."

"Oh God, Manny," Missie groaned. "What should I do? Help me . . . *please.*"

Manny had expected a longer struggle. He was relieved that it was over so quickly and that his 10 percent commission was safe for another three years.

"My advice, darling, is to grab it. That'll only be one picture . . . there'll be plenty more . . . this lot is where you belong . . . you're 'their little girl,' remember? . . . So *The Green Shoot* may turn out to be the kid's picture, but what the hell! You're still young and still beautiful . . . it's not over yet by a long shot. . . . I'll call 'em tomorrow and tell 'em they have a deal. . . . Be good now . . . stay happy." He left.

The phone rang, and Vergis answered.

"That was Chuck, Miss Missie, dailies in five minutes, projection room twenty-four . . . Alvin's outside."

"Give me a big drink," said Missie. "I'll take it with me. . . . Back in an hour. . . . Be an angel and wash my hair at home for me, so I can fall into bed . . . I'll get Alvin to take you downtown."

"Sure thing," said Vergis, "no trouble at all . . . be glad to."

The dailies were drawn out by the inevitable postmortem, and it was eight thirty before Missie and Vergis drove out of the studio gate.

The young Texan was on hand to say good-night and give the call for the morrow.

"Usual time," he said cheerfully, "five thirty makeup, and it's your big address to the miners."

Back at the house "He" was waiting. He looked very handsome with his curly black hair, white teeth, and blue eyes blazing out of a sunburned face. Her heart lifted when she saw him, but it immediately sank back again when she realized he was dressed for going out to dinner.

He hugged her and told her she looked great but that she

ought to get the show on the road because they were late already.

Whether he had forgotten to tell her about the dinner or whether she had forgotten what he had said was of no importance. Hedda's words had been eating into her all day. "He's already cheating on you." She *had* to go with him.

"Give me half an hour," said Missie. "I must see Sharon and take a bath . . . call them up and explain . . . I'll be as quick as I can. . . . Vergis, you go on home with Alvin, honey. I'll come in half an hour early tomorrow, so we can wash my hair before makeup."

"OK . . . 'night, Miss Missie, see you tomorrow."

A few minutes with a sleepy Sharon, a quick bath and change of makeup and a hurried selection of clothes left Missie in a second trough of exhaustion.

In a reckless gambling mood, she swallowed the reserve pill which Frankie had given her for "emergencies" and ran downstairs. "He" was waiting impatiently at the wheel of her convertible.

As he drove, she once again began to feel lifted far above her petty problems. She gazed down from Olympian heights on the scene of her jealousy and listened in a floating, gliding way to her own voice as she calmly asked the opening question. "How was the golf?"

"Great." He laughed. "I was really hitting it good today . . . made a little dough!"

"Many people at Lakeside?"

He paused for a beat. "I guess so," he said.

"This is the moment of truth," thought Missie. "It doesn't hurt much after all." Very deliberately she said, "I called the club a couple of times, but they couldn't locate you."

"Perhaps time is elongated by drugs," she thought. She had heard it sometimes was, but it still seemed an eternity before he answered in an offhand way.

"Pity you didn't call Hillcrest. We decided to play there instead."

The party was a buffet-style affair for about forty people. Missie, the only well-known Hollywood face, was instantly the center of attraction. The rest were the Bel Air Bay Club group with a sprinkling of Easterners out for the winter—all ideal prospects for "His" real estate promotions—and Missie, sipping champagne, watched with a distant fascination as he moved effortlessly from one group to another. Hers were not the only female eyes that followed him, she noted with a mixture of pride and apprehension.

The pill and the champagne kept Missie "up" like a Ping-Pong ball on a water jet, but in the back of her mind the dictatorial voice of studio discipline was ordering her "Go to bed . . . go to bed."

Around eleven o'clock she whispered to him that she must leave. He reacted like a spoiled child interrupted in mid-angel-food cake.

"We've only been here an hour and a half, for God's sake! . . . There's a whole raft of people I want to talk to."

"*Please,*" she begged. "I've got to get some sleep. . . . I have a really tough day tomorrow."

"Oh, OK." He pouted. "Let's go then."

Missie said her good-byes and found her wrap. "He" kept her waiting in the doorway while he lingered. Particularly drawn out, she noticed with a little stab of worry, was his farewell performance for the benefit of a tall, sultry beauty from Philadelphia.

During the drive back to her house Missie snuggled against his shoulder, but there was no response, and she could feel his frustration.

"You go on back, darling, if you want to," she said.

"No . . . it's OK," he said shortly.

Missie longed to be enveloped in her soft sheets, to lie back and wallow in oblivion. She also longed to feel his warm body beside hers, but that stern studio voice was insistent: "Get some sleep! Get some sleep!"

There was an awkward and inconclusive embrace between them in the hallway, and Missie turned to go upstairs.

"I'll be up in a little while," he murmured, moving toward the drink tray.

In her room the sight of the turned-down double bed and shaded light overwhelmed her with fatigue. She glanced at the bedside clock—it was almost midnight. Automatically, she set the alarm for 4 A.M., then remembered about her hair and changed it to 3:30. She took off her clothes and climbed into bed, too tired to remove her makeup or to switch off the bedside light. For a while she lay there, waiting for the sounds of mounting footsteps; then in her mind she saw, like an illuminated scroll, the long, long speech she would have to deliver the next day before hundreds of "miners." She turned her head from side to side to try to erase the words; they would not go away. She tried to relax for sleep and at last reached out her hand for the pills which "Needle Ned" had prescribed.

"I'd better take two," she said to herself, "to knock down those damn things Frankie gave me," and as she swallowed them, she put a third—"in reserve"—beside the water glass. Then she switched off the light.

Dimly, she heard the handle of her bedroom door turn, but she was sinking down into a deep black pit. Faintly she heard the door click, and then an eternity afterward, far, far away, she heard the self-starter of a car and in the dim distance the sounds of its wheels crunching the gravel as it disappeared down her driveway.

Manny had been well pleased with the speedy conclusion of his business with Missie.

"Lucey's," he said to his chauffeur.

When he entered the small grottolike restaurant opposite Paramount Studios, it took a few seconds for his eyes to become accustomed to the gloom.

The dim lighting was not accidental. Lucey's was the favorite rendezvous of the starlets and young actors from the nearby studios, the Italian food was inexpensive, the steaks were good, and the kidneys grilled in their own natural cradle of fat were delicious.

While he waited for the young actor, he asked the waiter to bring him the daily trades. He sat back and perused the castings, assignments, the hirings and firings and the comings and goings announced in the *Hollywood Reporter* and *Daily Variety* and made a few entries in his notebook.

The young actor sent a message to say they were working a little late but that he would be over in fifteen minutes.

"He won't be that considerate once he hits the big time," thought Manny grimly.

The restaurant was filling up, and the discreet little alcoves around the main floor became nests of opportunity; at the exposed tables in the center, out-of-towners sat, taking their time over long drinks and trying to spot celebrities in the smoke-filled gloom. Manny glanced idly at them, and his attention was caught by a young girl sitting quietly with an older woman. As a flesh peddler he was normally as resistant to the lure of it as an attendant in the Louvre is to the "Mona Lisa," but there was something haunting about this girl's unaffected beauty and her almond-shaped gray eyes.

His perusal of the girl was ended by the young actor who arrived precipitately, very conscious of the fact that he was being seen in the company of such a powerful agent. With his customary dispatch, Manny got down to business. "Would you like me to handle your career?" he asked.

"*Would* I?" the young man yelled. "I can't *believe* it!"

When he had calmed down, he began to worry about his present agent. "He's been so good to me . . . lent me dough when I was broke . . . he's my friend."

Manny listened dispassionately; he'd heard it all before.

The boy's scruples quickly evaporated as he contemplated his good fortune. He sat in the alcove shiny-eyed with excitement.

Manny rose to leave. He could chalk up a successful day and he wanted his dinner, but his departure was delayed by the arrival of the middle-aged woman from the center of the room. She addressed the young man. Behind her stood the beautiful teenager who had momentarily aroused Manny's interest.

"We're from San Diego," said the woman, "my daughter and I, we came up for the day to do a bus tour of the studios . . . it's a big racket really, we never got to speak to any of the stars, they're always roped off . . . Caroline here was real disappointed . . . she's movie-struck, you see . . . well, now we've seen *you*, our day has been *made!*"

"Me?" said the young actor in surprise.

"Oh, yes," chimed in the girl, her face glowing. "Mom and me went to see a musical last night, and instead they showed a sneak preview of your picture—you know, to test the audience reaction and that—and after, they gave us cards to fill in saying what we thought about it, and we thought you were *wonderful,* didn't we, Mom?"

"Yes, just *wonderful,*" said the mother, "and we loved the picture, too . . . we filled in the cards like that."

Manny stood quietly watching the young girl; he knew now why her looks had intrigued him. The young man was flushed with pleasure and preening himself before her excited eyes.

"Well . . . gee! Thanks!" he said, and stuck out his hand.

"Good-bye . . . congratulations, young fella," said Manny at the door of Lucey's. "We'll be seeing a lot of each other from here on."

He watched the young actor walking on air toward the parking lot; then, after a moment of decision, he turned back into the restaurant and invited himself to sit with the woman from San Diego and her daughter.

"Does Caroline want to become a film actress?" he asked.

"She dreams of nothing else, day and night," said the mother.

"Bring her to see me tomorrow at eleven o'clock," said Manny, handing her a business card. "You can check up on me any way you like before then . . . I can arrange for Caroline to make a test for *The Green Shoot* . . . it's the best part ever written for a young girl. If she does it, she'll steal the picture from the star."

4
Hedda and Louella

HOLLYWOOD invented a macabre party game called Airplane. This concerned a sizable transport which, owing to some mechanical defect, was destined to take off and never again to land, its crew and passengers doomed to fly around and around forever. The game consisted of providing tickets for those the players felt they could well do without. Hedda Hopper and Louella Parsons, unassailably the two most powerful gossip columnists in the world, had no difficulty whatever in finding space and, a refinement of torture, were usually allotted seats next to each other.

Compared to Lucretia Borgia, Lady Macbeth and others, Louella and Hedda played only among the reserves, but with their 75,000,000 readers all over the world, they wielded and frequently misused enormous power. Only Hollywood could have spawned such a couple, and only Hollywood, headline-hunting, self-inflating, riddled with fear and insecurity, could have allowed itself to be dominated by them for so long.

The reader must try to visualize that at every Hollywood breakfast table or office desk the day started with an avid perusal of the columns of Louella Parsons and Hedda Hopper. The fact that many had paid their press agents large sums of money to make up lies and exaggerations and then plant these items with Louella and Hedda detracted nothing from the pleasure they got from seeing this nonsense in the morning papers—they even believed it when they saw it.

81

A large part of their columns was pure fabrication, as I can witness. At one point Lord Beaverbrook asked me to cable a Hollywood page twice a month to the Sunday *Express.* My first article was on Clark Gable, and my second about Gary Cooper, but I soon realized that I could not wear two hats—I could not keep friends and at the same time disclose their innermost workings to several million readers—so I asked for and was given my release from the arrangement. However, before I could deliver the first article, I had perforce to become an accredited card-carrying member of the foreign press in Los Angeles.

At that time 500 journalists were encamped around Hollywood, covering the goings-on in the movie capital. My name was added to the mailing list, and every day thereafter bundles of gibberish arrived at my home, churned out by the public relations officers of studios, including, to my great delight, pages of complete fantasy about myself which had been dispatched by the Samuel Goldwyn Studios, to which I was under contract.

It took guts and ability for Hedda and Louella to rise to the top of this inkstained pile of professional reporters, and it took tremendous stamina and craftiness on their part to remain there for a quarter of a century.

Louella, short, dumpy, and dowdy, with large brown eyes and a carefully cultivated vagueness of smile and manner, was a Catholic, married three times, first to a real estate man, secondly to a riverboat captain, and thirdly to a doctor who specialized in venereal diseases. From the earliest days she had been a newspaperwoman and during her Hollywood reign was one of the star reporters of the W. R. Hearst publishing empire. Her flagship was the Los Angeles *Examiner.*

Hedda, who came on the scene later, was tall, thin, and elegant, with large blue eyes and a brisk, staccato way of demanding replies rather than asking questions. Of Quaker stock, she had been married only once to a four-times-divorced stage actor twenty-seven years her senior, whom she herself had divorced when she caught him cheating on her at the age of sixty-three. An ex-chorus girl, she graduated to small parts on Broadway and in films and was a washed-up middle-aged Hollywood character actress when she took to

journalism as a last resort. Her flagship was the other local
morning paper, the Los Angeles *Times*.

They were an unlikely couple, but they had one thing in
common—they loathed each other.

Hollywood folklore insisted that Louella held her job with
W. R. Hearst because she knew literally where the body was
buried. In 1924 Hearst had organized a trip aboard his yacht
Oneida. Among others on board were Louella and the producer Thomas Ince. Far out in the Pacific, so the story went,
Hearst entered the cabin of his mistress, Marion Davies, and
found her thrashing around naked beneath a similarly un-
clothed Ince. An altercation followed, during which Hearst
shot Ince. He then carried the body on deck and dumped it
over the side. Louella, who was dozing unseen in a deck
chair, was supposed to have heard the splash and reached
the rail just in time to see the dead producer bobbing past,
and Hearst was supposed to have told Louella to keep her
mouth shut, in exchange for which she was promised a job
for life.

The two major flaws in that story were, first, that Ince left
the yacht in San Diego suffering from indigestion and took
the train to Los Angeles, where he died two days later of a
heart attack, and secondly, that Louella Parsons was never a
member of the yachting party. The truth of her beginnings
with Hearst was that she was a very good reporter who appreciated the excitement that was being generated by the infant film industry and Hearst knew a good reporter when he
saw one.

Hedda's emergence as a newspaperwoman came some ten
years after the beginning of Louella's reign as the undisputed queen of the Hollywood scene. In 1935 Hedda was in
trouble. She was fifty years old and a very bad actress. She
was a striking-looking woman, however, who spent every
cent on her clothes, sparkling company too, always equipped
with the latest juicy pieces of information, but she was hardly
ever offered a part in films. She somehow kept going, doing
anything that came along, including modeling middle-aged
fashions and a stint with Elizabeth Arden, and on the proceeds she managed to give her son a good education and to
run an attractive little house near the Farmer's Market. She

had some staunch friends, among them the beautiful and talented writer Frances Marion, who took her along with her on trips to Europe. On one of these she picked up a bogus English accent, complete with the broadest A in the business. On her return she informed me that London was "ARBSOLUTELY FARNTARSTIC."

Another champion of hers at that time was Louella Parsons, who frequently mentioned her activities in her column and introduced her to W. R. Hearst and Marion Davies. It was at the Hearst ranch at San Simeon that a fellow guest, Mrs. Eleanor Paterson, the publisher of the Washing *Times-Herald*, became so captivated by Hedda's brittle and spicy observations about Hollywood that she invited her to write a weekly newsletter, and Hedda's first step toward becoming Louella's archrival was taken.

Once it was available for syndication, the number of newspapers subscribing to Hedda's column was far from spectacular until lightning struck in 1937—she was bought by the Los Angeles *Times*. Now she was read by everybody in the motion-picture industry, and overnight sources of information were opened to her that had remained firmly closed when her output was only being glanced at in remote corners of the country. As news and gossip flooded in on Hedda from hundreds of press agents and private individuals, her column received a blood transfusion and improved immeasurably. Within a very short time it was syndicated in as many newspapers all over the world as that of an increasingly resentful Louella Parsons.

The arrival on the Hollywood scene of a second queen who had to be pandered to, pacified, or prodded posed some very tricky questions for the publicity-hungry citizens. How to plant a story with one while still keeping the amiability of the other? How to arrange a private showing of a new film for one without offending the other? And above all, how to give the story of an impending marriage or divorce to one without incurring the implacable wrath of the other? It seems incredible, but in a town with a herd instinct and a concentration of insecurity, it needed only one of these ladies to hint that an actor or actress was "box-office poison" for contracts to be terminated and studio doors to be slammed. Discretion was, indeed, the better part of valor, and the great majority of us played a humiliating game of subterfuge and flattery, having long since decided that it was far less troublesome to have them with us than against us. If they were susceptible to flattery, they were also very astute, and it was fatal to try to get by with an untruth—for that there was no forgiveness.

They could help careers, and they could hinder careers, and they could make private lives hell, but if there was talent, they could not stop people from getting to the top, and, as Hedda knew from experience, if there was no talent, they could not manufacture it.

Hedda should have been the easier to deal with. Having been so long a frustrated actress herself, she understood, but she was unpredictable and ruthless in her championship of causes and in her attacks. With her private list of "pinkos," she made Senator McCarthy sound like a choirboy.

Louella was a much softer touch, easily humored by a bunch of roses, but also erratic because she was apt to listen to the last voice before her deadline, and many of her scoops were a long way off target as a result. On one occasion she announced that Sigmund Freud, "one of the greatest psychoanalysts alive," was being brought over from Europe by director Edmund Goulding as the technical adviser on Bette Davis' picture *Dark Victory*. This posed a difficult logistical problem because Freud had been dead for several months.

When conducting interviews for her big Sunday full-page story, Louella, in her comfortable house on Maple Drive, invariably set the oldest of tongue-loosening traps—she plied her subject with glasses the size of umbrella stands, filled to the brim with whiskey or gin—but often she trapped herself by keeping the subject company and her notes became illegible.

Hedda used the same technique and plied her subjects with booze, but she shrewdly sipped tonic water herself. She always swore that her short marriage was the only sexual foray of her life; she certainly had a long procession of admirers, but she stoutly maintained that she had preserved her near virginity against overwhelming odds, and probably because of this puritan outlook, she attacked ferociously those she suspected of any extracurricular activities. She infuriated Joseph Cotten and greatly disturbed his wife, Lenore, when she printed heavy hints that Joe had been caught by the Malibu Beach patrol in the back seat of his car bestride the teenage Deanna Durbin. Joe Cotten, the epitome of the Southern gentleman from Virginia, warned Hedda that if she added one more line on the subject, he would "kick her up the ass"! Sure enough Hedda went into action again a few days later, and the next time Cotten saw Hedda's behind entering a smart Hollywood party, he lined up on the target and let her have it.

In spite of this lesson, she became a little power-mad and soon after the war laid herself wide open to lawsuits when she wrote a book, *The Whole Truth and Nothing But.* In it she wrote that she had summoned Elizabeth Taylor to her house and tried to dissuade her from marrying Michael Wilding because not only was he too old for her but he had also long indulged in homosexual relations with Stewart Granger. She had some qualms about printing this passage, however, and one Sunday afternoon she called me and asked me to come see her urgently.

Her address had changed with her fortunes. She had left the Farmer's Market neighborhood and was now settled in a charming white house on Tropical Avenue in Beverly Hills— "The House that Fear Built" she called it. As usual, I was given a hefty gin while Hedda toyed with tonic. Then she came to the point.

"Isn't it true," she asked, "that Michael Wilding was kicked out of the British navy during the war because he was a homosexual?"

When I had recovered from the shock of this nonsense, I told her of Michael's gallant record and explained the true meaning of being "invalided" out of the service.

"Well"—she sniffed—"I know that he and Granger once had a yacht together in the south of France, and I know what went on aboard that yacht."

"So do I," I answered, "and it's a miracle that the population of France didn't double."

She let out her great hoot of laughter and then read me the passage she had written.

I told her I thought she was mad to print it and was bound to get sued if she did, but she said that the publishers wanted her to spice up the book and be more controversial. "They won't sue me," she said airily, "it would only make it worse for them to drag it into court—they'll be sore for a while; then they'll forget it."

In any event, Hedda and her publisher were sued for $3,000,000 and had to cough up a hefty settlement and an abject apology.

The two ladies were made of very durable material. Producing an interesting column every day and a feature story on Sunday entailed an immense amount of hard work and very long hours. True they employed legmen and legwomen, who scurried about on their behalf digging for gossip, but all the openings and major social events they attended themselves. They also manned the telephones for hours each day, sifting pieces of information and tracking down stories. Each nurtured an army of part-time informants who worked in restaurants, agents' offices, beauty parlors, brothels, studios, and hospitals, and no picture started shooting without its complement of potential spies eager to remain in the good books of Hedda and Louella.

Neither of them was above a little gentle blackmail through the suppression technique. People dreaded an imperious telephone message—"Call Miss Parsons/Hopper—urgent"—but it was better to comply because at least there was a chance to stop something untrue or damaging from being printed; if the call went unanswered, the story was printed without further ado.

COLUMNIST: Who was that girl you were nuzzling in that little bar in the San Fernando Valley at three o'clock this morning?

ACTOR: I was with my mother.

COLUMNIST: You were *not* with your mother, you were with Gertie Garterbelt. I suppose she told her husband you were both working late?

ACTOR: Well, we were—we just dropped in for a nightcap on the way home.

COLUMNIST: According to my information, you had one of her bosoms in your hand.

ACTOR: It fell out of her dress. . . . I was just
             helping her put it back in.
COLUMNIST: Rubbish! . . . But I won't print because I
             don't want to make trouble for you.
ACTOR: Bless you—you're a doll.
COLUMNIST: Got any news for me?
ACTOR: Afraid I haven't right now.
COLUMNIST: Call me when you hear anything, dear.
ACTOR: (wiping brow): You bet I will.

And he would, too.

Both had their favorites, and these were the happy recipients of glowing praise for their good looks, talent, kindness, and cooking, but when they fell from grace, retribution was horrible—and millions were informed that they could do nothing right. Sometimes, however, because of the good ladies' antipathy one toward the other, pedestals broken by one would be pieced together by the other, and life for the fallen idol would go on much as it had before.

Jealousy might have been the reason Hedda failed to appreciate great creative talent, but Louella had no excuse for joining her in scoffing openly at such giants as Garbo, Hepburn, Olivier, and Brando, and out of the ranks of the supertalented, each chose a target for real venom. For Louella it was Orson Welles; for Hedda—Charlie Chaplin.

When she discovered that *Citizen Kane* was modeled on her boss, W. R. Hearst, and Marion Davies, Louella screamed in print like a wounded peahen and flailed away at Welles on every occasion, accusing him of avoiding war service, stealing Rita Hayworth away from brave Victor Mature (who was in the Coast Guard), and dodging taxes by moving to Europe. She pilloried RKO Pictures, which had financed the film, and, backed by the power of the Hearst press, campaigned so effectively to have the picture destroyed before it was shown to the public that the heads of the industry got together and offered RKO $3,000,000 for the negative. Fortunately, the offer was spurned, and a movie milestone was preserved, but Welles was only infrequently invited to display his talent in Hollywood thereafter.

Hedda's stream of bile played for years upon Chaplin. She hounded him in print because of his avowedly liberal politics and for the fact that after making a fortune in the United States, he was still, forty years later, a British subject, and, having been herself married to a man twenty-seven years her senior, for some reason she nearly went up in flames when she heard that Eugene O'Neill's eighteen-year-old daughter, Oona, was planning to marry Chaplin, who was thirty-six years off the pace. When she published a string of stern warnings and dire prognostications, harping always on Chaplin's suspected preference for young girls, Chaplin ignored Hedda completely and went ahead with his wedding plans.

One day a weeping pregnant girl appeared on Hedda's doorstep and announced that she was the bearer of startling news—Chaplin's child.

According to Joan Barry, she had been engaged by Chaplin to play in a film with him. She had been seduced by him, and when she became pregnant, Chaplin canceled the film and had her arrested on a vagrancy charge, for which she had received a suspended sentence.

Hedda reacted like a firehorse. She took the girl to a hospital and had her examined. She was indeed pregnant. Then she dispatched her posthaste to Chaplin's home on Summit Drive to tell him that "Hedda Hopper knows everything." Chaplin's answer to that was to call the Beverly Hills police, who arrested Joan Barry and put her in jail for three weeks.

Thanks to the publicity, however, Chaplin was now involved in a paternity suit, and Hedda crowed when his marriage was postponed. She may have stopped crowing when blood tests proved that Chaplin could not have been the baby's father, but she bypassed this in her writings and concentrated instead on the fact that Joan Barry had been awarded child support. Chaplin rose above the whole episode, however, gave no indication that he even knew of Hedda's existence, and made the announcement of the new date of his marriage—in Louella's column.

If our heroines were long on self-importance, they were also the possessors of very short fuses when it came to having their legs pulled. Thanks to the aforementioned carefully cultivated informers, stars heading for an illicit love affair ran the risk of reading about it before they had undone the first button, and happily married couples having a difference of opinion about the number of shots taken on the eleventh green at the country club could read the next morning about their impending divorce.

Ida Lupino and Howard Duff had been happily married for several years; so had Hjördis and I, but for some reason both couples had lately been subjected to a spate of printed rumors, so we decided to have a little fun with Hedda and Louella. We chose as the battleground Ciro's, the "hot" restaurant of the moment and one of the most spy-infiltrated, and after dinner at Ida's home, I called the headwaiter.

D.N.:   Could you keep a table for me around midnight?

HW: Oh, yes, indeed, Mr. Niven—it'll be a pleasure—on the dance floor . . . and for how many?

D.N.:   (in conspiratorial tones): No . . . not on the dance floor . . . in a dark corner . . . just for two—*you* understand.

HW: Oh! Yes, indeed, sir, just you and madam . . . leave everything to me.

Around midnight I arrived with Ida Lupino on my arm, and the headwaiter's eyebrows shot up into his hairline. Vibrating with suppressed excitement, he led us to a dark corner at the far end of the room and stood with eyes glistening as Ida started nibbling my ear.

Somebody wasted no time in getting to the phone because by the time Ida and I had finished our second drink a battery of photographers was massing in the bar.

Howard and Hjördis timed their arrival perfectly, and the entire restaurant watched spellbound as a jittery headwaiter led them to a table as far away as possible from Ida and myself.

They made a lovely couple, and out of the corner of my

eye, I could see Howard draping himself over Hjördis like a
tent.

Howard had quite a reputation as a brawler, and as I was
pretending to be quite high, there was an expectant hush
when Howard, judging his moment with great expertise,
suddenly pushed his table over with a crash and rose to his
feet, pointing at me across the room with a dramatically accusing finger.

Hjördis tried to restrain her partner, as did Ida when I
staggered to my feet, though I thought Ida overacted a bit by
screaming, "No, no! Darling! You must flee! . . . He'll kill
you!"

Shrugging off the ineffectual clutching hands of women
and waiters, Howard and I advanced upon each other from
opposite sides of the restaurant. The place was deathly quiet,
and the photographers, headed by the veteran Hymie Fink,
moved expectantly into position for the scoop when like two
cowboys in the classic ending of Westerns, stalking each other down the empty street at sunset, we moved inexorably forward through the crowded and silent tables. At the edge of
the now-deserted dance floor, with eyes immovably locked,
we removed our jackets and rolled up our sleeves. Then we
advanced again and circled each other a couple of times. You
could have heard a pin drop; people at the back were standing on chairs. Suddenly, we sprang, grabbed each other
around the waist, kissed on the lips, and waltzed slowly
around the floor. A disappointed headwaiter set up a new table for four, and the ensuing revelry was recorded by the
more sporting among the photographers, but the two queens
of the columns were not amused. . . . I got calls from both
the next day telling me that they would not tolerate being
woken up in the middle of the night over a false alarm.

Louella and Hedda were not averse to a little "payola."
Louella had earlier conned important stars into appearing
on her radio show, *Hollywood Hotel.* Hedda had been less successful with her program, *Hedda Hopper's Hollywood,* but later
made a successful transition with it to television, where she
"persuaded" the biggest names in movieland to appear with
her. This program stole a lot of viewers away from the Great

Stoneface (Ed Sullivan), appearing at the same time on a rival network, and Sullivan complained bitterly that he was paying full salary to the performers on his show whereas Hedda was paying nothing to the lineup she had announced for hers—Gary Cooper, Judy Garland, Joan Crawford, Bette Davis, Lucille Ball, and Charlton Heston.

Some of Louella's payoffs were subtle: She persuaded Twentieth Century-Fox to buy the film rights to her unfilmable autobiography and made it quite clear to producers that whenever her husband, Dr. Harry Martin, was hired as "technical adviser" on their films, they would not lack for publicity.

Being a "clap" doctor, "Dockie" Martin was a very useful member of the community. Venereal disease increases in direct proportion to promiscuous fornication, so with Hollywood not being famous for the chastity of its citizens, it was inevitable that through the good doctor's waiting room passed some of the most famous private parts in the world. Many sufferers who had survived Dockie's extremely painful pre-penicillin treatments were understandably worried, in view of his marital setup, that news of their misfortunes might leak to the press, but the doctor in his bedchamber or in his cups stoutly stood by his Hippocratic oath.

Dockie, who resembled a gone-to-seed middleweight, was a heavy drinker, and people with uncomfortable appointments ahead of them on the morrow watched apprehensively as he consumed huge quantities of alcohol on the eve of the encounter.

It was on just such an occasion, during a dinner party, that he slid quietly under the table. Two men moved to pick him up but were stopped by Louella, who said, "Oh, let poor Dockie get a little sleep—he's operating in the morning."

Irving Thalberg and Norma Shearer chartered a yacht and took a party of us one weekend to Catalina. The doctor was determined to catch a fish during the four-hour crossing to the island and sat in a wicker chair, trolling a big white bone lure astern. A steward kept him topped up during the voyage with a steady stream of his favorite beverage—gin fizz. After a couple of hours he turned to me.

"Hold the rod for me, willya, Dave? . . . I've gotta take a leak."

No sooner had the doctor's head disappeared belowdecks than with a bang! and a screech! a twenty-pound tuna hit his lure. By the time a relieved doctor reappeared his fish had been brought to gaff, and the yacht was once more gathering speed.

Almost exactly two hours later a now well-oiled physician asked me once more to hold his rod. Bang! Screech! It happened again, but this time he heard it and came weaving back on deck with his dress not adjusted, causing Eddie Goulding to say in a pained voice, "Dockie, please do up your fly; we've all *seen* Louella's column."

Later that day, when we dropped anchor in Avalon Bay, Dockie rowed Louella ashore in the dinghy "to have a couple of snorts at the hotel." When they returned, not only was his oarsmanship most peculiar, but on arrival he ungallantly stepped onto the gangway ahead of his wife, at the same time pushing off from the dinghy. Louella, dutifully and equally unsteadily following her husband, stepped into forty fathoms of water, which was embarrassing for her because she couldn't swim. Goulding and I fished her out.

Louella and Dockie were a devoted couple, and evenings at their home were relaxed and unpretentious. The conversation was strictly movie shop. At Hedda's, evenings were gayer, brighter and, because of Hedda's friends and interests outside Hollywood, more cosmopolitan and much more stimulating.

She was a sparkling hostess, chic, gay, witty, and acid. She used a great variety of four-letter words and enjoyed hearing her two poodles sing to her piano playing. Hedda always stated that she would make up for her late arrival in competition with Louella "by outlasting the old bag." By the mid-forties both ladies were nearing seventy, and some heavy bets were laid in movieland as to which one would run out of steam first, but seemingly indestructible, they continued to work punishing hours, and their columns were still widely read despite a certain erosion of readers. The old stars who had played the publicity game with Louella and Hedda were fad-

ing fast, and the new ones—Brando, Holden, Newman, and
Dean—and the young producers and directors found it old-
fashioned and unnecessary to bother about Hedda and
Louella. The war was over; tastes were changing; like most
royalty, they were an anachronism; and anyway, newspaper
circulations were dropping all over the country. But if Hedda and Louella recognized all this, they gave no sign of it except, sensing perhaps that they were entering the last few
furlongs, each redoubled her efforts to outdo the other, and
oneupwomanship became the order of their day.

The super love goddess Rita Hayworth decided to take her
first trip abroad and asked my advice on a trip around Europe. Knowing how genuinely shy and gentle she was and re-
specting her longing to avoid the goldfish bowl of publicity, I
worked out a complicated itinerary for her, starting with a
small Swedish liner to Gothenburg, quiet country hotels and
mountain villages all the way south, and ending up in an oasis of Mediterranean calm, the Hotel La Reserve in Beaulieu-
sur-Mer.

Rita departed with a girlfriend and the works of Jean-Paul
Sartre. Everything went beautifully according to plan, and
after three leisurely and peaceful weeks, she arrived radiant-
ly relaxed at La Reserve. The champion charmer of Europe,
Prince Ali Khan, saw her walk in, and a new chapter was added to Hollywood history.

It was indeed a romantic match, and Hedda and Louella
spent frustrating weeks angling for invitations to the wedding. The ceremony was to be held at L'Horizon, the Ali's
pink villa near Cannes—an enchanting place to look at from
the sea with its feet in the blue water, but a difficult place in
which to carry on a conversation when the express trains to
Italy thundered past the kitchen door.

The Ali had no intention whatever of having a Hollywood-
style wedding, and all newspaper reporters received a blank
refusal to their requests for inclusion on the guest list.

Hedda and Louella could not believe that this treatment of
the press included them, and they were particularly irked
that with their immense power, their supplications received
the same cold shoulder as that turned toward the local re-

porter from Nice *Matin*. Poor gentle Rita with her inbred Hollywood fear of Hedda and Louella needed all the Ali's Olympian calm when threatening and ominous calls came from Beverly Hills, but she held her ground, and neither was invited to the wedding. Both ladies, however, goaded by their powerful employers, headed for the south of France, hoping for a last-minute breakthrough.

Louella, much to Hedda's chagrin, persuaded Elsa Maxwell, the famous party giver and sometime columnist, to take her along with her to a large buffet luncheon at L'Horizon a week before the wedding. Once she had her foot in the door, Louella pulled out all the stops, and appreciating the pressure that was piling up on Rita, the Ali finally agreed that Louella's name could be added to the wedding list.

If Louella was in a position to crow, Hedda was more than ever determined to square the account. She harangued the frustrated French reporters milling around Cannes, Antibes, and Juan-les-Pins. "How disgraceful," she told them, "that such favoritism is being shown to an American journalist."

At last, an embittered Parisian newshawk broke the deadlock. He unearthed a Provencal law from Napoleonic times which stated that no wedding could be held in private if one citizen objected. Dozens of citizens—reporters from all over France—signed the objection, and the local mayor announced that the wedding must be held in public at the *mairie*. Hedda had squared the account, but both she and Louella, after all their efforts, had to swallow their pride and join a cast of thousands hoping to catch a glimpse of the bride and groom.

When Louella reached the age of eighty-one, she was still writing her column, but the flagship of her syndication fleet was foundering, and one day it sank without trace. The Los Angeles *Examiner* ceased publication, leaving the Los Angeles *Times* as the sole morning newspaper in the city. Louella retired, and the stripling seventy-six-year-old Hedda had realized her wish—"to outlast the old bag."

She continued writing her column till the age of eighty-one, when illness incapacitated her, but she went down firing broadsides from her deathbed.

"I hear that son of a bitch Chaplin is trying to get back into the country," she told all and sundry. "We've *got* to stop him!"

Neither of them would have won a scholarship at MIT, or even obtained good marks for grammar, and most of their crusades turned out to be a waste of ink. Chaplin returned in triumph to receive a special Oscar in Hollywood; Orson Welles was forgiven; *Gone with the Wind* rose above the fact that David O. Selznick had "insulted Hollywood by employing an English actress to play Scarlett O'Hara"; Ingrid Bergman overcame the screams of outrage caused by her romance on Stromboli; Senator McCarthy inevitably became a nasty word; and Brando continued to be Brando.

Hedda and Louella had power out of all proportion to their ability and a readership out of all proportion to their literacy. They had delusions of grandeur and skins like brontosaurs, but they were gallant, persevering, and often softhearted. They interfered in casting and were partisan in politics; they helped some beginners and hindered some established filmmakers, but they could not be faulted when it came to their devotion to Hollywood, and they tried daily to preserve it as it stood—a wondrous structure of corruption, fear, talent, and triumphs, a consortium of Dream Factories pumping out entertainments for millions.

Perhaps they did not do much good, but on the other hand, they didn't do much harm either, and it's a good thing they were both spared the spectacle of the once-mighty Metro-Goldwyn-Mayer in its death throes auctioning off Fred Astaire's dancing shoes, Elizabeth Taylor's bra, and Judy Garland's rainbow.

5
Degrees of Friendliness

REPUTATIONS and fortunes were made out of movies by producers, directors, and actors, but if they had not had good screenplays to work with, they would have sat around picking their noses. For some incredible reason, however, the writers were treated by the studios as second-class citizens, grossly underpaid, housed in rabbit-warren offices, ordered to punch a time clock, and instantly blamed if a director or a star could not cope with the matter in hand. "Get the goddamned writer on the set" would be the cry. As a result of this folly a permanent state of war existed between some of the best brains in the world and the movie moguls.

Counterattacks were launched. Charles MacArthur introduced an illiterate London-born garage mechanic to L. B. Mayer as "the hottest playwright in England since George Bernard Shaw," and the young man was promptly given an office and $1,000 a week.

Wilson Mizner announced that working for Warner Brothers was like fucking a porcupine—"it's a hundred pricks against one"—and William Faulkner, rebelling against the Metro-Goldwyn-Mayer edict that writers must be in their miserable little broom-closet offices, pounding their typewriters from nine till six, demanded that he be allowed to work at home. Two months later, after frantic nonproductive phone calls and a spate of telegrams to his Hollywood apartment, someone remembered that he lived in Mississippi.

Samuel Goldwyn early on appreciated and paid for the

writers' true worth and, as a result, attracted the best, among them Somerset Maugham, Maurice Maeterlinck, Robert Sherwood, Sinclair Lewis, and Lillian Hellman.

Writers, being human and usually broke, scenting the easy money to be picked up in Hollywood, had packed up their typewriters and headed west. Once there, they separated into two main groups, those who blessed Hollywood for pay- ing them money and those who cursed it for the same rea- son. There was also a third group, headed by the hornet Eve- lyn Waugh (who insulted my nice black housekeeper by re- ferring to her as "your native bearer"), which grabbed the Hollywood gold and departed at high speed to rail against the place and to denigrate its inhabitants.

Of the various writer cliques, the Garden of Allah set was the most flamboyant—living in small, badly furnished stucco cottages, clustered around a central kidney-shaped pool, a well-frequented bar, and a suspect dining room which dis- pensed instant ptomaine poisoning.

Lodged there myself for a while, I became a sleepless wreck from the nights made hideous by the laughter, battles, and mating cries of Robert Benchley, Dorothy Parker, Charlie MacArthur, Donald Ogden Stewart, and others, all alumni of the Algonquin Group from New York and a fas- cinating mixture of talent, booze, eccentricity, and liberal ideas. They were regarded with some alarm by Hollywood.

"Mr. Stewart, I feel so silly with you dancing in that long black overcoat. *Please* take it off."

He did—and was stark naked.

Charlie MacArthur found a way to travel back cheaply to New York. He contacted the local undertakers and asked them to let him know if any Eastern families required an es- cort for their loved ones who had died in California.

On one trip, according to the Garden of Allah barman, with the casket in the goods van, Charlie got waylaid by friends during the Chicago stopover and decided to take in the Kentucky Derby. The corpse went with him on the side trip to Louisville.

Dorothy Parker specialized in making "immortal" quotes.

Rollicking, pear-shaped Robert Benchley hated birds.

"They're not too bad in profile, but have you ever seen the sons of bitches head on?"

He called me early one morning when I was away in San Francisco. "Is it raining up there?" he asked.

"No, it's lovely," I assured him.

"Raining like hell down here," he said and started to laugh. "You know that little pathway outside my bungalow? Well, it's got a lot of water on it right now." Another paroxysm of mirth. "A bird, a big black bastard with a yellow beak, just came in for a landing, and it skidded and sat right on its ass!"

And one writer wandered about the garden bemoaning the fact that he owed his teenaged son $40,000.

"I wanted him to get off his ass during the summer vacation," he said, "so I told him I'd double anything he earned. Well, the little son of a bitch wrote a pornographic book, and it's a best-seller."

The thing that worried the man most was the research that must have gone into his son's literary effort.

In the summer of 1939 Samuel Goldwyn called me to his office. I was about to make *Raffles—The Amateur Cracksman* for him.

"I'm not happy with the script," said Goldwyn, "so I'm going to put back the start for a few days and get a new writer on it—Scott Fitzgerald. He starts tomorrow."

That same day I ran into a producer, Walter Wanger. I had lately finished a picture for him.

"How's *Raffles* coming?" he asked.

I told him the latest news, and he was horrified.

"Fitzgerald! Forget it! He's nothing but trouble. I just had him with me on location in New England, and it was hopeless. Drunk as a skunk the entire time, missing trains, getting lost, insulting people. He never wrote a line I could use. Finally, I kicked him off the picture."

Merritt Hulbert, the head of Goldwyn's story department, was an ex-editor of the *Saturday Evening Post*.

"Fitzgerald is a lush," he said when I questioned him, "and he's never made it as a screenwriter, but he's written some beautiful stuff in the past. We bought a lot of his short stories for the *Post.*"

I had never read it, so he handed me a copy of *Tender Is the Night.*

"Mr. Goldwyn has given him the job because he feels sorry for him, but I don't think he'll come up with very much for this picture. Your agent talked Mr. Goldwyn into it," Hulbert added.

"Scott's a drunk, but he's still a brilliant man. Also, he's sick, so be nice to him," said my agent, Leland Hayward.

Fitzgerald is impossible for me to describe because he gave the impression of being absent, and he looked so frail that he seemed to be floating: mid-forties, Valentino profile, rather weak mouth, and haunted eyes. He carried a large writing pad and a cardboard container of Coca-Cola bottles when I first saw him and made a little nest for himself in a corner of the sound stage.

After a few days' delay, the picture had finally started shooting with, as far as I could judge, only minimal changes to the original script. I introduced myself, and Fitzgerald rose from his chair, which, as he was over twenty years my senior, surprised me; then he passed me a bottle of Coca-Cola—a strange gesture at eight thirty in the morning.

"I drink dozens a day," he explained, and added, with a flash of fun in the vacant eyes, "It's all I *can* drink these days."

I offered him the use of the icebox in my comfortable dressing-room suite, a short distance away. He gratefully availed himself of this and, as the picture progressed, of the divan bed that stood near it. He rested a lot.

Scott Fitzgerald did not contribute very much in the way of sparkling dialogue in the weeks to come, and if ever the director asked him for a quick change of a line or a piece of business, he looked scared and dithered, but he never took a drink. He just melted into the background, scribbling away on his big writing pads and, to the annoyance of the sound man, coughing continually.

At lunchtime he liked to come across the street with me to the Mimosa Café, a crummy Chinese restaurant, frequented by bookies and minor crooks; while I ate, he gulped down more Coca-Colas.

"I'm on the wagon for good," he said.

Actually, I found him rather heavy going, with his long silences and tales of bad luck at the hands of the movie moguls, but his was a genuine frustration because he had really studied filmmaking, was fascinated by the medium and, unlike many of his contemporaries, did not feel that all producers were illiterate half-wits.

I mentioned, one day, how much I had enjoyed *Tender Is the Night*, and he was galvanized. He suddenly came alive; he could not believe that a spoiled young actor had ever heard of it, let alone wished to discuss it. Little did he know that I had read it the night before, simply and solely to give myself some conversational ammunition.

He told me how pleased he was to have the job on the picture because he could now afford to put his automobile back on the road. When I looked disbelieving, he said that no writer worth a damn misses a chance to utilize his own experiences however dire: "that is why I have made Raffles explain to his friend that he has to do something desperate because he's just hocked his convertible."

In the middle of the filming Hitler attacked peaceful Poland and unleashed the horror of World War II. I told Fitzgerald that as soon as the picture was finished, I would go back to Europe and volunteer for the British army.

He was fascinated by this quixotic decision and became very maudlin about it, declaring his intention of coming with me.

"I missed out last time," he said wistfully. "I left it too late. I didn't join up until 1917—I never got to go overseas." He became quite dreamy-eyed about the impending heroics with his mind firmly focused on Agincourt and white chargers.

Just when I was beginning to like a lot, and perhaps understand a little, this strange, haunted, withdrawn, and massively insecure man, Goldwyn fired him.

Goldwyn had told him that he was contributing little to the picture and, in particular, had taken exception to a love scene Fitzgerald had written for Olivia de Havilland and myself:

RAFFLES: Smile!
DE HAVILLAND: (pressing closer . . . smiles)

RAFFLES: Wider! I'm going to ask you a *very* important question.

DE HAVILLAND: (expectantly) Oh! Darling!

RAFFLES: Tell me . . . who is your dentist?

Fitzgerald took his dismissal calmly. "It always happens," he said and buoyed himself up with the thought that, thanks to Goldwyn, he could now afford to work full time on a novel which he had started and upon which he had presumably been using up his yellow pads at a great rate.

I thought no more about him till one day, at the tail end of the production, we were doing a cricketing sequence—supposedly at some English county house which I was about to rob, and the game, in 110-degree heat, was being photographed on a polo field in Pasadena.

The director, Sam Wood, had been taken ill, and the great William Wyler had taken over. He knew nothing about cricket and had set things up like a baseball game, leaving me to unravel the shambles.

Just as we got things straightened out, a cry rose from the outfield, and the actors froze in their unaccustomed white flannels. "Hey, hey, my buddy! . . . I've been looking all over for you, buddy! Where the helluvya been, buddy?"

Scott Fitzgerald came tottering across the green turf like a stage drunk, weaving in great arcs.

Wyler, a meticulous professional, not renowned for his patience, was compassion itself, while I, profoundly embarrassed, like a little boy attempting to get rid of a piece of sticky paper in a breeze, tried to disentangle myself from my clinging visitor.

At last, I persuaded him to go and rest in my caravan till we had finished the day's work. He was escorted there, cosseted and given refreshment by Irving Sindler, the propman, but this retreat was only agreed to after much loud bartering, on condition that I would accompany him later to Don the Beachcombers to "drink all the rum in California."

Don, a thin, good-looking, philosophical, raffish character, was just that—a genuine beachcomber.

He owned a minute bar on McCadden Place just off Hollywood Boulevard which could accommodate, at most, twenty people. There he mixed his own inventions, delicious and exotic drinks composed of various rums, fruit juices, and flower petals. He served these wearing white dungarees and a dirty white undershirt. Frequently, he was fined for causing a nuisance; he had installed a powerful watering system above his establishment and delighted in requests for tropical rain, turning it on and deluging the passersby.

When Don had made enough dollars from dispensing his marvelous concoctions, he hung a sign outside the door of his bar—GONE TO THE ISLANDS—and off he went: to remote parts of Hawaii, there to sit on white sand beneath the palm trees and drink rum from coconuts. When he was broke, he returned to McCadden Place and removed the sign.

I spent the greater part of that night with Scott Fitzgerald listening to an outpouring of woe, charm, lost-youth sadness, boasts, family disasters, nostalgia, fears, hopes, pure babbling, and a lot of coughing. I suppose to me, numbed by Don's endless ministrations, it was, by turns, flattering to be the confidant of a man twice my age and a crashing bore to be pinned against the end of the bar, the recipient of so much self-pity and so many intellectual rationalizations. I longed to go to bed.

I never saw him again.

A little over a year later, at the height of the London blitz, I read that back in Hollywood, "the unemployed writer" Scott Fitzgerald had died of tuberculosis and that he had left behind him a brilliant, unfinished novel, *The Last Tycoon*. Later I learned that Dorothy Parker had looked at his coffin and quoted from *The Great Gatsby*: "Poor son of a bitch."

An endless stream of writers washed up on the Hollywood shores. Some were unappreciated, most were underpaid, and a few could hardly be trusted to address an envelope.

The refugees from Hitler arrived in droves and headed for the Hollywood Hills: Thomas and Heinrich Mann, Leon Feuchtwanger, Franz Werfel, Bruno Frank, Emil Ludwig, and Bertolt Brecht. When Erich Maria Remarque was not wrapped around Marlene Dietrich or other local beauties, he acted as a sort of liaison officer between the German-speaking foreigners, the Garden of Allah set, and Musso and

Frank's Restaurant on Hollywood Boulevard, where the brilliant William Saroyan and Budd Schulberg made their headquarters. Sooner or later they all showed up, a tidal wave of talent.

Besides Fitzgerald, the American writers who came and went while I was there included Hemingway, Thornton Wilder, Zane Grey, Robert Sherwood, John Steinbeck, Irving Stone, Raymond Chandler, George Kaufman, Moss Hart, Lillian Hellman, John O'Hara, Irwin Shaw, S. N. Behrman, Elmer Rice, Paul Gallico, and a thousand others; and the British contingent alone contained, among others, Maugham, H. G. Wells, P. G. Wodehouse, Hugh Walpole, J. B. Priestley, Graham Greene, Arnold Bennett, R. C. Sherriff, Christopher Isherwood, Eric Ambler, and Frederick Lonsdale. It was the greatest convention of brilliance ever assembled, but so much was watered down, wasted, or filtered out by megalomaniac producers that tragically little of the output of these famous authors ever reached the screen.

The writers, for the most part, swallowed their pride and rolled with the punches.

Clifford Odets gracefully admitted that he appreciated the money because "of thirteen plays I have written, I have made a living out of only two."

Nathanael West agreed: "Before I came here I tried to work seriously at my craft but was unable to make a living."

James Hilton murmured, "A movie writer must make his own reckoning as to whether he would rather say, a little less exactly what he wants, to millions or, a little more exactly, to thousands."

George Bernard Shaw was more cynical and, after listening to Samuel Goldwyn expatiating on the art of making pictures, closed the conversation by saying, "That's the difference between us. . . . You talk of art, Mr. Goldwyn, I think of money."

It was left to the rebel William Faulkner to lay it on the line: "I get sick of those people who say if they were free of Hollywood what they'd do. They wouldn't do anything. It's not the pictures that are at fault. The writer is not accustomed to money. It goes to his head and destroys him—not pictures. Pictures are trying to pay for what they get. Frequently they overpay, but does that debase the writer? Nothing can injure a man's writing if he's a first-class writer. If he's not a first-class writer, there's not anything can help it much."

The writers of Hollywood, however opulent they became, clung tenaciously to their prerogative to be inquisitive crusaders and could not keep their pens shut when they sniffed the whiff of suppression.

Less than two years after the end of World War II the first microbes of a foul disease that was to spread across the fair face of the United States surfaced in Hollywood. Senator Joseph McCarthy and his two loathsome lieutenants, Cohn and Schine, had not yet succeeded in infecting the land with McCarthyism, but a cry of "There are Reds under Hollywood's beds" was raised in Washington, and the House Committee on Un-American Affairs opened an investigation on Communist infiltration of the motion picture industry. Immense publicity was generated by the ensuing circuslike proceedings under the chairmanship of a highly biased gentleman named Parnell Thomas. Richard Nixon was a member of the investigation team.

Some full-blooded support for the theory that Hollywood was in grave danger of becoming a tool of the Communist Party was given by a long list of "friendly" witnesses, including L. B. Mayer, the head of MGM; Jack Warner of Warner Brothers; Walt Disney; Gary Cooper; Robert Montgomery; Adolphe Menjou; George Murphy, later U.S. Senator from California; Ronald Reagan, who became governor of the same state; and Ginger Rogers' mother, who remained Ginger Rogers' mother. Between them these "friendly witnesses" named a few of their fellow workers as Communists and pointed to a larger group as "acting like Communists." Before long, all these people were paraded before Parnell Thomas and Co.; many became known as the "unfriendly witnesses."

Hollywood, by instinct and common sense, was a town largely disinterested in politics; it was a community dedicated to the manufacture of mass entertainment for people all over the world, regardless of how they voted, but it was also traditionally relaxed about those who took their politics seriously. Of course, we know that a few among us were Communists, but we also knew that others were Holy Rollers and that quite a number practiced black magic, but so long as the Communist Party was officially recognized by the government and not outlawed in the United States, Hollywood did not feel that people who felt strongly enough to join it should be treated like criminals.

So the great majority watched sadly while a small minority tore itself to pieces. It all seemed so unnecessary, because it was quite impossible for a tiny group of writers, directors, and actors to subvert for Communist propaganda the motion-picture industry when the whole business was in the hands of a dozen men.

The writers and directors could possibly inject small doses of Communist ideology into innocent-looking scripts, and perhaps the actors might be capable of giving an innocuous line a sinister twist, but the producers controlled the finished pictures, and there was just no way that the Seven Dwarfs could be Reds under Snow White's bed unless Walt Disney wanted them there.

The macabre farce unfolded, and Parnell Thomas allowed the friendly witnesses to make opening statements but denied the same opportunity to the unfriendly witnesses.

The crunch question which the unfriendly witnesses all faced was this: "Are you now, or have you ever been, a member of the Communist Party?"

If a witness stated that he was a Communist, he was then required by Parnell Thomas to inform on his fellow party members. If he declined to do so, he went to jail for contempt. If he denied that he was a Communist and was then proved to be a party member, he went to jail for perjury, and if he refused to answer the question at all, he could go to jail for contempt of Congress.

In the end ten witnesses went to jail, the best known of whom were the writer John Howard Lawson, whom Parnell Thomas ordered to be forcibly removed from the witness stand by armed guards when he insisted loudly that his rights as an American citizen were being invaded; Dalton Trumbo, the writer, who was refused an opportunity to cross-question witnesses when they stated that he had Communist Party affiliations; the writer Sam Ornitz, who was also forcibly removed after an altercation with Parnell Thomas; the well-known director Eddie Dmytryk, who, because he claimed constitutional immunity, was refused a chance to cross-question witnesses; and the writer Ring Lardner, Jr., who was denied the opportunity to read a closing statement in his own defense.

Two breaths of fresh air blew through the committee room when Eric Johnston, the president of the Motion Picture Association, and Dore Schary were called as witnesses. Somehow they managed to be neither "friendly" nor "unfriendly" and to get in some fairly sharp criticism of Parnell Thomas' handling of the investigation. "Don't put any American who is not a Communist in a concentration camp of suspicion," warned Johnston, and Schary, who was the head of production at RKO Studios, made it quite clear that he would not hesitate to hire a Communist unless it was proved that he was a foreign agent and pointed out that the Supreme Court had ruled that an employer could not refuse a man work because of his political convictions. Schary's attitude so infuriated the columnist Hedda Hopper that from then on she waged a campaign against him, accusing him of everything "pinko" and only stopping short of announcing that he himself was a paid-up member of the party.

As Hollywood had predicted, the top brass of the industry stoutly denied that any Communist propaganda could possibly get by them, and Hollywood was indignant when Parnell Thomas handed down his report on the investigation: "The outlines and pattern of Communist activity in the industry was clearly disclosed." When the unfriendly witnesses returned from jail, they were promptly blacklisted by the studios and were only able to work abroad or by using false names. One writer won an Oscar with a pen name which caused an embarrassed lull in the proceedings on Academy Award night, when the winner's name was announced.

Apart from that, the only fun Hollywood extracted from the whole unfortunate episode was when it learned that at the very moment the Unfriendly Ten were being released from prison, Parnell Thomas was himself being locked up for padding a government payroll with fictitious names and keeping the salaries for himself.

So much for the curtain raiser. Three and a half years later there was a much bigger investigation, covering not only Hollywood, but the whole spectrum of the entertainment industry; it lasted from March, 1951, to November, 1952. Almost a hundred witnesses appeared before the chairman, John S. Wood, and his committee: they were roughly divided between "friendlies" and "unfriendlies." The names of the witnesses were more illustrious, the committee members more reasonable, and most of the acrimony and ill temper displayed before by both sides were avoided.

This time nobody went to jail.

In three and a half years, times had changed. Not, let it be said, thanks to Senator McCarthy's myopic misrepresentations, but by the actions of the Russians themselves, who by focusing the attention of the free world on their own brutal purges and the Berlin Wall among other things, had made it painfully obvious to Americans that their brave allies of World War II still had a highly unattractive side to them.

It had become increasingly difficult to justify the U.S. Communist Party, and many of its Hollywood members, including a large percentage of the original Unfriendly Ten, this time around not only told the committee how disenchanted they had become with it, but were happy to help along its demise by volunteering a list of erstwhile friends who were still members.

Directors Eddie Dmytryk, Elia Kazan, and Frank Tuttle and actor Sterling Hayden were not thought of highly in Hollywood for "shopping" their friends, but their motives, as they described them, seemed perfectly sincere. Sterling Hayden had doubts about his behavior, however, and later described his effort as a "one-shot stoolie show," but those who knew him for an extremely honest human being and a courageous fighting man who had spent many months in Yugoslavia during World War II with the partisans behind the German lines realized that he was once more putting country before self and self at great risk—this time from the blacklist.

The Hollywood blacklist swelled considerably during these

second hearings. Those who were exposed as present or past members of the Communist Party or who refused to answer the crunch question as to whether they were or not risked the total eclipse of their careers, and those who "squealed" risked, in addition, the hatred of their fellows and the cold shoulders of the pious noninvolved, and by the time the John S. Wood investigation had finished, McCarthyism was in full spate and the Hollywood blacklist was bursting at the seams. All unfriendly witnesses were automatically blacklisted but a sort of gray list was reserved for some friendly witnesses as well. The smell of fear was everywhere.

The actors suffered most. They could not change their names or their faces, and for several years they endured terrible hardships; many saw their careers collapse completely.

The writers suffered less financially because they could always go on writing under assumed names. Many did so abroad, but it was humiliating and soul-destroying work, and no one will ever know how much inventive and progressive talent during that period was stifled and stultified.

The tiny Communist group in Hollywood was certainly crushed like a beetle as a result of the two investigations, but it was never proved that it was even remotely possible that it could have "infiltrated" the motion-picture industry.

Hollywood was deeply wounded, however, and for years friendships, careers, marriages, and reputations lay in tatters as the arguments waxed and waned about who had behaved well, who had behaved badly, and who had saved their skins at the expense of others. "It is not enough to have informed. . . . You must also have talent!" became a favorite slogan on the walls of Warner Brothers.

Since I had worked with dozens of friendlies and unfriendlies, it was horrifying to see what happened to some of them as a result of the investigations and the spreading disease of McCarthyism. The bigger they were, the more likely they were to survive. The small ones mostly went under, and some, completely unconnected with the whole operation, suddenly found themselves under suspicion. No explanations were given; no responsibility was accepted; no one felt safe.

F. Hugh Herbert was the highly respected president of the Screen Writers Guild. I had done a play and a movie of his and was a great admirer of him and of his work.

As vice-president of Four Star Television, I was always on the lookout for good short stories for the many series our company was producing.

"Help yourself," said Hugh, when I was discussing this with him. "I have a whole trunkful of them. Take any you like."

I spent some time at his house reading through his output and soon found one that was perfect.

Nat Woolf was our contact man at the advertising agency which had provided the sponsor for the series in question.

When I told him I had obtained a story by F. Hugh Herbert, he was elated, and when he read the story, he agreed with me that it was exactly right for the show.

A few days later Nat came to see me at my house and was evidently embarrassed.

"That story of Hugh Herbert's, it's not going to work, I'm afraid," he said.

"Why not?" I asked. "You said you loved it, and you're the one I have to clear it with."

"It's not the story," said Nat. "It's Hugh."

Then I dragged out of him the fact that "someone," and Nat refused to say if it was someone at his agency or with the sponsoring company, had said, "We don't want anything from F. Hugh Herbert because he's a Commie."

I roared with laughter. "There's no way Hugh could be a Communist!" I said. "I've known him personally for years, he's president of the Screen Writers Guild, and his name never even came up in connection with the committees."

Nat was very uncomfortable. "Well," he said, "I'm not happy about it either, believe me. I think it's a load of crap, but you'll have to look for another story."

Hugh Herbert was incredulous when I told him; then he laughed; then he became very angry indeed.

"This is the sort of thing I hate with every bone in my body," he said. "Will you tell them you insist on doing my story and then ask for their reasons in writing if they refuse? I've got over two million dollars in the bank, and I'll happily spend the lot to find the son of a bitch who started this campaign against me."

In any event, Hugh Herbert never did find out. In due course I received a letter from the agency regretting that the first appraisal of F. Hugh Herbert's short story had been a trifle hasty and that they had decided that they would like me to present an alternative property for consideration. I did, I sent three more of Hugh Herbert's excellent stories and received three more refusals.

The fourth Hugh Herbert story I presented was accepted with alacrity. It did not make Hugh or Nat or myself feel any better when I confessed that I had changed the name of the author.

6
Errol

*I*T was a typical warm, scented south of France evening. It was, also, an ostentatious, scented south of France party, taking place in the beautiful gardens of a monstrosity of a house constructed at the turn of the century, with the maximum of financial outlay and the minimum of taste, by a Belgian textile millionaire. Now the place had been rented by a socially ambitious American couple—he the head of a proliferating conglomerate, she, on a voluntary basis, writing for a New York fashion magazine.

Not knowing any of the local residents or the so-called beautiful people from Paris and Rome, the American couple had cut the corners by hiring an international pederast, who had at his fingertips a list of the sort of people they believed would be good for their image.

The house and garden had been facelifted and lit by a decorator brought from California. Maxim's in Paris had provisioned the extravaganza, and a hot "group" from London had been flown down to ensure, with the aid of electronic equipment, that conversation would be cut to a minimum. The wine flowed, and the beautiful people, miming that they were having a marvelous time, pointedly ignored their host and hostess and paraded around, smiling vacuously at each other.

The evening brightened for me in the early hours when a young couple approached. She was a very beautiful Italian

113

actress with whom I had made a film not too long before; he was tall, extremely good-looking and had something about him that seemed vaguely familiar.

The girl smiled her beautiful smile, all lovely white teeth and glowing brown satin skin, and embraced me warmly as she breathed in my ear an introduction to the young man behind her. I put out my hand, which he seemed not to see.

"I know you were a friend of my father," he said in a loud voice. "Please don't mention his name to *me*." I replied, perhaps a trifle tartly, "That would be difficult because I haven't yet heard *yours!*"

The Italian girl made a quick up-rolling-of-the-eyes "sorry" and steered the young man away. Intrigued, I cornered the pederast and requested information.

"Why, that's Sean Flynn," he said. "Isn't he *beautiful?*"

Yes, undoubtedly he was, and it is sickening to think that as of this writing he is still "missing believed dead" as a particularly gallant news photographer in Vietnam.

Errol Flynn had indeed been a friend of mine; for a while a very close friend. We started together in Hollywood at exactly the same time.

The great thing about Errol was you always knew exactly where you stood with him because he *always* let you down. He let himself down, too, from time to time, but that was his prerogative and he thoroughly enjoyed causing turmoil for himself and his friends.

When we started off in the Hollywood studios, the flacks went to work on us. I was publicized as the "son of a famous Scottish general" (in actual fact, my father had been killed in 1915 with the rank of second lieutenant), and Flynn was widely reported to be "as Irish as the potato and coming straight from a successful career with the Abbey Players." By some inscrutable logic, Warner Brothers decided that Errol would be more palatable to the American public as an Irish potato than as himself—an Australian whose upbringing had been in Tasmania and New Guinea.

I first met Errol in Lili Damita's bungalow at the Garden of Allah in the summer of 1935.

Lili was a beautiful hourglass-shaped creature who epitomizcd the sexy French cover girls of *La Vie Parisienne*, but she was also one of those insecure ladies who feel the necessity to be surrounded by devout homosexuals, and as her usual little coterie was around her that night, for a while both Flynn and I thought the other was a fag.

After sniffing suspiciously, we got this sorted out, and a tour of the dives off Hollywood Boulevard became the logical outcome of the evening. Flynn had that day completed his first part under his contract with Warner Brothers, playing a corpse on a marble slab in *The Case of the Curious Bride*, so we had much to celebrate, and during our foray he unburdened himself of his obsession with Lili. Their love affair blossomed quickly thereafter, and they were soon permanently bedded down in a house in the Hollywood Hills—an adventurous move at the time because Hollywood was still reeling from the highly publicized excesses of the "Silent Days," and the spectacle of two people openly living together was both abhorrent to the hypocritical big studio brass and a salacious bonanza for the gossip columnists.

"Tiger Lil," as Errol called her, taught him a great deal about living and living it up, but a quick marriage in Arizona did nothing to dispel her pathological possessiveness, and in the next few months, during a spate of Herculean battles, Flynn drifted away from her. The truces between the battles became shorter and shorter, and one day Flynn called me and asked if I would like to set up a bachelor establishment with him. "Let's move in together, sport," he said. "I can't take that dame's self-centered stupidity for another day."

We rented 601 North Linden Drive, Beverly Hills, from Rosalind Russell, chartered a nice understanding black housekeeper, and pooled the expense.

Flynn was collecting rather more from his contract with Warner Brothers than I was receiving from Samuel Goldwyn, so he forked out more in rent and insisted that he had prior claim to the largest bedroom, the one which housed the double bed. Flynn was fairly tight about money matters, so although on state occasions I was allowed to borrow his room, it was only in consideration of a small readjustment to our financial arrangement.

One winter's evening I came back from work, and as I

turned my car into the driveway, I perceived a sinister figure, his hat pulled down over his eyes and with the collar of his camel's-hair overcoat turned up; he was lurking in the bushes by the kitchen door. Never the bravest of men, I let myself in hurriedly by the front door and went looking for reinforcements in the formidable shape of Flynn. I discovered that he was not yet back from his studio, so I took a hefty nip from the whiskey bottle ever present on our hall table and went out to deal with the intruder. I stalked him successfully and grabbed him from behind. He turned out to be the highly erudite and popular producer Walter Wanger. He was in a very nervous condition. Wanger was very much in love with the gorgeous Joan Bennett, and in matters pertaining to her, he suffered from a very low threshold of jealousy. As I released him, he blurted out that he knew that his loved one was upstairs in the big double bed with Flynn. I was able with truth to tell him that Flynn was not in the house, but I withheld the information that downstairs in the living room awaiting Flynn's arrival was Joan.

Wanger, mollified, left, and Joan, rather precipitately, left soon after.

Flynn was lucky that day because a short time later Jennings Lang, an agent, also raised Wanger's possessive instincts to a high level and one evening in the parking lot in front of the offices of the Music Corporation of America, Walter produced a revolver from the pocket of his camel's-hair overcoat, took careful aim, and shot Jennings Lang in the testicles.

Ten or fifteen years before Robert Mitchum was unlucky enough to be arrested for puffing on a joint in a house in Laurel Canyon, Errol had introduced the stuff into the life of 601 North Linden. Under the name of kif he brought it back from a trip to North Africa and was apt to offer it around, saying rather grandly that the painter Diego Rivera had introduced him to it in Mexico. Smoking it or chewing it, however, was a nonrisk pastime in those days, war on pot having not yet been declared.

I gave it up early on, chiefly I think because I was already hooked on something probably far more lethal—scotch—but

Flynn pressed on, and twenty years later, at the last meeting I was to have with him, he told me that apart from mainlining heroin he had by then used everything, including, as an aphrodisiac, just a pinch of cocaine on the end of his penis.

In those prewar days, Errol was a strange mixture. A great athlete of immense charm and evident physical beauty, he stood, legs apart, arms folded defiantly and crowing lustily atop the Hollywood dung heap, but he suffered, I think, from a deep inferiority complex—he also bit his nails. Women loved him passionately, but he treated them like toys to be discarded without warning for new models, and for his men friends he really preferred those who would give him the least competition in any department.

He was not a kind man, but in those careless days he was fun to be with, and those days were the best of Flynn.

Humility was a word unknown to Errol. He became a big star overnight with his first Hollywood superproduction, *Captain Blood*, but it never crossed his mind that others—the producer, the director, the writers, the technicians, and above all, the publicity department—might have had a hand in his success. It all went straight to his head, and by the time I joined him in his second superproduction, *The Charge of the Light Brigade,* he was cordially disliked by most of his fellow workers—particularly by the extras.

Guts he always had. We were seated on our chargers in front of 600 of the toughest "Western" riders and stunt men in the business when Errol let his reins go slack and busied himself with mirror and comb before a close-up.

The "soldiers" had been equipped with rubber-tipped lances to cut down accidents in the impending "charge." One of them leaned forward and waggled the rubber tip of his lance in Errol's horse's behind.

The animal reared up, and the star of our film looped the loop, landing flat on his back to the accompaniment of roars of laughter.

Errol got up slowly and dusted himself off.

"Which of you sons of bitches did that?" he asked quietly.

"I did, sonny," said a large broken-nosed character. "Want to make something of it?"

"Yes," said Flynn. "Get off your horse."

The man did with winks at his cronies. . . . He was taken
to the infirmary ten minutes later, and Errol's stock rose dramatically.

Errol always said that physically the toughest picture he
ever made was *The Charge of the Light Brigade,* and he had a
point. We spent several months at Bishop, California, in the
dusty, windy foothills of Mount Whitney.

The location started easily with decent late autumn weather and with the only hotel in town taken over for the exclu-
sive use of the company, but after a week shouts and profani-
ties at two o'clock in the morning alerted us to the fact that
someone had put a match to the place. It burned to the
ground very quickly, providing us with the last warm evening we would spend for the rest of the engagement, and
thereafter in tents and other miserable makeshift accom-
modations far out in the desert in sandstorms or high up in
the freezing winds blowing off the mountain snows, we shiv-
ered and grumbled in our thin tropical uniforms. Flynn's big
love at this point, apart from an unrequited obsession with
the leading lady, Olivia de Havilland, was Arno. Arno was a
schnauzer, and Flynn adored the dog, so much so that he
fought a duel over him.

The owner of the local bar in Lone Pine, a large oxlike mo-
ron of permanent belligerence, objected to all dogs, particularly those lifting their legs on the corner of his building. "To
teach the sons of bitches to find someplace else to piss," he installed a steel plate on the sidewalk and another on his door-
post, both wired to a battery inside the establishment. Poor
Arno came bouncing along as we were about to enter the bar
and lifted his leg in the danger area. The amber arc completed the circuit, and the luckless animal, collecting a high
voltage shock in his offending organ, was hurled into the air
and went careering off down the street, howling with pain
and terror. Flynn strode into the bar, and the place fell quiet.
The customers were evenly matched, local cowhands and
ranchers and a sprinkling of tough stunt doubles from our
picture. All prudently remained on their stools while Flynn
took the barman apart. It was a bloody battle, Flynn reveled

in it, and Arno was the last dog in Lone Pine to get shock treatment in his private parts.

Flynn loved fighting. He took it seriously and kept himself in a permanent state of readiness at 601 North Linden by sparring twice a week in the garden with Mushy Callahan and other professionals. John Huston also liked a good punch-up now and then.

On one famous occasion he and Flynn decided that they were bored at a Hollywood soiree. "Tell you what, kid," said Huston. "Let's get the hell outta here and go down to the bottom of the garden and just mix it a little. Whaddya say?"

"You're on!" said Flynn, and while the rest of the guests tried to concentrate on their dinner, the sound of strife filtered through the open windows as Flynn and Huston whaled away endlessly at each other. They both ended up in the Cedars of Lebanon Hospital for emergency repairs.

Barroom brawls were a specialty with Flynn. Sooner or later every well-known actor, particularly those specializing in tough roles, received a drunken shove in the back and heard the inevitable challenge: "Okay, sonny boy, let's see how tough you are." Gable, Cagney, and Bogart perfected sensible and peaceful ways of ridding themselves of these nuisances, but Flynn would gleefully wade in to the attack.

He met his match once. His beloved Arno fell overboard and drowned, and a particularly nauseating gossip columnist named Jimmy Fidler wrote a snide piece about Flynn's failing to rescue his dog. We spent a whole evening looking for Fidler, and when we found him sitting with his wife in a nightclub on the Strip, Flynn flattened him with a single punch. Mrs. Fidler, however, stuck a fork in Flynn's ear, and they both took him to court for assault.

Mike Curtiz was the director of *The Charge* and his Hungarian-oriented English was a source of joy to us all.

High on a rostrum he decided that the right moment had come to order the arrival on the scene of a hundred head of riderless chargers. "Okay," he yelled into a megaphone. "Bring on the empty horses!"

Flynn and I doubled up with laughter. "You lousy bums," Curtiz shouted, "you and your stinking language . . . you think I know fuck nothing . . . well, let me tell you—I know FUCK *ALL!*"

Toward the end of the picture Errol and I were placed in a large basket atop an elephant; for some obscure reason Warner Brothers had decided to twist history and to let the Light Brigade charge across the North-West Frontier of India instead of the Russian Crimea. The scriptwriters had been ordered to insert a tiger hunt into the proceedings to warm things up, and we were shooting this sequence at the studio instead of in open country. This proved just as well because the elephant, driven mad by the arc lights, and by Mike Curtiz's megaphone, went berserk and dashed madly all over the back lot trying to scrape off the basket with us inside it against trees, archways, and the side of the fire station.

Studio workers scattered like chaff as we trampled and trumpeted our way toward the main entrance, and only the astute closing of the gates by the studio police stopped us from careering out into the traffic of Pico Boulevard and heading for the Punjab. It was a most unattractive interlude.

When the charge itself was shot, one man was killed and many more were hurt, but the wretched horses suffered most. Curtiz ordered the use of the "running W," a tripping wire attached to a foreleg. This the stunt riders would pull when they arrived at full gallop at the spot he had indicated and a ghastly fall would ensue. Many horses broke legs or backs and had to be destroyed. Flynn led a campaign to have this cruelty stopped, but the studio circumvented his efforts and completed the carnage by sending a second unit down to Mexico, where the laws against maltreating animals were minimal, to say the most.

Perhaps it was the proximity to so many horses that caused it, but by the end of *The Charge* Flynn was really beginning to feel his oats. He sensed that Jack Warner was building him up to be the top box-office star of the studio, and he reckoned he could begin to throw his weight about. It started in the usual way with demands for a more lucrative contract, for a larger dressing room and all the trimmings, but as the years went by, Jack Warner found he was reaping the whirlwind he had sown. Flynn's pictures brought in millions, but he made a habit of breaking down the door of Warner's office when he was kept waiting for an appointment. Their contractual battles became legendary. It was a love-hate relationship, and there was admiration on both sides, but in the end King Jack ridded his court of his "turbulent priest."

After *The Charge* with the proceeds of a greatly increased contract, Flynn had bought himself a 65-foot ketch, which, after some hulk he had once owned in New Guinea, he named *Sirocco*. I was presented with a white T-shirt with her name proudly embossed across my chest, and we put to sea every weekend accompanied by helpful female "crew members." As I have already indicated, Flynn was never happier than when witnessing the discomfiture of his friends. One of my chores aboard *Sirocco* was the mixing of the drinks—a full-time job. As there was only a primitive refrigerator aboard, a large block of ice was purchased at the beginning of each voyage. In a rough sea, I was steadying the weekend block with my left hand while hacking off suitable chunks with an ice pick held in my right. *Sirocco* gave a violent lurch, and I found that I was unable to remove my left hand from the ice. Looking down, I noticed with a sort of semidetached interest that I had plunged the ice pick right through my middle finger.

I yelled to Errol to come and to get ready with the first-aid kit. He was delighted at what he saw.

"Hey, that's *great*, sport," he said. "Don't pull it out yet, we must show this to the girls!"

Impaled on the ice block, I waited below while Flynn rounded up the "crew." Much to his delight, one of them fainted when she saw what had happened.

Flynn read somewhere that a man named D'Arcy Rutherford had invented a new sport in the south of France—water skiing—and he showed me pictures of Rutherford skimming along behind a speedboat off Eden Roc.

"Look, sport," said Flynn, "we've *got* to try that," and he designed a pair of very painful, heavy wooden skis which the studio carpenters knocked together for us. The following weekend we tried them out off Catalina Island—they worked. There is no record to prove it, but I am pretty sure that on that day in the mid-thirties, Flynn and I introduced water skiing to California and maybe even to the United States.

Be that as it may, on that memorable weekend, Ronald Colman aboard his *Dragoon* was anchored in a nearby cove a couple of miles away from *Sirocco* in Avalon Bay, and we decided to give Colman and his guests an exhibition of our newfound sport. Flynn was driving the speedboat when we arrived, and my girlfriend for the weekend was sitting beside him. I was slapping merrily along on the heavy boards astern. After we had suitably impressed the customers aboard *Dragoon,* Flynn pulled a typical "friend-discomfiter," and instead of stopping or turning back toward Avalon, he headed out into the open sea. By now I was getting very tired indeed. I signaled to him to stop, and about half a mile from *Dragoon* he obligingly did so. I sank gratefully into the blue water and waited to be picked up. As the boat came near me, Flynn pulled in the towrope. "So long, sport," he called. "Why don't you drop in on Colman for a nice cup of tea? Betty and I are going back to *Sirocco* to take a nap." Betty, I noticed with some annoyance, seemed to be putting up only token resistance to this infamous suggestion, and with a roar of laughter, Flynn swept away, leaving me to face a long swim in mid-Pacific. However, it was a lovely afternoon, there was no adverse current, the sea was warm and oily calm, and when I wanted to rest, I had only to use the skis to support me. So I took my time, paddling gently along, rather enjoying my languorous journey.

About half the distance to *Dragoon* was covered when I got a nasty feeling that I was no longer alone. About ten yards on my right was a very large shark, its greasy black dorsal fin undulating above the surface as it moved effortlessly through the water.

Panic gripped me. I stopped swimming and tried to push the skis beneath my body for protection. With the uncoordination of fear I let go of one of them, which drifted toward the shark. The brute immediately flicked its giant tail and changed course to investigate. Some half-wit once said that you can frighten sharks away by splashing violently and making a noise . . . it's nonsense. . . . I splashed and shouted like a maniac, but my shark just came closer to find out what all the fuss was about. With one ski now beneath me, I hoped protecting my underbelly et cetera from being ripped away, I paddled slowly, gibbering with terror, toward Colman's yacht.

The shark in increasingly close attendance accompanied me the whole way. I prayed that he would remain on the surface, and I never took my eyes off his fin. Periodically, I yelled "Shark!" and "Help!" at the top of my lungs.

At long last I saw field glasses pointing in my direction and stopped paddling when Colman and a sailor jumped into the tender and started up the motor. Only when they were right on top of him did the shark lose interest in me. Then, with a mighty swirling convulsion, he slid into the depths below.

Aboard *Dragoon* a much-needed tumbler of brandy was pressed into my hand while I borrowed somebody's hand mirror to see if my hair had turned white, and when Flynn came over later to pick me up, I had a few words with him. He hooted with laughter. "Jesus!" he roared. "I wish I'd seen *that!*"

I planned my revenge carefully. First I enlisted the help of a writer friend, that redoubtable Teddy bear John McClain, who came up with a short script in which the leading part would be played by the unsuspecting Flynn.

McCLAIN: Oh, Errol, on Friday, my aunt from Marion, Ohio, is coming out with her daughter Eunice, and they'd just love to meet you—especially Eunice. You remember Eunice, don't you, Dave?

NIVEN: I certainly do! . . . Really gorgeous! . . . But don't let Errol get near her—she's just the age he likes.

McCLAIN: Now, Errol, goddammit, you keep your cotton-pickin' hands off my niece!

FLYNN: (with famous smirk): I'll do my best, fellers, but don't bank on it.

NIVEN: Why don't you bring them both over to

North Linden for drinks on Saturday, John?
You'll be there, won't you, Errol?
FLYNN: You're damn right!

After that it was just a case of subtle reminders and praise for Eunice and her measurements.

McClain and I enlisted a high-class whore of about thirty-five for the part of the aunt, and she in turn undertook to appear with a real stunner of seventeen in the role of her daughter. I was to be the director.

On "F Day" I left the Westside Tennis Club first and drove to North Linden at high speed, to rehearse and position my waiting actors. McClain and "Eunice," a sexy-looking blonde with the most awful hog-calling voice I had ever heard, I stationed at the bar. Then I moved the sofa so that it would be in full view through the curtains of the garden window and ordered the "aunt" to join me outside.

When Flynn came into the room, the "aunt" breathed in my ear, "Wow! He's really something!" I shushed her, but I had to agree. Errol was a magnificent specimen of the rampant male.

McClain as an actor was nervous, I noticed, but that is often the way with writers. Luckily, his poor performance went unnoticed by Flynn, who had eyes only for "Eunice." Nor did he seem to hear her blaring voice and preened himself outrageously in front of her. "Eunice" almost stole the show. She gave a stupendous performance, undulating with suppressed desire, making rapturous quick intakes of breath every time Flynn came close to her and darting the pink tip of her tongue between sensuous lips.

We had two phones in the house, so when I was satisfied that all was going according to plan, I nipped around to the kitchen and dialed the number which rang in the bar. McClain picked up the phone, and I listened carefully to hear him get off his most difficult speech.

McCLAIN: Hello! . . . Oh, Auntie, it's you. . . .
          Where are you? Oh, at the hotel. . . .
          Okay. . . . I'll come right over . . . no
          problem. . . . I'll be there in fifteen min-

utes. (Turning to Eunice) Eunice, I'm just
going to pick up your mother at the Bel Air
. . . back in half an hour.

EUNICE: (ogling Flynn): Take your time, Uncle
John. I'm sure Mr. Flynn will take good
care of me.

McClain made his exit and joined the "aunt" and myself
outside.

McClain had given Eunice some carefully worked-out
speeches here to make her seductive and to lure Flynn deli-
cately across to the sofa—they were wasted. Before she could
get the first line out, she found herself on that sofa and her
skirt over her head.

This was a tricky time for the poor girl because if she gave
in too quickly, the whole structure of the piece would be suspect. Flynn took her desperate time-consuming moves, the
maidenly hauling down of her skirts, her frantic hitching up
of panties, and her wild hand slapping as the real thing and
pressed home his attack with admirable expertise. The
watchers at the window were in agonies of suppressed laughter and when Flynn leched into her blond curls, "Oh, Eunice,
we only have about twenty minutes," I stuffed a handkerchief somewhere down around my tonsils. I pulled myself
together, and once Flynn was well and truly in the saddle, I
sent in my reserves.

McClain and the "aunt" made a dramatic entrance just at
the high point of the performance.

AUNT: Eunice! What *are* your doing?
EUNICE: (peering out from beneath Errol): I don't
know, Mom, ask Mr. Flynn.
AUNT: Mr. Flynn! Get off my daughter *Immediate-
ly* and explain yourself.
FLYNN: (buttoning up desperately):
Oh! . . . Oh! . . . I lost my head . . . I
lost my head.
AUNT: Eunice! You're a mess! Go to the car and
wait while I have a word with Mr. Flynn.
McCLAIN: Come, niece (then, turning ponderously

	toward Errol) Flynn! . . . You swine! (Exeunt)
AUNT:	Now, Mr. Flynn, I'd just like you to explain yourself.
FLYNN:	(shaking head and muttering) I lost my head, I lost my head!
AUNT:	(slowly) I sent Eunice out because (grabbing at his fly) I want a bit of that myself!

CURTAIN

During the years McClain and I occasionally dusted off the script and recast the principals with great effect.

Christmas in Hollywood was like something from another planet. Festoons of reindeer and giant bells were first stretched across Hollywood Boulevard in late November, and thereafter lighted trees proliferated in the snowless gardens of Beverly Hills. All work stopped or rather staggered to a halt during the late morning of Christmas Eve, and the rest of the day was dedicated to parties—parties on the set, parties in the producers' offices, the directors' offices, the stars' dressing rooms, the cutting rooms, and the casting office. Everyone at the studio expected presents, from the night watchman to the chief of police, and from the head of the studio to the lowliest secretary, but the biggest outlay was in the realm of personal gifts to friends and business acquaintances.

One was constantly getting caught short. I once gave Miriam Hopkins half a dozen handkerchiefs, and she gave me a Studebaker. All in all, it was a difficult and expensive time.

Errol and I decided that the whole Peace and Goodwill Department was getting completely out of hand. So we decided to buy no personal or business gifts at all. Instead, we invested in some fancy wrapping paper, yards of multicolored ribbons, and several dozen greeting cards. We then sat back at North Linden Drive and waited for the deluge. As the presents poured in, it was a simple matter to rewrap them, add something personal on a card, and dispatch them elsewhere.

Trade was brisk for several days before Christmas, and all

went well till someone sent us a case of champagne, which we gratefully opened instead of sending on its way. After that we became careless. Our rhythm faltered, and the operation lacked synchronization with the embarrassing result that Walter Wanger received a beautiful black silk evening wallet on which, in gold lettering, was inscribed "To D.N. from W.W."

I never quite understood Errol's hero worship of John Barrymore. Still of blazing talent and unquestioned, if somewhat blurred, profile, Barrymore seemed to go out of his way to shock and be coarse. He was also conspicuously unclean and smelled highly on many occasions.

He had an abiding love of the theater and treated filmmaking as a financially necessary evil. Watching him work, I was amazed at the carefully arranged phalanx of boards, some stationary, some held aloft by moving stagehands, and all bearing the lines John Barrymore was required to speak during the scene at hand.

Painstaking rehearsals went into the placing and progress of these boards to enable the great man to move freely about during the playing of a scene without giving a hint that he was reading the whole thing.

Like boys who go to complicated lengths to cheat in exams, it would probably have been less time-consuming and nerve-racking to have learned the lesson in the first place, but Barrymore was adamant and had a stock answer when anyone dared to make such an observation.

"My memory is full of beauty—Hamlet's soliloquy, the Queen Mab speech, the fifteen-minute monologue by King Magnus in *The Apple Cart,* and most of the Sonnets . . . do you expect me to clutter all that up with *this* horseshit?"

Barrymore had a tempestuous marriage with a lady named Elaine Barrie, and their partings and reconciliations were joyfully reported by the nation's press.

After a spat in New York, he boarded the train for Los Angeles. Elaine Barrie by leapfrogging over him in a series of plane trips tried to head him off and, surrounded by a snowballing number of reporters, made dramatic appeals from wayside railway platforms across the country while her husband gazed down dispassionately upon her from the safety of his locked stateroom aboard the Santa Fe Chief.

The Barrymores' progress west was followed avidly in the daily papers, and "The Caliban-Ariel Chase," as it was labeled, came to an end at San Bernardino, the last stop before Los Angeles, when at last Barrymore unlocked his door and allowed his wife to ride the remaining sixty miles in his company.

Shortly after this interlude Flynn took me to lunch with Barrymore at the Brown Derby in Beverly Hills. This restaurant was designed so that everyone could see everyone else; the tables were set at a series of semicircular brown leather banquettes, the backs of which fitted uncomfortably into one's lumbar region. The waitresses, all would-be actresses, wore very short bell-shaped and highly starched skirts and spent much time dropping and provocatively retrieving forks and spoons before the tables of producers and directors. Barrymore caused a stir as we entered, and he boomingly table-hopped his way to our corner.

He was a fascinating ham, and everything he did or said was accompanied by rolling eyes and extravagant gestures. His beautiful voice was pitched for the most effect, and he was far from reticent about its reaching the farthest corners of the room, particularly when Flynn asked him a loaded question: "But tell us, Jack, what do you *see* in Elaine?"

Barrymore banged the table, and the glasses jumped. Heads turned, and conversation stilled.

"You want to know what I see in my wife?" he roared. "Well, I'll tell you! You put it *in,* and it goes right through the main saloon and into the *galley;* then the cabin boy comes down a ladder and rings a bell. . . . In other words, you stupid bastard, *IT FITS.*"

Errol had sporadic reconciliations with "Tiger Lil" during his tenancy of 601 North Linden, but they amounted to little and did not seem to interfere with the main trend of his activities—a big turnover was the thing, with the accent on youth. One afternoon he said, "Come on, sport, I'm going to show you the best-looking girls in LA." We headed down Sunset Boulevard, and I thought he was taking me to the theater of *Earl Carroll's Vanities* which boasted an illuminated sign over the stage door: THROUGH THESE PORTALS PASS THE MOST BEAUTIFUL GIRLS IN THE WORLD.

He glanced at his watch.

"They should be coming out any minute now," he said, and stopped the car.

We were directly opposite the Hollywood High School.

Out came the girls, and they were indeed an eye-catching lot with their golden California suntans, long coltlike legs, and high, provocative breasts. All were made up, and many clutching their schoolbooks to their curves looked eighteen or nineteen. Flynn sighed and shook his head.

"Jail bait," he said. "San Quentin Quail. What a waste!"

A patrol car pulled up behind us, and a cop got out. "You fellows waitin' for someone?" he asked.

"No, Officer," said Flynn, "we are just admiring the scenery."

"Beat it," said the cop.

Early in 1939 Errol surprised me by informing me that his marriage was patched up "for keeps." "There's a whole new deal coming up with Lil," he said. "I'm going home."

601 North Linden was disbanded, and we went our separate ways.

During the inevitable wrangle over the "damages" we had done to Rosalind Russell's house during our long tenancy, tightfisted Flynn, who had been stupid enough to sign the lease, met his match. Our landlady had counted every piece in the woodshed when we moved in, and although we had constantly replenished her fuel supplies, in addition to other damage, we were asked to pay for thirty-seven small logs.

The following year we made *Dawn Patrol* together at Warner Brothers. Edmund Goulding directed, and it was a most happy assignment except that I could not help noticing that Flynn had really got the "star" bit between his teeth and was beginning to behave outrageously to the people who employed him and even toward some of those who worked with him.

In September, 1939, Hitler invaded Poland, and before

World War II ended six years later 55,000,000 lay dead.
How to behave as a young man when your country is invaded
or in danger is a very personal decision, and anyone who
rushes off brandishing a sword should never point a finger of
scorn in the direction of those who decide not to do so.

I decided to go, and Flynn decided to stay—it was as simple as that.

During my absence a lot of things happened to Errol.
Britain and Australia were at war with Germany and Italy,
but he had no intention of being called to the colors. He felt
no loyalty to Britain, and little to Australia; the United States
had given him his big chance, so he took out American citizenship. Then the Japanese bombed Pearl Harbor, and
young Americans started flocking to the recruiting offices.
Errol hesitated, but he was confronted by "Tiger Lil" with a
baby boy, Sean, in one hand and, in the other, one of the
most punitive settlements ever handed down by the notoriously tough California divorce courts. But working on in
Hollywood, Errol misguidedly accepted a series of war films
in which he appeared playing highly heroic roles: *Dive Bomb-
er, Edge of Darkness,* and *Objective Burma* to name a few. The
press reacted angrily to his efforts, particularly in belea-
guered England, where Zec, in the 4,000,000-circulation
Daily Mirror, depicted Flynn in a half page cartoon, dressed
in battle dress, seated in a studio chair with his name sten-
ciled on the back and in his hands the script of *Objective
Burma.* On the studio grass beneath his chair was a multitude
of tiny crosses and, beneath the jungle trees, stood the ghostly form of a soldier. The caption read: "Excuse me, Mr.
Flynn, but you're sitting on some graves."

Errol retreated to a mountaintop. High up on Mulholland
Drive he built a luxurious one-floor bachelor pad. It had a
Finnish sauna bath and a battlefield for a bed with a mirror
on the ceiling. It had glorious views of the San Fernando Valley below and some stables in which highly illegal cockfights
were staged on Sunday evenings, but apart from the inevitable girls, it became, according to Flynn, "the mecca of pimps,
bums, gamblers, process servers, and phonies." It also became a refuge for the great John Barrymore, whose end was
visibly drawing near. For a while he lived up there with Er-

rol, but there was general relief in the household when he left and the frame of the living-room window could be re-varnsihed because during his visit Barrymore had made it a nightly habit to urinate out of it in the hopes, he said, of spraying Warner Brothers Studios in the Valley below.

Errol liked to tell of arriving home drunk after drowning his sorrow at Barrymore's demise. According to him, he let himself into the house and in the dark living room with the picture windows presenting a panoramic view of the whole glittering San Fernando Valley, he beheld John Barrymore sitting in his usual chair with a drink in his hand. He thought it was a ghost, but on closer inspection Errol claimed it turned out to be Barrymore's corpse, which his cronies had persuaded the undertaker to lend them for a few hours.

Errol never explained satisfactorily why any undertaker would jeopardize his livelihood by breaking the law and handing over a body to anyone other than the next of kin, nor could he convince me that it had been medically and physically possible to overcome rigor mortis so conveniently.

Late in 1942 high jinks aboard *Sirocco* boomeranged on Errol, and he was arrested on four charges of statutory rape.

In the state of California statutory rape meant that a male had fornicated with a female below the age of eighteen. The fact that the lady in question had long since been deflowered and, far from withholding her consent, had entered enthusiastically into the proceedings made no difference, and conviction carried a sentence of five years. Looking back on many weekends aboard *Sirocco,* I could not remember any "crew members" flashing their birth certificates as they trooped expectantly up the gangplank.

It seemed obvious that Flynn was being framed, and young America was aroused. William F. Buckley, Jr., then at prep school, told me later that he had joined A.B.C.D.E.F., American Boys Club for the Defense of Errol Flynn. The accusing girls, Betty Hansen and Peggy Satterlee, had always looked like sophisticated well-upholstered twenty-two-year-olds, but for the trial the prosecution ordered them to take off their makeup, do their hair in pigtails, wear bobby socks, and carry schoolbooks.

It didn't work. The jury, confronted by the masterful tactics of Jerry Geisler, saw through the camouflage and pegged the girls for what they really were. Errol was acquitted, but the stigma of rape was attached to him. He never shook it off, and for years he gritted his teeth when hailed with cries of "In like Flynn!"

The long trial over, Errol married again—a quiet, pretty girl, with an uptilted nose, Norah Eddington—but by now he was so dependent on his bachelor life on Mulholland Drive that his new wife lived in a little house in Hollywood and never became the chatelaine of his mansion on the mountain. In 1945 Norah gave birth to a baby girl, but she and Flynn continued to live apart.

Errol was stuck with making a lot of Westerns, which he hated doing, but they made money for the studio and amid renewed sounds of strife he bowed to Jack Warner's directive and walked through his roles with haughty disdain. He also discovered vodka in a big way and proceeded to drink it as though it were going out of style. At seven o'clock in the morning he was gulping it down in the makeup chair—mixed fifty-fifty with 7-Up.

It was not a happy man I found upon my return to Hollywood at the beginning of 1946.

Miraculously, Errol still looked in good physical shape and gave the outward impression of being the same, insulated with charmingly cynical self-sufficiency, but there was something infinitely sad about him, something missing, and behind his eyes there was a shield—I could no longer see into his face.

With pride he showed me the spread on Mulholland Drive and, having discarded *Sirocco* as a bad dream, with loving care introduced me to every inch of his new "wife," *Zaca*—a 120-foot schooner which he had found in San Francisco. She was a dream, and he had spent a small fortune refitting her.

"And let me show you the house flag," he said as he unfurled a symbolic crowing rooster. "A rampant cock, sport, get it? That's what I am to the world today—goddammit—a phallic symbol."

He didn't smile as he said it.

Perhaps I had become smug, self-satisfied, and "square" in

the years I had been away. I had come back with a beautiful young wife and two tiny children, and I found I had little in common with the group which now surrounded Errol—hangers-on almost to a man.

The worst, I thought, was Bruce Cabot, an actor who specialized in playing villains, who drank hard, played golf beautifully, and gambled prodigiously, but who had a nasty habit of being absent when the debts were being settled. Flynn was always good to Cabot and never failed to keep him afloat or to see that he was lucratively employed in Flynn pictures, but it was Cabot in the end who delivered the unkindest cut of all—"Et tu, Bruce?"

Because of the implications, Errol tried hard to get away from making sex-symbol pictures, but they made money, and the studios kept him churning them out till the pointed fingers and the snide "rapist" cracks so depressed him that he drank more and more and even contemplated suicide, on one occasion sitting up all night with a bottle of vodka in one hand and a loaded revolver in the other.

Occasionally and unexpectedly during this low period Errol came down from his mountaintop to see us, and I would arrive home from work to find him playing with my little boys or helping my wife get supper. His tremendous charm enveloped us all like a tent, and he in his turn seemed to extract a certain peace from the closeness of our family. "This is the life, sport," he would say. "You've really got it made."

Norah had a second baby, and Flynn made a stab at family life for himself. He suggested that she move into Mulholland with their children, but the invitation came too late, and they were divorced. Errol, more restless than ever, then took *Zaca* through the Panama Canal and headed for the Caribbean where he fell in love with Jamaica and looked for a while like settling down, but he pulled up the anchor, set sail for the Mediterranean, and tried his hand at a new role—as international playboy in competition with Rubirosa and Freddie McEvoy.

He gambled, drank, fought, and became the target for every freeloader and trollop between Malaga and Taranto. He seemed to have lost all interest in making films, and although he still had a contract to make several more with Warner's, he never ran out of excuses for not returning to do so, but *Zaca,* with her large crew and complement of guests, was costing him a fortune, and it finally dawned on him that if he didn't make films, he didn't get paid.

Good luck, which Errol was beginning to believe had deserted him forever, appeared out of the blue in the shape of a lovely and calm young actress from New York—Patrice Wymore. She became an island of peace and common sense in the middle of his sea of false values, and eighteen months after his divorce from Norah, Errol and Patrice were married. On the day of his wedding in Nice with his adoring new wife holding his arm and looking trustingly up into his face, he was handed a document that turned him to stone—a seventeen-year-old French girl named Denise Duvivier was accusing him of something she said had occurred aboard *Zaca* one year before: RAPE!

All over the world headlines once more attacked, ridiculed, and pilloried Errol, but Patrice behaved immaculately, and sat beside him during the preliminary inquiry holding his hand. After visiting *Zaca* and asking Denise Duvivier a few searching questions about the small shower cubicle in which she insisted the action had taken place, the judge ruled that the girl had never even set foot aboard.

Patrice persuaded Errol to return to Hollywood and work out his contract, but when they arrived there, she was appalled by the inroads that had been made into his capital by lawyers, courts, wives, mistresses, alimonies, and, of course, the hangers-on, so when Errol went back on the payroll, she persuaded him to grab the weekly checks and buy land on Jamaica—the island of his dreams.

This advice Errol took, and by the time his contract was finally terminated (in the course of one last convulsion with Jack Warner) he was the owner of more than 5,000 acres, but he still had not cleared up his astronomical debts. Convinced that his career and earning power were over, he had no intention of doing so, and as Patrice had produced a baby, the three of them took off in a hurry for Europe to live on *Zaca.* "Let Tiger Lil and the whole goddamned lot of them come after me and try to collect," said Errol. "I'm sick of being taken."

First stop was Rome, where Errol put up half a million dollars—all the cash he could raise—as a half share in the costs of a picture, *William Tell,* but his Italian partners walked out, the picture collapsed halfway through, and Flynn found himself more in debt than ever. He cabled an SOS to his business manager in Hollywood, Al Blum, and discovered that his trusted adviser had just died—a blow not softened when he learned that in his last few weeks Blum had used the power of attorney Flynn had conferred on him to make some very peculiar financial arrangements which had effectively scraped the bottom of Errol's barrel. He also learned that "Tiger Lil" had taken possession of Mulholland Drive.

This was Flynn's lowest ebb, and it was then that his great friend Bruce Cabot showed his hand.

Flynn had brought Cabot over from America to play an important part in *William Tell.* When the picture collapsed, Flynn flew to the Geneva banks to try to salvage it. He returned, empty-handed, to find that in his absence the man he had befriended for years had sent around a process server for unpaid salary and had removed his car and his wife's and his baby's clothes.

Flynn never went to look for Cabot—he was afraid he might kill him.

For four years after the demise of *William Tell,* Flynn was a floating, boozing bum. He made some trips to Jamaica to try to keep hold of his land and was able to convince the banks there that its value had increased. He also made a couple of disastrous films in England for which he was happy to be paid a fraction of his former salary.

Most of the time *Zaca* remained tied up in the minor ports of the Mediterranean while her owner caroused and brawled, intent, apparently, on his own self-destruction. Vodka and other stimulants made terrible inroads into his health, his looks were fading fast, and with one exception, Hollywood washed its hands of Errol Flynn. Sitting in his beautiful house above Beverly Hills, surrounded by a most enviable collection of paintings, was a quiet, almost professorial man named Sam Jaffe—a highly successful agent. He had not forgotten Errol Flynn, and he had a hunch. He packed, left for Europe, and tracked Flynn down in Palma de Majorca.

He cajoled Flynn, and he appealed to his pride, and the loyal Patrice helped him. Flynn pulled himself together and before long was back in Hollywood, making a picture, *Istanbul.* He was not playing a beautiful young sex symbol anymore. He was playing himself, a middle-aged rake with the remains of elegance stamped on a face that had been lived in, and he loved doing it. After *Istanbul,* his old antagonist Jack Warner offered him the part of John Barrymore in *Too Much Too Soon.* Drawing heavily on his personal experience of the man, he turned in a performance that delighted critics and public alike. Next came *The Roots of Heaven*—another role from the same mold to be shot in Africa with John Huston directing and $4,000,000 being spent on the production.

In 1958 I met Errol by chance in London. Ten years had passed since I had last seen him, and it was a joyful reunion. We lunched, largely on Pouilly Fumé, at a little place in Soho, and I cannot pretend that I was not shocked by the physical change; he had been doing himself grave damage, the face was puffy and blotchy, and the hand that had once held the bow of Robin Hood could not have put the arrow through the Taj Mahal at ten paces, but there was an internal calm and a genuineness about him that I had never seen before.

He brought me up to date about all his wives—he had just separated from Patrice, and he talked wistfully of how hard she had tried to help him and how impossible he must have been to live with. He told me with pride of his children, especially of Sean, and when he spoke of Jamaica, he positively glowed.

Then he said something very unexpected: "You know, sport, I've felt a heel about you for ten years. When your wife died in that accident when she'd just come out to California, I never did a goddamned thing to help, did I? Never came to see you or anything. Well, I wanted to, and I thought about it all the time, but I couldn't bring myself to do it—I don't know why. . . . Anyway, I always wished I had."

We filled our glasses and sat in that wonderful silence that old friends can afford.

After a while I said, "I see you've still got a couple of lawsuits going and all the usual tax problems. You seem very relaxed about everything—how do you do it?"

"I've discovered a great book, and I read it all the time—it's full of good stuff," said Errol.

I looked at him inquiringly.

"If I tell you what it is, sport, I'll knock your goddamned teeth down your throat if you laugh."

"I promise," I said.

"It's the Bible," said Flynn.

On the evening I finished writing down these inadequate words about Errol Flynn, I left my house on Cap Ferrat and took the footpath around the end of the point, the one used by the *douaniers* in their search for smugglers. When I came to the Baie de Villefranche, I had a glass of wine with my friend Bidou in his little quayside bistro, before walking on past the old fishing village with its sun-washed houses and festoons of multicolored laundry, past the fourteenth-century fort to the Vieux Port. Very much the second-class citizen in these days of smart marinas is the old port of Villefranche. It gives refuge to elderly fishing boats and to a few seedy private yachts. In its little boatyard, a big Piggiotti 35-knot cruiser was being repainted by some shifty-eyed Algerians. Moored near her were two or three impounded motor cruisers which had been caught smuggling dope from North Africa. I wandered along the old seawall, looking down at the sad and rejected little fleet sheltered below: many were for sale. Rigging and mooring ropes slapped and creaked in the rising mistral. The place was full of ghosts.

Suddenly, I felt goose pimples rise up all over me. A large dismasted hulk lay before me. Her teak decks gaped to the sky, the planks of her sides were thinly covered with a cracked and flaking grayish paint, but despite the old bus tires that did duty as fenders swinging on frayed ropes along her sides, she still had a defiant elegance enhanced by her bowsprit still rigged and thrusting out belligerently before her.

My eyes followed along her beautiful, if aging, lines. I knew now what I was going to see, and there it was, proudly emblazoned on her great arclike transom:

7
"Mr. Goldwyn"

WHEN a history of Hollywood is written, the name of Samuel Goldwyn is bound to get top billing.

For half a century he towered like a colossus above his contemporaries, and the results of his taste and his single-minded determination to settle for nothing short of his own ideas of perfection are preserved for all to see.

It was long a habit among the jealous and the snide in the Hollywood jungle to ridicule Goldwyn and try by the all too easy manufacture of Goldwynisms to diminish his stature. "Include me out," "I'll tell you in two words—im-possible," "A verbal contract is not worth the paper it's written on," "We can always get more Indians off the reservation," and "We've all passed a lot of water since those days" have become part of the Goldwyn legend, but who can claim to have been present when these pearls of wisdom were dropped? Another Goldwynism faithfully repeated to me during the shooting of *The Real Glory*—"Elevate those guns a little lower"—was actually an Andrew Jacksonism which erupted from the lips of the future seventh President of the United States at the Battle of New Orleans in 1815. I was under contract to Goldwyn for fifteen years, and I only heard him produce one malapropism, and as it could not by any stretch of the imagination chip a piece off the colossus and as it occurred in the presence of thirty witnesses, I will quickly get it out of the way.

139

In 1946 for some reason to do with a visit to the American Pacific Fleet in San Diego, Field Marshal Montgomery appeared in California, and Goldwyn gave a dinner for him.

Because of Montgomery's foolish military whim about being punctual, the guests were selected from among the more reliable of the local citizenry. The field marshal arrived on time, wearing his blue patrol uniform, and on his left breast were several layers of medal ribbons. The guests were smartly seated at rows of small tables for four and six. Frances Goldwyn placed the field marshal on her right, opposite her she positioned Gary Cooper's wife, Rocky, and on the fourth chair, because he had served under Montgomery, sat the author. Small talk and Hollywood gossip washed over Montgomery's head; he only came to occasionally when the word "shooting" was used, so Frances became increasingly nervous and signaled to Sam to cause a diversion.

Goldwyn, at the other end of the room, obediently rose from his table and beat a knife against a wineglass. The clatter was cut to a minimum, and we braced ourselves to hear the inevitable words of welcome to the distinguished guest.

Goldwyn cleared his throat.

"It gives me great pleasure tonight to welcome to Hollywood a very distinguished soldier . . . ladies and gentlemen, I propose a toast to Marshall Field Montgomery."

A stunned silence, during which Frances Goldwyn sat very still, looking as though she had been hit with a halibut, was finally broken by Jack Warner, who cracked, "Montgomery Ward, you mean."

Like many others, Goldwyn did have a problem remembering names. Joel McCrea, who was under contract to him at the same time as myself, was invariably referred to as Joe McCreal, and his European public relations chief, the impeccable and immaculate Welshman Euan Lloyd, became resigned to being addressed as Urine. Goldwyn was no mean wit. When I was leaving Hollywood to go off to Montgomery's war in September, 1939, I went to Sam's office to say good-bye. He was very put out that I was leaving voluntarily and not waiting until I was called up, so he put me on suspension till the end of the war or of my life, whichever came sooner, and said, "I'll cable Hitler and ask him to shoot around you."

Goldwyn was a zealous preserver of a buck. In July, 1939, I paid the first down payment on a New York Life insurance policy. Exactly a year later and shortly after Dunkirk, I received a reminder from New York Life warning me that my second installment was now due and that if it was not paid very quickly, I would lose the coverage and the first installment. As Russia was still an ally of Germany and Hitler was opposed only by Great Britain, I did not rate my chances of survival as a soldier too highly and sought to do my dependents a good turn.

I cabled Leland Hayward, my agent, asking him to see if Goldwyn would advance the money against my suspended contract.

Goldwyn had been reading the daily papers and apparently had also evaluated my chances. He refused, and unable out of my soldier's pay to preserve the policy myself, I lost it.

Six and a half years later, when I returned to the Goldwyn fold, a forgotten, broke, and valueless commodity, Goldwyn somberly pointed out that during my absence there had been a change in the law as a result of which my suspended contract had lapsed. Then, unpredictable as always, he laughed at my stricken face, gave me a new five-year contract at a greatly increased salary, and lent me enough money to make the down payment on a house.

I purposely placed the start of these notes on Goldwyn at one of his dinner parties because a special determination of his was to be a great gentleman, and in his own home he was. An impeccable host, even if an hour before he had been banging his office desk and hurling imprecations at you across it, once at his house on Laurel Way, he would meet you smiling at the door, look after your every need during the evening, and personally escort you to your car when it was time to depart. People found this Jekyll and Hyde quality disconcerting because the reverse could happen, and despite their being lulled into a sense of false security during a cozy dinner, accusations and abuse could be awaiting them at the Samuel Goldwyn Studios first thing the following morning.

The key to understanding Goldwyn was to know that his total obsession was making pictures of which he could be proud, and apart from his private moments with his family, every waking minute of his day was dedicated to that end alone.

Above average height, deep of chest and high of voice, he was always dressed in suits, shirts, and shoes of perfect fit, clothes being one of his few personal extravagances. He also took great trouble to see that he remained trim. His light, almost spartan luncheons at the studio were served in his private dining room, invariably with his wife in attendance, and every evening on his way home, he ordered his car to stop as soon as he reached the city limits of Beverly Hills so that he might walk briskly the remaining mile and a half to his house.

Head high and eyes glazed in thought as he strode along, he had a habit of talking to himself and frequently became so engrossed in his own conversations that he ignored the salutations and greetings of aggrieved neighbors.

I never dared play gin rummy or backgammon with Goldwyn because I had heard tell of some nasty feuds and vendettas that had come the way of some who did, but then in everything, competition was his lifeblood, and to win was essential. Playing croquet with Sam could be a real "hazard."

He had a beautifully manicured lawn, and the best players in Hollywood gathered there on Sundays, but it was necessary to have an extra man stashed away in the trees because after disagreement Sam frequently stalked into the house and locked the front door. On particularly fraught occasions he dispatched a butler to fetch the drinks into the house after him. Nobody would have accused him of actually cheating at games—he just *had* to come out on top. I was playing a single at tennis with Goldwyn one day, and Fred Astaire (in reserve in case of emergencies) was watching. It was the first serve of the match, and I delivered a perfect ace into the corner. A puff of white dust arose to acclaim my feat.

"Doubles," said Goldwyn, and marched purposefully across to the other court.

Fred witnessed another bit of Goldwyn gamesmanship on a golf course. Sam sliced his ball into some trees, and it ended up in a virtually unplayable position. Fred grabbed my arm, shaking with laughter. "Look at him," he said. Goldwyn very methodically was moving stones and fallen branches and

placing the ball in a position from which he had an uninterrupted view of the green. Then he produced a wooden tee
from his pocket and put the ball upon it.

"Sam!" I yelled. "You can't *do* that!"

"I know," he shouted back. "My caddie *told* me I
shouldn't."

If he was competitive at games, he displayed the toughness
of stainless steel in business, and the fields were littered with
the vanquished. Ronald Colman, after years under contract
to him, refused even to speak to him again, and Eddie Can-
tor swore that working for Goldwyn put him in the hospital.
In Goldwyn's office the rows with his top director, William
Wyler, were so noisy that Merritt Hulbert, a distinguished
editor of the *Saturday Evening Post,* who had become the head
of Goldwyn's story department, asked to have his office
moved to another floor. "Quiet story conferences make quiet
pictures," retorted Goldwyn firmly, but eventually he and
Wyler arranged a truce.

"Look, Willie," he said, "from now on when we meet, we
each put a hundred-dollar bill on my desk, and the first one
to shout loses his money."

"OK," said Wyler.

As a result, Hulbert stayed on in his office while, next door,
appalling insults were traded in whispers.

I don't believe that Sam was rude on purpose. I think his
thoughts flashed through his head with lightning speed, and
sometimes he just didn't give his tongue enough time to
check its possible effect on people. Once he shook the normally imperturbable Laurence Olivier by being too quick on
the verbal draw. Goldwyn came on the set on the second day
of shooting, having just seen the rushes of the first day's
work on *Wuthering Heights.* We all stood nervously around
waiting for the great man's comments.

He put his arm around Olivier's shoulders, and Larry prepared himself for the compliments which he thought must
surely be coming his way.

"Willie," said Goldwyn to Wyler, who was hovering nearby,
"would you look at that actor's *ugly* face?"

(Olivier told me that he objected chiefly to being called
"that actor.")

Goldwyn had immense presence and a great dignity. His walk was athletic and always brisk. He lifted his heel at each stride. His head was almost completely bald from an early age, and his eyes were dark, small and deepset. His jaw was pronounced and very determined indeed. Employees from top to bottom at his studio were in awe of him for a very good reason—there was not a technical job on the lot that he could not fill perfectly himself. He was well aware of his awesome presence and seldom visited the sound stages because he knew that his appearance there sowed instant alarm and a feeling of impending doom in the breasts of one and all.

Directors, actors, cameramen, and sound technicians who had not reached the high standards he demanded of them were "sent for"; invariably they returned looking as though they had witnessed a terrible accident on Santa Monica Boulevard.

He never asked the banks to put up the money for his productions; however expensive, the sole financier of a Samuel Goldwyn film was Samuel Goldwyn himself. "The banks can't afford me," he said.

He had a deep and abiding interest in seeing that he got full value for his every dollar. It was not only we in his immediate vicinity who came under the microscope; exhibitors all over the world who showed Goldwyn's pictures received personal calls at all hours, demanding explanations of the finer points of their bookkeeping.

Little Samuel was born in 1882 in the Warsaw ghetto. At the age of eleven he ran away from home and found sanctuary with relatives in England, who quickly "placed" him as a blacksmith's assistant. He saved enough in the smithy for a steerage passage to New York, where an Irish immigration official, unable to cope with his unpronounceable Polish name, told him that from then on he would be known as Samuel Goldfish.

Young Sam migrated to Gloversville, New York, and became a glove salesman; a very good salesman, he sold enough gloves to be able at the age of twenty-eight to marry his first wife, Blanche Lasky.

In 1912 Samuel Goldfish decided that he could not look

another glove in the face and that his future lay with the infant motion-picture business. His brother-in-law, Jesse Lasky, was a vaudeville producer, doing quite well, so he was not overly tempted when Sam proposed that they should join forces and take a gamble. Lasky, however, conjured up a possible partner in the shape of an actor and a writer of vaudeville acts—one Cecil B. DeMille.

DeMille fell for Sam's idea, and a year later the two of them prevailed on Lasky to put up $25,000. DeMille was dispatched to Flagstaff, Arizona, to direct their first picture—a Western with William S. Hart, *The Squaw Man.* Flagstaff was chosen because with the exception of Death Valley, it was reputed to have the lowest rainfall in the United States.

In any event, it poured with rain there for five consecutive weeks and a dispirited DeMille moved on to the more salubrious climate of California, whence he wired his partner that he had "rented a barn for $75 a month in the middle of an orange grove in a place called Hollywood." Hollywood was born.

The Squaw Man was a success, and with Samuel Goldfish handling distribution and exploitation, the company made twenty-one films that first year, but success bred mergers, and mergers bred palace revolutions, and Samuel Goldfish became allied with a theatrical producer from New York, the quiet, self-effacing Edgar Selwyn.

Using half their respective names, in a moment of mental aberration, they registered their combine as "The Selfish Company," but wiser counsel prevailed, and the halves were reversed. The Goldwyn Company flourished and its name became a household word, whereupon Samuel Goldfish, with what quiet, self-effacing Edgar Selwyn described as a piece of monumental commercial treachery, nipped down to City Hall with his lawyer and legally took the name of Goldwyn for himself.

The Goldwyn Company boomed, and more palace revolutions followed. Goldwyn discarded his wounded partner, Selwyn, but was himself bought out by new associates who merged the Goldwyn Company with Metro and L. B. Mayer.

Goldwyn agreed to this merger but cagily insisted that his name should remain in eye-catching sloping letters between the stereotyped ones of Metro and Mayer. Then he left METRO *Goldwyn* MAYER with their snarling lion trademark and became in 1924 what he was to remain until his retirement in 1965: the greatest independent producer the world has ever seen.

After Goldwyn became an independent producer, he joined forces for a while with other independent producers—Douglas Fairbanks, Charlie Chaplin, and Mary Pickford. Together they formed the United Artists Company to distribute their products, and among them they bought studios on Santa Monica Boulevard. Before long Goldwyn realized that he was the major contributor to the company's output and in a final major convulsion, unloaded his partners, plus the United Artists Company, and wound up owning the studios.

The aforementioned palace revolutions assuredly occurred because if Goldwyn found it difficult to work with partners, the partners found it just too nerve-racking working with him.

Around this time, having for several years been divorced from Blanche, Sam married a calm and beautiful young actress—Frances Howard, who presented him with an enchanting heir and provided him with a quiet, uncomplicated home and an enduring Hollywood marvel, a happy married life.

The house in the hills they built together on Laurel Way was a charmingly unpretentious white structure surrounded by an attractive garden, a pool, and a tennis court—the croquet lawn came later. Decorated by Frances with a light and happy touch, it had, apart from a few good Impressionist paintings and a comfortable projection room, none of the traditional trappings of the vintage movie mogul.

Goldwyn loved this sanctuary and guarded it jealously against all intrusion. One evening sitting on the veranda with him, inhaling the smell of magnolia blossom in the clean champagne air and enveloped by my boss' very considerable charm, I pointed out to him the splendid spectacle of a family of quail parading across his lawn. Father was in front, proudly bearing his antennae headdress, mother fussily at the back, and in between, in strict line-ahead formation, were eight scuttling little babies.

"They don't belong here," said Goldwyn coldly.

The Goldwyns entertained quietly: no big ostentatious parties, no monstrous striped tents covering a boarded-over swimming pool—just a few friends on a Saturday evening invited to enjoy dinner and afterward a movie or cards.

All the top producers and stars had movie theaters either inside their houses or as outcrops of their playrooms and pool houses; this was known as the Bel Air Circuit, and a menace it was, too. The competition to display the latest film to weekend guests was intense, and to obtain them, a great deal of rank pulling and subtle blackmail was employed.

Producers, directors, and actors quailed when they learned that their lifeblood was about to be poured out at one of these private showings where months of effort could easily be ruined if their film was heckled, mocked, and torn to shreds by loudmouthed and overlubricated know-alls talking back to the screen. The reputation of a picture was frequently blackened before the paying customers had a chance to judge for themselves, and it was not uncommon for a studio head, hearing of the hostile reception thus accorded one of his productions, chickenheartedly to downgrade the exploitation budget he had already apportioned to it.

This never happened in Goldwyn's house. Once the guests were comfortably seated, Sam manned the sound controls himself, Frances settled herself, full length and rug-covered on a sofa, and the film, good or bad, was unfolded with honor and dignity. Afterward Goldwyn might invite discussion of its merits or demerits, but always his was the most generous and constructive of criticism. Secure in his own integrity as a filmmaker, he felt no need to chop down the opposition.

"The play's the thing"—Goldwyn early believed that Shakespeare had a point there. Although he produced only two or three pictures a year, he entered into long contracts with big established stars such as Ronald Colman and Gary Cooper and signed with a view to building them up to follow in the footsteps of their betters, a small band of unknowns, but his major outlay was always in the direction of the authors, and frequently, he would have several screenplays prepared by different writers from the same material; then he would choose the best and make his picture.

Employed by Goldwyn, but never incarcerated in the chicken-coop writers' buildings, the iniquitous "script batteries" of the major studios were, among others, F. Scott Fitzgerald, Robert Sherwood, John Huston, Maurice Maeterlinck, Lillian Hellman, Ben Hecht, and Thornton Wilder.

Could such a man *really* have held the following conversation with Edward G. Robinson?

ROBINSON: Sam, my studio is going to make *The Merchant of Venice*. They want me to play Shylock. Should I accept?

GOLDWYN: Screw 'em. . . . Tell 'em you'll only play the Merchant.

Robinson swore it happened.

I doubt it.

Goldwyn had an instinct, an instinct about everything to do with filmmaking. As far as music went, for example, he was incapable of differentiating between *Firebird* and "The Flight of the Bumblebee," and Al Newman, the musical director on many of his pictures, told us that Sam had congratulated him on his "wonderful new sounds" when by mistake he had played a new composition backwards on the sound track, but Sam in his own inscrutable way was right— the sounds fitted the scene, so Newman just accepted the praise and kept his mouth shut.

If Goldwyn surrounded himself with the best creative talent that his own money could buy, his formula for making a successful movie was deceptively simple:

1. Forget what other people are making.
2. Never worry about trends.
3. Buy a property that *you* think will make a good picture.
4. Hire the best writer or writers to give you a screenplay.
5. Employ the best director to translate that screenplay onto celluloid.
6. Give him the cast he wants and the cameraman he believes in.

7. Control the whole thing yourself, and *above all, take the blame if it goes wrong.*
"Goldwyn is not an easy man to work for. . . ." For half a century that remained the understatement of the year. Many people suffered under his arrogance and bullheadedness; tact was a word unknown to him, and his feuds were deep, bitter, and sometimes endless, but he, too, was fallible, and in spite of a spectacular string of successes, he inevitably suffered a few disappointments. In 1934 he signed the Russian actress Anna Sten, who had appeared in a silent version of *The Brothers Karamazov.* She duly arrived in America long on avoirdupois and short on English. Goldwyn uncorked a costly campaign of publicity and to no avail employed a regiment of physical culturists and several Professor Higginses. He then threw the result into the hesitant arms of Gary Cooper. "Coop" reeled under the impact of his leading lady, who remained resolutely incomprehensible for several films. The whole operation cost Goldwyn a small fortune. Gable he once turned down because "his ears are too big," and after buying the *Wonderful Wizard of Oz,* he decided that it would never make a picture and sold it, a cut-rate bargain, to MGM.

One setback he sustained particularly irked him. He was trying to coax the elusive Garbo into working for him. He managed to lure her up to his house for dinner—a most carefully prepared meal catering especially to her Nordic taste—intending once she had thus been softened up on smorgasbord and "Jonson's Temptation" to persuade her to sign a contract. After dinner, however, Garbo spent two hours talking to his Swedish cook, then slipped out through the kitchen door and went home.

Goldwyn could extricate himself from apparently impossible situations with the dexterity of Houdini. At great expense he bought the hit Broadway play *Children's Hour.* As it was about lesbian schoolmistresses in a girls' school, it was not surprising, in those days, that the Hays Office flatly refused to let him make it into a film.

Undaunted, he changed the title to *These Three* and had the plot altered to focus on the problems of two sex-starved schoolmistresses competing for the affections of a rampant schoolmaster. With Miriam Hopkins, Merle Oberon, and

Joel McCrea in the leading roles, the picture was a huge success.

Sam early learned to make the newspaper correspondents his friends and never repeated an early error when he "gave away" Vilma Banky, one of his first stars, at her marriage to her leading man, Rod La Rocque. The ceremony took place at Goldwyn's studio, and the suspect molars of several reporters flew apart when they bit into cakes and fruit provided by Sam's plasterers and painters. Thereafter Goldwyn's publicity department was geared to promoting Goldwyn the producer. The stars, directors, and authors he employed became of secondary importance, and the result of this, coupled with the almost unbelievably high standard of his product, was that all over the world distributors fought to obtain the next Samuel Goldwyn Production before he announced what it was about or who would appear in it.

"The Goldwyn Touch" was legendary, and he spared no expense to perpetuate it. "Good taste" were his watchwords on the screen.

We were rehearsing that subtle fantasy *The Bishop's Wife* (all Goldwyn pictures were carefully rehearsed in their entirety before shooting started). I was playing the Bishop, Loretta Young, the wife, and Cary Grant, the Angel. Bill Seiter, normally a director of broad comedy, was at the helm.

The day before shooting was to start, Goldwyn decided that the interiors of the Bishop's house were not ecclesiastical enough and ordered several sets to be torn down, redesigned, and rebuilt. For three weeks, while this was going on, production was halted; then, two days after the cameras finally had a chance to turn, Goldwyn decided that Seiter's hand was a little too heavy on the tiller; he was removed, paid his full salary, and after a week Goldwyn hired Henry Koster to start again from scratch—with another two weeks of rehearsal. All this must have cost Goldwyn several hundred thousand dollars, but in the end, he got what he wanted.

Always a perfectionist, when we were preparing a picture in which I had to age from twenty-five to seventy, Goldwyn talked me into having my hair bleached white for the last scene instead of wearing a wig. He examined the result of several trips to a women's beauty parlor, ignored the fact that my own dog had attacked me on sight the night before, and said, "It looks good. Now we have to slow down your movements as the old man."

So saying, he ordained that sixty pounds of lead should be distributed in the soles of my shoes and about my clothing. When he called me again to his office to inspect the result of his brainstorm, I arrived like a heavily handicapped racehorse.

An argument developed over the physical fatigue that I stoutly held would prostrate me during the long, hot hours of shooting. During this altercation I sprang from my chair to make my point and strode briskly about his office, but Goldwyn was right: My spring had become a rheumaticky rise, and my stride a stately totter. As a result of carting that lead around for weeks, I was a gibbering wreck by the end of the picture, but on the last day of shooting Goldwyn came on the set and gave me a complimentary lecture about how I had proved the necessity of always having a completely natural makeup.

"Well," I said, "I'm glad you're happy. Now what are you going to do about my hair?"

"What's the matter with it?" asked Goldwyn.

"I want it put back the way it was," I said.

"What was it before?"

"I can't remember—a sort of rich mouse color, I think."

Bob Stephanoff, the makeup man, was instructed to dye me back to normal, but it came out jet black and shiny, like that of a Japanese general, and during two weeks' holiday in Bermuda, the salt water and sun turned it into a metallic magenta. I was stuck with it it for about a year, and the review of our joint efforts which I liked least came from the Los Angeles *Examiner:* "a pity Goldwyn allowed Niven to ruin his performance by wearing an appalling wig."

This, of course, is not intended to be a portrait of Samuel Goldwyn. At most, it is a few hesitant lines of a preliminary drawing, because in spite of many years of close association with him, I was never able to see him clearly. By an accident of birth, I was not born Frances Howard or Samuel Goldwyn, Jr., and I suspect that only they could do so.

To me he was like crème brulée—rock hard on the outside

and surprisingly soft underneath. When he first pulled me out of the extra ranks and offered me a contract for seven years starting at $100 a week, I was in such a hurry to sign it, before he changed his mind, that I failed to notice that he had reserved the right to drop me at the end of every three months during the first two years and that I would have to face twelve weeks of layoff without pay each year. I just grabbed the contract gratefully and signed it with a heart pumping at the realization of the unbelievable good fortune that had befallen me. Then I walked to Hollywood Boulevard and did something I had always wanted to do: I went to the Ford dealer and flashing my golden credit card—my contract with the great Samuel Goldwyn—pointed to a two-seater convertible and said, "I'll take *that* one." Then I drove slowly back to the studio to display my shiny beauty before the admiring employees in the casting office.

Bob McIntyre, the kindly head of that department, looked embarrassed.

"Take it back again, son," he advised. "Mr. Goldwyn has just called down. You're on layoff for six weeks."

So much for the hard outside, but the gooey inside was often revealed by massive and unpublicized blood transfusions to charities and by unexpected generosity to the people who worked for him as lesser employees at his studio. To them he was a father figure who demanded and got an awesome standard. They gave him their best, and he looked after them. They loved him and would not hear a word against him, especially from the smart manufacturers of Goldwynisms. For a beginner it was incredible luck to be picked off the floor by Goldwyn. From 1935 to 1950 I had happy times with Goldwyn and sad times, some dizzy heights and some heartbreaking lows: arguments, battles, silences, suspensions, handshakes, meanness, sudden generosity, rages, and sunny smiles. In the end I repaid the man to whom I owed so much by getting too big for my boots and was, with great justification, fired. Only then did I really find a friend.

It is just possible, in spite of what I have intimated, that Sam perpetrated more Goldwynisms than I thought. If so, then I was the recipient of one sent by cable. It was delivered

to me in London during World War II at a time when selected actors were released from military service to make films
considered to be of importance to the national war effort.

PARAMOUNT INQUIRING IF YOU COULD OBTAIN RELEASE FROM
ARMY TO PLAY J.M.BARRIE'S HERO QUOTE THE ADMIRAL CRICH-
TON UNQUOTE. GOLDWYN.

I still prefer to think the slipup was at Western Union.

8
"The Emperor"

IN the summer of 1947 I was settling myself luxuriously into a booth in the bar of Romanoff's Restaurant in Beverly Hills. It was lunchtime, and the smartest, the chicest, and the owners of the best-known faces in Movie Town were arriving in droves, pausing to make their "entrances" into the main dining room. It was nice to be in the dark air-conditioned cool of the bar, nice to be out of the glare of the midday sun, above all, nice to be in the company of the diminutive proprietor of the joint—His Imperial Highness, Prince Michael Alexandrovich Dmitri Obolensky Romanoff.

"Old boy," my diminutive host intoned in his deep, slightly "off" Oxford voice, "your Emperor has ordered an ice-cold bottle of Dom Pérignon and some grouse which were flown in specially this morning from your native Scotland."

He extracted a monogrammed cigarette from a heavily embossed golden case (monogrammed with the imperial *R* of course), and I noticed once more that his thumbs arched back when he was gesticulating, almost to his wrist—a sign of great generosity, it is claimed, and with Mike Romanoff it was often proved.

The headwaiter approached with a deferential inclination of the head.

"We must find room for this party, Mr. Romanoff. They're very important . . . eight of them."

"Who are they?" demanded Mike.

"Oilmen from Texas and society people from Pasadena—very rich."

"Peasants," said His Imperial Highness. "Fuck 'em."

Ten minutes later the scene was repeated. "Very important, Mr. Romanoff—Main Line society people from Philadelphia."

"*Canaille!*" said Mike from the imperial tumbrel.

"And there's a general waiting in line too Mr. Romanoff . . . from St. Louis. . . ."

"Cannon fodder," commented the prince, "from the Interior, too," he added with disgust.

Harry F. Gerguson of Chicago, as Mike was known in the records of the New York police department, had also been described officially by Scotland Yard as "a rogue of uncertain nationality." He had been jailed countless times in the United States and in France and had received two suspended sentences in England. He had been deported regularly from all three countries and twice on transatlantic liners had been caught, a first-class stowaway using empty cabins. In December, 1922, unable to prove his American citizenship, he was held on Ellis Island. He escaped, by swimming he claimed, to the Battery. It is a matter of record that he disappeared from Ellis Island at that time, but it is equally true that without water wings, he could never swim a stroke. All his crimes had been what he termed "moves of self-preservation"—failing to return things he had borrowed without asking, selling *objets d'art* which did not belong to him, and passing enough dud checks on both sides of the Atlantic to provide his own ticker-tape parade. All these misdemeanors had been perpetrated in what he considered the best possible cause—to help Harry F. Gerguson live in the style to which Prince Michael Alexandrovich Dmitri Obolensky Romanoff would have been accustomed.

There was absolutely no malice in the man, and even when he had been at his most reprehensible, he had behaved like a latter-day Robin Hood, extracting cash from the wealthy and joyfully sharing the benefits accruing therefrom with his friends.

Many people who had been "taken" by Mike became his

most ardent supports, and slowly he had evolved from being a full-time impostor and international con man into the honest burgher of Beverly Hills who was pouring ice-cold Dom Pérignon on that warm July day.

The headwaiter approached again and whispered in his ear, jerking his head disapprovingly toward the bar.

"Give them my Imperial greetings," said Mike, without hesitation, "take them to the best table you have, and serve them anything they want; then send the account to the Winter Palace."

I watched the headwaiter approach two men at the bar and recognized them as a well-known actor and an excellent writer; both had served with gallantry with the Marines on Okinawa, and Mike was one of the few who cared that since their return to Hollywood they had found themselves largely forgotten and the going very rough.

I first met Mike in New York at the tail end of Prohibition; we frequented the same speakeasy, Jack and Charlie's at 21 West Fifty-second Street, where I had just been taken on as their first salesman of legitimate booze. I was not selling very much, so after his initial effort Mike realized that putting the bite on me for ten bucks was living in Mother Hubbard Land, and we became good friends in need. He never seemed to lack for invitations to meals, but he was very reticent about where he lived, and depending on whom he was talking to and his estimate of their gullibility, he operated a sliding scale of claims of kinship to the murdered czar. It fluctuated wildly. Sometimes he was the czar's nephew, occasionally his half brother, often he was the son of Prince Yusupov, who had pumped booze and bullets into Rasputin, and on particularly low-risk occasions, he became Yusupov himself. When he operated in the " Interior," he occasionally dropped his Russian connections, and in Chicago he took on a British aura, sticking closely to the Duke of Wellington, wearing a monocle and calling himself Sir Arthur Wellesley, Count Mornington, or plain William Wellington, Esquire, but he sometimes got his priorities a little mixed and referred to the Prince of Wales as "my cousin David."

In spite of his acquired accent, Mike's heart was never English, and as the years passed, it seemed as though he increasingly came to believe a large part of his Romanoff fantasy.

With New York harboring countless Russians of noble birth, Mike was again and again denounced as an impostor, but on such occasions he conducted himself with such immense dignity that he added to his growing coterie of admirers, who remember with awe his occasional courageous defenses of his indefensible situation and his battles against appalling physical odds in a number of barroom brawls. A particularly unattractive verbal confrontation occurred when somebody invited the Grand Duke Dmitri of Russia to meet his kinsman. The grand duke peered suspiciously at the top of Mike's hairbrush crew cut and spoke to him rapidly in Russian. Mike made for the door, raising a languid hand to silence him.

"I don't think," he said, "that we should insult our hosts by talking in any language but theirs."

Afterward he confided that he had never much cared for that branch of the family.

For anyone with Mike's flair and humor it was inevitable that sooner or later he would feel the call of the Hollywood wild, and in 1927 His Imperial Highness arrived aboard the Santa Fe Chief, took a large suite in the Ambassador Hotel, and started dispensing princely amounts of champagne and caviar to all and sundry. Vowing haughtily that the Romanoffs never dirtied their fingers with common currency, he tipped headwaiters and bellhops with great abandon by check and, at the end of his visit, signed his bill with a flourish and departed for pastures new.

The prince was lavishly entertained by Hollywood hostesses, and Warner Brothers begged him to be their technical adviser on *The Desired Woman,* a picture with a Sudanese background and a British army foreground. Mike admitted modestly that he had indeed served with the British army in the Great War and that it just so happened that he knew the Sudan like the back of his hand. He pulled down a royal salary for many weeks and became much sought after by the studios as technical adviser on all pictures with Russian or British overtones. These for a while he haughtily turned down and undertook instead a lecture tour of Pasadena, Whittier, Santa Barbara, and Pismo Beach—his subject "Russia Past and Present." When the proceeds from the tour dried up, Mike took a calculated risk and accepted one of the studios' offers. It proved his undoing. An old friend of the late czar—an ex-general, named Theodor Lodijensky—was working as an extra on the film, and he promptly alerted the Los Angeles *Examiner.* The next day a front-page story exposed Mike as an impostor, and he was publicly defrocked.

Finding Southern California suddenly uncomfortably warm, Mike decided to disappear for a cooling-off period, and the "Interior" was soon papering itself with his dud checks. He kept on the move, however, and, apart from the odd night in jail, largely stayed ahead of the sheriff, and from his uncomfortable perch on various flatcars, he enjoyed uninterrupted views of a large portion of the United States. But if the authorities found it hard to catch up with him, that ghastly creature bearing scythe and hourglass was breathing down his neck. Well into his forties by now, Mike was longing to settle in one place, and soon he was back in Los Angeles, broke as usual but with a new light in his eye— he had determined to stop moving and to go straight.

Mike's true genius was his ability to make admiring and staunch friends out of the very people who had the best reasons for disliking or distrusting him. His turn into the straight was a gradual one. Instead of borrowing money, he now preferred winning it at backgammon or chess, at which he was an expert, playing several games at once all over the country by telegram. Throughout his metamorphosis, he clung tenaciously to his Romanoff fantasy, but however much he believed it himself, he now traded on it openly and encouraged people to play false court to him and became more widely admired, feted, and entertained as a famous impostor than he ever had been in the days when he was accepted as the real thing.

He foreswore his time-honored role of freeloader and now, if he joined a friend's table for luncheon, he would meticulously pay his share if he was in funds; if not, he would sit nibbling a roll and sipping a glass of water. We knew better than to press him.

Twentieth Century-Fox employed him occasionally as a reader of possible film material or as a synopsis writer, and he acquitted himself well there and at other studios, but on Friday nights we made a point of avoiding him because payday to Mike was merely an excuse to entertain his friends at the Trocadero, snapping his fingers and ordering large quantities of the best wines to wash down out-of-season delicacies.

By 1939 I was living in comfort in a small house on the beach at Santa Monica. Mike was a frequent and most welcome visitor; he never borrowed money but occasionally asked if he might have the loan of a bed "on which to lay the Imperial head." He made the trips to Santa Monica by bumming lifts. One day he drove up to the door in an immense drophead Duesenberg.

"Greetings, old boy," he said smugly.

"Who did you borrow it from?" I asked.

"It's mine," said the prince, "I bought it last week."

"I don't believe you," I said ungraciously.

Mike frowned his displeasure at my bad taste. "Allow me to show you the pink slip."

He then displayed the coveted document proving that he had indeed made the purchase.

I goggled.

"Where are you sleeping?" I asked.

"Why, in the Duesenberg, of course," said the Imperial motorist.

Even though by now he was playing his impostor role for a different effect, he still used the trappings of his calling, wearing an Old Etonian tie one day and a Brigade of Guards scarf the next. His conversations still pulsated with "when I was up at Oxford," "during my time at Sandhurst," or "he was a classmate of mine at Harvard."

It was no easy job to catch him out; many tried and failed. There were dozens of witnesses to prove that in 1923, for a few months at least, he had indeed studied at the Graduate School of Arts and Sciences at Harvard, and I heard an old Etonian question him about Eton.

"Who was your housemaster?" he asked.

"You mean who was 'me tutor,'" countered Mike swiftly,

and followed up his advantage by saying, "I suppose you'll be asking me next if I went to Thomas' in the High Street to get my hair cut."

As an ex-Sandhurst man myself I found his knowledge of the goings-on, the military procedure, and the habits and hideaways of the cadets at the Royal Military College to be just as extensive as my own, and I did not doubt that when he poured out the names of officers, cadets, and staff of his supposed period there, he would have been correct down to the last hyphen and decoration.

"How many schools and colleges *have* you attended?" I asked him once.

"Let me see," said Mike. "St. Paul's, Andover, Choate, and Harvard in the United States. Eton, Harrow, Winchester, Oxford, Cambridge, and Sandhurst in England and, of course, the Sorbonne and Heidelberg. Believe me, old boy"—he chortled—"this business of being an impostor is a full-time job!"

It was Mike's British accent that always fascinated me. I could never put my finger on it. It was the sort of camouflage that English curates perfect to cover up honest Cockney voices. This "plummy" delivery never left Mike, and even on the very few occasions, those testing times when he took a glass or two too many, it remained as much a part of him as his bristly crew-cut pate and his military mustache.

I could never discover whence this strange sound originated. The secret of its source was locked away in the same little mental strongbox in which he kept the key to his whereabouts during the blood-drenched years between 1914 and 1918. The twin mysteries have never been solved, but during his many unveilings as an impostor, Mike stated under questioning that he had passed World War I as an officer with a British regiment in France or with Allenby in Palestine; he also claimed that the eastern front had enjoyed the benefit of his presence and expertise as a Cossack reconnaissance captain (though his horsemanship was later proved to be on a par with his prowess at swimming). He hinted at driving a taxi for the French army during the epic defense of Paris and vigorously defended his right to wear in his buttonhole the red ribbon of the Légion d'honneur, but whether or not he gathered any decorations during that period it was certainly then that he acquired his British accent and his military mementos.

In 1937 Mike struck gold. He obtained an option on the lease of a defunct restaurant on the Sunset Strip. His friends became stockholders in the shoestring enterprise, and the place reopened in a blaze of black ties, mink, well-known faces, and publicity.

The invitation was a classic:

> I AM COMMANDED BY HIS IMPERIAL HIGHNESS PRINCE
> MICHAEL ALEXANDROVICH DMITRI OBOLENSKY ROMANOFF
> TO REQUEST YOUR PRESENCE AT A SOIREE HE IS GIVING IN
> HIS OWN HONOR
> . . . COUVERT FIFTY DOLLARS
> BRING YOUR OWN WINE AND KINDLY FEE THE WAITERS
>
> HARRY GERGUSON
> COMPTROLLER TO THE IMPERIAL HOUSEHOLD

Le tout Hollywood turned out in force, and so many people brought wine that few realized the place had no arrangements whatever for cooking. A sparse menu was serviced by a nearby hash joint on a strictly cash basis (the money collected for the first two couverts started the ball rolling), a riotous evening was had by all, and enough money raised to install a kitchen and launch Mike on a fabulously successful career as a restaurateur.

In 1939, when I was headed for Europe and the British army, Mike came to say good-bye and gave me some advice: "If you become an officer, invent a pair of trousers that immediately drop around your knees when you are ordered to charge. Then you just say 'On! On! Men! Don't wait for me. I'll catch you up.'"

He also gave me a hand-knitted balaclava helmet ("saved me near St. Petersburg, old boy") and a large blue and white spotted scarf with a burn in the center ("mustard gas . . . Cambrai . . . silk is the only thing against it"). I lost the hand-knitted balaclava helmet, but I still have the blue and white spotted scarf; a laundress told me that careless ironing was responsible for the burn.

Restaurateur Mike prospered during World War II, and by 1945 he was firmly established as the owner-manager of the highly lucrative Romanoff's in Beverly Hills. The imperial *R* was emblazoned on the front door. When he branched out into an even larger and more elaborate establishment, his loyal staff and clients and the imperial *R* made the move with him. Around that time he also started a subsidiary on an escarpment near Palm Springs called Romanoff on the Rocks, accumulated a bulldog named Confucius, and an extremely attractive young wife, Gloria. His Imperial Highness had made the big switch from con man to capitalist and, in a strange reversal of form, had not lost a friend in the process.

Mike loved children, and one of my reasons for visiting him on that hot summer's day was to thank him for yet another kindness toward mine. As a widower I had been finding it a difficult job to bring up two small boys and at the same time earn my living. Friends had come to my aid, and Mike, with a constant flow of ideas, had been in the van of the rescue operation.

The evening before, I had arrived home from work to find the children waiting at the garden gate, shiny-eyed with excitement.

"Mr. Romanoff took us on a treasure hunt! Look what we found!" and they proudly displayed ropes of pearls, huge rubies, and handfuls of "doubloons."

Mike had staged it all meticulously, arriving unexpectedly with a picnic basket and a carefully drawn pirate's map of a lonely part of the beach ten miles away near Trancas. There had been clues and red herrings and arrows made of pieces of driftwood, and finally, after a long search, the corner of a treasure chest had been spied just showing above the sand in a pirate's cave. Mike must have spent hours arranging it all, but he brushed aside my thanks. "The pleasure was all mine, old boy . . . children are nature's gentlemen . . . I far prefer their company to that of grownups."

Over luncheon I sought to enlist Mike's help for a project of my own. Robert Laycock was coming to visit me, and I wanted Romanoff's to cater a party I was planning for him.

"Ah, and how is young Bob?" asked Mike the minute he heard the name. "I haven't seen him since he was at Eton."

"Now, Mike," I said patiently, "Bob Laycock is twenty years

younger than you. You were never at Eton with him or anybody else for that matter."

Mike looked pained.

"I did not suggest that young Bob was a schoolmate of mine—I merely mentioned the fact that I had not seen him since he was at Eton."

It was always fun to play along with Mike, so I gave him a cue. "And where did you meet him while he was a schoolboy?"

"At Wiseton, of course, he was home after the summer half and Sir Joseph had invited me for the weekend for a spot of country house cricket."

Wiseton was indeed the Laycock home in Lincolnshire, and Sir Joseph was certainly Bob's father, so I could not suppress a start of surprise. Mike noticed this and pressed home the advantage.

"Yes, old Joe and I were very close and Kitty, too, of course . . . too bad she lost a leg on their honeymoon."

Mike had obviously had reason somewhere along the line to research the Laycock family very carefully, but the mental picture of him in blazer and white flannels, sitting in a deck chair, sipping tea and eating cucumber sandwiches while waiting his turn to bat, was too much even for me.

"Mike, please," I said, "please don't get into a thing with Bob Laycock about his mother having only one leg because he may not appreciate it, and he's a very rough character indeed—he was the chief of all the Commandos, you know."

"And the youngest general in the British army," said Mike, unmoved. "I'm very proud of him."

I shook my head. "Mike, please, on this one occasion, *please* don't press your luck." There was a pause.

"After luncheon," said my host, "we will go to my house—I have something to show you which may put your mind at rest."

Back at Mike's white stucco residence on Chevy Chase Drive, he took me up to his bedroom; there he nonchalantly displayed a pair of ivory hairbrushes. The ivory was a little yellow with age, but what brought me up all standing was the insignia in worked silver on their backs. It was something I knew very well—the crest of the Laycock family.

"A present from old Joe," said Mike smugly.

Bob Laycock duly arrived on his visit, and the party as catered by Romanoff's was a great success. I had warned Bob about Mike and hoped against hope that Mike would stay off the subject of Wiseton. Far from it. For a large part of the evening, Mike cornered Bob, who seemed to be enjoying thoroughly the company of the mini-monarch from whose expressive gestures I could see from across the room that both cricket and hairbrushes were being discussed at length. Nothing awful happened, however, and the happy guests finally departed. After they had gone, Bob and I had a nightcap and held the usual postmortem on the evening.

"What did you think of Mike?" I asked.

"Fascinating," said Bob. "He had me stumped completely. There is no question but that he has been to Wiseton and no question at all that he has played cricket there. There is also no question that long ago a team of Durham miners came over to play. I well remember it because Father was so furious. When they left, it was discovered that someone had swiped his favorite hairbrushes." Prince Michael Alexandrovich Dmitri Obolensky Romanoff remained enigmatic when I tried to pump him.

"Golden days, old boy," was all he would say dreamily. "Golden days."

He steadfastly refused to answer my question: "What was Harry F. Gerguson of Chicago doing down a Durham coal mine?"

9
Two Queens

CONNIE

AT five o'clock on Sunday afternoons in the late thirties, tennis courts would empty and streets would become thinly populated. America liked to be by a radio set at that hour so it could listen to Edgar Bergen and his wooden top-hatted and monocled ventriloquist dummy, Charlie McCarthy.

The audiences for the big radio shows were enormous with 40,000,000 or 50,000,000 addicted to the like of Cecil B. DeMille's *Lux Radio Theater* and the *Lucky Strike Hit Parade,* but just as the advent of sound had a winnowing effect on the popularity of the silent film stars, so was the arrival of television destined to put an end to the careers of many radio personalities. Bob Hope, Jack Benny, George Burns, Gracie Allen, Jimmy Durante, and a few others made the transition with flying colors, but Edgar Bergen went under because people thought they could see his lips move when Charlie McCarthy was talking, and they were distracted by his strained smile and bobbing Adam's apple. Gravelly-voiced Fred Allen, who headed a wonderfully well-written weekly show which included Allen's Alley, a street peopled by hilariously contemporary characters, faded away because he was unveiled as a crotchety, sour-faced man with a bad complexion, and the longest-running show of all, heard nightly for twelve years—*Amos 'n' Andy,* the comic antics of two blacks in the Deep South—disintegrated when the cameras disclosed the fact that the well-known voices had been issuing from two whites.

After the big radio shows had departed, the performers were long remembered with affection complete with their signature tunes and sayings:

"Thanks for the Memory"—Bob Hope
"When the Blue of the Night Meets the Gold of the Day"—Bing Crosby
"Inka-Dinka-Doo"—Jimmy Durante
"Wanna buy a duck?"—Joe Penner
"Vas you d'ere, Sharley?"—Jack Pearl
and the squeals of Baby Snooks—Fanny Brice

Even the Morse sender which the gossip columnist Walter Winchell used to attract attention to his scurrilous gibberish was mourned in some quarters:

Tap. Tap. Tap.   "Good evening, Mr. and Mrs. North America, and all the ships at sea. Let's go to press!"

During World War II radio's foreign correspondents became household pets, William Shirer, Charles Collingwood, Cecil Brown, and Quentin Reynolds to name some of the most beloved, and the defiant growl of Churchill became as much a part of America as President Roosevelt's Fireside Chats beginning "My friends," but it was the deep clear voice of Edward R. Murrow broadcasting from London during the 190 days of the blitz which brought tears to American eyes. "This is London. . . . I am speaking to you from a city in flames."

Radio acting was not easy, the trick being to sound as though you were not reading, even though many rehearsals had bred overfamiliarity and suddenly a simple word could stare up at you from the page—an unrecognizable jumble of letters. Radio actors were a fascinating breed—performers who lived by their voices alone, never seen by their admirers and often preferring it that way. There was, for instance, one middle-aged lady whose minimal physical attractions were compensated for by the fact that she could produce the most seductive tones ever to come out of a twenty-year-old. Several times I was called on to play ardent love scenes with her, and for a young film actor, it required the marshaling of every reserve of imagination to be able to speak adoringly to her over the top of a microphone while averting my eyes from the gray roots of her hair and the heavy deposit of dandruff on her shoulders.

Some radio actors could produce twenty or thirty accents and dialects, while comedy voices were the forte of others, among whom the most sought after was Mel Blanc, famous for supplying the endearing quack words of Donald Duck and the strange mechanical sounds of Jack Benny's Maxwell automobile. But the backbone of the dramatic shows was the sound-effects men. These individuals were highly regarded by the studio audiences who watched their every move as from a forest of gadgets they coaxed the sounds of popping corks, electrical storms, galloping horses, crying babies, crashing aircraft, escaping steam, and burning buildings, but sometimes they elicited a response from their admirers which puzzled the unwary performer. Struggling through the thornbushes of the North-West Frontier with Victor McLaglen in *Gunga Din,* I was panting as ordered by the script and whispering "audience orientation" dialogue. "Phew, this undergrowth is heavy." To which McLaglen replied, "So's this dynamite I'm carrying, but we'll teach 'em a lesson with it when we get to the fort up ahead there in the clearing . . . don't make a sound." It was supposedly a tense and exciting moment, but the studio audience was tittering loudly, and we did not have far to look for the reason. The sound-effects man was simulating the heavy crackling of the bushes by wrapping toilet paper around his microphone.

The studio audience became specialists in their field. They lined up from early morning outside the enclaves of the Columbia Broadcasting System and the National Broadcasting Company on Sunset Boulevard, waiting patiently for free passes to see their favorite shows and to watch their favorite performers. Radio producers were pleased to see these "professional" audiences because they paid for their free passes by enthusiastically obeying the instructions waved aloft on boards emblazoned with LAUGH! or APPLAUSE! A select few could be relied on to sniffle.

The big radio shows carried tremendous publicity value, and the movie producers were delighted when their stars were offered the exposure. Some shows were popular with the top film performers, others, if possible, they avoided like the plague, but Louella Parsons had a blackmailing show called *Hollywood Hotel,* and a few years later Hedda Hopper, the other all-powerful columnist, came up with her own con game—*Hedda Hopper's Hollywood.* The big stars, goaded by their studios, performed on these programs at great inconvenience and for no salary because the chickenhearted producers believed that refusal to "lend" their stars would bring swift retribution in the shape of bad publicity and poor reviews.

The revulsion of the big film stars against the Parsons and Hopper shows was widespread, but they lined up happily to be heard on the big dramatic offerings or even as guest stars on comedy programs with Bergen, Crosby, Benny, or Hope, being well aware that exposure to the listening millions in well-written and well-produced material could do their film careers nothing but good. Some, like Constance Bennett, were a trifle condescending in their attitude toward what they considered the poor relation of the entertainment world, and this was a hazard for which I had been ill prepared when my first boss, Samuel Goldwyn, gave the electrifying news that he had lent me to the *Shell Hour* to play opposite the most highly paid film star in the world in selected love scenes from Pirandello.

Constance Bennett I had long worshiped from afar. She seemed to me the quintessence of a movie queen. She radiated glamor from her exalted position in the Hollywood firmament, and everything about her shone! Her burnished head, her iridescent skin, her jewels, her famous smile, her lovely long legs, and the highly publicized fact that she pulled down thirty thousand bucks a week. If Marlene Dietrich possessed a Cadillac the length of a subway train, driven by a chauffeur named Briggs who had a mink collar on his uniform in winter and a brace of revolvers on his hips, and Jeanette Mac-

Donald was ferried about in her conveyance by a smart gentleman who shared the front seat with a large gray and white sheepdog, then Constance Bennett was out of place in anything but her Rolls-Royce, a shiny black beauty of a phaeton, with *her* chauffeur sitting outside in all weathers while she sat behind in a velvet-lined compartment decorated on the outside with yellow wickerwork. I was excited at the thought of what the next few days had in store for me, but the Shell people were overwhelmed to have such a glamor queen on their program, and their awe of her seemed to inhibit them from giving her precise calls to rehearsal.

"Here's her home number, Dave," said the director ten days before the fatal Saturday. "Why don't you give her a call, then go over to her place and kinda kick it around together before we start full rehearsals Tuesday?"

Over the first weekend I familiarized myself with the scenes, and on Monday, about midday, I dutifully called Constance Bennett's house.

"Miss Bennett does not awaken before three o'clock," said a butler. "Kindly leave a message and your phone number with her secretary." He switched me over. I explained to the secretary the reason for my call. She was sympathetic but unimpressed.

"Well, there's plenty of time, isn't there? . . . The show's not till Saturday, and it's only radio! . . . We'll call you later."

I hung around my boxlike apartment for the rest of Monday, but nothing happened. On Tuesday morning early the director called me.

"How's it been goin', kid?" he asked, and from the anxiety in his voice, I knew that he too had enjoyed little contact with his star.

"Jesus!" he shrieked when I told him. "The first rehearsal's at two o'clock."

Later he called back and said that it had been canceled for that day but that he had arranged an appointment for me at Constance Bennett's house on the morrow.

"And you'd better be there," he snarled as though I were responsible for the nonevent so far.

As ordered, I reported at a most attractive house in Carolwood Drive at eleven o'clock on Wednesday morning. The butler showed me into a library, where I read magazines till two o'clock. At three I heard a car leave, and the butler brought me a tuna fish sandwich and a glass of beer.

"Miss Bennett has fittings at the studio," he said. "She said she was sorry to miss you and to come back tomorrow at the same time."

"I'd like to speak to the secretary," I said.

"She's gone, too," said the butler. "Coffee?"

On Thursday morning about ten o'clock the secretary called. "Sorry to disappoint you," she said. "Miss Bennett can't make it today, after all, but you have an invitation to lunch tomorrow, two thirty and bring a tennis racket." She hung up.

Nobody called from the *Shell Hour,* so I decided they must have been keeping themselves abreast of events.

I awoke on Friday morning in a highly nervous condition. One did not fool around with Pirandello, even if one was reading it, and certainly not in front of 20,000,000 people. The dress rehearsal with full orchestra and effects was scheduled to begin the following morning at ten o'clock, and the show itself would be broadcast at five that evening. Much depended on my forthcoming luncheon date with the star.

I arrived on the dot of two thirty to find a couple of dozen people already sampling various beverages on the patio. The secretary introduced herself and presented me to the others. It was a friendly and extroverted group, and I was able to relax. The talk was mostly about a poker game the night before at which, I gathered, my hostess had been the big winner. Good-humored threats of revenge were being issued, but La Bennett did not hear them—she was sleeping peacefully upstairs. After luncheon her resident and permanent "beau," the romantic-looking Mexican actor Gilbert Roland, took me by the arm. "Let's get some exercise, amigo," he said, and led me down to the tennis court.

We played singles and doubles till the light began to go. As it faded, I remembered Pirandello, and my nerves started twanging anew. I enlisted Gilbert Roland's sympathetic help. "I'll talk to her," he promised.

Up at the house people were arriving for cocktails, and a

poker game was already under way. At the table I noticed
Myron Selznick, the top agent in Hollywood, Joseph
Schenck, the head of Twentieth Century-Fox, and Irving
Berlin. Constance Bennett was also there. I had seldom seen
a more beautiful human being: straight, shiny, very blond
hair, pencil-thin brows over big, blue, intelligent eyes, a fine-
ly chiseled face with high cheekbones, and a rather determined jaw. Her skin was creamy white, and her beautifully
slim body was encased and encrusted in and by the latest in
fashion and the most expensive in jewelry.

Gilbert chose a lull in the action and bent over her. She let
out a peal of delicious laughter, waved gaily at me, and
turned her concentration once more to the business in hand.

"She says," said Gilbert, "why don't you go home and
change. It's buffet supper, and she's running *The Good Earth*
afterward. She'd be delighted to have you join us."

"My God," I croaked, "what about tomorrow? . . . We've
got to do that show!"

"You only have to *read* it, amigo," said Gilbert, "but I'm
sure she'll find time to run it through with you during the
evening."

By the time I returned an hour later forty or fifty people
had converged on Carolwood Drive and presupper conviviality was in full swing. The poker game was still in progress
in the cardroom, and from the totally engrossed expressions
of the players I judged it unlikely that much rehearsing of
tomorrow's radio show would be taking place. The buffet
supper came and went. *The Good Earth* with two good Jewish
actors, Paul Muni and Luise Rainer, looking determinedly
Chinese while swatting away at swarms of MGM's homemade
locusts, was dutifully applauded, and around two o'clock in
the morning the party began to thin out. I checked on the situation in the cardroom—it was unchanged, and the sight of
discarded ties and jackets, plus the presence of plates of
sandwiches and the monumental size of the pots, made it obvious that it would remain that way for some time to come.

At four o'clock I went home, none too relieved by Gilbert's
latest piece of information: "She can't quit now because she
was such a big winner last night. . . . She says she'll be
ready at nine o'clock in the morning, so you be here then.

. . .You can drive down with her and run it through a couple of times down at the studio before the rehearsal. . . . Don't worry, amigo, it's only radio!"

I couldn't sleep and had visions of a promising career going up in smoke, so I worked till dawn on the scenes determined by now to embark upon a policy of *sauve-qui-peut.*

Sharp at nine, eyes blinking in the blinding California sun and shaking with black coffee and Benzedrine, I rang the doorbell at Carolwood Drive. A housemaid looked surprised. "I've an appointment with Miss Bennett," I said.

The girl motioned me toward the still heavily curtained library redolent with the smell of after-party staleness. I couldn't believe my eyes. In the cardroom beyond, I beheld the poker game still going full blast; the players, with the exception of Constance Bennett, looked haggard and blue of jowl.

The hostess saw me and announced, "Last hand, fellows. I have to go to work."

Soon it was over, and an hour later I found myself seated in the Rolls-Royce phaeton beside an incredibly beautiful and apparently well-rested Constance Bennett. She must have been made of different stuff because with her unlined face and clear blue eyes she looked as though she had awakened from a dreamless sleep of at least ten hours.

During the twenty-minute drive to Vine Street, she filled me in on the outcome of the marathon game. "Poor Myron," she said, "I think he really will quit now. . . . He lost almost a hundred thousand bucks, but you can't mix martinis and cold hands . . . not with that group, you can't. . . . He was that much ahead at one time, but at the end he blew it."

At the radio studio everyone was determinedly trying to look as though he was not at panic station. We were at least two hours late for dress rehearsal, but such was the awe in which my glamorous partner was held by the executives of the *Shell Hour* that they welcomed her as though she had come to inaugurate a new wing of the building. Waiting, too, were several hundred of her fans, screaming her name and begging her to spare them a smile, pleading for autographs and apparently undismayed by the fact that they were kept at

a respectful distance from their idol, having been herded
since early morning into a prisoner of war cage of high wire
netting.

The director fawned on her and immediately acceded to
her request that for the next half hour she and I should be
left undisturbed in her dressing room so that she could
"check a few things in the script."

Constance Bennett was completely composed as she took
her first look at Pirandello's lines which she would be delivering later in the day to the expectant millions. Totally absorbed, she read for a few minutes then stopped and
frowned. In silence she leafed ahead through the rustle-
proof pages; then she threw them in the wastebasket.

"I'm not going to do this shit," she announced.

The producer and director were summoned; so too was
the advertising agency man. She would not tackle Pirandello,
she said, under any circumstances. A dew of sweat stood out
on the assembled group. "But, Miss Bennett, it's almost one
o'clock, and we go on the air at five," pleaded the director.

"Too bad," she answered.

"The orchestra has been rehearsing since eight this morning," murmured the producer.

"They get paid," said the star.

"Shell will cancel the account," groaned the man from the
advertising agency.

"Screw Shell," said Miss Bennett.

For half an hour the men pleaded and cajoled but at one
o'clock with air time a scant four hours away, the men agreed
that she could instead play a couple of scenes from the picture she had just finished at Twentieth Century-Fox. Quite
apart from the hideous spot into which this last-minute
switch now put me (a situation which nobody even mentioned), there was the question of obtaining the permission
of Twentieth Century-Fox.

"You go ahead with that," said C. Bennett loftily. "Just call
Darryl Zanuck; we'll go on back to the house and grab a bite
to eat while we read through the scenes together. I have
some scripts up there. You'd better send someone to pick
one up so you can find out what it's all about. . . . Let's go,"

she said to me over her shoulder and headed for the door. As we departed, I saw the director conversing with the orchestra leader; their faces were a very odd color.

Constance B. smiled charmingly at her caged fans on her way to the Rolls-Royce, and on the long drive back to Carolwood Drive she remained cool and confident. She patted my wet hand. "Don't be nervous," she said. "These are great scenes, you'll love them."

Around two o'clock I was given a hamburger which turned into a bicycle in my stomach, and between bites I read the scenes. They were light and airy and, compared to Pirandello, much easier to play. I felt a little less apprehensive of my impending ordeal, but my optimism was short-lived when the *Shell Hour* spoke to Constance Bennett. They were desperate: Nobody at Twentieth Century-Fox except Joseph Schenck or Darryl Zanuck could give the necessary permission; Zanuck was on his way to Santa Anita Racecourse, and even if they could locate him there, it would be too late. Schenck was at his home, and no one would give out his private number.

"Leave it to me," said the star. She glanced at the clock; it was almost three o'clock. Already the lines would have formed outside the radio station. She couldn't find her phone book, and the secretary was off for the day. Several calls later the secretary was tracked down, loudly relaxed at a liquid brunch in Santa Monica, but the whereabouts of the book were wrung out of her. It made no difference. Schenck, according to someone at his house, had given strict instructions not to be awakened till four o'clock. "He got home real late," said a soft black voice. "I know that, goddammit," said La Bennett loudly. "C'mon. Let's go."

"Where?" I asked, panic rising.

"To Joe's place," said La Bennett. "I'll wake the son of a bitch up."

The chauffeur of the Rolls, spurred on now by a far less relaxed employer, catapulted the phaeton with smoking tires through Holmby Hills, but to no avail. We arrived to a head-on confrontation between a big film star and the stone-faced entourage of a big producer. His butler, the gardener, and a private detective lurking in the bushes all made it crystal clear that they had not the slightest intention of waking their boss before the appointed hour.

The big star wheedled, threatened and ranted. "But he was still in my house at nine o'clock this morning," she yelled, stamping a pretty foot.

They were unmoved. "Sorry, Miss Bennett . . . orders is orders!"

Finally, she gave up. "Let's go," she growled. "Back to the studio."

The Saturday afternoon traffic by now was bumper to bumper, and every light seemed to be red. Down in Hollywood an expectant audience of hundreds was settling itself, twittering with excitement at the prospect of seeing its own Constance Bennett, and millions all over the country were gathering around their radio sets to hear her voice. "We'll stop at Schwab's Drugstore," she said. "You go call those creeps at Shell and tell 'em it's Parendillo or whatever the hell his name is."

From a pay booth I called the *Shell Hour,* and a noise like boiling water issued from our producer, but I promised that I would indeed "get that bitch down here in fifteen minutes."

By the time we had run the gauntlet of the swollen number of her fans behind the wire netting (and I had to admire her—she smilingly took her time and even signed a few grubby slips of paper poked at her through the holes) it was less than half an hour before air time, and she was swept off to her flower-filled dressing room, where she nonchalantly changed her makeup and put on a stunning silver lamé dress. I sat bolt upright on a wooden chair, alone in a corner of the stage, avoiding the hostile glances of the orchestra, and with trembling fingers and unseeing eyes pretended to be working on my script.

At a quarter to five the curtain rose, and the announcer warmed up the studio audience with a few nervous jokes, explained to them how much their applause would contribute to the listeners' pleasure, extolled the beauty, brilliance, and dedication of our hardworking star and introduced the orchestra leader and the director. This individual found time to hiss at me, "You both work on the same mike . . . take stage right so she can show her best profile . . . when there's a music bridge, sound effects, or pause, watch me for your cue before you start speaking and . . . God help us all!"

Five minutes before air time the announcer remembered me and told the studio audience that the young man playing opposite Miss Bennett came from the Abbey Players in Dublin—a black lie which aroused little response.

Thunderous applause and gasps of admiration then greeted the appearance of the star. She smiled beautifully and calmly settled herself on a chair next to mine and crossed her impeccable silken legs. After what seemed an eternity, the red sign ON THE AIR flashed; a fanfare, and the announcer began extolling the smiling efficiency of the Shell station attendants, the unequaled excellence of their product, and the cleanliness of their lavatories. Another fanfare, followed by a moving introduction of the main event, and Constance Bennett and I were alone in the center of the stage, facing each other and twenty million Americans over the top of the microphone.

I didn't feel anything very much: I was numb with terror. I had to speak first; the director signaled frantically to me to begin. I stared back at him like a dog watching a snake; then I looked across at my partner, hoping that miraculously some of her superhuman calm might rub off on me. What I saw made me relax completely. She was human, after all—she was pale green and shaking like an aspen .

GARBO

In our itchy fustian trousers and jackets of the same material stained at the armpits with salty sweat rings and redolent of a hundred earlier occupants, we extras working on a Marie Dressler potboiler were making the most of our short lunch break on the MGM back lot, stretched out on the grass and foraging dispiritedly among the unappetizing contents of small cardboard boxes provided for our refreshment.

A dusty road separated the well-tended campus lawns on

which we sprawled from the fronts of a row of prim New England clapboard houses. They had no interiors and no backs.

"Here she comes!" somebody announced in an excited whisper, and the message spread with the rapidity of a forest fire among the half hundred depressed citizenry.

"Who?" I asked my neighbor, a large Mexican lady of uncertain cleanliness who, I had noticed, earlier in the day, when pinned against her in a doorway, had a cluster of blackheads between her bosoms.

"Garbo!" she replied, rising to her feet. "Every day at lunch time she takes her exercises."

The road at its nearest point to us was fifty yards away, and the extras, with one exception, making no move to close the gap, stood respectfully and watched in fascinated silence as a slim figure wearing dark glasses, a baggy sort of track suit, and a large floppy hat strode purposefully past. Upon the hardened, cynical faces of those long exposed to every great star in the business were looks of wonderment and awe. Suddenly the spell was broken. A young boy broke from the ranks, and brandishing a pencil and a grubby piece of paper, he ran across the grass toward the dusty road. "Miss Garbo!" he called.

The trim figure missed a beat and stiffened perceptibly; then she accelerated by lengthening her stride; as the cantering youth closed the gap, she broke first into a trot, and finally, as he gained upon her, she opened the throttle and, leaving him pounding along in her wake, disappeared at a graceful gallop toward the sanctuary of the main studio and her dressing room. She had never looked around, but she had the radar system of a bat when it came to avoiding contact with a stranger.

When the panting and crestfallen boy returned, the Mexican lady cuffed him hard and shook him. "Why you not leave her alone?" she demanded loudly. "She likes be *private!*"

She did indeed, and the studio was filled with stories of her determination to preserve her privacy. She liked to work always with the same crew and demanded that the redoubtable Bill Daniels photograph all her pictures. A great professional, she seemed perfectly at ease among others working on the same film, but as Bill said, "She could sniff an outsider a mile away, and if anyone, no matter who, came on the set to get a peek at her, she'd sense it even with a coupla hundred extras around and she'd just go and sit in her dressing room till they'd been put out."

Stories of her elusiveness were legion, and much enjoyment was extracted from the names, "Gussie Berger" and "Harriet Brown," under which she booked hotels and travel arrangements. The great Garbo quote "I want to be alone" was probably never uttered by her, but there was no question that she was a loner—painfully shy with people she did not know and preferring her own company to that of most people. "Making a film with Garbo," said Robert Montgomery, another star at MGM, "does not constitute an introduction." Garbo had an icy look in her eyes when anyone sought to impose upon her, as, according to studio gossip, Groucho Marx discovered one day. He saw a well-known figure approaching in slacks and floppy hat, waylaid her, bent down in his famous crouch, and peeked up under the brim. Two prisms of pure Baltic blue stared down at him, and he backed away, muttering, "Pardon me, ma'am. I thought you were a guy I knew in Pittsburgh."

When the talkies came in, there were many casualties among the great silent stars, but none suffered a more dramatic and humiliating decline than John Gilbert. The established number one male box-office attraction of the MGM Studios was wrecked upon the rocks of his first talking film, mistakenly titled *His Glorious Night*. Gilbert did not have a voice of great resonance, he had a light, pleasant voice, but somehow it did not suit the dark, flashing eyes and gleaming white teeth of the great screen lover, in addition to which sound in its infancy was unreliable in the lower registers and poor John Gilbert's first squeaky declarations of passionate love brought down the house. He was allotted no more roles by the studio where he had reigned supreme for so long, and stories abounded that the studio heads were trying to break his very expensive contract by trapping him with whores or getting him drunk in public and then invoking the morals clause whereby an actor undertook not to bring himself into disrepute with the public. In fact, the poor man was so desperately humiliated and unhappy that he refused to be seen in public, but his drinking bouts in private became legendary.

Garbo and Gilbert, some years before the debacle of *His Glorious Night,* had embarked on a highly publicized love affair. Too highly publicized perhaps for Garbo's taste because at the very moment when Gilbert thought that all was set for a wedding and a honeymoon in the South Pacific aboard a yacht specially and romantically outfitted for the occasion, Garbo had taken to her heels. Gilbert, thereafter, married twice elsewhere, but both marriages fell apart, and with his career in tatters he was badly in need of a friend.

Garbo at the height of her popularity was preparing to make *Queen Christina,* and Laurence Olivier with great fanfare was brought over from England to play opposite her, but for some never fully explained reason, the studio decided at the last minute that he was wrong for the part and sent him home again. To see such a glorious opportunity blown away before his eyes and before the eyes of the world must have been a body blow to a young actor as yet unknown outside his own country, but Olivier, blessed with a massive talent and a highly justified faith in himself, returned later to Hollywood to take his pick of the best roles at all the studios. MGM, in the meanwhile, received a body blow of its own when Garbo informed it that she would make *Queen Christina* only with . . . John Gilbert.

The picture was a triumph for Garbo, but Gilbert's performance failed to rekindle the flame with his fans, and he sank back once more into despondency. Around this time (1935) Ronald Colman, who had befriended me, took me frequently to Gilbert's house to play tennis. The house, which was later purchased by David Selznick when he married Jennifer Jones and completely modernized and rejuvenated, was in Gilbert's day a somber place, a rambling Spanish-style structure at the end of a long winding and highly dangerous mountain road with only the flimsiest of barriers at hairpin bends to save one from terrifying drops.

From the property the view was spectacular; below as though photographed from an airplane lay the whole of the Los Angeles Basin, ringed on the left by the high snow-topped mountains and to the right clamped against the great horseshoe of the Pacific Ocean with Catalina Island like a giant humpbacked whale anchored fifty miles offshore. The decor in Gilbert's time was heavy and the gloom of the place was intensified by curtains permanently drawn against the light. When he showed up to play, the tennis was desultory, but the conversation, bonhomie, and refreshment were abundant. In his mid-thirties he was a man of sparkling good looks, but his good humor and laughter seemed dredged up with great effort. Often he did not appear at all, and Colman and I would take a swim in his sad leaf-filled pool. Once or twice I caught a glimpse of a beautiful face watching us from a window, and on one occasion, as we were climbing into Colman's car, a figure in a man's shirt, slacks and a big floppy hat approached from the scrub-covered hills and, with head down, hurried past us into the house.

"When Jack's drinking, she goes walking," said Colman phlegmatically. John Gilbert made only one more film before his heart gave out—*The Captain Hates the Sea.* Columbia Studios chartered a liner and dispatched an entire film unit and a troupe of hard-drinking actors to complete the picture at sea. It proved an expensive experiment, the filming became ever extended, and finally, as the budget was revamped with sickening regularity, a desperate head of production cabled the director far out on the Pacific: RETURN IMMEDIATELY. THE COST IS STAGGERING. He received a laconic reply: SO IS THE CAST.

I was afforded one more mini-glimpse of the famous recluse when Edmund Goulding, the director, invited me for a weekend at his desert retreat above Palm Springs. I arrived hot and dusty after a long drive, and Goulding pointed the way to his swimming pool in the palm trees below. "Go and cool off," he ordered.

As I neared the pool, it became apparent that standing in the shallow end was a naked female figure. As this incident took place in the mid-thirties, the reader will understand that I retreated to the house and asked my host for a clarification of the situation.

"Oh," he said, "it's only Garbo. She's staying somewhere down there and uses the pool when she feels like it."

I hastened once more down the garden path, but I was too late. All that remained was the disturbed surface of the water.

Garbo was finally dethroned as a working actress but remained inviolate as the most mysterious personality in Hollywood's history.

Her dethronement was sudden and remarkable because she apparently went down without a struggle. It could have happened to anyone—and frequently did. She chose the wrong film. Certainly in her position she could have refused it, but because it was wartime, she had agreed to do the sort of picture that was cheering people up—a farce.

Nothing in show business is more horrendous than a farce when it is not funny, and *Two-Faced Woman* was a four-star, fur-lined, oceangoing disaster. It also contained a surprising quota of "dirty" dialogue, was banned by the Legion of Decency, and roasted by the press with one eminent reviewer referring to Garbo's appearance as "embarrassing—like seeing Sarah Bernhardt swatted with a bladder."

The actors have always been the principal targets when shows flop, and they accept this as an occupational hazard—the producers rarely get blamed—but Garbo, instead of sweeping *Two-Faced Woman* under the rug of her memory, drawing comfort from an unassailable record of success, and being more selective in future, just stopped making films.

Certainly she was intensely shy and as sensitive as a seismograph, but it was an extraordinary abdication and rocked Hollywood to its foundations. Possibly she reasoned that she had always longed for privacy, she could certainly afford it, and to quit at the very pinnacle may have seemed to her the ideal time to go—no one could find out. She did not go far— just to New York—and she came back occasionally to haunt Hollywood like a lovely ghost and nonchalantly pushed aside a hundred offers to return to the screen. Only once was she tempted, by the producer Walter Wanger, who had a moment of glory when he was able to display a contract on which she had affixed her name, but she never went before the cameras. Hollywood could not believe that she would not make a well-timed comeback, not to do so was contrary to all Hollywood thinking, so the longer she stayed away, the stronger and stranger with every passing day grew the Garbo myth.

About five years after Garbo's retirement I purchased an old house in Pacific Palisades with "all mod cons, views, ocean and mts." It had been built by Vicki Baum, the author of the best-seller *Grand Hotel,* which had been made into a hit film starring Garbo. A neighbor of ours there was a rarity—a Hollywood hermit.

Richard Haydn first made his name imitating fish. "I was standing on a street corner as happy as could be, minding my p's and q's, when a large man tied a horse and cart to me. I uttered a cry. A passing fishmonger said 'Why! that is the mating call of the Goo Boo or Blushing Fish!' I was *amazed.*"

Richard's act as "Mr. Carp—the only living Fish Mimic" went down to history, and Hollywood commandeered him. He became a much sought-after director, as well as character actor, but his joy in life was to be completely alone, tending the most beautiful concentration of flowers and plants in any garden in California. I suspected that he went near the studios only in order to earn money to buy seeds and fertilizer, and it took weeks of patient prodding and the absorption of countless rebuffs on our part before this enchantingly fey creature could be persuaded to visit our house. When he finally became tame enough to do so, he appeared unexpectedly, saying, "Come quickly. I *must* show you my phlox and scabiosa." I had an urge to call the doctor.

One evening Hjördis and I were sitting on our terrace, watching the ostentatious setting of the sun upon the distant Pacific and listening to the weird yelping of coyotes in the hills around us, when Richard Haydn materialized. His eyeglasses glinted mischievously.

"I've brought someone who says she spent some of her happiest days in this house," he announced. "She would like to see it again if it's not inconvenient."

Birds of a feather had evidently flocked together because behind Richard stood Garbo.

I don't remember what she wore on that occasion because I was so stunned by the beauty of her face. She was utterly unaffected and completely easy and relaxed with a spontaneous and highly infectious laugh. My wife, being Swedish, took over the tour of the house, and by the time they came back the two of them were jabbering away like two Scandinavian conspirators. Garbo told us about our house during the Vicki Baum days—it must have been a fascinating place, a rendezvous for Leopold Stokowski and a host of European writers and artists.

During the years to come Garbo often came to see us. Always the same, of undiluted beauty and spontaneity, but always something was held back in reserve. She reminded me of a child living in her own secret world, and with childish directness she came and went as she wished, swam when she felt like it or when she missed the rains of her native land, walked about under the lawn sprinklers, but no amount of pleading on behalf of our Swedish cook could coax an autograph out of her. "I never give autographs or answer letters," she said firmly.

Normally an infallible way of getting to know someone and of ferreting out their good and bad points is to be cooped up with them for several days aboard a small and unreliable sailing boat. I forget who organized the trip, but Hjördis and I, Garbo and a friend of hers, who claimed he could navigate, set off for a few days in a small sloop I chartered in San Pedro. It was a miracle we survived the experience because on the first evening out the wind dropped at dusk, the engine failed, and Garbo's navigator friend got loose among the schnapps bottles. Trying to find Catalina Island with ourselves a forlorn little speck on the ocean, we were not reassured when he informed us that we were several miles north of the Grand Canyon.

Eventually we found the island, which was lucky because the next stop would have been Japan, and there spent a most enjoyable few days. Garbo was going through a health food period and tried to interest us in the contents of a brown paper bag she had smuggled aboard—foul-looking walnut burgers fried in sunflower oil. Her swimming outfit was far more intriguing—a white bathing cap and a pair of boy's swimming trunks. Throughout the cramped trip she had been a model crew member, the fountainhead of gaiety and fun, uncomplaining and always courageously volunteering to help in our many emergencies, but when we docked once more at San Pedro, I realized that I knew her no better than when she had first bobbed out from behind Richard Haydn, and the only thing I had discovered about her was that she did *not* have big feet.

The jealous always try to detract from beautiful women, but Garbo's beauty was so unassailable that the jealous, in desperation, pointed at her feet. "They're *big!*" they exulted.

Actually Garbo's feet were beautifully shaped and long, in correct proportion to her height, but she had an unfortunate habit of encasing them in huge brown loafers which gave the impression that she wore landing craft.

Robert Taylor, who played opposite Garbo in *Camille,* told me it was a fascinating and totally satisfying experience except for her fixation about having comfortable footwear.

"There she was," he said, "playing love scenes and death scenes with me and wearing these gorgeous crinolines, but all the time I *knew* that underneath she had on a crummy old pair of bedroom slippers."

Garbo was in our house one summer evening when the time came for Hjördis and me to leave for a large cocktail party which we had promised to attend. We explained the situation to our visitor, who asked who was giving it, how many would be there, and so on.

As it was to be at the home of a close friend who was celebrating the end of a long suspension by his studio, we were able to supply the answers and to hazard a guess that about a hundred people would be on hand.

"May I come too?" Garbo asked suddenly.

We were stunned and wondered what had brought about such a phenomenal "turn up for the books."

The party, when we arrived, was in full and boisterous swing, and when Garbo walked into the garden chockablock with young filmmakers, the effect was magical. They just could not believe their eyes. For a while she was left in a clear space, chatting happily with people she had worked with, but gradually as the throng pressed ever closer in its enthusiasm, her eyes took on the look of a hunted fawn, and suddenly she was gone.

Garbo's visits to California became rarer, but the myth remained as deeply entrenched as ever. The newspapers showed pictures of her fleeing from their photographers in European cities and printed reports of her aimlessly and alone walking the New York streets or haggling over the price of carrots and small antiques, and her apartment was reputed to contain a priceless collection of Impressionists stacked on the floor and all facing the wall. At the end of the period covered in this book we found ourselves in a house in the south of France. To our joy we discovered that Garbo was installed in a house on a neighboring promontory, the guest of a Russian-born New Yorker—George Schlee. The property was ideal for her, isolated and perched high upon jagged rocks far from prying eyes. In calm weather she could descend some steps into the blue Mediterranean, and when it was rough, she could take her beloved exercises in the pool. Schlee was the ideal companion for Garbo, a cosmopolitan of immense knowledge, charm, kindness, and understanding. She seemed completely happy in his company and, after the passing of several years, more beautiful than ever. One day, when they were at our place, we laid out food and wine in the garden on an old table among the olive trees, but an unseasonable rainstorm arrived just as we were about to sit down to luncheon. "Help me carry everything into the house!" I ordered, grabbing something light.

"Nonsense," said Garbo firmly. "We put it all under the table and eat it there."

People who have climbed a cliff and are resting peacefully on the summit have been known to glance casually down into the void below and for the first time realize to their horror that they suffer from vertigo. With knees of jelly, pounding hearts, and spinning heads, they then inch their way down and never climb again.

I often wondered if something of the sort had overtaken Garbo at the pinnacle of her career, so seeing her before me, carefree and happy, munching away contentedly with the rain cascading off the table, I decided it might be a propitious moment to try to find out.

"Why *did* you give up the movies?" I asked.

She considered her answer so carefully that I wondered if

she had decided to ignore my personal question. At last, almost to herself, she said, "I had made enough faces."

"A riddle wrapped in a mystery inside an enigma" was how
Winston Churchill described 170,000,000 Russians. And one
lovely, lonely Swede, too, perhaps?

10
Summit Drive

RONALD COLMAN

$\mathcal{I}$N Beverly Hills, Summit Drive was well named but not for topographical reasons. It was a short street winding up a valley from Benedict Canyon. There were only six estates on the ridges on either side of this valley, but in prewar days in these six houses, hidden by magnificent specimens of sycamore, pine, eucalyptus, jacaranda, chestnut, and oak, reposed some of the crown jewels of Hollywood.

Up Summit Drive, the largest estate of all was at the bottom on the right, a rather untidy, comfortable, secluded, rambling hideaway belonging to one of the Hollywood pioneers—Harold Lloyd.

On the ridge opposite his estate was a more imposing structure—a large "stockbroker Tudor" edifice complete with beams, eaves, sloping roofs, ivy, and mullioned windows. From the stately wrought-iron gates at the entrance, a winding driveway led to the house past beautifully manicured lawns flanked, not by orange trees, brightly colored hibiscus, oleanders, or trumpet flowers, but by dark foreign-looking yew hedges. Waiting, somberly dressed, at the top of the drive would be a diminutive general factotum named

189

Tommy. "Mr. Colman," he would intone reverently, "is in the library. Pray follow me."

Ronald Colman, if not a recluse, had a mania for preserving his privacy—understandable really when one remembers that on any given day, hundreds of fans would be cruising, goggle-eyed, around Beverly Hills in limousines, jalopies, or buses equipped with loudspeakers, clutching in their hands the maps they had purchased for $1 from beery ladies parked beneath beach umbrellas at the city limits: "Maps of the Movie Stars' Homes." Many of these documents were wildly inaccurate, and the guides of conducted tours were also badly informed. Important putts on the greens of the Bel Air Country Club were frequently muffed by prominent local citizens, thanks to a blaring voice from the nearby road describing their distant clubhouse as "the palatial home of the beautiful platinum bombshell—Jean Harlow . . . where champagne flows and anything goes."

Colman, a quiet man, was English. He had been recruited from an obscure position on Broadway when, panicking at the sudden event of talking pictures, Hollywood had convinced itself that none of the "silent" stars could talk. The choice of Colman as a standard-bearer was fortunate because he was indeed the possessor of a matchless speaking voice, plus darkly handsome good looks, massive charm, and great acting ability. He was also the lucky owner of a pair of dark-brown eyes, dark eyes being much the most photogenic and expressive on black-and-white film—the worst were the pale-blue ones which looked washed out and somehow dishonest. The owners of dark eyes also suffered much less from the sun arc lights which were capable of burning the skin of the eyeballs. "Klieg eye" was a painful and unattractive occupational disease.

Ronnie Colman lived alone in the large, rambling pseudo-Tudor house, surrounded by a beautiful collection of Chippendale and Sheraton furniture; only English painters of the eighteenth and nineteenth centuries graced the walls, and the rooms were comfortable in a leathery sort of way. The place was masculine to a fault and screamed out for a lady of the house. Ronnie, under heavy camouflage in the late thirties, was laying the foundations of just that. Having lately tottered away, mentally bruised, from a most unhappy marriage, followed by an extremely painful divorce, he was highly nervous of any further entanglements, but egged on by his close circle of men friends, he was hesitantly chipping away at his mental barriers. The chipping soon passed the stage of wishful thinking, and working at night, he knocked a large hole in the wall bounding the back garden of his estate. Tommy produced some hinges, cement, and a heavy oak door, and the beautiful actress Benita Hume, who lived in a small Spanish-style house immediately behind Colman's kitchen garden, was able to come and go in the greatest secrecy.

This delightful intrigue by Hollywood's most eligible bachelor ended, as his friends always hoped it would, with the gate being removed, the wall being bricked up again, and Benita moving into the manor house as the second Mrs. Ronald Colman.

The misogynist Colman slowly thawed out under the warmth, gaiety, and humor of Benita. The small coterie of his old-time friends was enlarged, a daughter, Juliet, was born, and the house was filled with flowers and laughter, but if the flowers were usually stocks, roses or chrysanthemums, the mirth too remained predominantly British.

Colman was never part of the "British Colony" as personified by the Hollywood Cricket Club, Ernest Torrance's Sunday afternoon tea parties, and the tournaments on C. Aubrey Smith's croquet lawn, but his old American friends, William Powell, Richard Barthelmess, and the cowboy star Tim McCoy, found themselves outnumbered by the Nigel Bruces, the Basil Rathbones, and Herbert Marshall with a bewildering succession of wives and mistresses.

Christmas dinner at the Colmans' was a permanent fixture. On went the dinner jackets, down went the turkey, plum pudding, and champagne, and out poured the speeches.

After dinner the women withdrew, and over port and brandy, the older men reminisced while the younger ones, Brian Aherne, George Sanders, Douglas Fairbanks, Jr., and myself, remained respectfully silent because mostly they talked about the Great War: Colman had been gassed in it,

Rathbone had won the Military Cross, Nigel Bruce had absorbed eleven machine-gun bullets in his behind, and Herbert Marshall had lost a leg.

Before his second marriage Ronnie had invested large sums to protect his beloved privacy. First, he bought the San Ysidro Ranch in the hills above Montecito 100 miles north of Los Angeles. This was no cattle-raising spread; it consisted of several hundred acres of gently sloping land. Immensely tall eucalyptus trees framed the property, on which were groves of oranges, avocados, and lemons, and hidden among these were twenty or thirty white-painted frame bungalows with private gardens and verandas. There was a main dining room and bar, tennis courts, stables, a swimming pool, and a stunning view of the mountains and ocean. It was a Mecca of calm to which the same clientele returned faithfully each year at the same time like the swallows to Capistrano. A hundred years before, Robert Louis Stevenson had loved the place, and the little cottage in which he wrote many of his works was preserved with pride. Later Galsworthy wrote much of *The Forsyte Saga* in the same cottage, and J. F. Kennedy spent some of his honeymoon there.

Ronnie's second investment in peace and quiet was a box of oil paints and an easel, a less costly extravagance than his third—an 85-foot copper-bottomed ketch, *Dragoon*. No sailor himself but cosseted by Tommy and an excellent crew, he liked at sundown to sit at the wheel with his yachting cap at a rakish angle, a large whiskey and soda in his hand, and fulminate against Samuel Goldwyn, for whom he had worked for many years and at whose hands he vowed he had suffered unimaginable injustices. Apart from Goldwyn, I never heard Ronnie say an unkind word about anyone.

Bill Powell loved the sea as much as I did, and we were frequently invited aboard *Dragoon* for weekend trips to Catalina or the Santa Barbara islands.

One cold October evening *Dragoon* dropped a lonely anchor in a little bay off the sheltered eastern coast of Santa Cruz Island. We had enjoyed a couple of days' fishing en route, but the heavy autumn swells had made most anchorages among the islands uncomfortable sleeping places, and we looked forward to a good night's rest ashore at Eaton's Fishing Camp.

Expectantly, therefore, Ronnie, Bill Powell, and I climbed the hundred rickety wooden steps from the landing stage to the small cluster of cottages roosting on the rock face above, owned and operated for many years by Mrs. Eaton.

Santa Cruz Island was large and was a privately owned cattle and sheep ranch. The Eaton family had long held the only concession of any sort allowed on it.

The widow Eaton was a wild-eyed, harridan-type woman with straggly gray hair, dirty fingernails, and a gray woolen sweater which made one's eyes water, but the beds she assigned to us looked clean, the water was hot, and in the dining hut the menu promised a welcome change from the baked beans and corned beef dispensed by Tommy.

Nobody was there but us.

After taking showers, we repaired to the dining hut, and while Mrs. Eaton and a gap-toothed Mexican were preparing our meal, we relaxed around a roaring fire. The conversation, as usual, was about movies, which was unfortunate because having plonked down our plates, Mrs. Eaton suddenly fixed us with her mad eyes.

"You guys movie folk?" she demanded belligerently.

Feeling uninvolved, as I had as yet hardly appeared on the screen, I looked at my companions, two of the biggest stars in the business, and waited for their modest acceptances of the fulsome compliments that would soon rain down upon them.

"Yes," said Powell, "we are—er, in a small way."

Mrs. Eaton was instantly transformed. She grabbed up our sizzling steaks and headed for the kitchen.

"Clear that goddamn table, Ramon," she shrieked at the Mexican. "No film people set foot in my camp . . . fuck off, the lot of you!" She started pulling us out of our chairs. "Get off this island—I hate you all, you're a bunch of no-good chiselers . . . the dog gets your steaks."

A mangy, twitching mongrel lying in front of the fire opened one unenthusiastic eye.

"Here," she babbled, ripping our wind jackets off hooks. "Take your goddamn coats and get the hell outta here."

She started raining blows on our retreating backs.
"Why, madam. . . . Why?" asked Colman, trying to lend
some dignity to our retreat. "What have we done to you?"
"Barrymore!" she yelled. "Ever heard of a creep called
John Barrymore? . . . Well, ten years ago the bastard
dropped anchor down there in a big white schooner . . . he
came up to the camp for supper, he and his lousy
friends . . . my little girl was here on vacation; she was gorgeous and only seventeen. She waited on table at the Happy
Halibut Seafood and Steak House at Pismo Beach. This
drunken shitheel, Barrymore, was old enough to be her
granddad, but he kept making passes at her. Finally, she
says, 'Mom, I've been invited off to the yacht for a beer,' and
off she goes. . . . I never seed hide nor hair of her since.
. . . That goddamned Barrymore sailed away that night
with my little girl, and I never seed her no more."
   Tears were pouring down the woman's dirty cheeks, and
she kept shoving us through the door.
   "She married some fella . . . a cameraman or some such,
they told me . . . she never wrote to me, and she never
come back . . . I hate all of you . . . get off my camp, you
lousy bums, and stay off of it."
   As our crestfallen and stomach-cheated trio clambered
down the dark rotting steps, we were bombarded with half
grapefruits, empty beer bottles, and cries of "Lousy actors—
who needs you?"

   Harry Cohn, the foulmouthed and dynamic head of Columbia Pictures, once enlisted Colman's help in another situation that called for quiet charm. Cohn had fallen in love
with "The White Cliffs of Dover," a piece by Alice Duer Miller, but was meeting resistance from her because she feared
that he might not have the taste and finesse to translate it to
the screen. Colman was shooting a picture at Columbia, so
Cohn begged him to invite Alice Duer Miller to the studio,
give her luncheon, show her around, and generally soften
her up. "Tell the old bag how goddamned taseful I am," said
Cohn. "Shit! I'm making the *Lost Fucking Horizon*, ain't I?"
   Colman dutifully did his best, and Alice Duer Miller was
visibly weakening during luncheon in his dressing room. Af-

terward he took her on a tour of the rabbit warren of a studio, avoiding its seamier parts.

He thought she might be impressed by a walk through the writers' building because on the doors were the titles of forthcoming productions and the well-known names of those slaving over the screenplays within. The place, smelling of coffee, was impressive with its air of quiet concentration, and the steady clacking of typewriters underlined the industry of Harry Cohn's employees.

"This picture will be going into production soon," said Colman, pointing to a door on which was written:

TOM BROWN'S SCHOOLDAYS
Writers—TOWNE AND BAKER

Alice Duer Miller was genuinely delighted. "Why, that's just wonderful! They are going to make a film of that . . . what a charming idea!"

At that moment the door flew open, and out rushed the diminutive Gene Towne. He grabbed Colman by the lapels of his jacket. He was glassy-eyed with excitement.

"Hey, I've got it! Goddammit, I've got it! It wasn't the boys who did it—the sons of bitches—it was the masters, the bastards!"

"The White Cliffs of Dover" was, not surprisingly, made by Metro-Goldwyn-Mayer.

I had first met Colman in the pre-stockbroker-Tudor period, when he lived a hermitlike existence in a cul-de-sac above Hollywood Boulevard, Mound Street. I was still an extra.

I was taken there by Alvin Weingand to make up a four at tennis. After that I was invited back often, but *only* for tennis. Tommy each time would meet me at the gate, escort me through the back garden to the court, and escort me out again at the end of the game.

The players were always the same—Weingand, Colman's agent Bill Hawkes, Clive Brook, Warner Baxter, Colman, and myself. I was much the youngest, so usually I was teamed with Colman, who had, I noticed, rather flat feet; he left most of the running to me. When he finally became convinced that his inner self would not be imposed on by me, I was no longer escorted by Tommy to the gate at the end of a game—I was invited inside for a drink, and a lasting friendship slowly developed.

In all the years I knew him he was only interested in one woman—Benita. His favorite film leading lady had been lovely Alice Terry, a blithe and free spirit whose weakness was eating cream cakes.

Her studio remonstrated with her about this. "You can't do that and remain a star," they told her.

"All right," she replied. "I shall make a million dollars as fast as I can; then I'll retire and eat cream cakes."

According to Ronnie, she did just that. She no longer read the scripts the studio sent her.

"Just tell me two things," she said. "Do I have to get wet or ride a horse?"

If they said no, she would agree to make the film.

The last Ronnie heard of her, she had made her $1,000,000, had retired to the San Fernando Valley, and was up to her armpits in cream cakes, as happy as a clam.

Ronnie tried hard to further my fledgling career and when he was about to make *Lost Horizon* with Frank Capra, he did all he could to persuade Capra to cast me in the role of his younger brother. Capra reacted kindly to the suggestion but, after meeting me, was only moderately impressed. He did, however, say that he might give me a test the following week.

For six days I never moved more than a few feet from the phone, but it never rang. On the seventh day I concluded sadly that my chances were slim and decided to go fishing. Before I left, I took a small precaution in case by some miracle Frank Capra still might call and asked a girlfriend to stay in the house for me. If Capra rang, she promised to drive north of Malibu and to wave a sheet from the cliffs of Point Dume (pronounced DOOM—and for me it very nearly was).

The all-day boat from Malibu Pier pulled out on the dot of seven o'clock. It was a beautiful still morning with the sun just rising above the sea mist, not a ripple on the surface, just a long, lazy swell.

The fishermen were a jolly cross section of locals from Las Tunas, Santa Monica, and Venice, retired businessmen, carpenters, garage mechanics, house painters, and the like on their day off, with a sprinkling of college kids stealing a day away from their classrooms. We started fishing about three miles offshore, and while the live bait was being chummed overboard to attract the big fish, several fishermen, with a conspicuous lack of husbandry, started munching the contents of their lunch boxes, and beer cans were being opened freely even at that early hour. All in all, it promised to be a good day.

Suddenly, the water all around the boat erupted as a school of yellowtail tuna found the sardines and anchovies. The fishermen, with eager cries, flung aside their sandwiches and started overhead casting, with gleaming silver spoons—a dangerous time, that early first excitement, when the inexperienced caster frequently hooked somebody's ear with his backswing, but that morning no ears and a lot of fish were caught, and everyone was happy.

By noon the schools of big fish had completed their feeding, and we moved in toward the kelp beds off Point Dume, to tackle the bass and halibut. The sun was beating down, and the swells were heavier. A few fishermen changed color and became strangely silent. Such had been my total absorption that I was halfway through my lunch before I remembered my arrangement with the girlfriend and the sheet signal.

I alerted the captain, and he made a comic announcement over the loud-hailer, asking everyone to keep an eye open for a flapping sheet.

"How the hell are you going to get ashore, Dave?" he asked.

"I'll swim," I said blithely. "It's only a couple of hundred yards."

"More like five," said Jack doubtfully, "and don't forget that kelp . . . it can really hold you . . . that swell's real heavy."

Half an hour later a cry went up: "The sheet, Dave! . . . the sheet!"

My heart nearly stopped beating. There, far away on a bluff, stood a leggy blonde waving frantically.

A test with Frank Capra! For an important role in one of the biggest pictures to be made that year! Hurriedly, I stripped down to my underpants, and to the encouraging yells of "Attaboy, Dave!" and "Good luck, kid," I dived over the side and headed for stardom.

The kelp beds which form an unbroken chain along hundreds of miles of California coastline are about 200 yards in diameter; the great golden-brown slimy weed branches out to cover the surface, and the thick, weaving roots go down to the ocean floor a hundred feet or more below. Kelp feels very unpleasant to the naked body and has to be navigated carefully from open patch to open patch. It is not advisable to fight it or panic, or one becomes entangled.

In the middle of a clearing, I was resting, floating on my back before tackling the next slippery barriers, when I thought of the sharks. Suddenly, about six feet away from me there was a swirling commotion, and a black shiny head with two huge eyes and a bristling mustache shot out of the water. When my heart restarted, I saw it was a baby seal, and it wanted to play. It swam all around me and under me and stayed with me all the way to the clear water on the beach side of the kelp beds. In fact, its presence gave me courage because by now I had heard the ominous sound of heavy surf—big oily swells rising and falling several feet in water a hundred feet deep are transformed into a series of giant foaming rollers when they arrive at a sloping shore.

From the tops of swells I obtained momentary glimpses of the girl and two men scrambling down a cliff path. I paddled on, but I still had quite a way to go. I was tired after my long struggle through the kelp. I was growing cold, too, and my fingers were curling up toward my palms. I began to wonder if I had made a horrible mistake.

Looking landward from the top of one swell, I could see a dozen more, and the farthest ones were curving out of sight away from me. Plumes of spray from their crests were flung back by an offshore breeze. For a few minutes, listening to the alarming pounding of the surf, I rested beyond the broken water, conserving my strength. I had decided to ease my way in, then swim fast with the last unbroken swell. This would carry me ten or twenty yards shoreward. The next one would break, and I would body-surf with it in the approved style, sliding, head down, from the crest. This, I guessed, would take me safely to the beach.

I guessed wrong.

Suddenly a mountainous surge gathered beneath me, and I found myself propelled forward in a crest of foam. I struggled, head high, for a lungful of air and somehow got into my surfing position. I was whizzing beachward at an alarming rate. Feeling myself sliding down the far side, I raised my head again for another much needed gulp of oxygen and beheld a horrifying sight: Beneath me, about fifteen feet below, was nothing but sand liberally sprinkled with stones and small rocks. I had picked up the surfer's nightmare—a big shore breaker. The giant wave flung me onto the hard, unyielding foreshore. Tons of water crashed down on top of me, turned me over and over, and ripped me out again along the ocean floor. My mouth and nose were full of sand and water. The breath had been knocked out of my body. I was inside a giant washing machine. I tried to swim to the surface, but everything was dark brown. I didn't know which way up I was. Somehow, with bursting lungs, I found myself on the surface. I was picked up by another roller and flung once more shoreward. Providentially, this wave broke behind me and bore me along, rolling me over and over like a log almost to the high-water mark.

The girl and the men dragged me up among the stinking decayed seaweed, where someone turned me face down and pressed the water out of my lungs. Then I was sick. My chest had been almost stripped of skin.

The girl drove me home, anointed me with iodine, and bandaged me. Then I called Frank Capra's office at Columbia Studios.

Capra had gone for the day, but his secretary was still there.

"Oh, you shouldn't have bothered to rush back from your fishing," she said. "Mr. Capra just wanted to tell you that he will not be making your test because he has cast John Howard in the part."

DAVID SELZNICK
AND *The Prisoner of Zenda*

Colman was not put off by Capra's indifference, though he was full of misgivings when I landed a small contract with Samuel Goldwyn, and when he was preparing for his next picture, *The Prisoner of Zenda,* he walked across Summit Drive and talked about me to the producer, David O. Selznick.

Selznick lived fifty yards away in a white, brightly decorated, rambling one-story house; a belt of towering trees marked the boundary between his property and that of Harold Lloyd. The gardens were full of color, and the place was equipped with the inevitable pool and tennis court. There was no front gate; one turned off Summit Drive into a semicircular driveway.

Selznick was a huge giant panda of a man, standing about six feet two and permanently struggling with a weight problem. He wore thick glasses and had thick, curly hair. He chain-smoked incessantly, had a broken nose, a wild sense of humor, a great deal of kindness, a weakness for dry martinis and terry-cloth bathrobes, and a completely nonexistent sense of punctuality.

Not even his friends, and he had hundreds of them, could have called him handsome, but such was his charm that it never crossed one's mind that he was anything else. Selznick was married to dark, flashing-eyed Irene, the daughter of the all-powerful chief of Metro-Goldwyn-Mayer, the foxy, mercurial and frequently vindictive Louis B. Mayer.

Selznick's courting of Irene must have been a nail-biting period. When it came to the affairs of his daughters Irene and Edith, Mayer made Papa Barrett look like Winnie-the-Pooh. His ambitions for Edith were shaken to the core when she announced her intention of marrying quiet, witty Billy Goetz, who had just lost his job as an assistant studio supervisor, and when the young couple asked for an unobtrusive wedding, Mayer nearly blew a gasket.

After endless arguing, they reluctantly agreed to what he thought was more fitting to *his* station, an overproduced publicity-oriented bash at the Biltmore Hotel, but as a reward he presented them with a hefty chunk of stock in a new film company which he was largely financing—Twentieth Century-Fox.

If he swallowed with difficulty the marriage of Edith to Bill Goetz, he found the possibility of a match between Irene and David Selznick totally indigestible. "That schnook, that bum" he called David, "that son of a Selznick." David's father, Louis, had been a partner of Mayer's in earlier days, a partner, according to Hollywood legend, who had been unloaded and destroyed by massive jiggery pokery. This belief was certainly held by David and his brother, Myron, a powerful agent, both of whom had sworn to get even on their father's behalf.

Myron was often successful at this and, by manipulating his stable of sought-after stars, was able, from time to time, to give his father's old enemy a right royal financial screwing. David, of course, did not fall in love with Irene in order to do his bit in the Selznick-Mayer war, but he did cause the enemy great anguish. Mayer did all he could to dissuade Irene from the enterprise, and his house shook with emotional scenes, but Irene was unmoved, and finally he gave his consent.

Mayer genuinely admired David's success as head of production at RKO Studios, and once he realized he had lost the battle for Irene, his search for good potential manpower overcame his personal distaste, and he offered David a comparable job at MGM plus, as an inducement, the same amount of stock in Twentieth Century-Fox that he had lately given to the other newlyweds. Selznick spurned the stock offer, took the job, quickly turned out a string of great successes, and then announced that he was leaving MGM to form his own production company.

L. B. Mayer did everything in his considerable power to hold Selznick, but David was wary of him. Above all, he was wary of the aforementioned vindictiveness, of which a classic example surfaced when Mayer fell in love with a beautiful young actress, Jean Howard. Mayer put a detective on her trail to report on any extracurricular activities on her part. Not only were the reports "positive," but Jean fell in love and married Charlie Feldman, a handsome, moderately successful young agent, so Mayer promptly barred Feldman and all his clients from MGM Studios and tried to persuade the other company heads to do likewise.

Charlie Feldman refused to panic and kept his ears open. When he heard that Garbo, the brightest jewel in L. B. Mayer's crown, was scheduled to make *Conquest* and would do so only if a newcomer from France, Charles Boyer, played opposite her in the role of Napoleon, he talked Boyer into letting him handle his affairs. Garbo would work only with Boyer, but Boyer would speak to Mayer only if his agent was present, so Feldman was back in MGM Studios; he took great joy in putting the boot in, and Boyer wound up being paid almost twenty times his former salary.

Selznick stuck to his guns, left MGM, and even won the final jackpot. In a bewildering series of plots and counterplots, he maneuvered Mayer into lending him Clark Gable, the biggest box-office star at MGM, for his picture *Gone with the Wind.*

Colman's good words on my behalf fell on receptive ears, and one Sunday I received an invitation from Irene Selznick to come play tennis. I arrived at two thirty to find David Selznick in the hall, wrapped in a terry-cloth robe, consuming a plate of smoked salmon, cottage cheese, and pumpernickel.

"Like some breakfast?" he asked cheerfully.

I had just finished lunch, but I thought it might be diplomatic, so I accepted.

"Ronnie Colman talked to me about you," he went on between mouthfuls. "He thought you could play Fritz von Tarlenheim . . . I'll kick it around with John Cromwell tomorrow—he's going to direct—but don't raise your hopes too high because I'm aiming for an all-star cast. I've signed Madeleine Carroll to play Princess Flavia opposite Ronnie, Mary Astor will play Madame de Mauban, Raymond Massey I'm negotiating with for Black Michael, and I may bring Doug Fairbanks, Junior, over from Europe, if he can tear himself away from Gertie Lawrence, to do Rupert of Hentzau. Dear old C. Aubrey Smith wants to play Colonel Zapt, which will be great, so that leaves Fritz."

He stared at me for a long time over the top of a cup of coffee, and I sat there thinking about the last two times I had seen him—lying flat on his back, having been knocked cold at Hollywood parties. Both David and his brother, Myron, compounded their weakness for dry martinis by having very short fuses when arguments started, and they were continually getting into fights which they lost. Chronically bad performers in the noble art, they were further handicapped by very short sight, so the locals when challenged by one of them had a way of bringing matters to a speedy conclusion by first flicking off their eyeglasses and then delivering a quick one-two punch.

The crash of falling Selznicks was frequently heard around midnight in Hollywood high society.

"It might work out," said Selznick suddenly.

He lit a cigarette and rose, his bathrobe fell open. "Oops, sorry," he said. "Let's go down to the court and see who's there."

I followed him past rows of bookcases and out into the garden.

Some good tennis was being played by a men's four and some spectacular ladies were watching, including Marlene Dietrich, Paulette Goddard, and Claudette Colbert.

David and Irene Selznick introduced me around and made me feel completely at home. Never for one moment during that long day was I allowed to feel out of it in the presence of an endless procession of the mighty and the talented of Hollywood. I was pressed to stay for drinks and then for a buffet supper and a movie and, like many before me, fell completely under the spell of David Oliver Selznick.

When he bade me good-night, my heart jumped. "Good night, Fritz," he said. "I'll talk to Cromwell tomorrow. Maybe we'll make a test."

All went well. A test was made, and during a game of gin rummy, probably as part of the stakes, Selznick acquired my services from my boss, Samuel Goldwyn.

The Prisoner of Zenda, the classic story of intrigue and high adventure in Ruritania, was an ideal film subject. Donald Ogden Stewart and John Balderston turned out a masterful screenplay full of duels, chases, coronations, and ballroom spectacles.

Selznick assembled the cast he had hoped for, and for four

months a great time was had by all. Usually when one makes a film, it is a little like being too long on an ocean voyage. At the end of the trip, total strangers who have been thrown together for several weeks part, swearing eternal allegiance to each other, but never doing much about it. *Zenda* was different. Everyone became friends and remained so.

Colman was the leader and very much the star—a most serious and dedicated performer who was never his easygoing self until the end of the day when Tommy would come and lead me to the star bungalow to join him in his ritual six o'clock "beaker."

Madeleine Carroll was a procelain beauty of great sweetness and fun, and Mary Astor, who looked like a beautiful and highly shockable nun, had a sweet expression and a tiny turned-up nose and made everyone feel she was in desperate need of protection. In point of fact, she was by her own admission happiest and at her best in bed. She was also, it turned out, highly indiscreet and confided all in her private journal, starting each revealing daily entry "Dear Diary. . . ."

"Dear Diary" right in the middle of the picture caused a major reshuffling of the shooting schedule because it was stolen and turned up as prime evidence in a highly publicized divorce case, and Mary had to give evidence.

If "Dear Diary" caused a stir among the *Zenda* company, it was nothing to the upheavals and near heart attacks it perpetrated throughout the upper echelons of the film colony. Mary, it appeared, had been a very busy girl indeed, and her partners had gleefully been awarded marks in "Dear Diary" for performance, stamina, et cetera.

After being absent for days in a blaze of scandal and being laid bare (to coin a phrase) for all to see, Mary returned to the set of *Zenda,* looking just as sweet and demure as ever, and everyone, as usual, desperately wanted to protect her.

C. Aubrey Smith was over seventy when *Zenda* was made, six feet four, ramrod straight, alert and vigorous. Never did he forget a line or misunderstand a piece of direction. Unfailingly courteous, kind and helpful, he was beloved by all.

Every Sunday he ordered me to turn out for the Holly-

wood Cricket Club, I always called him "sir," and though
dreading long hot afternoons in the field, I obeyed.

His great, craggy face was frequently creased by worry because he loved England very deeply, and as it was early in
1937, he had little faith in the way Neville Chamberlain was
coping with the Rome-Berlin Axis and Germany's anti-
Comintern Pact with Japan. Refusing to read the "local
rags," the Los Angeles *Times* or the *Examiner,* trusting only
the London *Times* to keep him up to date, and with airmail
across the Atlantic almost nonexistent, Aubrey was usually
eight to ten days behind a crisis. Nobody spoiled his fun by
telling him the news, so it was almost two weeks after it had
happened that the old man flung down his morning paper
and boomed across the set, "The bloody feller's done it!"

"Who, sir? What, sir?" we chorused.

"That whippersnapper Hitler! He's marched into
Austria!"

John Cromwell, the director, was highly respected and
highly efficient, but he was a little low on humor, which created certain hazards for Raymond Massey and Doug, Jr., two
of the most inveterate gigglers in the business.

The scene at the state ball was most important. Colman,
masquerading as the king, was proposing to Princess Flavia
in a small anteroom. Outside, a courtier was eavesdropping.
At the end of the long intimate love scene this courtier, a
large fat man with a mauve face, had to hurry to Fairbanks,
Massey, and myself, waiting in our resplendent uniforms at
the bottom of a long flight of steps at the entrance to the castle. On arrival he had to say two words: "Good news!"

It was what is known as a production shot, designed to give
richness, size, and color to the film by showing the maximum
number of people in their magnificent costumes and the
most advantageous views of the extravagant sets.

The famous Chinese cameraman James Wong Howe had
excelled himself, and by a "marshaling yard's" arrangement
of tracks and overhead trolleys, his cameras were able, all in
one flowing movement, to witness the love scene, then follow
the mauve-faced courtier through several anterooms filled

with beautifully gowned ladies and bemedaled gentlemen across a giant white marble multipillared patio, around a lily pond on which cruised haughty black swans, thence up a flight of ornate stairs into the candlelit main ballroom, where 300 couples of the handsomest and most glamorous extras were executing a carefully rehearsed waltz.

Past the minstrel's gallery the mauve courtier hurried, on through the kitchens and vestibules, followed everywhere by a battery of wondering eyes—what would his message be?

Finally, the big moment came. Satin-breeched flunkies flung open the huge main doors, and as the tension mounted, he ponderously descended 120 steps to our little group waiting at the bottom.

"Good news!" he said loudly, and we reeled back. It was bad news for us—he had a breath like a buzzard.

When the courtier tramped back to his starting position for the next run-through, we dared not look at one another. Fairbanks, I sensed, was beginning to vibrate, and out of the corner of my eye, I could see that Ray Massey was making a great production of polishing his monocle.

We suffered through half a dozen more rehearsals and six more broadsides from "Halitosis Harry." By the time John Cromwell was satisfied and ordered the first take we realized we were doomed. A sort of schoolboy hysteria had gripped us, and although we still avoided one another's eyes, we knew we could never get through the scene.

"Let's pretend it's drains," I whispered.

We could hear the love scene being played in the distance, and with dread we followed the sounds of the courtier's slow progress toward us. The orchestra in the ballroom fell silent as he approached the end of his journey so that his two golden words could be recorded for posterity.

The doors above us were flung open, and our tormentor, relieved to be at the end of his complicated trip, descended smugly toward us.

"Good news!" he said.

We greeted his announcement with gales of pent-up laughter.

"Cut! What the hell's going on?" demanded a furious

Cromwell, rushing up, but the more angry he became, the more uncontrollable became our mirth.

Fairbanks behaved in a most craven manner. "Ask Mr. Massey what's wrong," he blurted out with tears streaming down his face. "He's the oldest."

Ray's suggestion didn't help at all. "Gee, Mr. Cromwell, perhaps it would give us a kind of springboard if the gentleman *whispered* the line."

The whisper brought us a whiff of pure phosgene.

In the end Cromwell rearranged his shooting schedule so that our reactions to the fateful "news" could be photographed the following day when, as he succinctly put it, "You bastards will have had a whole night to calm down."

Hollywood always felt that the leading characters of costume pictures should be seen riding prancing, frothing, and often unmanageable steeds, so when we came to the shooting of the coronation procession, I had a few words with the head wrangler, some currency changed hands, and I was mounted on a nice quiet old mare. Unfortunately, she was in heat. Trotting through the cheering citizens beside the golden coach bearing Ronnie and Madeleine, resplendent in cuirass and silver helmet topped by a golden eagle, I was blissfully unaware of danger gathering like a storm astern of me. Ray was riding a large black stallion.

A high-pitched whinnying rose above the screams of hurriedly departing townsfolk, and about six feet of easily identifiable stallion equipment passed me like a torpedo. I turned in my saddle to find thrashing hooves and gnashing teeth all around me. Far above, I saw Ray's horrified face. Not wanting to go down with the ship, I hurriedly disembarked by flinging myself to the ground, leaving my mare to her happy fate and Ray to a ringside seat. For a while it looked as though he were riding a rocking horse.

David Selznick's *Prisoner of Zenda* was a triumphant success, critically and financially, and a testament to what happens when a producer infuses all those around him with loyalty, enthusiasm, and a real joy in their work.

Fifteen years later L. B. Mayer decided to make some easy money and ordered a remake of *The Prisoner of Zenda*. Feeling that he could not improve on the way his son-in-law had captured the Anthony Hope classic, he insisted that the new version be made with identical sets, word for word, shot for shot, and close-up for close-up; it had to be exactly the same as the old one, but with new faces. He cast Stewart Granger in the Colman role, and James Mason misguidedly attempted to follow Doug, Jr. To David Oliver Selznick's great amusement the result was a critical and financial disaster.

Douglas Fairbanks

At the top of Summit Drive stood Pickfair, a walled estate that had long been the focal point of all that meant Hollywood.

The home of the two biggest stars of silent pictures, Douglas Fairbanks and Mary Pickford, Pickfair had hosted the most ostentatious parties and royal entertainments of the great dawning of Hollywood.

The "King of the Silent Films," the most popular male star in the world, hero of such muscular, exciting, and intentionally amusing spectacles as *The Three Musketeers, Robin Hood, The Mark of Zorro, The Black Pirate,* and *The Thief of Bagdad,* had married "America's Sweetheart"—a Hollywood bonanza!

Fairbanks had a hold on the filmgoers of the world, young and old, that has never to this day been equaled. Mary Pickford, too, "Little Mary of the Golden Curls," had her own immense and devoted following. The marriage had ended in divorce the year before I arrived in Hollywood, and the Pickfair I saw was a sad, overfurnished, and melancholy place of memories and closed doors. Mary was a wan and gallant little hostess, relying more and more on the companionship of a serious curly-haired young actor-singer whom she subsequently married—Buddy Rogers. Fairbanks was far from wan and sad. He was being comforted in England by the glorious, willowy, lemon-meringue blond Lady Ashley.

Sylvia Hawkes had been a chorus girl and small-part actress till she met dull good-looking Lord Ashley. Before long, she met the far from dull, but equally good-looking, Sir Tim Birkin, a rich racing motorist, but a year after her divorce from Lord Ashley she upset the books by marrying Fairbanks.

Doug, an ex-Harvard graduate, was a chronic Anglophile. He openly and unashamedly loved the country, the people, the customs, and the climate. He rented a large country house in Hertfordshire, had his suits made by Anderson and Shepperd, his evening clothes by Hawes and Curtis, his shirts by Beale and Inman, his monogrammed velvet slippers by Peel, and he drove a Rolls-Royce. Although a self-confessed snob enjoying the company of the more flamboyant British aristocracy ("Burke's steerage," he called them), he never lost the common touch. He was worshiped wherever he went.

When he departed from Pickfair, Fairbanks moved down to a Santa Monica beach house with Sylvia and a huge oversexed mastiff called Marco Polo.

This dog was a bisexual menace: nobody was spared its attentions. It weighed about 200 pounds and pumped up and down indiscriminately on anything that moved.

Doug in his mid-fifties still had the figure of a young athlete, and he paid constant attention to keeping it that way. He took a sunbath daily in a small green canvas compartment in the garden, burning himself the color of chewing tobacco. He was curiously coy in the presence of the friends he invited to join him there, always covering his private parts with his two cupped hands.

Chuck Lewis, his personal trainer, was always in attendance, giving massages and organizing workouts, steam baths, tennis, golf, or long-distance swims. Doug enjoyed hugely displaying his acrobatic talents and watching those half his age trying to catch up with him. I nearly killed myself jumping off his high diving board onto the low springboard alongside, which he had assured me would give me a "real tremendous bounce." It did. I missed the water altogether and landed in some petunias below the drawing-room window. While we disported ourselves in the business end of the pool, Sylvia, ever careful of her famous creamy white skin, paddled about in the shallow end beneath a huge floppy hat. Douglas was an overgrown schoolboy reveling in practical jokes, simple and elaborate.

The simple ones ranged from giving people exploding cigars, lighting orange flash papers, playing ostentatiously with a twenty-pound cannonball, exchanging it unseen for a rubber replica, yelling "catch," and tossing it to some poor unsuspecting wretch, to disappearing beneath the dinner table on serious evenings, crawling on hands and knees, and gently opening the fly of a pompous man sitting between two equally haughty ladies at the far end.

The elaborate ones turned sometimes into expensive productions. He announced in the trade papers that Dr. Hans Strassmann, the head of the German film company UFA, was coming out to visit him. Then he arranged for a "professional insulter"—a small bald actor named Vince Barnett—to board the Santa Fe Chief at San Bernardino, the last stop before Los Angeles.

Barnett, in Tyrolean hat and green cloak, made a triumphant entry into the film capital, and Fairbanks welcomed him at Union Station with red carpet, photographers, and a large crowd. The next night Fairbanks gave a white-tie dinner, and everyone was in the know except Samuel Goldwyn. At the end of the meal, cigars were lit and speeches of welcome were made. The last guest called on was the unfortunate Goldwyn. When Barnett rose to reply, with a heavy German accent, he thanked all the speakers but said that he was a little surprised that Goldwyn had been invited to meet him because he considered him to be the least talented filmmaker in the United States. He went on to say that Goldwyn was famous for stealing actors like Gary Cooper away from other studios, that everyone in Berlin knew that the only reason he had brought the Russian actress Anna Sten out to Hollywood was "because he wanted to get into her bloomers."

Poor Goldwyn was slow to catch on, and it took Fairbanks a long, long time to put matters right.

Fairbanks was a low handicap golfer, an excellent tennis player, and a top-class performer with saber, épée, or foil.

His film duels were high spots in all his productions, and his daring stunts, as a matter of pride, he did himself, scorning the use of doubles.

One was really spectacular: Escaping from the heavies from a high balcony in *Robin Hood,* with both hands he plunged his sword into an eighty-foot-high velvet curtain and whizzed down to safety. He repeated this stunt in *The Black Pirate:* trapped in the highest crosstrees, he slid down a billowing mainsail and arrived safely on deck, leaving his adversaries in the rigging.

Plagued by questions on how his hands and wrists could possibly have been strong enough to keep the sword at exactly the right angle, he one day divulged to us that on the other side of the curtain and sail the swords had been bolted into a large board—but it was still a very dangerous descent.

Doug's prowess and ability aboard movie ships did not extend to his seamanship in real life. One Fourth of July he and Sylvia chartered a motor cruiser and invited a small group to sail with them to Catalina. The idea was to anchor on arrival alongside Cecil B. DeMille's sleek white three-masted schooner. Our captain had an ominous name—Jack Puke.

Except for the deckhand who really had been prostrated by seasickness, the four-hour trip to the island had been uneventful, and without difficulty, we located DeMille's schooner. Nearby was a large circular mooring buoy, and Captain Puke decided to attach his boat to the ring on top of it. With DeMille's smartly dressed guests applauding our arrival, we rammed this buoy at considerable speed because when Captain Puke rang down to the engine room for "full astern," the engineer was on deck picking his teeth and contemplating DeMille's yacht.

Finally, we maneuvered into position for someone to jump down onto the buoy and secure us. "Now," yelled Captain Puke.

"I'll go," said Fairbanks bravely. "Quick, David, up to the sharp end!"

I followed him to the bow, where he grabbed a rope I was holding and, with his famous grace and feline agility, leaped down onto the pitching buoy. Further applause greeted this effort, but it was premature because the rope turned out to be attached to nothing on our boat, and when the engineer at last obeyed Captain Puke's unnautical command to "BACK UP . . . YOU SON OF A BITCH!" we pulled away, leaving our host stranded.

I fetched him later in the dinghy.

Fairbanks owned a large country property near San Diego—the Rancho Santa Fe—and there he delighted, for short periods only, in the simplicity of ranch life, keeping us up all night coyote hunting, lying, heavily armed, in wet grass, waiting for the ghostly slinking packs to devour the dead chickens he had impaled on stakes.

His duck hunts were more civilized and of minimal danger to the timid mallard, teal, and widgeon which swarmed around the reservoir. He would wake us stealthily before dawn, in whispers distribute guns and ammunition, and then drive us three miles to the waterside in his Rolls-Royce with headlights blazing and radio blaring. No humans were shot either. Such heady stuff was it for an unknown young actor to be accepted by one of the Hollywood giants that it was some time before I realized that beneath all his gaiety, flamboyance, and love of youth, Fairbanks lived with a great sadness. He fought off the advancing years valiantly and perhaps a little desperately, but the afternoon light was already softening the contours of a career that had long been illuminated more brightly than any other in the history of the movies, and it was with a rather sad smile he bade me one day bend down and look at myself in the mirror top of a coffee table. The blood ran into my cheeks and under my eyes, and I found myself staring at a warthog.

"That's what you'll look like when you're fifty!" He laughed.

Still acclaimed, applauded, and stopping traffic wherever he went, even in the remotest parts of the world, he accepted the adulation with a flashing smile, but it must have been a knife in his guts to know that, at an age when his contemporaries in other walks of life were just reaching their zenith, he had already been turned out to grass.

CHARLES CHAPLIN

On the same side of Summit Drive as Pickfair and Ronald Colman's house sprawled an estate of about the same acreage as that of Harold Lloyd. . . . It also was owned by a founding father of Hollywood—Charles Spencer Chaplin.

It boasted stands of beautiful trees, green lawns sloping down to a swimming pool and, of course, a tennis court. The house was large, cluttered, of yellow-ocher color and Victorian design: high french windows giving on to the gardens retrieved it from being supersuburbia. Few people were invited there, not because Charlie Chaplin shunned all contact with the Hollywood he had done more than any other to change from a citrus-growing community into one of the biggest industries in the United States, but for two very basic reasons: The greatest public entertainer in the world had only a sketchy idea of how to entertain in private, and he was also allergic to laying out large sums of money for food and drink to be guzzled by those he reckoned to be passengers and noncontributors. He enjoyed going out, however, to selected houses, and nothing made him happier than playing the elder statesman, sitting in a chair after dinner, with the faithful at his feet, while he held forth with gestures and sublime caricature.

Not the greatest listener in private life, Chaplin was a great advocate of it as an essential part of the actor's equipment. One night Doug Fairbanks ran a film after dinner at the beach house, and in it was one of my earliest efforts. When it was over, the others made the insincere but flattering noises so dear to an actor's heart, but Chaplin sat still, saying nothing.

Finally, I plucked up courage to ask him what he thought.

"Don't just stand around like most actors waiting for your turn to speak," he said flatly. "Learn to listen."

The uncompromising directness of this excellent advice was typical of Chaplin. The folk hero of millions in every land, the tattered courageous little tramp who loved flowers and children and raised two rude fingers at the Establishment, he was in himself an extremely opinionated man with a highly developed sense of his own place in history. He loved being asked for advice and gave it freely.

Beside Fairbanks' pool one day, the playwright Charles MacArthur, who had lately been lured from Broadway to write a screenplay, was bemoaning the fact that he was finding it difficult to write visual jokes.

"What's the problem?" asked Chaplin.

"How, for example, could I make a fat lady, walking down Fifth Avenue, slip on a banana peel and still get a laugh? It's been done a million times," said MacArthur. "What's the best way to *get* the laugh? Do I show first the banana peel, then the fat lady approaching; then she slips? Or do I show the fat lady first, then the banana peel, and *then* she slips?"

"Neither," said Chaplin without a moment's hesitation. "You show the fat lady approaching; then you show the banana peel; then you show the fat lady and the banana peel together; then she steps *over* the banana peel and disappears down a manhole."

Chaplin was devoted to Douglas Fairbanks and never wearied of telling that it was Fairbanks' business antennae which had sensed the fact that with Mary Pickford the three biggest stars in the business were overpricing themselves so heavily that producers, seeing little profit from their pictures, would soon be unwilling to employ any of them.

"It's simple," Fairbanks had said. "We cut out the producers; then we make our own pictures and employ ourselves."

The result had been the highly profitable United Artists Company.

When Fairbanks was around, Chaplin delighted in telling stories against himself because Doug, with his schoolboy humor and infectious laugh, was the world's best audience.

Egged on by Doug, Chaplin reenacted, one evening, an embarrassing arrival in the little French port of Cagnes-sur-Mer.

Aimee Semple McPherson was a beautiful blonde with a fascinating superstructure. She was also an evangelist with a faithful following of thousands who called her Sister, subscribed $1,000,000 to build her Angelus Temple in down-

town Los Angeles, and watched breathlessly as she publicly
baptized immense truck drivers swathed in see-through
sheets.

"Come to Jesus!" she would cry.

The faithful also purchased a license for her Angelus
Temple Radio Station and financed her personal travels "to
the Holy Land."

One day Aimee Semple McPherson disappeared, and
headlines screamed that she had been kidnapped on her way
to Mecca. These were later reoriented toward suicide, mur-
der, or simple drowning beneath the Santa Monica Pier, but
in point of fact she had run away with the burly operator of
her radio station.

During one of her aforementioned travels to the "Holy
Land," "Sister" Aimee had joined Douglas Fairbanks on a
yacht he had chartered for a Mediterranean cruise. Another
guest had been Chaplin.

Wherever the yacht anchored, thousands had lined the
shoreline, hoping for a glimpse of their heroes, and landing
for a stroll or a little shopping had produced mob scenes
reminiscent of a DeMille epic, so they worked out a careful
plan to enjoy a quiet picnic in the hills behind Grasse. The
yacht anchored a mile offshore. The crew reconnoitered the
little port and reported nobody about except a few fishermen. A car was ordered to wait at a certain flight of steps
with engine running, and the party, complete with rugs and
picnic baskets, descended into the motorboat for the trip
ashore.

For dinner, the night before, however, they had eaten a
mound of mussels and, just as they rounded the breakwater
and slid into the calm water of the little harbor, one of these
shellfish struck.

Chaplin felt two fists clenching and unclenching around
his intestines. He broke out in a sweat and knew that he must
immediately get to a toilet. He was in agony.

The launch came alongside the landing, and Fairbanks
stood up to help Aimee Semple McPherson ashore—he was
instantly recognized.

"Dooglas! Dooglas!" yelled a fisherman, dropping his rod

and disappearing at high speed into the nearest bistro. Out poured the inmates; children were dispatched to spread the glad tidings to the village.

"Dooglas! Dooglas!" chanted the swelling throng. Bathers and tourists, attracted by the cries, circled excitedly at the perimeter of the crowd like sea gulls around refuse.

"*Regardez!*" yelled someone, excitedly pointing at a bent-over figure clasping his abdomen in the stern of the boat.

"*C'est lui! C'est Charlot!*"

Chaplin was undergoing paroxysms of pain.

"*Où est le lavabo?*" he croaked in faltering French. Fairbanks, already ashore, turned and was so unnerved by the sight of his friend's ashen face that he released his grip on the evangelist, who slipped and baptized herself between boat and landing.

The populace applauded: "*Formidable! Bravo! Bravo!*" They were convinced that high comedy was a way of life with the world's two greatest entertainers.

Fairbanks tried his hand at enlisting the help of the crowd. "*Le can pour Charlot!*" he shouted. "*Où est le can?*"

Chaplin tried sign language to help things along and, clasping one hand to his stomach, pantomimed the pulling of a chain with the other. This really brought down the house.

"*Bravo, Charlot! Bravo, Charlot!*" the crowd shrieked, delighted at the prospect of a free show beyond their wildest expectations, and convinced that they were about to witness some marvelously inventive comic ending; so they helped him from the boat and carried him shoulder high to an evil-smelling cell at the far end of the port.

Inside, in the most appallingly insanitary surroundings, nature took its long and horrendous course to the accompaniment of at first encouraging, then impatient, and finally disgruntled shouts, clapping hands and time beaten upon the door and walls: "CHAR-LOT! . . . CHAR-LOT! . . . CHAR-LOT!"

When Chaplin finally emerged from his noisome sanctuary, the shadows were lengthening on the little port. As he boarded the waiting launch, the fallen idol was treated to turned backs, shrugs of Gallic dismissal, and mutterings of "*Ce Chaplin . . . il est rien.*"

I recounted to Chaplin some of the experiences I had endured in the "meat market," the loathsome practice of some directors when casting the smaller parts of their films, calling twenty or thirty "possibilities" to the sound stage and making each in turn play a key scene *in front* of the remainder, finally dismissing all except one.

Chaplin told me that this embarrassing and unfair system was a legacy from Broadway and that it had not changed since he had come to New York in 1913 with Fred Karno's *A Night in an English Music Hall* (another member of that small troupe had been Stan Laurel, later of Laurel and Hardy). Chaplin was interviewed by William Gillette, a great actor-manager of that time, who was casting for *King Henry V,* and twelve nervous young actors were lined up on the stage, hoping for the microscopic part of Williams, one of the English soldiers.

Gillette, an intimidating figure draped in a long black coat with a fur collar, addressed the group.

"Gentlemen," he intoned, giving full range to his famous voice, "I shall approach each of you in turn and say, 'The dauphin is dead!' Your reply will be one word: 'Dead!' He who makes the most of that one word will play the part of Williams."

The group of young hopefuls shuffled nervously about. At the farthest end of the line in a black suit with a high white stiff collar stood Chaplin—by several inches the shortest.

"The dauphin is dead!" boomed Gillette at the first actor, but the young man was so terrified he just managed to roll his eyes and emit a pitiful squeak: "Dead?"

He was dismissed. "The dauphin is dead!" roared Gillette, but the next actor decided that an English soldier would be delighted at the news. "Dead?" he asked, smiling happily as though his stock in the Union Pacific Railroad had risen twenty points. He too was dismissed.

As the line was thinned out and an impatient Gillette drew inexorably nearer, Chaplin became increasingly nervous.

Eight actors had been dismissed with ignominy, taking with them every inflection and every nuance with which he had hoped to embellish the word "Dead." Three more dismissals followed in quick succession, and the diminutive Chaplin found himself alone on the stage confronted by the towering figure of the now-exasperated actor-manager.

Gillette looked down with distaste upon the sole survivor. "The dauphin is dead!" he yelled.

Chaplin's mind went blank.

He shook his head mournfully from side to side, then clicked his tongue loudly on the roof of his mouth. *"Tch! tch! tch! tch!"* he went.

Gillette slowly raised his arm, pointed scornfully to the exit, and Chaplin, not for the last time, disappeared alone and with dignity into the sunset.

Feeling himself pilloried too long in the American press for not taking out his U.S. citizenship, for his leftist political views, for his former love affairs with young actresses, and finally for his marriage to the teenaged daughter of Eugene O'Neill, Chaplin folded his tents and one night silently stole away to live peacefully in Vevey, a small, sleepy town on the shores of Lake Geneva.

Reclining in a hospital bed into which Chaplin had inadvertently put me, I read of his sudden departure and was amazed because a few hours before I had been playing tennis with him on Summit Drive.

A highly organized man, as his military-style withdrawal demonstrated, he liked his tennis games neatly arranged. With a clearly defined preference for winning, he had given me as a partner for the afternoon's sport Tim Durant, a slow-moving elderly man, later famous as the galloping grandfather courageously flogging also-rans around the Grand National Steeplechase. As his own partner Chaplin had invited none other than Big Bill Tilden, questionably the greatest tennis player the world had ever seen.

Tilden served first to me, and because of his great height, the ball came out of the sun. I never saw it—but I *heard* it as it went by and became embedded in the wire netting behind me.

Durant fared no better, and Chaplin looked smug.

"Thirty-love," he crowed.

For the next serve to me, Tilden decided to be kinder and instead of acing me with another bullet, he uncorked a delivery that had so much spin on it that the ball was egg-shaped as it floated over the net. When it hit the ground, it shot straight up in the air above my head. With visions of smashing the Great Tilden's top-secret delivery, I leaped in the air and flailed at it.

I thought I had received a blow with an ax behind my leg, and I fell to the ground writhing in excruciating agony. I had not pulled a tendon; I had snapped my entire calf muscle clean in half.

Tilden was galvanized into action. He leaped the net. "I know what it is," he said. "Quick, somebody, get adhesive tape!"

Chaplin disappeared toward the house, and with hindsight, I suppose he must have done some unpacking. At any rate, the most appalling pain I have ever experienced was relieved when he reappeared.

"I'm going to tape your heel up as high as it will go," said Tilden. "That'll point the toes down and make the muscle go slack. It'll help the pain; then we'll put you in the hospital."

He did as he promised; then he and Durant carried me to his car and drove me away. My final view of Chaplin, with his last day's tennis in California ruined, was of a small, white-flanneled figure disconsolately hitting balls against the green canvas of the backing.

Within a few hours, Hollywood's one true genius was gone forever to the land of peace, understanding, milk chocolate, and all those lovely snowcapped tax benefits.

11
Mary Lou

IN the earliest days of Hollywood the professional extra did not exist. If a director needed bodies to fill out the screen, he dispatched his assistant to find them. For a while onlookers and others in the vicinity, with nothing better to do, enjoyed the experience of appearing in front of the camera—for fun. Later they demanded to be paid, and the going rate became 50 cents a day. This munificent offering attracted every drunken bum and panhandler in the area, and the streets around the studios became clogged with flushed citizenry with outstretched hands. The producers then invented the bullpen, a sort of central corral into which, early each morning, hundreds of eager bodies were herded, and from which, as the day progressed, assistant directors siphoned off the types they needed.

As the original Hollywood studios became bigger and new ones sprang up all over the sprawling Los Angeles area, each studio built its own bullpen and used, in addition, the services of independent hiring halls in downtown Los Angeles.

By the mid-twenties Hollywood was attracting a tremendous monthly influx of young hopefuls, from trained or semitrained actors and actresses to what seemed like every beauty contest winner in the world—and all with a one-way ticket.

By 1926 the studios realized that their prehistoric methods of hiring extras must be revised; potential talent was being

221

trampled underfoot by the bums and panhandlers in the bullpens and hiring halls, and no coherent records were being kept.

The time had come to move from utter chaos to simple confusion, so the Central Casting Corporation was born.

A filing system was at last instituted, but an "open door" policy still persisted, and by 1930 an unwieldy 18,000 names were on the books and Hollywood film actors found themselves members of the most overcrowded profession in the world. A few, very few, percolated upward from the crowded extra ranks, among them Carole Lombard, Joel McCrea, Paulette Goddard, and Lucille Ball, but the chances of such success were microscopic, and the luck had to be colossal. Much talent withered and died from frustration.

Central Casting made ineffectual efforts to stem the surging tide of the star-struck and, in the early thirties, hung over the front door a large banner upon which was emblazoned a piece of advice which I noticed with some alarm when I joined a long rain-soaked line awaiting registration: DON'T TRY TO BECOME AN ACTOR. FOR EVERY ONE WE EMPLOY WE TURN AWAY A THOUSAND.

We newcomers had been warned, but worse was to come; within a few weeks the pay of the extras was arbitrarily cut by 20 percent.

It was grim. The wage for a crowd extra fell below $3 a day, and Central Casting reported that, including the highest paid of their 18,000, fewer than 60 extras were earning more than $2,000 a year; the rest were averaging less than $500.

Most of us were forced to take part-time jobs, and we became carhops, manual laborers, shop assistants, janitors, or waitresses; I worked on a fishing boat. Many went on relief.

The lucky ones among us who received studio calls were expected to report for work at 6 A.M., to accept inedible meals when it suited the producers, to continue working, or rather to continue being herded about like cattle, till all hours of the night with no additional pay and to report again at 6 the following morning. For the same pittance we had to work right through the night on Saturdays, and we had to face the fact that on days when shooting was canceled at the last minute because of bad weather, a drunken leading man, or "acts of God" (a favorite studio ploy), we would be sent home without touching a cent. There was no compensation for the hours of travel spent on the erratic transportation system of the metropolis, and if we got hurt during filming, there was no redress except by suing the studio heads, which was tantamount to asking them if they would kindly find room for more names on their blacklists.

The powerless and leaderless extras became desperate. They were saved by their more opulent fellow actors who conceived the idea of a Screen Actors Guild to give protection to all film performers in Hollywood. Leading man Leon Ames, comedian James Gleason, and the glowering figure of Frankenstein's Monster Boris Karloff were the founding fathers of the movement, and the first to join them "to help the less fortunate than ourselves" was that splendid old gentleman C. Aubrey Smith.

His example lit the torch, and Gary Cooper, Clark Gable, Spencer Tracy, Paul Muni, James Cagney, Robert Montgomery, Fredric March, Groucho Marx, and many other great stars quickly affixed their names to the crusade which resulted by 1935 in the producers' being forced to recognize the guild and to treat their highly profitable cattle more like human beings.

The ambitious mass of extras registered at Central Casting were divided into four classes:

1. *Dress extras.* These owned garments for every occasion: ball gowns, white tie and tails, riding habits, clothing for business, weddings, graduations, beaches, racetracks, et cetera. The more outfits they owned, the more often they worked. They numbered only 200 or 300 and were a very upper-class closely knit group in extra land. They were led by a dignified dowager named Mrs. Wickes, a tall, professional-looking gentleman named Larry Dodds, and an elderly white-mustachioed ex-Indian army man known as Major. They were paid $10 per day, lived in a country-house atmosphere, and played bridge endlessly among themselves, gossiping and chattering together, spurning the common box lunches and munching goodies from their picnic baskets. Mostly, they

were devoid of all acting ambition and, like all extras, had only a sketchy idea of what masterpiece they were currently engaged upon.

2. *General extras.* These could look presentable and move well in street clothes or uniforms.

3. *Atmosphere or crowd extras.* And comprising nine-tenths of the main herd of cattle. We were rounded up and mercilessly harried from morning to night by brash young assistant directors. In this group we were classified ethnically— Latin, Middle Eastern, Far Eastern, Asian, Indigenous U.S. (white, black, or red). My card was stamped "ANGLO SAXON TYPE 2008."

4. *The "shit kickers" or cowboy extras.* These habitually hung out in "Gower Gulch," on the corner of Gower Street and Sunset Boulevard, strategically placed between several bars and the small independent studios which churned out cheap Western quickies.

In addition, the studio gates were daily besieged by crowds of freakish opportunists hoping to catch the eye of directors being signaled through in their limousines: giants, dwarfs, midgets, the grotesquely ugly, the fat, the emaciated, the maimed, and those waggling newly arrived bosoms and bottoms.

All registered extras followed the same routine: Between five and eight o'clock every evening we would call Central Casting and state our names and classifications.

At the other end the operators—and there were dozens of them working frantically at a huge board—would check the latest requirements:

Paramount	180 Indians
Universal	25 Greeks
RKO	150 Asians
MGM	200 Nondescripts
Fox	230 U.S. (white)
	25 ″ (black)

Then, till the quotas were filled, the first to call who fitted the required groups would be hired and told where to report on the morrow.

With up to 18,000 inquiries coming in for an average of 800 jobs, the evening hum of disappointment rising from the switchboard was numbing.

"Nothing, call later. . . . Nothing, call later. . . . Nothing, call later"—but most people continued calling till at long last the switchboard went dead.

After years of exploitation, it is not hard to imagine how much the extras relished getting a little back from the producers; even the snooty dress extras indulged in this game. They were periodically called to "dress parades," where before an audience of casting directors and assistant directors from all the studios they displayed their entire wardrobes and, according to the number of changes they could muster, were marked down for future calls. By deft maneuvering in the changing rooms, it was possible for them to arrange for one cutaway or white fur stole to appear on a dozen different backs with most beneficial results.

We of the lower classes found more plebeian ways of revenge.

It was a simple matter to show up early, for example, at Paramount for a big crowd call to collect our voucher (which had to be dropped into a box at the end of the day's work for later payment), to entrust this document to a chum to drop with his, and then hotfoot it over to another studio, draw another voucher there, and collect a second day's pay for one day's work.

The obvious refinement of this was to do no work at all at any studio and still get paid for a full day's labor. A group of us perfected this, and when employed on the back lot at Metro-Goldwyn Mayer, we were able to put it into practice. We had loosened some boards and rearranged some wiring in the high surrounding fence. At 6 A.M. we drew our costumes and our pay vouchers and showed up with hundreds of other Friends, Romans, Countrymen, or whatever. Later we drifted lavatoryward and kept going to the escape hatch in the fence, where we stripped off the studio clothing, and in our bathing costumes (thoughtfully worn underneath) joined a friend in his convertible for a lovely day at the beach. Toward evening the reverse procedure was employed, and we arrived back in ample time to drop the vouchers and hand in our costumes.

If we worked later than expected, damp salty swimsuits beneath breastplates or doublets and hose became itchy reminders of a golden day of hot dogs and surf enjoyed at L. B. Mayer's expense.

One athletic girl, Mary Lou, was an avid beach lover and an eager recruit on these expeditions. Like thousands of others among the extras, she had come to Hollywood with stars in her eyes, but a veteran of three years in Hollywood, she had still not spoken a line, and she was becoming disillusioned.

"I've tried it all," she told me. "I've worked at night in acting classes and theater groups, and I've paid those phony makeup schools that guaranteed employment, but no talent scouts ever came near me. I've been on parties with producers and gone to Vegas with casting directors, and I've held my nose and laid some of the creepiest agents in the business, but no dice, nothing ever happened."

She was a beautiful, open-faced girl, tall, creamy-skinned with wide, almost golden eyes and rather broad shoulders. We called her Miss Corn on the Cob because she had once won a high school beauty contest in her small farming community in Iowa. She was a quiet, private person, mysterious and aloof, and no matter how well one knew her, a part of her was always held in reserve. Going through a bad financial patch, she was evicted by her landlady and showed up at my little Hollywood pad till things got better. To start with, this unexpected bonanza went the traditional route, and she shared my bed, but even there she held back, and I had an uncomfortable feeling that she was merely paying rent. After a few days we made other sleeping arrangements, which included a mattress for me on the floor.

We remained good friends but it was infinitely frustrating to see such a gorgeous creature wandering about in all sorts of provocative stages of undress, cooking things and tidying up, and to have to face the fact that my romantic or sexual fulfillments were subject to the most stringent rationing, and I was quite relieved when she got a job on a long location picture and left.

Paulette Goddard at Fairbanks' beach house.

König's deck hand and friend

The White Ball. David Niven, Merle Oberon, and Irving Thalberg as invited, Norma Shearer in flaming red.

The "Who is your dentist?" scene by Scott Fitzgerald with Olivia de Havilland.

Clark by author's pool.

Flynn on *Sirocco*.

Flynn in the garden of 601 North Linden Drive.

Edmund Goulding and Douglas Fairbanks, Jr., at "Welcome Home" party for David Niven after World War II.

Hedda Hopper (right) eavesdropping on Louella Parsons.

Marlene Dietrich in a rare sporting moment.

Marlene's car and Briggs, her chauffeur.

Opening of original Romanoff restaurant with Jacqueline Dyer, David Niven, and "The Emperor."

Gilbert Roland ("Amigo") and Cedric Gibbons (right).

Constance Bennett . . . she gleamed all over.

Garbo in *Camille*—glamor above decks, comfort below.

From the MGM release *Camille* © 1936 Metro-Goldwyn-Mayer Inc.

Ronald Colman, at ease in the mountains.

Photo: David Niven

Douglas Fairbanks and Sylvia visit *The Prisoner of Zendu* set.

Photo: Selznick International

C. Aubrey Smith and Mrs. Wickes, the social leader of the dress extras.

Photo: David Niven

Bogie at the helm of *Santana*.

Photo: David Niven

Betty Bacall with daughter Leslie. Photo: David Niven

Fred in orbit.

Fred and sailfish, Mexico.

William Randolph Hearst's castle,
San Simeon.

Marion Davies.

Cary Grant and Phyllis Brooks
"trucking" at San Simeon.

Dolores del Rio and Ce-
dric Gibbons.

"You're a member of the family now," said Lubitsch. Claudette
Colbert and Gary Cooper demonstrate the point.

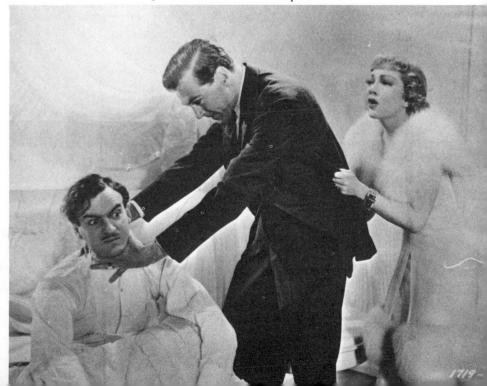

Bobbie Newton fishing in Colorado.

Ginger in *Bachelor Mother.*

"Coop" in unaccustomed outfit.

Photo: David Niven

Photo: Chris Ware,
Keystone Press Agency

Winifred (Clemence Dane).

Photo: David Niven

Lieutenant Colonel James Stewart USAF on leave during World War II at the author's cottage near Windsor, England.

Photo: courtesy Charles Feldman

John Huston directing Deborah Kerr and author in *Casino Royale*.

Beverly Hills, city limits.

Photo: David Niven

By a series of highly unlikely gyrations, the wheel of fate had picked me up, shaken me, rattled me, and finally spewed me upward from the extra ranks into the coveted strata of contract players, so at the end of 1935 I left my sordid little South Hollywood pad and rented a slightly larger and marginally less sordid one in a once-smart residential area on a North Hollywood hillside.

It comprised a bedroom below and a large living room above, complete with kitchenette and a permanently sealed picture window, through which, when I cleaned it, I could see at night the electrical rash of the Los Angeles Basin and by day in the far distance, the water tower of Metro-Goldwyn-Mayer Studio and the oil derricks beyond Culver City. I also had a small terrace.

Directly below me, in a beautifully manicured garden, stood a large cream-colored Colonial-style mansion with a pillared front entrance which I could not see and a private parking lot at the back which I could not only see but hear. Expensive cars backed and filled from early afternoon to dawn on its gravel surface; laughter and sometimes altercations disturbed my slumber.

Eddie, the mailman, brought me up to date when I asked him about my neighbors.

"Hey! Whaddya know!" He chortled. "You been livin' here a month and you don't catch on you're lookin' inta the back windows of a whorehouse! You want a piece of tail—you better get yer ass down there and talk to the Baroness—she's got the best-lookin' bunch of hookers in LA."

Thereafter I borrowed a pair of binoculars from the studio property department, hoping to catch a glimpse of some friend in action, or at least at pre- or postcoital parking, but the windows were heavily curtained, and as the days passed, I became disenchanted with the attractive girls and the well-heeled gentlemen who ebbed and flowed on the parking lot below me. I had not seen one familiar face.

One evening I received a shock: Mary Lou was locking the door of a green two-seater Pontiac convertible. I watched the familiar figure pass around to the front entrance; she did not reappear.

Thereafter I kept an eye open for that car, and when I

realized that it was a semipermanent visitor to the parking lot, my curiosity was understandably aroused.

I made some inquiries and learned from Central Casting that Mary Lou had withdrawn her name from their books. The next time I saw the green car, I left a note under the windshield wiper, indicating my whereabouts and suggesting that it was time we resumed contact.

One calm evening I was sitting content on my little terrace, sniffing a sunset scented by the orange blossoms of an adjacent grove, when there came a knocking at my door. Mary Lou walked in, looking ravishing. She settled herself down with a drink, crossed long silken legs, shook her sun-kissed hair and, without any prompting from me, brought me up to date.

She was an extremely forthright girl and explained her new life clinically and concisely. There were no excuses, and there was, apparently, no remorse.

"I'm a whore now," she announced cheerfully, "but I am also going steady with Bobbie."

"Who's Bobbie?" I asked.

"You'll see for yourself in a little while," she answered. "I gave up sleeping around when I met Bobbie because for the first time I had found someone who suited me in every way. With Bobbie it really *works.*"

"Are you in love?" I asked.

"I dunno . . . I guess so . . . Anyway, for the moment I've never been so happy. . . . I was really getting desperate in Hollywood. I was going noplace fast and not earning enough to pay my laundry. I didn't want to go back to Iowa." She paused, spread her hands, and smiled down at her white pleated skirt and expensive shoes. "Now look at me—I'm *loaded!*"

I looked at her, and she really was a dish.

"How does Bobbie feel about you being a whore?" I asked. "That's sleeping around, isn't it?"

"Just *great!*" She laughed and did not elaborate.

"Who is the Baroness?"

"Oh! You'll *love* her, she's a great old broad . . . she really is a baroness, too . . . German . . . she's like a mother to me." She giggled.

"I'll bet," I said sourly. "Is she the madam?"

"Yes, but she doesn't run it like a cathouse. She has a great bunch of girls working there, and it's mostly done on a 'date' basis. The guys call up for a date with one of us, and we have lovely apartments to entertain them in, and there's a butler and two maids and drinks and snacks. We get a lot of dough, and the fellows are nice too, mostly important businessmen from back East or society people from Pasadena, or Palos Verdes, and the LA Country Club. In fact, the Baroness won't accept anyone from the movie business; she says they're 'common' and talk too much, and she doesn't need them anyway."

A car stopped outside, and a horn honked.

Mary Lou's face lit up. She rushed to the door. A beautiful tall girl of about twenty-eight with close-cropped dark hair and wearing white slacks strode into the room.

"Hi!" she said. "I'm Bobbie."

When I saw Mary Lou's glowing face, I knew how a Brooklyn Dodger fan must have felt on hearing that his favorite pitcher had defected to the New York Giants.

The girls shared an attractive ground-floor apartment near the Garden of Allah, and there I was frequently invited for Sunday brunch. They were very happy together, and it was obvious that they treated their time spent under the roof of the Baroness strictly as office hours. They had no intention of breaking the old lady's number one rule: "Private telephone numbers are never under any circumstances to be given to clients."

The Baroness, they told me, sometimes sent her girls out on dates to private addresses but never to hotels, and she carefully vetted, personally, all prospective clients, inviting them around for afternoon tea to see if she "approved"; she had no intention of paying protection money to Mickey Cohen.

Bobbie was great fun and painted enthusiastically in oils. She explained that she ran the "correction unit" for the Baroness, and billed as "Deborah de Sade—strict disciplinarian," she climbed into her leather bra, open-sided leather shorts, high-heeled thigh boots, gauntlet, and black mask and meted

out lusty punishment with belt and whip to those who came
to pay for humiliation and pain.

"It doesn't mean a goddamn thing to me," she said. "It's a
pleasure to be able to help out the poor bastards. The funny
thing is most of them are big guys in business, running cor-
porations and that, and the moment I get through with them
or they've had enough of being kicked around the floor,
they're on the phone to their offices, cussing hell out of their
secretaries and issuing orders all over the joint."

Mary Lou was happy in her work, too. "The dates I have
really pay good money, and most of them are real nice. I
guess they're not getting it at home. Some of them just like to
sit around and talk—they must have lousy wives. Of course,
we have a few specialists—like Brenda,who was trained for
opera; she does specialties and hums 'The William Tell Ov-
erture' at the same time—but most of us are straight. The
humping doesn't mean anything to me, of course, but I've
finally become one hell of an actress! I give the best service I
can and help them out with their little problems.

"Quite a few like to dress up, and the Baroness always
sends those to me. She's given me a whole load of wigs and a
makeup table for them, and they'll take forever choosing
black underwear or a dress or a French maid outfit. I help
them with their eyelashes and suspender belts and tell them
how beautiful they look while they mince about in front of
the three-way mirror. . . . It's a lot easier, I can tell you,
than standing around on some goddamn hot movie set for
twelve hours a day to earn what I now give the maid for tidying up the room. . . . Those guys don't do anyone any
harm anyway."

One day I asked her how it could be arranged because I
had generated an overpowering curiosity about the Baroness. "How can I meet her?"

Mary Lou and Bobbie decided that the best plan would be
for them to tell her they had met a lonely young foreign visitor on the beach and ask the old lady if she would like to in-
terview him as a potential client.

So it was put in train, and a few days later I was bidden to
take tea with the Baroness.

I walked down from my aerie above and rang her front

doorbell. A butler dressed in white coat and striped trousers opened the door.

"I have an appointment with the Baroness," I said, and told him my name.

"Yes, indeed, sir," he said in a sibilant German accent. "Follow me please."

We passed through a large beautifully furnished hall and knocked upon a door.

"Mr. Niven," he announced, and bowed.

I entered a small, cool, tastefully decorated green-tinted sitting room, cluttered with pieces of Meissen china, silver, bric-a-brac, and a profusion of oval-shaped photographs of square-headed gentlemen with spiky mustaches and ironclad military expressions. Above the mantelshelf was an oil painting of a girl; her dark hair was swept up at the back, and the fact that it sat upon her head like an inverted falcon's nest did nothing to detract from the serene alabaster beauty of the aristocratic face beneath.

"Good evening, young man," said the Baroness, extending her hand. "Come and sit down."

She indicated an armchair facing hers.

"Mary Lou tells me you are English, so we are having my favorite tea—Lapsang Souchong. I am sure you will appreciate it."

The white-haired old lady smiled, and I saw how beautifully the young girl above the mantelshelf had aged.

She asked what part of the British Isles I was from and launched into rhapsodies over the good times she had enjoyed as a young girl when she had been presented at court.

"Ah, those beautiful houses! And those gay weekends! Chatsworth! Drumlanrig! Eaton! Belvoir! Badminton! It was all so elegant and carefree, and we loved each other so much—till that stupid Kaiser ruined everything."

I was fascinated by my chic, carefully coiffed hostess, and as I looked across the three-tiered silver cake dish, happily munching mille-feuilles I wondered if the other girls in her establishment would measure up to the beauty standards set by Mary Lou and Bobbie.

I asked how long she had lived in California, whereupon she treated me to a harrowing description of the Baron's

financial difficulties under the Weimar Republic when runaway inflation had cut the value of his Deutschmarks in half
every hour.

"In 1923 he sold his estates near Münster for what he
could get, and we moved here. He became interested in
growing oranges and walnuts in the San Fernando Valley,
but he passed away before he could get started." She sighed.
"It was difficult for me at first being alone in a foreign country, but I made friends quickly, and now I run classes in de-
portment and social graces for young girls. The house is always full of young people, and I am content. All work and no
play is not good for the girls, so I allow them to entertain
their friends here between classes, and they organize swimming parties and so on."

I was just about to ask her if I could meet some of her pupils when she forestalled me by pulling a bell cord. The butler appeared and bowed.

"Wolfgang, I believe Miss Tessa, Miss Judy, and Miss Mary
Lou are having a rest period at the moment. Tell them I
would like them to join me for tea." The butler bowed again
and withdrew.

"Dear Wolfgang," said the Baroness, "so loyal, he insisted
on coming with us when we left the Schloss. I would be lost
without him." She poured me another cup of tea.

"Mary Lou tells me that you are lately arrived and don't
know many people out here. That is why I have asked two of
her friends to join us—they are charming girls, rather shy,
but if you feel you would like to have a private word with
either of them and perhaps make a date with them?" She
wagged a finger. "I know what young people are!"

I went along with the game.

"I can't thank you enough, Baroness, it's most kind of you,
and I do appreciate it—but how can I, er, speak to one of the
girls and not hurt the feelings of the others?"

She smiled a sweet smile and waved a hand. "The girls will
be seated in those three chairs. If you feel you would like to
have a private word with one of them before you go, signal
the fact to me by turning the handle of your teacup in her direction and I will see that she stays after the others leave—no
feelings will be hurt."

The girls came in together, Mary Lou leading and obviously going to have a hard time not bursting out laughing. The
other two followed, and a most spectacular couple they were,
too. The Baroness had thoughtfully provided a choice of col-
oring so, as they seated themselves, Mary Lou's blond fresh
good looks were flanked by a sultry red-lipped, olive-skinned
brunette and a green-eyed redhead whom I remembered
seeing on several movie sets.

Both had spectacular figures, and their bosoms longed to
burst out of their flimsy dresses. All had nice "toothpaste ad"
smiles, they were carefully made up, and there was no hint
anywhere of a hard-boiled trollop.

Tea and cakes were dispensed, and Mary Lou opened the
ball game with a fast delivery. "Have you visited any of the
studios since you've been out here?" she asked innocently.

I ducked that one with a clever shake of the head, and the
conversation became more general.

The Baroness was kind and thoughtful with the girls, and
they obviously enjoyed her company. It was a well-mannered
and successful tea party, and only the muffled sounds of
footsteps above and the distant flushing of toilets reminded
me of my true whereabouts.

Discreetly raised eyebrows on the part of the Baroness signaled that she would like to conclude the business in hand, so
I turned the handle of my teacup firmly toward Mary Lou.
The Baroness rose, and we all stood. She glanced at a china
clock. "Tessa and Judy, darlings, I promised your mothers
you could be home early today, so you had better run along,
both of you."

The girls smiled good-bye and said it had been nice meeting me.

"Mary Lou, darling, I have so much to do. Why don't you
show your friend the house? He tells me he is very interested
in furniture. . . . Come and see me often, young man;
you'll always be welcome."

The Baroness elegantly lifted to me the back of her hand,
and I found myself bowing and kissing it. She swept regally
from the room.

Mary Lou collapsed into a chair with laughter.

"Jesus, isn't that some act? But you should see her when

she wants to get rid of someone—she's like a bouncer in the Bowery! Come on, let's go. You can see my workbench, and if Bobbie is not beating the bejesus out of some poor bastard, you can case her torture chamber."

Mary Lou's room was comfortable and functional. There was a large double bed and a thick run on the floor for the "rough trade." The aforementioned well-stocked dressing table, wardrobe, and three-way mirror for the fetishists were in evidence, as was an imposing selection of spiky high-heeled shoes and "kinky" underwear for Mary Lou's own use if such aids were requested by the customers. A bathroom was adjacent, the lighting was discreet, and the radio was tuned to the music station.

We sat on the bed, and a strangely silent Mary Lou held my hand. Then she started crying, quite suddenly, gently at first, then with deep, heaving shudders. In great embarrassment I tried to console her, but she turned her head into the pillow. "Go away," she sobbed. "For chrissake, *go away.*"

At the bottom of the stairs, Wolfgang materialized. He glanced at a pocket watch which he withdrew from his waistcoat. "The Baroness says you have most generously donated a hundred dollars toward the new pool house for the students," he said.

I handed over what amounted to my weekly salary, walked out into the poolless garden, and inhaled the warm Californian evening, thoroughly depressed.

I was sent away on a location picture in northern California for six weeks. When I returned, it was two days before I noticed an unnatural calm below me. The Colonial mansion was quiet; there were no curtains at the windows and no cars in the parking lot; pieces of newspaper were blowing about in the garden, which looked unhappy and deserted.

My little shack was the highest point, physically, of Eddie the mailman's morning round, and he made it a point to refresh himself there before proceeding downhill.

I heard him upstairs opening my icebox and joined him. He poured out a bottle of beer and brought me up to date.

"There's a carload of great-lookin' hookers loose around here someplace," he said. "They cleaned out the old lady below."

"Who? The cops?"

"Nah. The Mob . . . Bugsie Siegal, Mickey Cohen, and that bunch of hoods. Seems they wanted a big piece of the action down there, but the old dame just told them to go fuck themselves and closed up the joint in twenty-four hours. I seen a coupla big Bekins interstate vans loadin' on all her junk, and the girls were standin' around cryin'. Some people think she's moved to Vegas, but I don't think that's refined enough for her—my guess is Frisco. I feel sorry for them hookers, though." He shook his head sadly.

"Information" informed me that the phone had been disconnected, so I went round to Mary Lou and Bobbie's flat near the Garden of Allah. A suspicious Grant Wood-type lady wearing curlers and a flowered dressing gown opened the door a few inches.

"Yes?"

"I'm looking for the girls who live here—are they around?"

"No—they left town almost a month ago, and from what I understand from the folks around here, no one's going to miss them. . . . Whores!"

She slammed the door.

12
Bogie

*H*UMPHREY Bogart was born in December, 1899, which, up to a point, was perfectly all right with him. The thing he deeply resented about it was that it happened on Christmas Day. "Got gypped out of a proper birthday, goddammit."

Bogie's father, a well-to-do New York physician, was incessantly nagged by his wife. Bogie too enjoyed needling people, and he practiced it from an early age.

"Guess I inherited it from my folks—they were always griping at each other."

His famous lisp was caused by a badly performed operation on his lower lip in which a splinter of wood had become embedded.

"Goddamn doctor—instead of stitching it up, he screwed it up."

I asked him how the piece of wood had got into his lip in the first place. "Accident as a kid." He shrugged.

The Warner Brothers publicity department improved upon this and announced that it was a "shrapnel wound suffered in combat during World War I."

Bogie endured a well-to-do eastern seaboard upbringing, attended Andover, and headed for Yale. He didn't make it there, much to his mother's annoyance. She told him he was a failure and ordered him to go get himself a job. He complied, the next day enlisted in the U.S. Navy, and at seventeen and a half aboard the troop carrier *Leviathan* did indeed see service in the closing months of World War I.

After two years he was honorably discharged from the Navy and for the next eighteen months was employed as a runner for a Wall Street brokerage house. He didn't run fast enough apparently and resented openly the financial Establishment which employed him, so to the accompaniment of catcalls from his mother and with very little encouragement from his father, he drifted little by little into the theater.

First, he became stage manager to William Brady, the father of a school friend, who was producing plays in Brooklyn, and later he played his first part for the same suburban impresario in a play called *Swifty*. Opposite him was a young actress, Frances Howard, who left the production to become the wife of my own future boss—Samuel Goldwyn.

Bogie caught on in a small way and, by the age of twenty-six, was regularly employed in New York and the suburbs as a sleek juvenile lead complete with white tie, tails, and occasionally a tennis racket. These being the Roaring Twenties, he also set about making a name for himself in the speakeasies of Prohibition, where he took happily to the use of scotch. Although never at any time was he near alcoholism, Bogie maintained from then on an awe-inspiring level of consumption—he enjoyed it; he liked the taste of it; he approved mightily of its effect upon him—but he never allowed it to interfere with his work.

Bogie married a successful young actress named Helen Menken. The marriage fell apart after eighteen months, with Bogie blaming himself for putting his career before the possibilities of a happy home life—a lesson which remained unlearned because one year later he married another successful young actress, Mary Phillips, and promptly departed for Hollywood, where he had been offered a small contract.

The fulfilling of this long engagement 3,000 miles away from his new wife did nothing to help his new marriage or to further the career which he still found all-important, and on his return to New York he was only routinely surprised when Mary Phillips informed him that she had fallen in love with a New York-based actor, Roland Young.

The depths of the Depression coincided with Bogie's return to Broadway, and work for actors was scarce to nonexistent, but against this somber background Bogie and Mary made a brave stab at putting together the Humpty-Dumpty of their partnership. They moved into peeling, crumbling lodgings on the East Side and for a while were supported solely by Bogie's prowess at chess; he played for 50 cents a game in sleazy Sixth Avenue dives.

To be thirty-four years old, an unemployed married actor, small in stature, short on presence, with a pronounced lisp and little professional experience, must have been daunting even for Bogie, but he gamely plodded off on his rounds of agencies and producers' offices, and in 1934, a few weeks after the death of his bankrupt father, Bogie struck theatrical oil. Arthur Hopkins was casting *The Petrified Forest* by Robert Sherwood, and Bogie was given a chance to read the part of the sentimental killer, Duke Mantee. He shaved off most of his thick thatch of hair and delivered his lines with a snarl made even more menacing by his lisp.

Neither Hopkins nor Sherwood was impressed, and from the darkness of the stalls Bogie heard the dreaded "Thank you very much, don't call us, we'll call you." As Bogie slunk from the stage, renewed whispering broke out. Leslie Howard, the star of the play, had been sitting quietly in the back row. Now he moved forward and urgently begged the others to reconsider. He was convinced that Bogie was ideal for the part. Bogie read again, Sherwood agreed with Howard, and finally, Hopkins nodded his assent.

The play was a huge success, and Bogie made a personal success of enormous proportions. He was signed with Leslie Howard to make the picture for Warner Brothers at the end of the Broadway run, but when he and Mary in high excitement arrived in Hollywood, all set to knock the film world for a loop, he learned to his stunned dismay that the studio had decided to pay him off and put one of their biggest contract stars into the role of Duke Mantee—Edward G. Robinson.

Bogie had no intention of meekly swallowing this, his first taste of big studio duplicity, so he fired off an SOS to Leslie

Howard in England. Howard reacted immediately and unleashed a return salvo at Warner Brothers: "It's either with Bogart or without me."

Bogart it was, and film history continued smoothly on its way.

He never forgot, never ceased to acknowledge the helping hand he had received when he had most needed it and, as a gesture of his gratitude, named his second child, a girl, Leslie.

The brothers Warner, never renowned for the delicacy and foresight with which they handled their contract players, decided that they had hatched a golden egg, so Bogie was treated like a battery hen and in the next four years was forced to pump out no less than twenty-nine gangster films, in each of which he played a carbon copy of Duke Mantee; this nearly finished his career and completely ruined his marriage. Seeing nothing of her husband except glimpses of a zombie who worked punishing hours on Warner's production line, Mary took off for New York to do a play. Bogie was sad to see her go but consoled himself with an undulating blonde of conspicuous cleavage named Mayo Methot. Mayo was a hard case, a drinker who went refill by refill with Bogie, but unlike him, she was unable to handle it, and by the time Mary divorced Bogie Mayo was well on her way to alcoholism. In 1938 Mayo and Bogie married, and at a famously liquid reception the Russian actor Mischa Auer appeared from behind the giant wedding cake and danced before the befuddled guests stark naked.

Bogie settled down for the third time to married life, but his latest partnership soon developed into the toughest situation he had ever had to handle.

I witnessed some of it. I had met Bogie the year when he had been lent by Warner Brothers to Samuel Goldwyn to make *Dead End,* and one day we drank lunch together at the Formosa Café across the street, but we did not like each other very much. I found his aggressively tough and needling manner rather tiresome, and he obviously marked me down as a prissy Englishman. We parted with expressions of mutual respect and a determination from then on to avoid each other like the plague.

The next time I came face to face with Bogie he was underneath a table in the Restaurant La Maze on the Sunset Strip. This was a favorite hangout of the younger Hollywood group because it boasted the best music in town and the manager made a welcome specialty of keeping it off limits to the prying eyes of the columnists, possibly because the place also catered to the Mickey Cohen gangster element of Los Angeles, and indeed there had lately been a full-scale killing on the premises.

Bogie, like all movie mobsters since the beginning of films, was plagued by drunks who would lurch up to him in public, trying to pick a fight in order to impress others with how they had "taken care of the tough guy." Bogie was an adept at avoiding all forms of physical combat. It was not that he was cowardly; it was just that he was quite small—a bantamweight—who had not the faintest intention of being knocked around by people twice his size. His love of the needle, however, sometimes ended in dangerous brinkmanship.

That night at La Maze Bogie was confronted by a large man with a flushed face wearing an open-neck shirt turned down outside his jacket.

I was sitting in a corner with the "Oomph Girl," Ann Sheridan. Bogie with Mayo was a few tables away. We couldn't hear the confrontation, but we could see that the scene was developing along traditional lines. The large man was bending over their table and poking Bogie in the chest with a forefinger, Bogie was smiling insults, Mayo was rising like a ruffled hen turkey from her seat, and waiters were circling warily around, taking up action stations to isolate or eliminate the impending conflict.

Suddenly all hell broke loose. Bogie threw a full glass of scotch into his aggressor's eyes, and at the same moment Mayo hit the man on the head with a shoe. I caught a momentary glimpse of flinty-eyed characters rising purposefully from the table whence the large man had come and of a solid phalanx of waiters converging on the battle area. Cries of rage and alarm rose on all sides, and the air became thick with flying bottles, plates, glasses, left hooks, and food.

"Quick," screamed the Oomph Girl. "Under the table."

This was a suggestion with which I was only too happy to

comply, but for some technical reason, it was impossible to get beneath our own table, so we threw ourselves to the floor and crawled on hands and knees to a larger sanctuary a few yards away.

We had not been installed there for more than a few seconds before Bogie came padding in on all fours; he was laughing like hell.

"What's going on up there?" I asked.

"Everything's OK," he chortled. "Mayo's handling it. . . . I wish I'd brought a fork, though—I might be able to jab the bastard in the leg."

Mayo did indeed handle it. The attacker and his party were ousted, and the evening dusted itself off and returned to normal.

After that night Bogie nicknamed Mayo Sluggy, and she lived up to it. The skirmishes between the "Battling Bogarts," as the Hollywood press corps christened them, were noisy in the extreme, and complaining neighbors insisted that they were nonstop. Jealousy on the part of Mayo seemed to be the spark that ignited the flames—jealousy mixed with booze, a lethal cocktail, with Bogie playing his role of "stirrer." He and Mayo would drink: then her jealousy, generally of his current leading lady, would come to the boil, and Bogie would gleefully go into action, goading her till the bottles started whizzing past his head. It must have been a most exhausting period for him, and it was certainly dangerous, because on one occasion Mayo slashed her wrists, on another she set fire to their house, and on a third she stabbed him in the back with a carving knife. "Only went in a little way," he said as he was being stitched up.

The "Battling Bogarts" were still at it hammer and tongs in September, 1939, when, in a moment of military lunacy, I departed for Europe. I did not see Bogie again till I returned in 1946, but a great mutual friend, the writer John McClain, serving with the American navy, had kept me up to date.

Bogie, he told me, had widened the area of conflict and had decided to take on Jack Warner at the same time as he was conducting his running battles with Mayo. He had realized that he must get away from his gangster screen image because he saw clearly that with the wartime carnage being fully reported, the "Mob" in action had become tame stuff indeed, so he refused to work at all and was suspended. After much resistance from Warner, John Huston was allowed to put Bogie into *The Maltese Falcon,* a picture regarded at the studio with undisguised apprehension. With the success of this picture a new career opened up for Bogie, and in *Casablanca* he played a romantic soldier of fortune opposite Ingrid Bergman. He became the pet of the Warner Brothers lot, and a beaming Jack Warner told him he could have the pick of all the scripts.

As Bogie's film popularity soared, so his home life deteriorated. Mayo became a confirmed alcoholic; her looks and figure collapsed, and she made an increasing number of hideous scenes in public, but Bogie, trying nobly to keep the ship afloat, would never hear a word against her.

"She's an actress," he would say with menacing quiet, "a goddamn good one, but she's not working much at the moment, which is tough on her . . . understand?"

When Mayo heard this, she was apt to scream out that Bogie was "a Four-F coward and a phony," but somehow he got through the battle-scarred nights and still arrived on time for work early the next morning.

It couldn't last at that pace, of course, and when in 1944 Bogie made *To Have and Have Not,* he fell head over heels in love with his nineteen-year-old leading lady, an ex-theater usherette and cover girl, Lauren Bacall. Mayo's antennae picked up the message early, she scented battle and sailed into the studio, and Bogie's next love scene was interrupted by the strident voice of his wife inquiring how he was getting along with "that poor child half your age."

Betty Bacall was equally in love with Bogie, but all she could do was suffer and pray that Bogie could work things out so that he would be free to marry her. Bogie gave his marriage to Mayo another try to see if he could forget Betty, but it didn't work. Poor Mayo—her jealousy made her ugly, and her ugliness made her drink, and a guilt-ridden Bogie ducked her flying bottles and pretended not to hear her abuse, but even he was not made of steel, and his nerves finally cracked under the strain.

One morning in the studio makeup department, a girl was washing Bogie's hair. His chin was cupped sleepily in the aluminum bowl, and the hairdresser was proudly giving him the benefit of her best friction rub. Suddenly the poor creature stared aghast into the basin; then she let out a piercing shriek and fainted dead away. The entire growth of hair on the head of the most valuable star in her studio had come away in her hands. It grew back in time as his nerves recovered, but Bogie never again had the same luxurious thatch. From then on it always looked to me as though the cat had been at it.

Divorce became inevitable, and Mayo, a classic Hollywood casualty, departed for her Oregon birthplace, and there six years later, as the tragic decline accelerated, she died all alone in a motel.

When Betty and Bogie married in the Ohio home of Louis Bromfield, there was exactly twenty-five years' difference in their ages. This sparked off some spicy observations about "old folks' homes" on the part of Betty's father, and the Hollywood smart money went on an early breakup. The locals, over the years, had been afforded ample opportunity to study Bogie's form, but they underestimated Betty, who was an unknown starter. In spite of her extreme youth, she had a mountain of common sense and the guts to put it to work. She never kowtowed to Bogie, she never nagged him, and above all, she truly admired him as a man and as an actor. For his part he adored her and was proud of her looks, her honesty, and her spirit. He cut back conspicuously on his whiskey consumption because "Betty doesn't go for it too much, and it's no fun drinking alone." Her explanation was probably nearer the mark: "Bogie drank a lot because he was unhappy. Now he's happy."

This then was the couple that John McClain took me to visit when we both returned to Hollywood in 1946. Nobody likes being dropped in on, especially when tired after a long day's work, but Betty had arranged a surprise party for Bogie on his forty-seventh birthday—a potentially dangerous tactic.

When Bogie walked in and discovered thirty people hiding in cupboards, seated on toilets or under beds, he became loudly abusive, and it seemed that no amount of singing "Happy Birthday" could soften his attitude. Betty finally won the day by playing it his way. "All right then, you son of a bitch," she yelled. "You stay here alone, and we'll all go out for dinner."

He bared his teeth in the famous wolf grin and snarled, "Okay, you bastards—you're welcome." The party went on till dawn.

Bogie bought a sailing boat from Dick Powell, the 65-foot ketch *Santana,* and next to Betty, she became the most important thing in his life.

He was a first-class sailor, an ocean racer of repute, and his love of the sea was deep, almost mystical. Betty was smart enough not to be jealous of this other love and realized that he derived much peace and strength from his weekend voyages. Occasionally she went along, but mostly she encouraged him to go alone with Pete, his Danish crewman, and a couple of pals.

During his forty-seventh birthday party, Bogie learned that I, too, had sailed all my life, and his face softened.

"There's hope for you yet," he growled. "Come to the island next weekend."

I enjoyed the trip immensely, but I subsequently discovered that while I had been reveling in being told to take the helm or put up a spinnaker, I had, in fact, been under Bogie's microscope. His theory was simple—if a man could handle a boat in rough weather or be a good shipmate in days of calm, he should be awarded one star like a reliable restaurant in the *Guide Michelin.* If in addition, he proved to have interests, experience, and curiosity outside the small world of filmmaking and enjoyed a game of chess, he might receive a higher rating. I never learned my own classification, but imperceptibly almost, our understanding prospered from then on, and one day I looked up to find Bogie and Betty among my closest friends.

This was flattering because Bogie did not really like actors as a breed, and apart from Tracy, Sinatra, and Peter Lorre, he usually kept his distance, much preferring the company of writers such as Huston, Bromfield, Nunnally Johnson, Mark Hellinger, Alistair Cooke, and Harry Kurnitz.

On the many, many subsequent trips I had aboard *Santana,* I grew to realize what a very special man Betty had married. Things to Bogie were either black or white; he had little patience with the grays. To sort people out quickly, he used the shock technique. Early on in an acquaintanceship he would say or do something completely outrageous, and the reaction of the other person told Bogie most of what he wanted to know. People in movie theaters saw him as the personification of the tough and the sardonic, and up to a point they were not far wrong. He gamely presented the same facade in real life, but my own theory was that he worked to maintain it and had a difficult time covering up the fact that he was really kind, generous, highly intelligent, and deeply sentimental. Animals loved him, too—the best sign of all.

I think he had a horror of being unmasked, and being very publicity-conscious, he gradually eliminated nearly all contact with the press, preferring, if he had anything to say, to give it to one man who wrote a column in the New York *Herald Tribune*—Joe Hyams. Other people would then pick it up.

Joe was an intelligent and respected newspaperman, and he kept Bogie's image alive in exactly the colors Bogie wanted. Whether he was taken in by Bogie or whether his personal friendship impeded him in his reporting of some of the subtler shadings of his subject, it was hard to decide, but he certainly played the game according to Bogie's rules.

Bogie set himself up as a nonconformist, and this was no act. He really intended to do his own thing and despised those who pandered to the Hollywood code of good behavior.

"I'm not one of the boys next door. I leave that to all those good-looking bastards with their button-down shirts."

And he would go on his merry way, tilting at the windmills of convention, arriving at nightclubs with giant panda dolls, arguing with all and sundry, championing left-wing causes, and making heavily quoted statements about the unreliability of people who never drank.

Once, sitting on the deck of *Santana* in a quiet cove off Catalina Island, eating delicious lobsters caught in his illicit trap (his publicity incidentally stated that he never fished because he loved animals too much), I heckled him about his obvious determination to bend the rules.

"You're very clean about your own house," I said. "Why do you make such a point of going out to dinner unshaven and wearing a stinking old tweed jacket when you've been asked to arrive in a tuxedo?"

"The point I'm making," he said, "is that if I choose to show up unshaven and stinking, it's nobody's goddamned business but mine, and nobody gets hurt but me."

"Working on the Bogart image?" I asked.

"How far can you swim, you jerk," he countered, "because it's sixty miles from here to Santa Monica!"

Bogie one day was reminiscing on how great a part luck had played in his early days at Warner Brothers; he reminded me yet again that he had played *The Petrified Forest* only because of Leslie Howard's determination and added that he had got *The Maltese Falcon* only because George Raft had turned it down and *High Sierra* had come his way because Paul Muni had huffily refused it on the grounds that it had first been offered to George Raft. "But that's the way the piss pot cracks," he said.

I couldn't resist it, as I had been husbanding the dangerous morsel for years. "Now I'll tell you how you got an Oscar for *The African Queen* in 1951," I said.

"Please do," said Bogie with chilling calm.

"Because Bette Davis turned it down!" I announced smuggly.

When the explosion died away, I told him more.

C. S. Forester wrote the story in 1935, and Warner Brothers bought it for Bette Davis. In 1938 their producer, Henry Blanke, borrowed me from Samuel Goldwyn to play the Cockney "river rat" opposite her. The deal was signed, and bemused by my glorious opportunity, I had spent four weeks polishing up a Cockney accent. I even grew a beard which made me look like a diseased yak, but at the last minute, Bette Davis fell out with Blanke and told him she refused to be photographed out of doors (a likely story), so the picture was canceled and the property sold to Twentieth Century-Fox, where twelve years later John Huston unearthed it.

When I finished, I waited for the Bogie bombshell. It never came. He put a consoling arm around my shoulders and said very thoughtfully, "Kid . . . I think you would have stunk up the screen in that part." It was a hundred to one that he was correct in his assessment, but he was sensitive enough to know that when it had happened, it must have been a crumpling disappointment not to get the chance to find out.

Bogie, above all, loathed the phonies and the pretentious. At one evening party I settled down happily when I discovered that he was sitting opposite me and beside him was an overdressed lady from Cincinnati whose money had restored the façades of both her husband, a bisexual Roman count, and his crumbling palazzo.

"Do you have servant problems in Hollywood, Mr. Bogart?" she asked.

Bogie helped himself to some bread and made a large gray ball of it; then he shrugged.

"It's *quite* impossible in Italy now," continued the lady from Cincinnati, missing these first ominous signs. "We used to have only English, then they became impossible, so we took on Germans, but they became difficult, too, so we had to fall back on Italians—nothing but trouble."

"Too bad," said Bogie, fixing her with the needling eye I knew so well. "Whaddya got now?"

"Greeks," she said. "Of course, they're peasants and have to be taught everything from the start. I never let them near the nursery."

Bogie flicked the gray bread ball with his thumb and watched it perform a graceful parabola in the direction of John Huston at another table.

"Who looks after the kids?" he asked.

"Oh, I have a wonderful Dutch girl, and the children just *adore* her. She never complains and doesn't mind at all eating her meals off a tray. Of course, I overpay her, but it's worth it because I feel secure when I go to Paris. . . ."

I waited expectantly. The pause was long.

"Does she fuck?" Bogie asked.

Bogie had a slight predilection for that particular Elizabethan word and enjoyed the shock waves it could produce when used to the greatest effect. He once spent an afternoon in 21 in New York, flanked by John McClain, Quentin Reynolds, and myself drinking stingers and poring over various telephone directories. We worked out that by forging the signature of the Con Edison Company and sending 438 telegrams to selected officeholders in Radio City requesting them, for testing purposes, to leave their lights blazing at the end of the day, we could emblazon the word in letters sixteen floors high.

Sitting long evenings below decks in *Santana*, I was constantly amazed at the simplicity of Bogie's character; he just could not be bothered to camouflage his weaknesses. Although right at the top of his profession, he also possessed the actor's Achilles' heel—he was jealous and showed it.

The actor he admired most was Spencer Tracy. They were highly professional performers, and both despised the "stars" who were not. Bogie wanted to make a picture, *The Desperate Hours,* and the "dream casting" was to play Spencer and Bogie in the two tailor-made roles. Both were longing to do it, and both wanted badly to play with the other. Again and again, they met and got all steamed up about the prospect, but each time it mysteriously collapsed, the reason being that the moment they parted they quickly contacted their respective managers—neither of them would take second billing. They never worked together.

If he was childish about billing, which is something the public is blissfully unconscious of, he was also overly quick to react to the threat of "new faces."

"Why the hell don't they lift some of the old ones? All those bastards at the studios are trying to do is find fifty-dollar-a-week Gables, Coopers, and Bogarts." And he was positively vituperative about the Method acting of the New York Group Theatre and the Actors Studio—the "scratch-your-ass-and-belch school" he called them and had the lowest opinion of Lee Strasberg, the group's founder. Actually Bogie and Tracy, the down-to-earth-no-frills actors par excellence, had been performing naturally for years in just the way the pupils of these schools were now learning to do. Bogie had no time for people who took their talent for granted or for actors who denigrated or downgraded their own profession; he admired the ones who worked hard to improve what they had been given.

Bogie took me, when I was in a nasty financial bind, to see his business manager, Morgan Maree. From then on, Maree picked up my earnings, paid my bills, and worked out my taxes, but like Bogie, I was put on a tiny weekly allowance and only permitted to sign for necessities—no bar bills or things of that ilk. Bogie and I spent hours trying to work out ways to cheat Morgan, but over the years he was too smart for us and saved our collective bacon.

I don't for a moment believe that Bogie had any premonition, but he became increasingly exercised over the fact that a successful actor's life is a series of short bursts of high taxation with no chance to spread the earnings over the lean years. "I've got to get some decent dough put away for Betty and the kid." He worked continuously toward that end, making pictures through his own company and finally selling the company with the rights to all his pictures for a very large sum.

When the sale was consummated, Morgan Maree called to say that the check had arrived. Bogie rushed over. "Can I borrow it for an hour or two?" he asked like a child. Then he took Betty to lunch at Romanoff's and made a grand tour going from table to table, waving the check like a banner.

Being married to Bogie even for someone with the understanding and intelligence of Betty could have been no smooth ride. For a start he was as set in his ways as a streetcar and had an utter disregard for personal comfort. Betty was soon champing at the bit to break out of his small gloomy canyon house with its disturbing memories. For a long time her pleas for more elbowroom fell on deaf ears—"you were raised in one room in the Bronx, for chrissake, and there's nothing wrong with *you*."

Finally, with the help of the trusty Morgan Maree, who touched a nerve by persuading him that it would be an excellent investment—"something to leave to Betty and the offspring"—he forked out a down payment on a beautiful tennis-courted and pooled house in the high-tax-bracket area of Holmby Hills. Bogie felt he was being conned into joining the Establishment, which he wholeheartedly despised, and *Santana* for a while rocked with resentment, but Betty smiled like a big cat and smoothed him down and became pregnant a second time, and he grew to be obsessively proud of his new acquisition. He never dressed the part of a Holmby Hills squire and forever slopped about the place attired in a grisly selection of antiquated moccasins, sweaters, windbreakers, and dungarees—usually with a battered yachting cap on his head; dogs and cats were everywhere.

Betty was the perfect mate for Bogie, and as they were both completely honest with each other and utterly straightforward in their approach to life, the friction points were few and far between. Occasionally there would be an almighty explosion, but it never lasted long, and with the air cleared, life went on more smoothly than ever. Betty gave as good as she got, but she also understood his love of his men friends, his need for male companionship, and she appreciated his longing for arguments, though she was never too happy when his extreme needling tactics were used to provoke them. She never was just a decoration in her husband's home, though Bogie loved her to be beautiful and admired her looks, her taste, and her talent. He was, above all, proud of the fact that he had a partner with whom he could share everything good or bad. He never looked at another woman.

He was a good father, I'm sure, though his idea of entertaining his children on a free day was odd—to take them to lunch at Romanoff's. The lack of discipline was something he felt could be put right later by Betty. The longest wince I ever witnessed was the one which contorted the face of the elegant Noel Coward when little Stevie was introduced to him and piped up, "Hi there, Mr. Dog-do-in-his-pants."

Bogie, like Flynn, was always greatly amused by the discomfiture of his friends, and on one Fourth of July trip aboard *Santana* was at his sardonic best. We sailed over to Catalina Island and dropped anchor in Cherry Cove. As a special concession on the big national holiday Betty and Hjördis were grudgingly invited, too. This cramped the sleeping quarters considerably and, for me at least, turned the occupancy of the single confined toilet, with its unreliable hand pump, into a hazard of insurmountable proportions. To circumnavigate this embarrassment, in the early morning, I told Pete that I was taking the dinghy as I wished to take a little stroll. Silhouetted on the top of the barren hills of the Wrigley Ranch which surrounded the bay, I had spied the top of a large clump of bushes; donning a pair of red sailcloth slacks and a white cotton shirt, I rowed ashore and toiled up a precipitous goat track toward my objective. It was a long, hard, hot climb, and even at that hour I soon took off my shirt and rested awhile enjoying the sight below of fifty or sixty yachts floating lazily on the glassy slate-blue early-morning calm of the bay. On some of them people were already stirring, stretching and yawning and swabbing vaguely at decks; the boat noises took a long beat to reach up to me.

On arrival at the summit and just out of sight of the fleet below, I entered the clump of bushes.

I was making some preliminary adjustment to my red slacks when I had a nasty feeling that I was not alone. Five yards from me and regarding me with undisguised hostility was a monolithic Brahma bull—the sort of animal that drives rodeo riders into early retirement. Red slacks at half-mast, I hobbled a hasty retreat from the clump.

The bull followed. On the crest of the hill I stood facing it; it faced me. We both stood perfectly still. Then it lowered its head and pawed the ground, but I was so frightened that quite apart from the sack race impediment of my lower garments, I was unable to move. This then was the tableau, in perfect silhouette on the skyline, which the owner of *Santana* perceived when he rolled back the hatch and took his first tentative breath of fresh air.

Bogie took in the juicy situation at a glance and alerted Betty and Hjördis. Then he reached for his loud-hailer and addressed the awakening fleet.

"Now hear this . . . hear this . . . *Santana* calling all yachts. . . . Happy Fourth of July, folks! . . . This is the day we celebrate ridding ourselves of the British. . . . Just take a look up the hill, ladies and gentlemen . . . This production comes to you by courtesy of your friendly neighborhood Yankee."

Then the noise started—a cacophony of sound as loud-hailers opened up from all over the fleet, "Olé! Olé!" and many crude suggestions to do with my red slacks. By a miracle the bull instead of being maddened by the bedlam below became momentarily distracted; it stopped pawing the ground and looked uneasily toward the source of the interruption. When it turned its head once more toward me, the contact was broken. The bull made a noise, a snort of pure disgust, the sort of sound that daily help make when they give notice; then very slowly it turned away and lumbered off along the skyline. This elicited a veritable thunderclap of enthusiasm from below, cheers and bravos for me, catcalls and whistles for the bull. I hauled up and secured my red slacks (more applause and more tasteless instructions); then, idiotically, I decided to make a gesture of defiance toward the tail end of my departing antagonist. I flapped life into the white shirt which had remained clasped in my trembling hands and, for the benefit of my noisy aficionados, executed a few passes.

The crowd was delighted by my farols and largas and roared its approval of my series of veronicas.

Success went to my head. I turned my back on the bull to demonstrate the insulting pase de pecho. A roar of warning from the loud-hailers told me that the bull had got the message. He turned in a flash, and the earth shook under his charge. There was nothing for it—I flung away the offending shirt and went down that hillside the shortest way . . . straight—jumping, bumping, cartwheeling, and ricocheting. I don't know why I didn't kill myself, and Bogie spent most of his Independence Day happily pulling cactus spines out of the behind of a redcoat.

John Huston was always a joy to Bogart, probably his favorite companion and certainly his favorite director. Bogie could never measure up intellectually, but Huston stretched him to the utmost, and some classic discussions developed.

Director Huston got the most out of Bogie as an actor, and if they worked perfectly as a team and together turned out some classics—*The Maltese Falcon, The Treasure of Sierra Madre, The African Queen,* and *Beat the Devil* among others—the leg pulling was also mutually satisfactory. Huston was waiting to hear news about his induction into Special Services with the Army during World War II. The word came by phone when he was in the middle of directing Bogie in a small building. His escape had been carefully rehearsed— whom he shot, whom he knifed, and through which window he would jump, et cetera.

Huston never said a word about the receipt of his call-up, he just tripled the number of Japanese around the building, boarded it up with the hero inside, and left for Europe. A hastily summoned takeover director found a note on the door: "I'm in the Army—Bogie will know how to get out."

Occasionally, when in England, I had been invited by His Grace, the Duke of Marlborough to shoot birds at Blenheim Palace in Oxfordshire. I was not a very good shot; the duke was one of the best in the country. It was, therefore, with some surprise when walking up partridge across frosty stubble fields that I noticed the duke preparing to dispatch a high-flying pigeon which was heading for the line of guns. I was surprised because to everyone present, it was perfectly obvious that our host was taking aim not at a wood pigeon, but mistakenly at a carrier pigeon, hot winging it to its waiting owner somewhere in the industrial north. To general embarrassment the bird thumped to earth at the duke's feet. In the ensuing silence, I could not resist shouting down the line a vintage pigeon joke: "Are there any letters for me?"

I was not asked to shoot at Blenheim again, and indeed, two or three years passed before I set eyes on the Duke of Marlborough.

In London, Hjördis and I were having a midsummer dinner at Les Ambassadeurs with Betty and Bogie and John Huston. In mid-fun, I perceived that the immensely tall pink-faced duke had materialized beside me. Always fascinated by films and film people, he now made it obvious that he wished to meet my famous companions.

Hjördis he already knew, so I introduced him to the others. That done and a few pleasantries exchanged, he sought for a gracious exit line and said, "Well, David, when are you coming to shoot a pheasant with me?"

"Any time," I said blithely, "just give me a date and I'll be there."

"Ah, well . . . How about the, er, last week in January?"

"Splendid," I said, "thank you so much."

The duke rejoined his female companion at a nearby table; Bogie followed him with his eyes and then leaned toward me, the big needle poised.

"Hey, get a load of you! . . .Hobnobbing with the aristocracy! . . . Shooting goddamn pheasant with a Dook for chrissake . . . a lousy ham actor wearing a deerstalker!"

Huston was at that time enjoying full country squire status in the Irish bogs, so he put things in their correct perspective.

"It's not really much of a compliment, Bogie, being asked to shoot during the last week in January. The season is over by then, and a few bad shots are invited, the local butcher and people like that. They go round the outlying hedgerows and kill off the old birds—cocks only."

Bogie mulled this over and glanced somberly across at the duke's table. "Cocks only, eh?" he muttered.

The evening at our table resumed the course on which it had been set, and wine, arguments, and mock abuse flowed in an endless stream.

Finally, the duke and his guest rose to leave. His departure happened to coincide with some remark of Bogie's which amused Huston greatly. He threw his head back and roared with laughter. Unfortunately, he threw his head so far back that his chair overbalanced and he landed with a crash at His Grace's feet.

Huston caught sight of the ducal disapproval etched on the pink face far above him, and his laughter redoubled.

Marlborough stepped haughtily over the helpless body and said, loudly, to me, "I don't think much of your Hollywood friends. . . ."

People nearby heard his calculated rudeness, and there was a hush. Bogie was out of his chair like a terrier. He only came up to the duke's navel, so instead of grabbing him by the lapels and lifting him off his feet in approved movie tough-guy style, he grabbed the slack of his trousers somewhere around the top fly button; then he lifted, hard. The duke found himself teetering on tiptoes, his face congested with acute discomfort, and he started to splutter.

"Now get this, Dook," snarled Bogie in his most menacing style, "get this and get it straight! You quit insulting my pal with your goddam . . . COCKS ONLY!"

When Bogie released his hold, John Albert Edward William Spencer-Churchill, tenth Duke of Marlborough, Baron Spencer, Earl of Sunderland, Baron Churchill, Earl of Marlborough, Marquess of Blandford, Prince of the Holy Roman Empire, Prince of Mindelheim in Swabia, returned to terra firma and shook his ruffled feathers.

His companion plucked at his sleeve. "Come along, Bert," she said.

I don't remember when I first noticed Bogie's cough, probably sharing sleeping quarters with him aboard *Santana*. I expect I thought it was just a smoker's cough because he used up a great number of cigarettes—"coffin nails" he called them. But the cough slowly got worse, and Betty prevailed on him to see a doctor. The doctor made some tests and then called Bogie in to tell him the news—it was as bad as a man could hear.

There followed an eight-hour operation, and the slow slide began. "I've got it licked if I can put on some weight," he said. But as the weeks went by, he lost weight steadily. His eyes became enormous in his pitifully gaunt face, but his courage shone out of them.

At the funeral service on January 17, 1957, his friends were determined that his departure should be dignified and purged of all Hollywood gloss and bad taste, and we unceremoniously bundled outside into the sunshine several newsmen who had attempted to enter the church with concealed cameras.

John Huston was always the closest to Bogie, so it was right and fitting that he should write and speak a few words of farewell at the service. No one could have done it better, and he has most graciously given me permission to remember some of them here.

"Bogie's hospitality went far beyond food and drink. He fed a guest's spirit as well as his body, plied him with goodwill until he became drunk in the heart as well as in the legs.

"This tradition of wonderful hospitality continued on to

the last hour he was able to sit upright. Let me tell you at what effort it was extended through the last days. He would lie on his couch upstairs at five o'clock, when he would be shaved and groomed in gray flannels and scarlet smoking jacket. Then, as he was no longer able to walk, his emaciated body would be lifted into a wheelchair and pushed to a dumbwaiter on the second-floor landing. The top of the dumbwaiter had been removed to give him headroom. His nurses would help him in, and sitting on a little stool, he would be lowered down to the kitchen, where another transfer would be made, and again by wheelchair he'd be transported through the house into the library and his chair. And there he would be, sherry glass in one hand and cigarette in the other at five thirty when the guests would start to arrive. They were limited now to those who had known him best and longest, and they stayed, two and three at a time, for a half hour or so until about eight o'clock, which was the time for him to go back upstairs by the same route he had descended.

"No one who sat in his presence during the final weeks would ever forget. It was a unique display of sheer animal courage. After the first visit—it took that to get over the initial shock of his appearance—one quickened to the grandeur of it, expanded, and felt strangely elated, proud to be there, proud to be his friend, the friend of such a brave man. . . ."

13
The Pleasure of Your Company

CHRISTMAS parties! New Year's parties! Birthday parties! Parties to celebrate the end of a picture or a marriage, the signing of a contract, or the birth of a baby! There was always an excuse for a party in Hollywood. And at the end of a strenuous six-day week Saturday night was dedicated to letting off steam. The needle measuring Hollywood parties swung between orderliness and orgies.

Income tax was low, salaries were high, and if a few of those entertained could be deemed helpful to the career, the cost of the binge could be deducted from taxes, provided the presence of the helpful guests could be proved.

A good plan was to have the arriving guests sign the Visitors Book (it was risky to leave it till they departed at 4 A.M.), and an essential was to invite a few press photographers to record on film the presence of the "useful" ones. Hollywood, conscious always of its public image, indulged in a token purity at the beginning of most parties, and while the photographers were snapping away, glasses and bottles were kept out of sight and husbands, wives, and established "couples" sat close and smiled fondly at each other. Once the press had departed freedom of movement, speech, and behavior was restored, and the opportunity for all hell to break loose was welcomed with open arms and lifted elbows.

Parties, of course, varied enormously in size and content, from a super bash for 2,000 in costume at Marion Davies'

259

beach house to half a dozen eating Mexican food prepared by Aldous Huxley in his tiny stucco pad on the wrong side of the Beverly Hills tracks.

Some of the biggest party givers held annual events: Marion Davies to celebrate the birthday of her boyfriend W. R. Hearst, Sonja Henie to celebrate her departure on her spring trip to Norway, Joseph Cotten, who gave an all-day party each Fourth of July, and wealthy oilman Tex Feldman, who loved to illustrate the fact that every year Hollywood was full of sensationally beautiful girls.

The big black-tie parties for 200 or 300 usually followed the same pattern: Men in white coats parked the cars, the food and drink was catered by Romanoff's or Dave Chasen, the swimming pools were boarded over to make dance floors, and green and white striped marquees were erected in the gardens. In the early mornings, fights and scandals were frequent.

Basil Rathbone and his Russian wife, Ouida, were inveterate middle-sized party givers, and several times a year this kindly man, the highest-paid free-lance actor in the world, who specialized in playing mean, hiss-provoking villains, provided extravaganzas into which went a great deal of inventive thought.

He badly misjudged the climate one Christmastide, however, when he covered his lawn and driveway with 300 tons of snow trucked down at high speed and great expense from Big Bear, and we splashed and skidded through brown slush when torrential warm Southern California rain took care of the arrangements. The city of Beverly Hills sent Basil a ferocious bill for cleaning up the mess.

Many parties were given with full press coverage to publicize the emergence of a finished film, the theme of the production being worked into the decor.

The first night Deborah Kerr spent in Hollywood, I took her to one such affair being given by producer Nunnally Johnson. We arrived early and found lying outside his front door half a dozen sour-faced topless blondes with everything below their hipbones squeezed into shiny green fishtails.

"We're waiting to be carried in and propped up at the bar," they told us. Nunnally was launching his picture *Mr. Peabody and the Mermaid.*

Small parties, as usual, were the most satisfying, and many people were experts at giving them. They ranged from beach parties and full-moon searches for the mad grunion fish, which came in on one big wave, laid its eggs hurriedly in the sand, and departed on the next, to ranch parties in the San Fernando Valley—Western style. These were very popular, and Darryl Zanuck allowed us to ride his polo ponies through the darkened countryside after dinner.

Mike Todd, always flamboyant, had steaks flown out from Kansas City on his private plane for a party of six and proudly displayed them to Elizabeth Taylor, Eddie Fisher, Debbie Reynolds, Hjördis, and myself. He was going to cook them a new way, he announced, and at his barbecue pit on a hillside he left them surrounded by sauces, oil, and brushes; then he took us into the house to wait till his charcoal fire was perfect. A fox ate the steaks and Todd sent out for Chinese food.

Many, many houses had projection rooms, and a normal evening was twenty or thirty people for dinner and a preview of one of the latest films, but the wiser producers refused to expose their pictures on the highly critical and often destructive "Bel Air Circuit." David Selznick, when he married Jennifer Jones, moved into John Gilbert's old mountainside mansion and transformed it. The parties there were my favorite in the fifties—very relaxed and always an intriguing mixture of Hollywood and the big world outside. Bill and Edie Goetz too provided much fun for their friends among their staggering collection of Impressionists, and it was intriguing to see the works of Renoir, Picasso, and Toulouse-Lautrec wafted upward at the touch of a button to make way for the unrolling screen and the twin projectors moving into firing position through the gaps left on the wall.

The Goetz family lived in a splendid residence on the same street as Sonja Henie. It was a short walk to Sonja's annual party, but Bill wanted to drive his new Rolls-Royce. He drank too much, which was very unusual for him, and Edie issued the driving instructions for getting home.

"Just stick right on the curb," she ordered, "keep in low gear, and don't go more than five miles an hour."

Bill followed her suggestions to the letter, glued himself to the curb, and motored slowly into the back of a parked police car.

Speech-making was a grisly Hollywood habit, and in some houses one risked being called upon to say a few words after dinner.

Jack Warner was a popular, if high-risk, speaker, and at a dinner for Madame Chiang Kai-shek brought on a deathly hush by concluding, "So, folks, if you have any laundry, you know where to take it!"

Some comedians never let up even at parties. Sitting at a table with Red Skelton, I alerted him to the fact that a caterpillar was roaming around in his salad.

"HMMM . . . NICE," said Red, and ate it.

Streaking is an old sport. Carole Landis did it to great effect in the early evenings, but people swimming naked in a floodlit pool toward dawn merely drew attention to the lateness of the hour.

Smoking plants, other than tobacco, was not widely practiced, but parties were conducted in a sweet sickly haze in remote glens off Laurel Canyon, and in dim nightclubs, where jam sessions went on all night, joints glowed brightly in every corner. Cole Porter gave intimate dinners of great taste with masterpieces presented by his French chef washed down by wines to match, and after dinner, when he and George Gershwin and Irving Berlin tried out on each other their latest compositions for the great new musicals, we lucky guests were at jam sessions of the gods.

At one party champagne flowed out of a statue's nipples, and when a nude party was being held in a beach house, two guests slipped out and came back dressed as cops. A well-known character actor broke a leg when he jumped out a window.

Charlie and Ann Lederer gave a party for the Shah of Iran. When the incumbent of the Peacock Throne complimented Lauren Bacall by saying, "You were born to dance, Miss Bacall," she replied with gusto, "You bet your ass, Shah."

A white horse was the guest of honor at an indoor party with disagreeable results for the carpets, and when Premier Nikita Khrushchev of the USSR was guest of honor at luncheon in the commissary at Twentieth Century-Fox, this event, too, left a bad odor.

With the exception of Madame Khrushchev and her daughter, it was strictly a "men only" affair. About 300 of us were bidden to attend, and Frank Sinatra and I were detailed to sit with the two ladies and jolly them along with the help of an interpreter. This proved to be no chore. Madame Khrushchev was a sweet-faced motherly lady with an almost totally square frame encased in a black tent. Her grayish hair was pulled straight back into a bun; she smiled benignly at one and all and, within a minute of being seated, delved into a voluminous black handbag and passed to me across the table photographs of her grandchildren.

Her daughter was a quiet, thirtyish, large-nosed blonde, and both she and her fleshy husband, the editor of *Izvestia,* were equally affable. I asked Madame Khrushchev what they were planning to do after luncheon, and she looked very crestfallen.

"We were so much looking forward to visiting Disneyland," she said, "but the police have told us they cannot be responsible for our safety."

I passed this information on to Frank, who reacted in typical fashion. "Screw the cops," he said. "Tell the old broad you and I'll take 'em down there, this afternoon—we'll look after 'em."

I tactfully rephrased and then, via the interpreter, relayed this suggestion to Madame Khrushchev, whose face lit up at the idea.

She delved into her huge bag and scribbled a note to her husband, which was dispatched to the speakers' table. Khrushchev reacted angrily and signaled *nyet* to her with much wagging of a forefinger. When Spyros Skouras, the president of Twentieth Century-Fox, rose to make his address of greeting, he chose, with elephantine bad taste, to describe how he, too, had risen from being a workingman to become the head of a great enterprise and sought to draw a parallel between his rise and that of the guest of honor, who had gone from coal miner to become the most important man in the USSR.

When Khrushchev's turn came, he stood, obviously flushed with anger, and proceeded to rend the wretched Skouras. He also poured scorn on the perfunctory airport

welcome he had received that morning from Mayor Norris
Paulson of Los Angeles and ended by acidly observing that it
must be a sad state of affairs if living in Mayor Paulson's city
was so dangerous that Madame Khrushchev and his daughter would not be safe in a children's playground.

After this ill-fated and well-televised meal, a further risk
was taken by Twentieth Century-Fox. The publicity department, scenting a big break for their forthcoming picture
Can-Can, herded the visitors across to a sound stage where
Shirley MacLaine and a large troupe of carefully rehearsed
dancers were "just by chance" about to shoot a take of the famous dance by the same name.

The Khrushchev party were seated in a specially built box
and looked down with undisguised horror as Shirley and
Company, complete with garter belts and black fishnet stockings, kicked their legs, swirled their petticoats, waggled their
knees, and ended up with their skirts over their heads and
their bottoms pointing directly at the guest of honor and his
family.

As the publicity department gathered around for Khrushchev's eagerly awaited quote, he gave it to them in one
word: "DISGUSTING!"

There was a band of butlers headed by Marcel and Theodore who catered and served small parties. With their wives
or other female helpers they arrived during the afternoon
and took over, bringing with them hors d'oeuvres, bottles,
and food. They commandeered the kitchen and the bar. The
only information they required was the number of guests,
what liquor to serve, and whether to push it early on to get
the party going or to hold back and let nature take its course.

They knew all the guests, their preferences and dislikes,
and a great deal too much about their private lives, but they
were impeccable servitors and for a large sum relieved hosts
and hostesses of all worry. Nothing ruffled their calm.

Theodore, at the home of Frank Ross and Joan Caulfield,
demonstrated this when he was offering me a platter of
goodies during the cocktail hour around their pool. He
bowed and stepped back into eight feet of water. Somehow
he managed to keep his hold on the tray and, ignoring the
encouraging cries of the common herd, swam with it before

him to the shallow end, climbed the steps, and without any change of expression stalked majestically toward the kitchen. Later that night from inside a dinner jacket belonging to our host, he watched enigmatically while guests, in various stages of undress, ate little sausages, deviled eggs, and small squares of cheese off the bottom of the deep end.

Several rich neighbors from Santa Barbara and Pasadena gave parties because they enjoyed rubbing shoulders with "movie folk," and the "movie folk" went along because they enjoyed parties.

Dorothy Earel, a dark-eyed socialite beauty, invited us to come to the downstairs room of the Vendome Restaurant dressed as children. On arrival we were announced and discovered that we had to make our entrance down a canvas fire chute, but altercations broke out when it became apparent that at the bottom of the chute the Pasadena Polo fraternity was making book on which girls would not be wearing panties.

Errol Flynn once utilized a favorite Hollywood ploy on a pompous Washington diplomat who was pestering him for an invitation to a "real" Hollywood party. The man arrived at the appointed hour and was delighted when a gorgeous maid wearing nothing but shoes, stockings, and a little white cap opened the door.

"The undressing room is here, sir," she said, indicating a room full of discarded clothing.

"When you are ready, sir, I'll take you in to the party." She smiled seductively.

The man soon appeared naked, his eyes shining with excitement.

"I hope you'll have some fun, sir," said the maid. "Follow me, please."

He did, appreciating the sway of her hips and her twinkling behind.

She stopped at a door. The sound of revelry came from within. She asked his name, opened the door, and announced it. The diplomat charged in like a bull at a corrida.

Thirty people in full evening dress looked at him disapprovingly.

When Jimmy Stewart was getting married, about twenty of

us gave him a bachelor party in a private room at Chasen's. It followed predictable Hollywood lines with the usual jokes, speeches, and gags, including a huge covered dish which was put before the bridegroom-to-be; inside was a midget dressed as a baby.

I sat next to Spencer Tracy that night, and he gave me a jarring insight into his great personal problem.

"What is this?" he asked me, pointing to the dessert.

"It looks like a trifle," I answered.

He sniffed at a spoonful like a bird dog. "There's something in it," he said. "What is it?"

I, too, sniffed. "A touch of rum—I think," I said.

Spence pushed his plate away. "Jesus!" he said. "That's all I need—one mouthful of that, and I'd be gone for a week."

When I looked disbelieving, he elaborated. "I'm not kidding. I have to fight it all the time, I'm a real alcoholic, and just that little bit would start me off."

If parties were given to launch new films, they were also occasionally given to launch new faces.

When Sophia Loren first thrust herself, chest first, into the limelight, *le tout* Hollywood was invited to meet her by the producer of her first Hollywood picture, and an elaborate dinner was given. The photographers outnumbered the guests, but Sophia was delighted and, in a very low dress, gave them everything she had. Convinced that she was the possessor of a bad profile, Sophia, when making a film, liked to choose a spot about three inches to the right of the camera and play all her scenes to that spot, irrespective of where the other actors were standing, so facing a battery of still cameras on her introduction night, Sophia's highly professional eyes soon found a suitable spot which would ensure her best angle, and she directed her smiles accordingly. The popping bulbs reached a sudden crescendo, but Sophia did not realize till too late that she was being "outboobed." Bending low over her right shoulder, with the most famous orbs in the world gleaming in all their creamy glory, was Miss United Dairies herself—Jayne Mansfield.

An eccentric and lonely little old millionaire named Atwater Kent gave sumptuous parties at his statue-encrusted estate above Beverly Hills, Capo di Monte. No expense was spared, and a good time was had by all, but many people never set eyes on their host because he usually took refuge in a huge leather wing chair in a remote library and stayed there all night.

A majority of the guests never discovered why they had been invited, but they swallowed their curiosity and the Moët et Chandon and attacked the beluga with reckless abandon.

If occasionally the better-mannered would go to the remote library to seek out Atwater Kent and thank him, he was almost pathetically touched, smiled a wispy little smile, and marked them down in his heart as "friends." When he departed this earth, he left bequests to seventy-three "friends" and enjoined them to use the money "for happiness," something, perhaps, he had always been short of.

Two mature ladies from New York became the superhostesses of Hollywood: Lady Mendl and the Contessa di Frasso. They had nothing in common except New York beginnings, an urge to live in California, and a love of the questionable excitement generated by people in the film world.

Lady Mendl was born Elsie De Wolf, and after blossoming into a near nonentity on the New York stage, she became internationally renowned as an interior decorator, salvaging Louis XV's tumbledown Villa Trianon in Versailles from complete disintegration and making it a gem of beauty and converting two rat-infested East River slums into New York's most desirable quartiers—Sutton Place and Beekman Place.

At the age of seventy she descended full of vim and vigor upon Hollywood. With her nice elderly ex-diplomat husband, Sir Charles, she bought a really horrible little Spanish-style monstrosity in Beverly Hills and transformed it, by using a lot of trelliswork, mirrors, eighteenth-century French furniture, and clever lighting, into a mini-monument to good taste in the middle of the surrounding "Cape Cod style," "adobe style," "ranch style," and "Ye Olde Englishe style."

Her tight white curls she colored according to her moods, pale green, pink, or mauve; she wore gloves a lot and stood on her head in a corner after dinner. Her little house was Mecca for the young and unsophisticated, and she seemed, while fostering our romances and ambitions, to draw a curious strength from us. In spite of the daunting sight of the good furniture, we were encouraged to lounge around on comfortable chintzy sofas upon which were mounds of silk cushions with embroidered advice: "Never complain. Never explain."

Elsie Mendl's parties were small, the food was simple and beautifully cooked, and she loved to produce on each occasion somebody "new," a "new" face, a "new" talent, or a couple in the throes of a "new" romance.

She one day invited a group to meet the artist Ludwig Bemelmans, lately arrived from Paris. For the occasion she decided to offer a buffet-style dinner, and the young and unsophisticated duly faced a long white-clothed table upon which reposed a great array of chafing dishes filled with chicken à la king, goulash, vegetables, and fruit salad, surrounded by bottles of wine.

The buffet opened for business at nine o'clock, but there was as yet no sign of the guest of honor. By ten Elsie Mendl was visibly disappointed, and coffee was being taken in a general mood of anticlimax.

At last Bemelmans walked in, looking very small and round and bright pink. He was obviously splendidly drunk. "This," he said, pointing to a large, equally well-oiled individual behind him, "is Hank."

Hank was wearing a raincoat and a black hat. He lifted this hat to the astonished company.

"I have only one *great* parlor trick," he announced, "and that is my ability to remove a tablecloth from a table *without* disturbing the crockery."

With that, Hank took hold of a corner of the cloth and very slowly, like a fisherman on the Volga pulling in a net, and humming the while "Yo-ho heave-ho!" he yanked it toward him. Crashing down inexorably went the chafing dishes, the bottles, and the coffee cups; the amazed guests, ankle-deep in chicken à la king and fruit salad, watched fascinated as Hank lifted his black hat once more, put a fatherly arm around Bemelmans' shoulder, and departed saying, "Come, Bemie, we must away to pastures new."

Dorothy di Frasso was born in New York, and Hollywood legend had it that her father, Bertrand Taylor, onetime president of the New York Stock Exchange, had left her $12,000,000; in any event Dorothy was one of the early swingers. She first married Claude Graham White, the British adventurer who owned the first gasoline-driven motorcar in England and possessed the first British pilot's license; then she married good-looking, impecunious Count Carlo di Frasso, brought back to life his crumbling Villa Modama in Rome, and became an intimate of both Mussolini and Count Ciano.

When Dorothy descended on Hollywood, she did so without her husband and moved into a large Beverly Hills estate off Coldwater Canyon, filled it with Italian servants, and entertained nonstop. Luncheon parties melded into tennis and swimming parties, and the afternoon parties went on till the early hours of the morning.

Dorothy resented with a passion the passing of the years and, like Elsie Mendl, down the road, felt that the presence of the young and beautiful around her might help to keep at bay that threatening old gentleman with his hourglass and scythe.

She was a truly generous person and loved nothing more than to give pleasure and provide fun for those less well fixed financially than she. Cary Grant became a great friend, and she and Marlene Dietrich were inseparable. When Marlene in the mid-thirties made her historic appearance in a man's suit, thus liberating women and giving them the necessary lead to take to slacks, Dorothy egged her on to make her "outrageous" move.

Dorothy loved gossip and sometimes went to odd lengths to obtain it: At one of her parties she placed chairs and mattresses in pairs in secluded spots all over the garden and had them bugged—the result was scheduled to be played back at luncheon the next day to, she hoped, our great embarrassment. Luckily, Ann Sheridan found a bug in her mattress and rushed all over the garden alerting recumbent shapes. When Dorothy played the results the next morning, she heard nothing but salacious gossip about herself.

Gossip about Dorothy was never difficult to come by because she was nothing if not direct in her approach when she saw something she fancied.

On Friday nights she went regularly to the Hollywood Legion Arena to occupy her ringside seat at the fights. Lupe Velez, another extrovert, sat nearby, and the two ladies enjoyed competing for the limelight. Lupe, being Mexican, made all Mexican fighters her protégés, and if one lost, she would storm into the ring, flashing tantalizing expanses of thigh and buttock as she climbed the ropes and physically attacked the referee.

One night Dorothy noticed a handsome young Italian prizefighter named Enzo Fiermonte and decided that she too could be a racist. Throughout the bout she screamed advice and encouragement at the young man in his mother tongue while Lupe was shrieking at his opponent in Spanish. The Italian won, and Dorothy was out of her seat and into the ring before Lupe could move. A commanding figure with her blue eyes and sapphires to match, brilliant under the arc lights, she stood congratulating both Fiermonte and the referee.

Dorothy's relationship with the fighter was not a long one. She announced first that she was going to adopt him and later that she was about to marry him, but strangely weakened at his next appearance in the ring, he was knocked cold in the first round, and she never saw him again.

Early in her Hollywood days she met a gangling young actor from Montana and decided, though he was several years her junior, that she would dedicate a great deal of her time to polishing this rough diamond and turning him into a sophisticated man of the world. Gary Cooper resisted the polishing and remained his own man, but he enjoyed greatly his long liaison with the effervescent Dorothy, particularly African safaris and trips to the capitals of Europe. Well-publicized voyages these were, because Dorothy was not renowned for avoiding the attentions of the press, and they prompted Bill Goetz to remark, "The best way to cross the Atlantic is on the *Countess di Frasso.*"

One of Dorothy's maritime adventures made headlines. She had accumulated a young male companion from a most unexpected quarter. He was extremely good-looking in a dark, swarthy way and a very natty dresser. His name was Charles Siegal.

"Bugsie" Siegal was a gangster fairly high up in the California underground hierarchy, who had hitherto indulged his appetite for young blond actresses. This sudden switch to the titled hostess was an electrifying titillation for Hollywood, and much to Dorothy's delight it received generous coverage in the newspapers.

She stoked up the fires of local imagination by setting off on a four-month sea voyage with Bugsie, Jean Harlow's stepfather, Marino Bello, and his girlfriend.

The trip ended in charges of piracy and mutiny and suits for assault. There were whispers of the discovery of buried treasure in the Cocos Islands and the delivery of an illicit cargo to Louis "Lepke" Buchalter, another gangster currently on the lam, who was later strapped to the electric chair in Sing Sing.

Dorothy appeared before a federal grand jury and fended off all questions with wide-eyed innocence. Asked if she did not find it peculiar that she had been in the company of a well-known gangster, she said stoutly, "On the contrary, I was in the company of a *good friend,* and anyway, Mrs. Bello was there to chaperon me."

(What Dorothy did not mention was that Mr. Bello had married his girlfriend on the last day of the trip.)

Bugsie did not get off lightly. Not long afterward a man with a tommy gun walked up to a house in Beverly Hills, drew a bead on him through the window as he sat on a sofa in his living room, and squeezed off a long burst.

There was no malice in Dorothy. She was generous to a fault, and she was one of the first to "do her own thing." She died wrapped in a mink coat aboard a train between Las Vegas and New York. She left her entire fortune to her housekeeper and afforded Hollywood one last titillation and speculation—the fortune amounted to less than $40,000.

There was a very unattractive kind of snobbery about Hollywood's social life—the snobbery of success.

The guest lists to the highly publicized big parties reeked of it. The successful and the established were invited; the struggling and the passé were not. I was never invited when I was an extra, and later when I was invited, I don't remember seeing any extras as fellow guests.

This nasty differentiation percolated down to those invited

to most of the children's parties, unhealthy competitions to see who could provide the most exotic and novel entertainment for the pampered little creatures.

The kids were showered with expensive gifts and the latest in miniature fairgrounds and sideshows, ponies and motorbikes to ride, clowns to laugh at, orchestras to dance to, and a proliferation of conjurers, magicians, and illusionists to watch. Without doubt, the children would have been far happier turned loose in blue jeans and inventing their own games, but some were sent off to their parents' studios to be waved, ringleted, and made up, and all arrived impeccably dressed and surly, ready to face the inevitable photographers. Professional parents, who used their children for their own publicity, were among the sadder sights in Hollywood, because the kids sensed it and did not always forgive, and the list of bad parent-child relationships in Hollywood was long.

One Christmas I gave a party for my two small sons, and Tyrone Power offered to play Santa Claus. Ty was everybody's favorite person, and all agreed that he was that great rarity—a man who was just as nice as he seemed to be. With his flashing good looks, graceful carriage, and easy laughter, it was no surprise that he was a Pied Piper to women—they followed him in droves wherever he went—but Ty was a simple person, with a great down-to-earthness and modesty about himself. He lived a few blocks from me, and I went over to help him dress and brief him on the impending operation.

He was extremely nervous.

"This is worse than a first night on Broadway," he said, helping himself liberally to the scotch bottle. "I've never performed for a bunch of kids before."

I pushed and pulled him into the padded stomach, bulky red outfit, and high black boots rented from Western Costume Company and helped him fasten on a black belt, a huge white beard, and little red cap.

"Don't worry about it," I said. "It's all fixed. I've left the gate open at the bottom of the garden. I've rigged up some sleigh bells down there and stashed away the presents, and at exactly six o'clock we'll give 'em the bells; then you pick up the sack and make it up the lawn to the house—they're all expecting you."

"Oh, God!" Ty groaned. "Why the hell did I suggest this? Hand me that bottle."

Another hefty swig passed through the cotton wool beard.

"Whose kids are they, anyway?" he asked.

"Two of mine, Maria Cooper, Roz Russell's kid, the Fairbanks' and Deborah's, Loretta's and Jerry Lewis', Michael Boyer, and Edgar Bergen's little girl Candy, about fifty all together. You'll know a lot of them; the rest are neighbors."

"Fifty!" yelled Ty. "Hand me that bottle."

"Don't worry," I said. "I've written all the names clearly on each present. Just read 'em out, ad-lib a little, and don't forget to go HO! HO! HO!"

"Jesus!" said Ty. "Let's go. . . . I can't stand all this waiting around."

One last nip, and we were off: we took the bottle along.

During the five-minute drive to my house Ty begged me to let him off the hook. "Why don't *you* do it?" he asked. "It's your party."

"You suggested it," I said firmly.

By six o'clock Santa Claus was loaded in every sense of the word and, sack on shoulder, was hidden in some bushes at the bottom of my garden.

I tugged the string and pealed the sleigh bells.

Immediately excited cries broke out from the house, and little heads appeared at every window.

"Off you go," I said to my quivering companion. "Lots of luck!"

"Son of a *bitch!*" hissed Father Christmas, and he lurched off up the lawn.

When his shadowy form was spotted by the excited children, shrill shrieks and applause broke out. At that point I had intended to turn on the garden lights to illuminate the scene, but for some reason I missed the switch and turned on the sprinklers. With a crack like a pistol shot, geysers of spray shot out of the grass all around him, and Ty fell down. I readjusted the situation; Ty picked himself up, gave me a marked look, and squelched on toward the shining, expectant faces in the windows.

Like all actors, once the curtain was up and the adrenaline had started pumping, Ty was relaxed and happy in his work. "HO! HO! HO!" he boomed. "And *who* is this lovely woolly lamb for, eh?"—fumbling at the card—"Aha! I remember now. Candice Bergen. . . . Come here, little girl . . . HO! HO! HO!"

He was doing beautifully by the time I had sneaked in by the back door, seated in a big chair in the hall with excited children climbing all over him.

"And who is *this* gentleman?" he asked my eldest son, indicating me.

"That's my daddy," the little boy piped up.

"Well, now, I wonder if your daddy could spare old Santa a glass of lemonade. I've come a *long* way tonight."

A sizable bolt of scotch disappeared into the white foliage, and Ty became too sure of himself.

"Maria Cooper! *My,* what a pretty girl! HO! HO! HO! You tell your daddy that old Santa thought he was just dandy in *High Noon* . . . and ask him for Grace Kelly's phone number while you're about it. . . . HO! HO! HO!"

Maria Cooper was a little more sophisticated than the other children. "Where did you see the picture, Santa?" she asked sweetly.

"Oh," said Ty, pointing vaguely above him, "up there!"

After a while Santa made his good-byes and staggered off down the lawn. Some of the children cried when he left; one complained about his breath.

Back at the bottom of the garden, I helped him out of his outfit. He was as excited as if he had just given a triumphant Broadway performance of King Lear. "I really enjoyed that!" he said. "Weren't the kids a *great* audience!"

Up at the house he mingled unnoticed with arriving parents and was beside me when my youngest son emerged from a bedroom flushed with embarrassment.

"Daddy, Daddy! Guess *what* ? That Candy Bergen has been trying to *kiss* me."

Some Hollywood children *never* knew when they were well off.

14
The Ace

*E*UROPEANS, particularly the British, have a loathsome habit of arriving on American doorsteps bearing "letters of introduction," and upon receipt of these missives, Americans have an endearing habit of asking no questions and opening wide the doors of their boundless hospitality.

I had such a letter to Fred Astaire, from a slight acquaintance in England—Lord Graves (the only titled bookmaker to be found taking bets on the rails)—and I decided to present it one evening in 1935 after a hot game of tennis. I wandered over to the Astaire house, but I forgot to put my shirt on.

I rang the bell.

After a while the door opened and a doll-like, ravishingly beautiful redhead stared at me coolly. She looked about fifteen.

"Is Mr. Astaire at home?" I inquired.

"Who wants him?" she asked, raising eyebrows at my attire and sniffing slightly.

"Well, he won't know who I am, but I have a letter here."

"Who's it from?"

"Er, a bookmaker . . . Tommy Graves is the name."

"Your name?"

"No, the bookmaker's name."

The redhead looked at me with distaste, held out a slim hand for the letter, and started to close the door.

"I've met Mr. Astaire's sister," I added hastily, but as the words came out, I knew they were rash because under cross-examination I was bound to be exposed as having once been taken backstage for two minutes to her London dressing room when Adele Astaire was the toast of the town in *Stop Flirting.*

"Stay here," commanded the redhead icily.

From inside I heard her calling, "Fwed, Fwed, come quickly! . . . There's a perfectly *dwedful* man at the door without a shirt . . . he says he knows your sister and has a letter from a bookie called Gwaves."

From these unpromising beginnings, a friendship grew which perhaps meant more to me than any other in Hollywood.

The combination of Fred and Phyllis was a joy to behold. They blended together with an almost uncanny smoothness, though the mixture had been potentially an unreliable one: the highly bred New York society girl with no interest whatever in the theater or theater people and the dedicated professional entertainer born in Omaha, Nebraska, the son of a small-time brewer, an Austrian immigrant. Fred had been a vaudeville performer at the age of five, doing a touring act with his sister. They had worked hard, and their talents had not gone unappreciated for long. Soon Fred and Adele had taken both Broadway and London by storm, and when Fred met Phyllis at a Long Island luncheon given by Mrs. Vanderbilt, the Astaires' musical *The Bandwagon* was the hottest ticket on Broadway.

Fred immediately fell in love with the slim, steady-eyed girl who could not pronounce her *r*'s, but it took him two agonizing years to persuade her that marriage to an actor would not necessarily mean entering a den of iniquity.

RKO Studios offered Fred a contract, his first picture to be *Flying Down to Rio,* and he decided to take a flyer in the movies.

Would Phyllis give up her Long Island summers and winters in North Carolina and take a flyer, too?

"Yes, I will," said Phyllis to Fred's unbounded joy, and after a one-day honeymoon, the newlyweds flew to Hollywood.

Before Fred started work on *Flying Down to Rio,* in typical Hollywood style, his studio bosses decided first to lay off the bet they had made by lending him out at an exorbitant fee elsewhere, thereby securing his services free for themselves. Fred found himself reporting to MGM and ordered to do a couple of dances with Joan Crawford in her movie *Dancing Lady.*

In Fred's own words, "I didn't have much to do so I just did as I was told, but when I saw myself on the screen . . . gosh! I looked like a *knife.* "

Fred was just about to start filming *Flying Down to Rio* when that "perfectly dwedful man without a shirt" came banging on his door. He had actually started the rehearsals of his one number with the star, Dolores Del Rio, but he had already spotted that his best opportunity in the picture would be in the "Carioca," a subsidiary dance number which he considered the best thing Vincent Youmans had ever written.

A full-time worrier, Fred was very concerned about who would be his partner for this big opportunity. When he heard the name, he was overjoyed. It was to be an old friend and an excellent dancer whom Fred, a year before, had been called in to help when she was having choreographic troubles in her own Broadway show—Ginger Rogers.

As partners they caught fire in "The Carioca," and the rest is movie history, but Fred always swore that he "never realized we were starting something."

As their smash hits piled up— *Gay Divorcee, Roberta, Top Hat, Swing Time, Shall We Dance,* and many, many others—Fred and Ginger together became the top box-office attraction in the world, but Fred remained mystified by his success. "I'm just a hoofer," he said. Phyllis stayed outwardly aloof but inwardly glorying in his success.

"You go ahead, Fwed, and make the money . . . I'll look after it for you." She did too, quite brilliantly, spurning the local business managers with their get-rich-quick schemes of golf courses in Mexico, oil drilling in Mozambique and Black Angus herds on windswept Colorado escarpments. She talked quietly to friends in New York, made minute entries in ledgers the size of Ping-Pong tables, and enabled the family to live in comfort for the rest of their days.

Self-effacing Phyllis only infrequently visited the studio to watch Fred working, and there was a widely believed rumor that she forbade him to kiss Ginger. This was, of course, complete fabrication. Ginger and Fred had a mutual distaste for slowing things up with what Fred described as "long, mushy love scenes," but the rumors provoked a counterattack, and in *The Barkleys of Broadway,* they took a deep breath and were glued together in the longest and most unrelenting kiss so far recorded on film.

Fred invited me to RKO Studios to watch the filming of his "Cheek to Cheek" number in *Top Hat,* and Phyllis came with me. Fred spent a minimum of two months meticulously preparing his dance routines for each picture; then, on shooting days, he would run the pertinent number through for the camera, lighting, and sound experts, put on his costume, turn up the playback of the music, and usually have it "in the can" at the first take—the supreme professional. People begged for a chance to be present on those historic shooting days.

Phyllis settled herself down unobtrusively to watch Ginger and Fred do their run-through on the vast sound stage.

Ginger rehearsed in slacks, and when she appeared for the first take, she looked ravishing in a dress composed almost entirely of red feathers.

"She looks like a wooster," Phyllis giggled.

It transpired that the dress was only just ready in time owing to some sartorial hitch in the wardrobe department. The playback blared forth, and the dance started. Slowly, one at a time at first, the feathers parted company with the parent garment. Then, as Fred whirled Ginger faster and faster about the gleaming set, more and more flew off. It became reminiscent of a pillow fight at school, but they pressed bravely on with the number, and by the end Ginger looked ready for the spit.

Altercations broke out between the director, the cameraman, and the wardrobe mistress. Phyllis pulled my sleeve.

"Let's get out of here," she said. "Fwed will be so embawassed."

The Astaires took me down to Dolores Del Rio's house in a quiet street in Santa Monica. Dolores, a spectacular black-

haired, dark-eyed Mexican beauty with skin whiter than a
hen's egg, was married to good-looking military-mustached
Cedric Gibbons, the head set designer at MGM Studios.
Their house was covered with climbing plants of various
kinds, the choice of which perhaps contained a clue to the
odd relationship of the two householders. Dolores had a
large sunny room on the first floor containing a huge and inviting bed. Gibbie lived in comparative squalor in a small
room immediately below. The only connection between
these two rooms was by way of a stepladder which could be
lowered only when a trapdoor in the floor of Dolores' room
had been raised. There was a long stick in Gibbie's room with
which, we conjectured, he signaled his intentions or hopes by
rapping out signals on the floor of his wife's bedchamber.

Phyllis and Fred delegated me to find out more, but despite many happy hours spent in the company of Gibbie and
Dolores, they declined to unravel the mystery.

Serious music has an unfortunate effect on me unless I am
prepared for it. With Fred and Phyllis I went to Joan Crawford's house one night for dinner, a rather formal affair,
served to the four of us by white-coated menservants. Crawford, one of the reigning movie queens and a lady of extraordinary beauty and drive, had decided to branch out and become an opera singer in her spare time. She had taken a few
lessons locally and had made some ill-advised recordings of
the result with the MGM Studio Orchestra. After dinner she
put record after record on her solid mahogany radiogram,
and for what seemed a very long time, we were treated to her
interpretation of famous arias from *Tosca, Aïda,* and *La Bo-
hème.* As her courageous but fluctuating notes rose and fell,
Joan watched us keenly, and we, not daring to look at each
other, nodded appreciatively back. I was highly relieved that
Raymond Massey and Douglas Fairbanks, Jr., had not received invitations to attend.

Summit Drive appealed to Fred and Phyllis, not because of
its glittering inhabitants, but because of Phyllis' bird-dog
nose for good business. They occupied two houses on that illustrious street in fairly quick succession. Phyllis invested in
some choice acreage just below Pickfair, on the Colman

ridge. She divided this land in two and on one half built a nice, comfortable, easy-to-run family house complete with swimming pool and tennis court.

Fred remonstrated about the court. "I don't like tennis; everybody beats me," he complained.

"David and I will play on it," said Phyllis smugly, "and anyway, this house is not for us . . . it's for sale."

She then put the house on the market, sold it at a succulent profit to William Wyler, the director of *Wuthering Heights, The Best Years of Our Lives, Ben Hur,* and many other movie milestones, and built a second and bigger one on the other half of the land.

Peter Potter, the child of a brief former marriage of Phyllis', was a three-year-old when Fred and Phyllis married, a serious-minded citizen even then, destined later to serve many remarkably useful years as a law enforcement officer in Los Angeles and Santa Barbara counties. He was early fascinated by explosives. Fred misguidedly gave him a chemistry set on his tenth birthday, and quiet dinners at the Astaires' were thereafter punctuated by appalling explosions upstairs.

Once upon arrival at the house, I found the whole family in the living room, cowering behind sofas while outside a huge projectile lay hissing and smoking ominously on the lawn.

"Peter's wocket wefuses to take off," said Phyllis nervously. "It's been making that tewibble noise for ten minutes and it's pointing this way—can you do something bwave about it?"

Prudently, I waited till the noises ceased altogether; then I went out and stalked it. When I was about six feet away, the monster suddenly came to life with a burst of orange flame and an appalling *woosh.* It missed my head by inches, arched up high over the house, disappeared in the general direction of Pickfair, and Peter's arsenal was ordered to be dismantled.

Peter had been joined, very early on, by two enchanting Astaire children, Fred, Jr., and Ava, and it was impossible to find a more devoted family. Fred and Phyllis had everything in common, love of their three children, a longing for a peaceful life, a loathing of Hollywood parties and "chichi," and a fascination with horses and horseracing. This last resulted in the purchase of a ranch at Chatsworth in the San

Fernando Valley and the accumulation, by judicious buying and breeding, of a very handy string of racehorses.

One, Triplicate, bought as a three-year-old for $6,000, a beautiful animal with a coat of beaten bronze, went on to earn well over $250,000 in prize money, capturing, en route, the Hollywood Gold Cup and the San Juan Capistrano Stakes. Other horses they owned did well too, including one oddly named The Fag.

The ranch became the center of their lives. It was always spick-and-span, as I can witness, having been frequently bullied into painting and repainting what seemed like miles of white paddock fencing. Fred, one of the few people in the world about whom it could be claimed that he would never hurt a fly, in point of fact loathed the insects because they annoyed his beloved horses. He invested in electric "fly crematoriums" for the stables; any flies landing on their seductive surfaces were instantly incinerated. Another gadget was less successful. Fred loved the family maid, and he bought an electric carpet sweeper to ease her burden. Something went wrong, and the machine left tracks like a mowing machine on the rugs. The maid was in tears, so Fred trimmed the bristles of the revolving brushes down to nothing with his nail scissors. Little was swept thereafter, but the family maid was wreathed in smiles. Fred loved gadgets. He began losing his hair early, and although philosophical about it, referring to "my high intellectual forehead," he fought a permanent battle to try to maintain the status quo: hence the purchase of an electric hair restorer, a strange, throbbing rubber cap containing elaborate coils and impulses. He must have misread the directions and assembled it incorrectly because on opening night it went into reverse and yanked out a large proportion of what he had left. Fred dreaded "social" dancing, and Ava swore that the most embarrassing night of her life was at a debutantes' ball. There was a father-daughter dance, and according to his daughter, Fred, the focal point of all eyes, "tripped all over me." Above all, he dreaded lugging around a dance floor some eager matron or starry-eyed teenager who would breathe, "Gee, I just can't believe I'm dancing with the *great* Fred Astaire!" But an inhibited and self-conscious social dancer, he would occasionally "take off" in private. Coming home one night in 1950 and hearing loud canned music booming out of my house, I found Fred leaping from staircase to bookcase, to sofa, to floor, using my golf clubs as swords for a sword dance and Hjördis for a partner and, all the time, beating an incredible tattoo with his winged feet.

Since Fred was established as a dedicated worrier, it was inevitable, after a string of ten consecutive box-office smashes, that he would become convinced that he was due for a slump. The interest of audiences toward all musicals had indeed started, slowly, to erode all over the world, and as his last two pictures with Ginger had been merely "great successes" instead of "sensational hits," he talked so persuasively to his costar that she too decided that they might indeed have done enough together and agreed to a "trial separation."

Ginger chose to do a straight comedy, *Bachelor Mother,* with a new, young leading man—David Niven—and Fred took a whole year off to enjoy himself.

Ginger bloomed in her success as a straight actress, but poor Phyllis, instead of spending twelve months of hard-earned relaxation with her husband, found herself cooped up with a hand-wringing wreck who was convinced that he was permanently unemployed, could no longer hit a golf ball, spot a winner, or get a job, but the scene changed unexpectedly. Musicals became the perfect antidote to the grimness of the latest intercontinental lunacy—World War II. Suddenly they were back with a rush, and Fred, with a variety of sparkling partners (of whom Rita Hayworth was his favorite), found himself back on top of the tree.

With the war over, Fred was immediately consumed with renewed doubts about continuing dancing and even went so far as officially to announce his retirement. Photographs were flashed to a horrified public of Fred performing his "last dance," but "Somebody Up There" had no intention of letting Fred off the hook that easily and allowing him to spend the rest of his life with racehorses and mashie niblicks, so he sneakily arranged for poor Gene Kelly in the middle of rehearsals of *Easter Parade* to break a leg.

An SOS went out to Fred, and much to everyone's delight, including Gene's, Fred Astaire's "retirement" ended overnight.

Fred was such an honest person that he just could not believe it was fair that he should be getting such real pleasure out of working. More than 90 percent of the people of the world, he reckoned, were slaving away at jobs they hated in order to support themselves and their families. The most balanced of men in every sense of the word, he only once to my knowledge went mad. At dawn one day Fred called me and announced his mental aberration.

"I'll never know what made me do it," he moaned, "but I had this overpowering urge . . . so I got up in the middle of the night and drove all over Beverly Hills painting the mailboxes with my racing colors."

Fred never ceased to say that he was "the luckiest hoofer and luckiest guy in the world," and it seemed to his friends that he had indeed been dealt an unbeatable hand.

Apart from his soaring talent, this kind, generous, and gentle man had three children who adored him and whose adoration he had earned by being unfailingly understanding and helpful during their growing-up problems, their early careers and marriages. He had a home where he felt safe and at peace; he had his racehorses and had earned and kept money enough to minimize all the everyday problems. Above all, he had Phyllis, the vibrant, vital little auburn beauty he worshiped with all his heart. Theirs was the prototype of a gloriously happy marriage, but Fred, the worrier, deep down felt that his luck was too great, and that it was all too perfect, that something was *bound* to ruin it all, and, one day at Belmont Park Races, Phyllis, who had never known a day's illness, asked to be taken home. "I feel dizzy," she said.

The next day she felt fine, and Fred thought no more about it till a few weeks later, this time at Santa Anita Races, she said in a quiet voice, "I feel faint—please take me home." Fred went cold, and at his insistence Phyllis visited a doctor who ordered a series of X rays, the result of which was an emergency operation.

On a hot afternoon I sat with Fred in a small waiting room at St. John's Hospital, Santa Monica, during her five hours of surgery. Finally, relieved doctors came in and told him the good news. "Looks like we've got it all." They beamed, but their optimism was short-lived: Complications set in, and at 4 A.M. back she went into the operating room, and there was little hope of survival. Fred was numb, but friends can do nothing to help on these occasions—all they can do is stick around in case they are needed and try somehow to share the awesome helplessness.

As the cool, flower-scented California dawn broke, Fred was told that a miracle had happened. Phyllis had come through once more. Frail, waiflike Phyllis was made of stainless steel. Alone in a lead-lined room, she endured weeks of X-ray treatments, put on weight, and even joked about her past ordeal.

"The only time I thought I was in twubble was just before I went in for the second time . . . a lot of nuns came into my woom, knelt down, and started pwaying."

Two months of euphoric remission ended abruptly with further emergency surgery, and Fred's own words will postscript his lost happiness:

"She lapsed into a coma for several weeks. I *knew* she would snap out of it. She didn't. She looked like a beautiful child. She never lost her sweet facial expression. Phyllis . . . slipped away from us."

15
The Enchanted Hill

*E*VEN by the standards of Hollywood in the mid-thirties it had been a very heavy night.

It was after five o'clock, and already the sky was becoming lighter behind me as I sped, none too safely, westward down Sunset Boulevard. High in the hills to my right, the giant sign looked luminous in the ghostly predawn glow: HOLLYWOODLAND.

I was in a great hurry. I had to drop a Wampas Baby Star back at her mother's apartment in Beverly Hills, watch her sneak in, slippers in hand, then return to my own nest in Hollywood, shave, shower, and check in at the studios by seven o'clock.

I pushed the accelerator right down to the floor, and the passenger stirred uneasily as we whizzed through a red light. Suddenly she screamed, but I had seen it too. Slowly crossing the boulevard fifty yards ahead of us was a sizable building.

My unreliable brakes came through nobly, and we stopped with the radiator a yard away from a white front door. Angry men with lanterns surrounded us, including two in the uniform of the Los Angeles police department. When I was allowed to get a word in, I inquired why a large building was crossing a main thoroughfare.

"It's Marion Davies' dressing room," they said.

"Where's it going?" I asked.

"To Warner Brothers," came the reply.

It was too. After ten years as a top star at Metro-Goldwyn-Mayer, Marion Davies was literally moving house, and her fourteen-room bungalow was being towed in sections ten miles from Culver City to the San Fernando Valley.

Louis B. Mayer had stood blubbering at the main gate when this strange cortege had moved out of his studio. "The queen is leaving us," he wailed.

When she was eighteen and one of the most beautiful girls in New York, Marion Davies had a walk-on in a revue, *Stop! Look! Listen!*

William Randolph Hearst, the multimillionaire head of a vast publishing empire, saw her and promptly fell in love with her. She became his mistress, but there were snags to the smooth running of this arrangement because Hearst was thirty-four years older than Marion, he was also married, and the United States was still rigidly puritanical with regard to people "living in sin."

Hearst, however, decided that there was one code of behavior for himself and another for the rest, so he openly flaunted their relationship, and his presses pumped out praise of the talent of his beautiful girlfriend. Aided by that and a genuine flair as a comedienne, Marion quickly passed through the showgirl school of Florenz Ziegfeld, graduated to small parts in musicals, and arrived in the upstart film business. Hearst formed Cosmopolitan Pictures and, after a beginning on the East Coast, moved his production company to Hollywood. He longed to make Marion a big star adored by the public, and he very nearly succeeded, but the very intensity of his efforts upset the apple cart. Marion was perfect material for Lombard-type comedies, and the audiences warmed to her beauty, her charming little stammer, her naturalness, and her obvious sense of fun, but they became suspicious of the constant blast of publicity that issued from the Hearst press and sniggered openly at the sycophantic drooling of Hearst's super columnist, Louella Parsons, whose every description of a Hollywood gathering inevitably concluded with "and Marion has never looked lovelier."

Marion, an utterly genuine person, had no illusions about her talents and must have fulminated endlessly against

Hearst's efforts to promote her as a great dramatic actress. If his well-meaning interference in the choice of roles made things difficult for her, it was nothing compared to the way in which his meddling during production upset her directors. He rewrote scenes, ordered retakes, fired hairdressers, demanded that certain favorite pieces of his own furniture be used to dress the sets, and insisted, however out of place, that somewhere in the picture Marion should sing a song.

He loved her deeply and truly, and she repaid his devotion in kind. Above all, she loved him for himself, not for what he could do for her. She was not at all ambitious, and although she enjoyed the fun and camaraderie of making pictures, she did so to please him, not to polish her own ego, and large chunks of the money she earned she gave away to charity or to less fortunate friends. The one thing she wanted desperately for herself was his name, but although Hearst was reputed to have made a few halfhearted attempts to arrange this, it was denied her and she tried reluctantly to reconcile herself to the status quo.

It was important to Hearst that his mistress was not looked on by the world as just another ex-Follies showgirl, so he pressed on relentlessly to try to propel her right up to the number one spot in the Hollywood galaxy. MGM had been chosen by Hearst as the instrument for the push.

The presence of Marion Davies among L. B. Mayer's stars had guaranteed an incalculable amount of benevolent publicity in the Hearst publications, but matters had come to a head when Hearst insisted that Marion should play Elizabeth in *The Barrettts of Wimpole Street* and the title role in *Marie Antoinette*. Both had already been earmarked for the reigning queen of MGM—Norma Shearer, who happened to be the wife of Irving Thalberg, who happened to be the producer designate of these productions.

The negotiations, which had been long and acrimonious, had ended up with Hearst ordering Marion's bungalow to be towed across town to Warner Brothers and Norma Shearer's name to be banished from his newspapers and left L. B. Mayer using his main gate for a wailing wall.

Hearst's roughneck gold-mining prospector father many

years before had finally struck it rich. He didn't strike gold, but he hit on the next best thing, in enormous quantities—silver.

George Hearst, a firm believer in the future of the West, with the proceeds bought up large hunks of California, including, for 60 cents a time, 40,000 acres in San Luis Obispo County, stretching from San Simeon Bay to the Santa Lucia Mountains; there he developed a famous stock farm and constructed, on a grassy slope not far back from the ocean, a modest ranch house called the Hacienda.

Son William Randolph, at the age of twenty-four, refused to follow in his father's footsteps as a mineowner or a rancher and, already fascinated by the world of journalism, talked his parent into making him a present of a failing little publication, the San Francisco *Examiner*. His huge, sprawling, octopuslike publishing empire was born that day and was destined to become the largest consumer of newsprint in the world, but he never lost sight of that acreage in San Luis Obispo County. There he decided he would one day build his castle, and as his fortunes prospered, he assiduously bought up more and more land in the area till his holdings at San Simeon totaled almost 250,000 acres.

A man of incredible energy, he found time to weld his colossal empire, to rule it with a rod of iron, to revolutionize and sensationalize the whole spectrum of journalism, to oppose U.S. entry into World War I, to fight the League of Nations, to wage a private vendetta against both the British and the French, to warn the United States that the Brooklyn Bridge was about to fall down, and to run twice for mayor and once for governor of New York. At the same time he became the biggest collector of antiques and *objets d'art* in the world, ending up with a many-floored warehouse covering a whole city block in the Bronx and serviced by a permanent staff of thirty. It was stuffed to the roof with treasure, most of it still unpacked, including entire rooms, staircases, and ceilings, ripped from within the walls of disintegrating British, French, and Italian stately homes, plus one complete Spanish monastery with its stones still individually wrapped and numbered. He also collected real estate with the same abandon, garnering, among other choice plots, 1,000,000 acres in

Mexico, a hotel in New York and St. Donat's Castle, an eleventh-century pile in Wales, but in the middle of all these and a thousand other activities the apple of his eye remained San Simeon, and there as he had long promised himself, he constructed with loving care a castle of his own design.

On a craggy, treeless spur, high above the original Hacienda, he blasted rock, dragged thirty-foot trees over ranges of mountains, and slowly, securing for itself a spectacular 360-degree panoramic view of unmatched beauty, the incredible edifice arose.

The housekeeper of what Hearst liked to call La Cuesta Encantada—The Enchanted Hill—proudly boasted that the place cost $7,000 a day to run, not counting the mounds of fish and meat consumed by the packs of wild animals in the open range zoo which surrounded it.

At weekends it was full of guests, but for Marion, the chatelaine, it must have been a lonely mist-shrouded domain during midweek when the ocean fog crept clammily up the Enchanted Hill and she found herself alone, surrounded by forty pairs of see-all-miss-nothing eyes belonging to Hearst's hand-picked Filipino servants.

About a year after my early-morning near collision with her dressing room, I received a phone message: "Call Hacienda one immediately."

I enlisted the studio operator's help, and she informed me that it was the Hearst estate at San Simeon. "Miss Marion Davies is trying to contact you."

Marion sounded enchanting on the phone, and I greatly enjoyed my first exposure to her most attractive stammer. She invited me up for the following weekend and explained that Bill Hearst had suggested that I be part of the house party which she was organizing. "The boys will all be here," she said.

W. R. Hearst had five sons: George, the eldest, rather portly and distrait, Bill, Jack, and the twins, Randy and David. Their mother, Millicent, lived on a large estate at Sands Point, Long Island, and the fun-loving boys moved between these two poles of interest, intrigue, and luxury without, at least on the surface, the slightest dent in the armor of their common sense or their attitude toward their parents.

They were completely relaxed about the Hearst-Marion relationship, though it could not have been easy to assimilate it under the prevalent conditions. They were very fond of Marion, loved their mother, and adored and admired their father. San Simeon was their dream place, too, and there they were happiest.

They were contemporaries of mine, and Bill and his wife, Lorelle, I had come to know very well, so I was relieved that they too would be at the Ranch, as the castle was cozily referred to by the family, when I arrived for the weekend. I was fascinated and a little scared at the thought of meeting W. R. Hearst.

As a beginner in the film industry, I had necessarily become aware of the power of the press. In those days the Hearst press columnist, Louella Parsons, wielded undisputed and immense power mixed with a limited sense of right and wrong, so I thought it might do no harm to let drop in her ear that I would be spending a few days with her boss. I passed the happy word along to one of her spies at my studio and packed my bag.

The route north in early April was beautiful. For several hours I drove through hills still green from the rainy season; wild flowers grew in great profusion. At San Luis Obispo, I turned left to the coast road and drove for another hour through Morro Bay, Harmony, and Cambria till I reached the boundary of the Hearst ranch and found an unobtrusive sign: HEARST HACIENDA.

I turned right into the hills; far above me I beheld, in the glow of the sunset, the castle. I had heard many descriptions of it, some flattering, some derisory, but I personally found it breathtaking. It looked from the coast like a green oasis enclosing a white Spanish village, dominated by twin cathedral towers, and I pressed eagerly up the winding road. Signs were everywhere—"Animals have right of way"—and every mile or so it was necessary to open a heavy gate, and while one did so, it was advisable to keep a wary eye on the zebras, bison, ostriches, and water buffalo which stood around glaring balefully. I was passing through the largest private zoo in the world.

When I arrived at the castle, the boys met me and escorted

me through beautifully manicured flower gardens to the guest "cottage" which had been allotted to me—it seemed to my eye, as yet unaccustomed to the Hearst scale of things, to have the proportions of a mansion. They told me that the huge carved bed in which I was to sleep had belonged to Cardinal Richelieu. I have since read that Hearst always slept in Richelieu's bed. If he did, I certainly did not notice him that night, but then the thing was the size of a battlefield.

The sun was over the yardarm, and the boys watched expectantly as I unpacked. Sighs of relief went up when I produced the bottles of scotch and gin they had instructed me to bring.

We settled back with our drinks, and they explained the reason for their predinner thirst. Marion for years, it seemed, had been drinking too much, and W.R. had instituted a campaign to remove the temptation. He himself would mix an innocuous cocktail for the guests, wine would flow like glue during the meal, and afterward it might just be possible to extract an occasional glass of California champagne from the butler, but the "old man's" eye would be on everyone's intake, particularly that of Marion.

We had several more drinks; then I cleaned up for dinner, and munching handfuls of peppermints, we strolled past a treasure trove of garden statuary to La Casa Grande. The entrance was most impressive—a huge door topped by ornate balconies and a portico, flanked by the twin cathedral towers I had seen from the coast road. On top of each tower was a set of church bells encased in a circular colonnade capped by a beautifully proportioned dome and a crucifix. The overall effect was Spanish, and the detailed work in wood and stone was magnificent.

Inside the castle I was led into a cavernous reception hall which must have been thirty yards long and twenty across. The fireplace, in which enormous logs were blazing, was framed by a mantelshelf of gargantuan proportions; the ceiling was almost out of sight. On an immense Spanish table in the middle of this room stood a very large silver bowl full of fruit juice, and into this bowl, W. R. Hearst was pouring a thimbleful of gin. He, too, was huge; almost six feet six inches tall and shaped like an avocado, with sloping shoulders and sizable paunch. His straight grayish hair behind a high-domed forehead was plentiful, parted in the middle and falling forward in two unruly locks. He wore coat, trousers, and waistcoat of thick tweed of overcheck design.

When Bill introduced me, his father turned and treated me to a charming, if rather vague, smile, but his eyes beneath brows that sloped down in harmony with his shoulders were the bluest and the coldest I had ever seen. I had a nasty feeling that he knew about the empty bottles of gin and whiskey now reposing under Richelieu's bed.

He had a curiously high voice. A dachshund sniffed at his shoes. Marion bustled up, and I was captivated by her. She was all bubbling fun and laughter, and despite her fortyish figure, her long blond hair, huge baby-blue eyes, and sexy mouth and teeth made her seem fifteen years younger.

Introductions happened piecemeal, and of the thirty or forty present, I remember two or three mature ladies who were friends of Marion from her days in the *Follies,* one with a permanent leer caused by an erratic operation to remove the bags from under her eyes, Frances Marion, a talented screenwriter who had written many of Marion's movies, Gutzon Borglum, the Danish sculptor who was currently hacking the likenesses of four American Presidents out of the side of Mount Rushmore in South Dakota, and several gray, noncommittal gentlemen from the hierarchy of the Hearst empire, including Richard Berlin and his top columnist, Arthur Brisbane. Among this older group, I was excited to see Charlie Chaplin, though my excitement faded after dinner when he held court, telling long and surprisingly dull stories.

Guests at dinner were seated by Marion at the "longest refectory table in the world" in the longest dining room I had ever seen. The chairs were extremely uncomfortable, having been designed for knights who ate in their armor. Behind us, against the entire length of the walls, were monks' stalls of solid oak removed from some medieval house of worship, and high in the gloom above us, on long poles arching over our heads like swords at a military wedding, were several dozen beautifully embroidered banners from the leading families of Siena and Florence. Arranged at intervals of a yard or so down the center of the vast table were three-foot-high heavily worked silver candlesticks, and between these were surprising but somehow reassuring little outcrops of paper napkins, Worcestershire sauce and ketchup. W.R. liked to keep things simple at the Ranch.

Hearst sat at the middle of the table. Marion sat directly opposite him, and I noticed that his cold blue eyes, which had alarmed me earlier on, were looking warmly at her throughout the meal. In the middle section of the table, flanking W.R. and herself, Marion had parked the elder statesmen and stateswomen of the group, while the boys, their wives, and their friends, jogging the arms of the wine-serving Filipino servants in vain attempts to encourage respectable rations, were phased out into the half-light at either end.

There was no general conversation. The dinner itself was buffet-style and hearty—man-eating steaks, baked potatoes, salads, and desserts. Self-service from another large and well-laden table at the end of the room was the order at all meals, and throughout these repasts one became accustomed to yards of ticker tape and other pieces of hot news being slipped beneath one's host's nose by a male secretary.

After dinner we filed into the private movie theater and from deeply comfortable seats watched one of the latest as yet unreleased films, which were sent up every week to San Simeon by the major studios, hoping to garner some favorable publicity by this genuflection in the direction of the all-important Hearst press.

To an unknown young actor it was a revelation and a mixed joy to listen to the acid comments and catcalls that greeted some of the efforts that were selected nightly for dissection. It was a rough audience for a bad film, but the best audience in the world for a good one.

Well past midnight the film ended. W.R. and Marion disappeared inside a claustrophobic little elevator which held only two people and were borne jerkily aloft to his Gothic library, and there, before retiring four or five hours later to their "Celestial Suite," the charming, relaxed host of San Simeon surrounded by telephones became the dynamo, and some said the demon, who put the fear of God into editors, bankers, captains of industry, and statesmen all over the world.

When the cat was away, the mice began to play, and the young indulged in all sorts of harmless pursuits, moonlight swims in the giant marble and colonnaded outdoor pool or the gold-leafed indoor one, card games, music, and always dormitory-type raids, booby traps and water fights. W.R. knew everything that went on, and sometimes damage was extensive, but nothing was said, provided none of the three cardinal rules was broken: No drunkenness, no bad language or off-color jokes, and above all, no sexual intercourse between unmarried couples. This last was a strange piece of puritanism from a man living openly with his mistress, but it was rigorously enforced and any misdemeanor immediately punished by banishment, the offenders receiving a note with their breakfast saying that it would be advisable to make an early start. Nobody lingered, though all marveled at the efficiency of the local intelligence service.

Dorothy Parker was said to have received her marching orders—being sent down the hill, it was called—and bridled at the indignity that she felt had come her way for making love in the middle of so much beauty and treasure.

San Simeon lore had it that before her early-morning departure she opened the visitors' book and in it wrote:

> Upon my honor I saw the Madonna
> Standing in a niche
> Above the door
> Of a well-known whore
> And a first class son of a bitch.

On a subsequent visit to the Ranch I myself fell foul of the local Gestapo.

I had been encouraged to drive up from Los Angeles with a very beautiful girl. The first evening of the weekend had developed along normal lines, and when the movie and other jollities were over and I judged that everyone was sound asleep I set out from my guest cottage in the gardens intent on finding my friend somewhere high up in the main house.

During the evening this project had become a joint planning operation, and my partner in crime had given me minute instructions on the exact location of her bedchamber.

Undeterred by the fact that we had been alloted rooms at the farthest extremities of San Simeon, I tiptoed quietly along garden paths, inhaling the overpowering sweetness of night-scented jasmine, and gained the impressive front door of La Casa Grande. Inside, the great hall was warm and smelled of lingering cigar smoke; the embers of the dying logs still gave out a faint glow which helped because all the lights had been switched off. I groped my way around looking for some stone stairs and found instead the door to the two-seater elevator. This I entered and pressed the button that would propel me past the danger area of the Gothic library and the Celestial Suite. In the stillness of the night the elevator sounded like the elevated railway on New York's Third Avenue, and when it finally clanked to a stop, I stayed in it for an eternity, not daring to come out, and toyed with the idea of giving up the whole project, but as the girl had hinted that she didn't think I had the guts to try the assault on the stronghold, I decided to press on.

In the darkened elevator I had misjudged the number of buttons, so when I did emerge, I found myself on a veranda which had no place at all in our meticulous planning. I began to long for the safety of Richelieu's bed, but there was nothing for it. I had to go back into the elevator.

The noise going down was deafening, and I couldn't wait to get out of the damn thing, but I had once more miscounted and this time I emerged into a dank passage full of pieces of sharp masonry upon which I left the leading edges of my shinbones.

After two more clattering trips in the elevator I finally surfaced among acres of pitch-black and recognizable reception rooms where I blundered about until miraculously I bumped into the "longest refectory table in the world." I don't know how I did it, but I had found the dining room.

Almost prostrate with nervous exhaustion, I sank gratefully into one of the monks' stalls. From there I could work my way to the front door. I was saved!

Suddenly all the lights in the place went on.

I hastily prepared a thin excuse about foraging for a snack, but nobody appeared. In the full glare of the lights and in the certain knowledge that my entire promenade had been monitored, I summoned what dignity I could for the benefit of the watching eyes and sauntered from the room, humming a brave little tune. In case I was still under any misapprehension, the moment I swung the front door open an unseen hand once more plunged La Casa Grande into darkness.

I went unpunished for my nocturnal ramble and had the great good fortune to be invited frequently to the Ranch during the next few years.

Marion was always warm and gay. Even in repose she seemed about to burst out laughing. She was a sort of den mother to the young and was never happier than when she was fostering romances.

W. R. Hearst remained courteous, thoughtful, and charming, but I cannot claim that I ever came close to him. I was always in awe of him, despite the fact that he sought out the company of the young and encouraged us to talk to him.

Although at the time in his mid-seventies he was full of amazing physical energy. Picnics were organized which W.R. would lead in full Western costume, riding for hours to some remote ranch on the estate, where, as if by magic, everything had been prepared for the arrival of his troupe.

Playing tennis singles with him was something of a hazard because he plainly liked to come out on top, and as he had no intention whatever of running for the ball, he took up a strong position in the center of the court and waited for it to be hit within his reach. When this was achieved, he struck it very hard indeed and unerringly returned it out of one's reach. It was incredible to think that when this man was sitting on his father's knee, Abraham Lincoln was balancing a piece of paper on his own and drafting the Gettysburg Address.

I had heard much about Hearst's chronic anti-British feelings, and indeed a glance at any of his publications in those pre-World War II days showed how stubbornly he still held to them. Often I wondered why anybody with my blood was tolerated near him, but he never said a word of criticism to me and only once put my American loyalty in question.

In order to get rid of an extra who was pestering me on the set, I gave him $10 toward some fund for which he was collecting. He had mumbled something about the starving Mexican lettuce pickers of Salinas.

It turned out that along with dozens of other unsuspecting people I had suscribed to a Communist front organization.

Hearst's Los Angeles *Examiner* picked up the story, and along with such well-known "Communists" as C. Aubrey Smith, Ronald Colman, Basil Rathbone, and Cedric Hardwicke, I was pilloried in its columns for days.

"Who needs these British bums?" was the theme, if not the actual wording, of the attacks, and we were publicly hauled over the coals for taking jobs from clean-cut American actors and undermining the fabric of the country that had befriended us. It was, therefore, with some trepidation that I accepted my next invitation to the Ranch, but Hearst was his usual charming self and even singled me out for a personal tour of the cages of his favorite dangerous animals behind La Casa Grande.

W.R. loved animals great and small with a most endearing passion, but he could not bear their injuries or deaths. When the dining hall of La Casa Grande became infested with mice, far from destroying them, he left out tasty tidbits for them before retiring at night. When they multiplied alarmingly, he reluctantly agreed to have them trapped, provided they were not hurt. Special cages were constructed to capture them alive, and each morning resentful Filipinos emptied the catch into the front garden. The little captives, hardly believing their good fortune, then hotfooted it happily back in the direction of the kitchen entrance.

At the end of our walk he smiled his vague smile and said, "And when are you going to become an American citizen?"

I had been lulled into a feeling of false security by his charm, and while I fumbled around for an answer he continued. "After all, you *do* owe a great deal to this country, don't you?"

"I certainly do, sir," I said sincerely, "but I am proud of my own country, too . . . and after all, thousands of Americans work happily all over the world, but they don't feel they have to become British or Arabs or Chinese."

Hearst did what I least expected: He let out a high cackle

of laughter and patted me on the shoulder. "Good boy!" he said. "Good boy!"

If I had hoped that the "Limeys, go home!" trend in the Hearst press might abate as a result of my brilliant riposte, I could not have been more mistaken, and two years later, after Hitler marched into Poland, the crescendo was reached when President Roosevelt lent Britain fifty old destroyers and several thousand rifles, hoping to stave off the inevitable involvement of the United States. "Pulling the British chestnuts out of the fire!" proclaimed Hearst, and he stuck to his guns right up to the moment when the Japanese bombed Pearl Harbor. Then he put all his resources unreservedly behind an all-out war effort.

It seemed strange that a man of pure Anglo-Saxon heritage should conduct such a virulent crusade against the land of his forebears. Perhaps the fact that his wet nurse had come from Southern Ireland had something to do with it. Personally, I don't believe he was anti-British. I think he was just 100 percent pro-American.

When he sent his son Bill to England for the first time, he told him he liked the English very much but warned him to be careful. "They are charming," he said. "Don't let them charm you off your American perch."

W. R. Hearst's love for Marion was plain for all to see, and in spite of the difference in age, it remained so to the end. Marion's love was equally strong, but there was an appalling gap in her contentment. She longed to be Mrs. Hearst and knew it could never be. Probably therein lay the cause of her increasing reliance on the bottle to help her maintain her gaiety, and Hearst was permanently on tenterhooks because of her drinking. By all accounts he was far more concerned about that than any thought of losing her to a younger man. It seemed that she did occasionally have flirtations with actors in her films, but she must have known that information of such goings-on was bound to be relayed to W.R. even before the bed had been turned down; perhaps she hoped that she might spur him on to make the one move she longed for.

If one became a frequent visitor at the Ranch, one also became involved in Marion's near alcoholism. There was one heart-stopping occasion when she opened her handbag upside down during dinner, and after a loud crash of broken glass, the unmistakable smell of Booth's Gin rose from the stone floor. "My new perfume." She giggled nervously at W.R. He smiled indulgently across the table, but the hurt and the fear were in his blue eyes.

I, for one, cursed myself when I grew older and wiser because after dinner when the champagne went around, Marion would wink at one of her "trusties" and whisper, "Isn't it about time you went to the can?" This was the signal for a full glass to be left in there for her.

It seemed fun at the time to stoke up her fires of outrageous fun and laughter, and I got a kick, I suppose, out of feeling that I had outwitted one of the most powerful and best informed men on earth, but what a disloyal and crummy betrayal of someone who had shown me nothing but kindness and hospitality and what a nasty potential nail to put in her coffin.

On my visits to San Simeon the balance of the invited was always much the same: top-ranking employees from his empire mixed with authors, politicians, statesmen, explorers, and other figures of world renown, never anyone from the rich froth of international café society—they bored him to distraction—and old friends of Marion's from the theater and movies.

The boys invited their friends, and from their vantage point, it was fascinating to observe the imperfections and pretensions of the great and near great. Though I was not fortunate enough to be present when Albert Einstein, George Bernard Shaw, or Winston Churchill was a guest at the Ranch, it was tempting to speculate if it had ever been hinted to them that a good place to leave a glass of champagne was in the bathroom.

Hearst's preoccupation with furthering Marion's career had led him to surround her with the trappings he thought befitted a great film star.

In 1926, realizing that many of the Hollywood greats, including Douglas Fairbanks, Joseph Schenck, Will Rogers, L. B. Mayer, and Marion's great rival, Norma Shearer, owned beach houses at Santa Monica, Hearst set out to give her the most luxurious beach house of all. Marion went along with the idea, not that she particularly wanted it, but she knew that showering her with gifts gave Hearst great pleasure and also helped him paper over his conscience.

Hearst bought up the necessary beach frontage, including a small adjacent lot belonging to Will Rogers upon which he intended building a tennis court. The lot was worth a few thousand dollars, but Rogers had decided that Hearst should be taught that money could not buy everything, so each time Hearst made an offer, Rogers had put up the price. Finally, he accepted a round sum of $100,000, thereby learning what money *could* do.

Reminiscent, with its pillars, porticoes, and symmetrical wings, of Buckingham Palace, the white frame structure, named Ocean House, rose slowly on the Santa Monica beach, and Hearst filled it with treasure, sometimes driving the architect to distraction by mentioning that the shape of a particular room was dictated by the fact that he had already bought it intact in Europe, and now it was up to the architect to fit it into the house.

There was a ballroom, a gigantic staircase, fifty-five bathrooms, and lockers for more than 2,000 guest swimmers—it was not very cozy. The parties at Ocean House were on a different scale from those at San Simeon—they were strictly Marion, and there with gaiety, generosity, and bubbling fun she entertained her multitude of friends. Each year she gave a costume ball on W.R.'s birthday. There was a Forty-Niner Party; a Kid Party, when Gable came as a Boy Scout and Joan Crawford as Shirley Temple; an Early American Party, when Hearst dressed as James Madison; and a Your Favorite Movie Star Party, which saw Gary Cooper as Dr. Fu Manchu and Groucho Marx as Rex, the Wonder Horse. But the most lavish of all was the Circus Party.

Two thousand guests assembled. Cary Grant and Paulette Goddard arrived with a party of friends dressed as tumblers and, after days of practice, were able to make a most impressive entrance cartwheeling across the dance floor. Henry Fonda came with a group of clowns; Bette Davis was a bearded lady, Dolores Del Rio a bareback rider, and Claudette Colbert showed up as Pocahontas.

I forget what Marion wore, but I do remember thinking, in spite of his noble profile, how forlorn and self-conscious W. R. looked as the ringmaster.

There was a carousel and sideshows and prizes for the most original costumes. Among the less popular contestants for these were Errol Flynn and myself, who arrived dressed in baggy white suits and white peaked caps, inquiring where the elephants were. We carried shovels and buckets on which was painted "IT."

It was estimated that Ocean House cost more than $7,000,000 by the time it was completed and furnished. Gratuitous additions for me were a couple of white frame guest cottages. Bill Hearst talked to Marion, and for a while I rented one of these from her for a minimal sum. I shared it with two bachelor friends, and our parties, if not on the scale of the big house, were such that Carole Lombard nicknamed the place Cirrhosis-by-the-Sea.

We had this painted on a board above the front door, where it remained till Harry Crocker, a great friend of Hearst's, dropped by and suggested that I take it down.

"Imagine," he said, "how W.R. would react if he ever thought it was a crack at Marion."

Some days Marion walked down the beach and dropped in to see if her tenants were behaving themselves. Our free and easy life-style fascinated her and made her a little wistful, I think. She adored and revered W.R.—"Hearst come, Hearst served" was her favorite parting line when she terminated her visits. Occasionally, one heard rumors that she had cuckolded him, but in so doing, she somehow would have remained true to him. It would have meant nothing to her; she was just being generous and making someone happy. There was no bitchiness or underhandedness in Marion's makeup.

Undoubtedly, by the end of 1937 if I had had my eyes and ears open, I would have detected certain undercurrents at San Simeon. I would have realized that the gray, uncommunicative top brass of the empire was now outnumbering the friends of Marion and the boys, and I would assuredly have noticed that these men were looking drawn and worried.

I might also have spotted that Marion was antagonistic to

these same high executives, and I would certainly have sensed that this antipathy was heartily reciprocated, but never by word or deed would my shy, generous, courtly, and thoughtful host have alerted me to the fact that he was under an almost intolerable strain.

The Hearst empire was cracking up. The debts amounted to a monumental $126,000,000, and Hearst at the age of seventy-five was facing personal bankruptcy and the total dissolution of everything he had single-handedly built up.

I don't know if the boys realized how close above their heads Damocles' sword was dangling. If they did, they kept their own counsel, and the fun at San Simeon seemed to the self-indulgent guests to be as constant and unforced as usual, but behind the scenes W.R. was taking what must, for him, have been heartbreaking decisions. He formed a committee of his top advisers to take over his financial affairs with orders to cut away the deadwood and liquidate everything that was not making a profit, so during the next few months dozens of his favorite newspapers and radio stations were sold, much of his real estate went, and finally, his beloved collection was put on the market. No single antique dealer in the United States was able to cope with the thousands of items, so the accumulated treasure of the most prolific collector in the world ignominiously went under the hammer at Gimbel's and other department stores throughout the country. The castle in Wales did not find a bidder, nor did the 164,000 outlying acres of San Simeon itself, but one can imagine the wrench Hearst must have felt when his "committee" ordered him to divest himself of the very heartland of his empire. The animals went off to zoos in 1938, and a year later Hearst asked the bank for a mortgage on the Enchanted Hill itself.

The strain on Hearst and on Marion must have been crippling when stockholders, rivals, and even some of his own committee openly and most unfairly blamed her for his almost lunatic outpourings, but the unkindest cut of all came when he discovered that the mortgage he had finally obtained on the Enchanted Hill was held by his archrival, Harry Chandler, publisher of the Los Angeles *Times.*

If W.R. Hearst was made of very special stuff, so was his mistress. At the most critical point, when his aged head was only just above water, he needed just one more million dollars to keep afloat. Marion, without a moments' hesitation, pooled her film savings, jewelry and real estate investments and presented W.R. with a check which, over his vehement protestations, she insisted he cash immediately and for which she refused all security.

The empire shrank, but Hearst's remaining newspapers and radio stations were run with all his old vigor, and his feelings toward Great Britain remained unchanged.

In 1939, just before Hitler finally went berserk, W.R. addressed a stern radio warning to the American people: "It is no part of our duty to support the British Empire in her ambitious schemes to dominate Europe, absorb Africa, and control the Orient. England has never in our whole history extended any aid, comfort, or consideration to these United States of ours!"

When he made that statement, what was left of his empire was at the edge of the precipice, but a few weeks later mankind embarked on its bloodiest self-inflicted wound, and the Hearst empire was saved. With the outbreak of hostilities, profits from newspapers and radio stations soared, the 164,000 unsold acres of San Simeon were snapped up by the U.S. army, and a sizable and timely slab of hard cash came from, of all people, the despised British government, which took St. Donat's Castle in Wales and turned it into a training school for officers.

If 1939 was a turning point in Hearst's business career, it was also the harbinger of a particularly difficult time in his private life. The "boy genius," Orson Welles, descended on the film capital, and *Citizen Kane* was prepared in great secrecy at RKO Studios.

The screenplay was not written by Welles, as most people believe; it was the work of the hard-drinking, brilliant and erratic Herman Mankiewicz. It was directed and acted by Welles, and it was photographed by the young Sam Goldwyn protégé Greg Toland, whose deep-focus photography gave a three-dimensional illusion which brought paeans of praise from the industry.

The story, of an egomaniacal, power-mad, acquisitive publisher and his drunken blond ex-actress mistress living in a hilltop castle, left no one who saw it in much doubt as to who were the prototypes.

Hearst, when shown the picture, was furious; not for himself, because, as he had lately demonstrated during the near eclipse of his publishing world, if he could dish it out, he was perfectly prepared to take it, but the pointing up of the failure of comedienne Marion's career as a dramatic actress and the underlining of what was now becoming her near-chronic alcoholism were more than he could bear. He fought back savagely. The Hearst press was still a power to be reckoned with by the film industry, and a great deal of pressure was brought to bear on RKO. L.B. Mayer offered to pay the entire cost of the film if they would destroy the negative. They refused, and the film won international acclaim, not so much for its content, which was a very local affair, but for its brilliant revolutionary, youthful, and long-overdue approach to picture-making.

The name of Orson Welles was banned from all Hearst publications, and for a considerable time RKO Studios received no reviews whatsoever for their pictures, but *Citizen Kane* survived the onslaught and won the Academy Award for Best Picture.

When World War II ended, Marion was forty-eight years old, Hearst was eighty-two, and Ocean House was a beached white elephant. Marion sold it for a song to a developer, who turned it into a beach club which failed, and before long it was pulled down and made into a public parking lot, giving a local wag a chance to write, "Marion Davies' Beach House— no more—thousands homeless."

More and more, W.R. and Marion retreated to San Simeon, but the parties were fewer, and the tempo of the place was slowed to walking pace.

The remaining 75,000 acres still enabled Hearst to look to the horizon in any direction, and everything he saw except the ocean was his, and if the beloved animals were no longer surrounding him in various stages of freedom, in the evening light he could still look down from the Enchanted Hill and rejoice in the sight of herds of elk grazing peacefully on his golden slopes below.

Returned from the war which Hearst had so much hoped

his country could avoid, I did not see San Simeon again with
W.R. in residence. Bill Hearst I had met up with many times
in Europe where he had served as war correspondent, and
back in California, he became a great favorite with my wife,
Hjördis, and my two small sons at our house in Pacific Palisades. "Mr. Useless" they named him because he consistently
failed to demonstrate the tiniest glimmer of know-how or in-
vention when called on to assist in small household chores
such as changing a light bulb, controlling a runaway toilet,
changing a fuse or boiling an egg, but fun-loving, intelligent
and generous Bill, with big blue eyes as warm as W.R.'s were
cold, became "Mr. Useful" as far as reporting went and created a record in the chilliest weeks of the cold war, when he interviewed Khrushchev, Bulganin, Molotov, Zhukhov, Churchill, and Eisenhower.

There were those who said that W.R. Hearst had an over-
developed dread of death, and they argued in a rather con-
voluted way that it was this fear of the inevitable which drove
him to surround himself with the young and hinted that he
felt he could postpone the end so long as he continued making additions and alterations at San Simeon. Certainly I had
never seen the place without scaffolding enveloping some
corner of it, but if he harbored greater than normal appre-
hensions about the end, by all accounts, he covered them up
most gallantly when he realized that his time was approaching.

For most of his life he had suffered from a suspect heart
and in 1947 was struck down by a heavy attack. He was ordered to live the rest of his life near a specialist and realized
that his days at San Simeon were over.

Marion found a rambling Spanish house in Beverly Hills,
the gardens were touched up with a few pieces of his favorite
statuary, and a dozen of his faithful San Simeon retainers
were dispatched to prepare the place for their master.

How all-envelopng must his sadness have been when he
went down for the last time from his Enchanted Hill. For
four years in Beverly Hills he clung to life and with occasional spurts of superhuman energy still ripped off spiky direc-
tives to his editors and perpetuated one last, gloriously defiant act of horrendous extravagance when he bought fifty

thoroughbred Arab horses and ordered them to be sent to San Simeon, but in August, 1951, at the age of eighty-eight he finally gave up the struggle. Nobody knows what conversations took place during the last months between the frail and weakening W.R. and Marion, who had at last lost her long battle against alcoholism.

Probably she reiterated her dislike and suspicion of the committee; certainly the dying man saw only too clearly how desperately unprotected her life was soon to become. In any event, there was mystery and high drama from the instant of his passing.

A few months ago I was trapped halfway up a Swiss mountain in a two-seater chair lift. A sudden blizzard had so violently rotated the wind gauges on the pylons that the lift motor had automatically cut, and with my companion I was left swinging, perilously, seventy feet from the ground.

Stanley Flink, because he was an ex-paratrooper, was less terrified than I.

"I think we can jump from here," he calculated. "The snow looks deep enough, so we'll only break our legs . . . but if this goddamn chair comes off the wire, we'll go down in it and break our backs."

I had long since resolved to stay in the chair come what may, so I set about ensuring that Flink would not leave me in the lurch by hurtling to his own doom.

I started a jerky and strained line of conversation that encompassed the days we had spent together in Hollywood when Flink had been the resident correspondent for *Life*. Suspended from a wire that seemed in imminent danger of snapping and swinging wildly about with the horizontally blown snow blinding us and trying to rip the skin off our faces, Stanley Flink told me what had transpired in Marion Davies' house in Beverly Hills.

Marion had been at Hearst's bedside most of that last night. By dawn the old man was sleeping, and she was exhausted. The doctor gave her a sedative and told her to rest for a few hours. When she awoke, she found not only that W.R. had died but that the undertakers had obeyed prior instructions from the committee to remove the body—she was alone. As she recounted it, "The nurse said he was dead. His body was gone whoosh! . . . like that. Old W.R. was gone. . . . Do you realize what they did? They stole a possession of mine. He belonged to me. I loved him for thirty-two years, and now he was gone. I couldn't even say good-bye."

Flink found that the guards from around the house had been removed, and a *Life* photographer took a picture of the large four-poster in which W.R. had died. Sitting on it, whining piteously, was a little dachshund—Hearst's favorite animal and his only companion when the end had come.

The funeral, attended by the family and more than a thousand friends, rival press lords, and dignitaries, took place in San Francisco.

Marion was not invited.

W.R. had loved and admired his sons, and in his last days he must have been inordinately proud of them.

George with the San Francisco *Examiner* and Jack, aide to the Hearst newspapers' general manager, perhaps showed less flair as newspapermen than the twins, Randy, publisher of the San Francisco *Call-Bulletin,* and David, publisher of the Los Angeles *Herald-Express.*

Bill (Mr. Useless) was the star performer, publisher of the New York *Journal-American,* and being groomed to step full time into his father's shoes.

Much as the boys and their families loved the Enchanted Hill, not one of them fancied the idea of maintaining the castle and its remaining 75,000 acres.

In 1957 the state of California accepted the boys' gift of San Simeon, with 123 acres surrounding it, as a state park to be opened to the public.

At the end of that year Bill Hearst and his gorgeous second wife, "Bootsie," invited Hjördis and me to San Simeon for the last private weekend before it became public property.

Except for the giant great hall with mammoth logs blazing for the last time, La Casa Grande was dark and cold, so the four of us were housed in the largest guest "cottage," La Casa del Mar, a Spanish-style structure adjacent to the 100-foot marble outdoor Neptune pool.

For a few days we explored and played tennis and remembered the tournament organized with such helpful partners as Helen Wills, Bill Tilden, Fred Perry, and Alice Marble. We hiked and pretended we enjoyed ourselves, but Bill was obviously weighed down with a deep sadness which affected us all. In the evenings before simple meals in the "cottage," we mixed cocktails in the vast ghost-filled hall; the logs did their best, but there was a bone-chilling unhappiness about the place which Bill tried valiantly to exorcise by taking me down to the cellar on a foray for wine for dinner.

Below was a colossal underground depository, and I was amazed that W.R., with his well-known feelings about alcohol, would have laid down such a mammoth supply. We found there thousands upon thousands of dust-covered bottles. Nothing had been cared for, and the contents of bottle after bottle were quite undrinkable, including several cases of 1890 Tokay which looked and tasted like the bottom of San Pedro Harbor.

On New Year's Eve we drank beer and ate hamburgers in the "cottage," and at 10:30 P.M., too depressed to see in the New Year, we went to bed. The next morning the sightseers from their trailers and motels below arrived in buses and started filing through the gardens and reception rooms of La Casa Grande, gaping at the banners and the monks' stalls, nudging each other in their flowered shirts, giggling in the Gothic library, and posing in their ten-gallon hats beside the Neptune pool.

The state park guides seemed to be doing a well-informed job on the history of the place, but not one of them mentioned Marion Davies.

The sea fog slowly seeped up toward the castle. First the flower beds and "cottages" were covered; then the palm trees were no more. For a while the soaring twin towers made ghostly appearances as the cold mist swirled about them. Finally, they, too, were obliterated.

In silence, William Randolph Hearst, Jr., drove us down the road from the Enchanted Hill.

16
Our Little Girl
(Part II)

*L*ET'S pull 'em up and head back," said my companion, a general practitioner from Santa Monica. "It's gettin' late, and nothin' goin' to hit now."

We reeled in our lines, and he gunned the motor; it was four o'clock in the afternoon, and we'd been trolling for marlin since six o'clock in the morning. "Just one of those days, I guess." He sighed. "We might just as well break out the scotch!" We had an hour's run back to Balboa, so we settled ourselves comfortably, glasses in hand. Silence is not an embarrassment between friends, and we sat back contentedly watching the horizon astern thicken to purple as it prepared to receive the great red ball of the sinking sun.

"That's one hell of a profession you've gotten yourself into," said the doctor later with a smile. "D'you think you'll come out OK at the end of it?"

I asked him what he meant. "I have very little contact with people in the film business myself," he said, "but d'you have any idea how many wind up in our hospital as alcoholics, addicts, suicides, attempted suicides, or with breakdowns?"

"Just what I see in the papers," I replied.

"That's only the tip of the iceberg," said the doctor. "It's frightening! A guy at the hospital has written a paper on stress, there's a chapter on what it does to actors; I'll send it along to you."

I told him I hoped that I personally would survive; he

laughed and said, "Yes, you probably will, because you're perfectly happy sitting on your ass for ten hours holdin' a rod and not catchin' a fish."

Some weeks passed before I got around to reading about the dire effects of stress in the motion-picture industry. High-powered executives, it appeared, were prone to everything from heart attacks, to hemorrhoids and premature ejaculation. Agents and publicists cornered the market in ulcers, while writers and actors frequently became alcoholics or drug addicts. An alarming number of actresses, the article stated, either killed themselves, attempted to do so, or suffered nervous breakdowns. I was still not reading seriously until the writer provided an up-to-date casualty list starting back in the silent days with Clara Bow, Barbara La Marr and Jeanne Eagels—it was a profoundly disturbing catalogue of collapse, which included the names of many people I knew or had known.

The main point the writer made was that the players most likely to suffer were not the talented "personalities" such as Garbo, Joan Crawford, Bette Davis, Katharine Hepburn, Dietrich, Mae West, or Claudette Colbert, because they would always be able to adjust to the fact that each day everyone becomes twenty-four hours older; the targets for attack were the young, of minimal talent, who had been plucked from obscurity, spoon-fed on publicity, taught how to walk, to talk, to dress; and then how to undress and expose themselves to the world as sex symbols or love goddesses.

The article printed a lurid picture of what could happen to the mind of a female in her late twenties or early thirties who was beginning to realize, after years of adulation and secure in the knowledge that half the male population of the world wanted to sleep with her, that in fact her famous face and curves were showing signs of losing the battle against gravity, and to be told by her studio that her public was tired of her.

That, the writer concluded, would be a traumatic enough experience for anyone, but to have to cope with it in the full glare of publicity in front of millions of people could prove too much. She would have to fall back on her "real" self; if she discovered that her "real" self was absent because it had never existed, then collapse in some form would follow as the night the day. The article on stress went the same way as other sad-ending scenarios because I mentally pushed it aside. Famines in India seemed far away, too.

Three years had passed since I had first met Missie. "He," the boyfriend, had gone to jail for defrauding gullible ladies (including Missie). A third mate had given up the unequal struggle of being married to a sex symbol, and now she was married to a close friend of mine, a cameraman, one of the best in Hollywood, a master of diffused lighting, and in great demand by the female stars. Missie, by now twenty-eight years old Hollywood time (thirty-three Eastern Standard Time), was still a gay, sparkling creature, but according to local gossip, her thickening body was making her exceedingly jealous of her husband's proximity to the most glamorous ladies in the world, and lately, whispers had been filtering back from the South Pacific, where he was photographing an extremely predatory lady. Rumor also had it that the film Missie was currently shooting was a skid picture designed to be the last one at the studio where she had worked for fifteen years but which was now preparing to dump her. She seemed in good spirits when she called to invite me to a small party at her house a few days hence. "Just friends," she said, and she talked rapidly and at great length about its chances of success.

Missie was a meticulous and house-proud hostess, who took endless pains to ensure that her guests were happy and that everything—company, food, drink, and lighting—was as near as possible perfect. True, she was shooting a picture so as a mid-week party we did not expect a late or elaborate affair, but the twenty or thirty guests were a trifle surprised to find on arrival that Missie had ordered no food or made any apparent efforts to accommodate them. She was overly bright and gay and said she was delighted that we had all dropped by, but she still wore the sweater and slacks in which she had returned from work and had not removed her heavy studio makeup. It didn't matter. People disappeared to their houses and came back with ham and eggs, cheese, bread, candles, and a couple of cases of wine; the girls invaded the kitchen and calmed down Mae, the longtime "help"; and with Missie behaving like the most animated of guests, we ended up having a very good time.

As I drove home, I thought back over the evening and decided that Missie must have been high on something. I was perhaps a little surprised, because she habitually drank very little and I had never seen any signs of her taking drugs, but I dismissed it from my mind and went to sleep.

At six o'clock in the morning Mae called me on the telephone.

Mista David, you git over here *real* quick! . . . Somethin' terrible's happenin' to Missie."

"What?" I asked sleepily.

"She's *possessed*—that's what! . . . You git over here real *quick* now!"

Within twenty minutes I drove up to the little white garden gate and jumped out of the car. Mae was waiting for me. She was shaking. She clutched my arm and repeated over and over, "She's possessed! She's possessed! She's throwed me out! . . . I'm quittin'. . . . I'm quittin'!"

I tried to reassure her, but nothing would persuade her to come back into the house with me, so I took her key and watched her head quickly down the treelined street in the direction of Sunset Boulevard—she never looked back.

It was still dark, and no lights showed in the small house as I quietly let myself in the back door. I didn't know what to expect, so I stood inside the kitchen and called out softly a few times, "Missie, it's David!" There was no answer, then the sound of footsteps above. I pushed the swing door into the hall. Suddenly all the lights went on, and there stood Missie at the top of the stairs. Her hair was hanging down in straggly clumps; the mascara and makeup made a ghastly streaked mask down to her chin; one false eyelash was missing; her eyes were staring and wild. She was naked and looked quite, quite mad.

I had never seen real hysteria before and didn't know how to cope with it. I tried walking up the stairs toward her, but she backed away, screaming, "Go away! Go away! I hate you! . . . Don't touch me!"

When I tried to reason with her, she sat on the landing, alternately sobbing like a child and snarling down at me through the banisters like a caged animal.

I knew I must get her a doctor, but the very mention of the word brought on the most terrifying reaction. I knew also that she must be overdue at the studio makeup department, and any minute the assistant director would be calling up to find out if she had overslept; above all, I knew that if Missie had cracked up, no word of it must leak out to the press or she'd be finished in Hollywood.

In desperation I tried an offhand approach.

"Look, darling," I said, "you can sit up there on the floor as long as you like, but I'm bored, and I want to watch television."

At that hour of the morning in the early days of TV, there were no programs on the air, but I had a feeling that I must coax her downstairs and try to keep her busy. I switched on the set, which cracked and hummed and displayed nothing but horizontal lines, and settled myself on the sofa to watch them. After a few minutes the stairs behind me creaked, but I did not look around. I could sense that Missie was standing watching me. Then she came shyly into the room, like a child, and curled up on the sofa next to me to watch the blank screen with a funny private smile. We sat there together for a long while. Occasionally she would let out a peal of laughter and point at the set; sometimes she would shrink back in horror; once she screamed with fear and moved up close beside me.

Goose bumps rose on my back.

I put my arm around her naked body to protect her from whatever it was she saw in her poor faraway mind—she was icy cold.

The phone rang in the kitchen. I glanced at my watch. It was only eight o'clock, but I already felt I had been in that house for a lifetime.

Having succeeded, so far, in calming her by playing a game of lies, I continued by saying, "Oh, that's for me. . . . I'll be back in a second."

It was indeed Mac, the assistant director. He was in a highly choleric condition.

"Where the hell is Missie?" he demanded. "She's over two hours late!"

By a great stroke of good luck I had worked with Mac and knew him for one of that priceless breed of true professionals who can guide unsure directors, make life pleasant for actors, and save money for producers. Once he had identified himself, I whispered down the phone.

"Missie is sick, Mac, and it's real trouble, so for her sake don't say a word to anyone except the producer. . . . Who is he?"

Mac mentioned a fairly obscure name and added, "And he's a jerk."

"Tell him to come over right away," I said. "Not to come up to the house, just blow the horn in the street, and I'll come out to him."

I fetched Missie's husband's overcoat from the hall closet and joined her once more before the television set. She snuggled under the coat and clasped my hand. "Isn't she lovely?" she said, pointing at the empty screen. Around nine o'clock I heard the front doorbell ring. Missie was transformed.

"Don't let them in!" she pleaded. "They'll take me away!" I promised that I wouldn't let anyone in if she would be a good little girl and go up to her room and shut the door. I watched her still-gorgeous back view ascend the stairs.

On the doorstep I found a highly strung, fat, youngish man dressed in white slacks and a puce open-neck shirt. His black hair was slicked down, and his eyes were obscured by dark glasses.

"What gives, for chrissakes?" he asked, and before I had time to phrase an answer, he added belligerently, "And how did *you* get into the act?"

I brought Missie's producer up to date and told him that in my opinion she would be unable to report for work for some time.

"Are you screwing her?" he asked. "What the hell do you know about it? . . . You're not her goddamn physician. . . . Where is she? . . . I want to talk with her."

He was prevented from doing this and finally left, having jabbed a finger in my chest and promised to sue me, to call the police, to get me barred from all the studios and to "take care of Missie for fucking up *my* picture."

When he had gone, I found Missie cringing among the shoes at the bottom of her wardrobe.

After another hour of empty television I claimed an urge for a cup of coffee and left Missie reacting to the horizontal flashes while I headed for the kitchen and another whispered phone call, this time to the new head of her studio—a quiet, dignified man I had met only once.

He was light-years ahead of his image-conscious producer. "The only thing that matters is that girl's health," he said at once. "We'll keep the picture going and wait for her as long as we can; if necessary, we'll recast and reshoot Missie's part, but what about *her*?"

I underlined the urgent need for a doctor, and he instantly agreed to alert my old friend from Santa Monica, whose office, far from Beverly Hills, was unlikely to be infiltrated by gossip columnists' spies, eager for the hot news of an impending abortion, a drying out, or a breakdown. He also promised to locate Missie's husband and get him an immediate message, telling him, from me, in the most urgent but least frightening terms, what had happened to his wife and to urge him to return posthaste. We both agreed it would take him at least three days to make the trip.

Probably from her hours of naked exposure in a drafty house, Missie was coughing intermittently, so I told her that my doctor would be passing by to give me "an injection" and that I'd ask him to check her over at the same time and perhaps recommend something for her cold. To my surprise she agreed without much ado, but when I suggested that she clean up her face for the impending visit, it provoked another screaming spate of abuse: If I didn't think she was beautiful the way she was, why didn't I get the hell out? . . . Who'd invited me anyway? et cetera. After she calmed down, we returned to the television set, and Missie ate some cottage cheese.

The doctor arrived punctually, and I went down to the gate to brief him. He followed me into the house, and when Missie saw him administering my bogus jab, she held my hand during the proceedings. When he turned his attention to her, she babbled incoherently but allowed him to listen to her heart and lungs. He produced a bottle of pills and said to me, "She should take two of these every two hours. . . .She has the beginnings of a nasty infection there. . . .I'll drop by again around six."

Missie had been unnaturally calm during his visit but the

storm broke when he asked if she had a girlfriend who could come and sit with her "because you might feel drowsy and you don't want to take a fall."

She suddenly turned on the poor man and started belaboring him and pushing him toward the front door. She yelled and screamed and poured out torrents of abuse on him and on all her girlfriends, naming them one by one, reviling them and accusing them of plotting against her.

When she collapsed with the inevitable tear storm, she sobbed, "David's the only one I trust . . . and he's looking after me."

At the doctor's car he said, "There's no question . . . the girl's in big trouble and must go in for psychiatric treatment at once."

The responsibility was being lifted from my shoulders. I was relieved and said so, but he shook his head. "You told me it would be three days before the husband gets here, and by California law the next of kin is the only one who can sign her in. . . . Even I can't do it. Till he gets here, she *must not be left alone* whatever happens. And lock up all the kitchen hardware because she might do anything."

He paused and said kindly, "It's going to be tough on you, but you're the friend of the family, and it looks as though you're stuck. . . . How's the sex thing between you?"

"There isn't any," I said. "There never has been."

He opened the door of his convertible. "She's going to offer it to you," he said. "That's part of the pattern. If you accept, you'll make matters worse, and if you refuse, you'll still make matters worse because she'll feel rejected by the only person she trusts. . . . I don't envy you the next three days."

"What the hell do I do?" I asked. "I've only been here four hours, and I'm already exhausted. . . . I have my own life to lead, too."

"Give her those pills," he said, "and keep in touch with me. Remember, when they're like this, they're very, very cunning. Good luck."

He drove away.

Back in the house the nightmare took its course. First the phone rang, and a voice said, "Hold the line for Miss Louella Parsons, please."

It hadn't taken long; probably a secretary in the fat producer's office had heard him pressing the panic button. Louella's well-known drawl came over the phone. She demanded to speak to Missie.

"She sick," I said, putting on what I hoped was a Filipino houseman's voice. "She sleeping . . . she no come to phone . . . you leave message."

"Tell her to call Louella Parsons as soon as she wakes."

"Yes, ma'am," I said.

"Who was that?" asked Missie when I went back into the television room.

"Oh, just Louella," I said offhandedly.

Missie was instantly transformed. "Why don't you want me to speak to Louella ?" she yelled. "She probably wants to do a Sunday story on me. . . . You *know* I love Louella." She ran into the kitchen and started looking up the columnist's number. I grabbed the phone from Missie's hands, and a battle royal took place for its possession. She went for my eyes and testicles with fingers like hooked claws, so during the sobbing period that followed the encounter I took the doctor's advice and locked up all the sharp kitchen implements I could find.

The dreadful day dragged on. During the afternoon I finally persuaded her to take two of the doctor's pills, which she had hitherto regarded with the deepest suspicion, but first she wanted to take a walk around the small swimming pool. Stark naked as usual, she paraded about the garden, and I prayed that prying journalistic eyes could not see through the hedge. When the moment to take the pills came, she grabbed the bottle out of my hand and ran off like a naughty child, hid it behind her back, and demanded a kiss in exchange for it. This payment having been extracted, she deliberately emptied the contents of the bottle into the deep end of the pool.

The doctor paid his second visit, and Missie refused to let him inside the house, saying he was one of "Them." I managed to have a few words with him in the garden.

"I'll get you some more pills," he said, and showed me where he would leave them by the gate. "They're strong sedatives; it'll make your life much easier if she'll take them. . . . Is she eating anything?"

"Only cottage cheese," I told him.

"Try pounding them up and mixing them in there," he suggested. "Is she drinking?"

"She asks for a glass of wine now and then . . . is that bad?"

"Any stimulant is bad, of course, but don't refuse it—water it down."

He gave me news from the head of Missie's studio. "I'm in contact with him; he sounds like a good guy. He said to tell you that the husband is on his way. He's due in eight o'clock Sunday morning."

My heart sank—it was only Thursday evening.

"He said to tell you that he's put out a press release that she's in bed with a virus infection under doctor's care . . . good luck, Doctor!" He added with a smile, "Try to get a couple of those pills into her stomach, and take the phone off the hook."

Missie made the offer the doctor had predicted during our first night together.

"I've something for you," she said seductively, and ran upstairs, giggling.

Half an hour later she called down. Her face was cleaned at last, her makeup redone, her hair brushed and falling in a golden cloud over her shoulders, and she was wearing a short black see-through nightie. She looked lovely.

"Come and get it," she whispered from the top of the stairs, turning her back in a parody of sexiness and lifting the hem of the nightie. It was not an easy evening for me, to put it mildly, and it ended in a glass- and bottle-throwing scene with Missie ordering me out of the house, an instruction I longed to, but dared not, obey.

The pills did not seem to have much effect on Missie. Around midnight she ate some cottage cheese which contained a couple and drank some wine into which I had stirred a third, but they slowed her down for only an hour or two; then she was as bright and demanding and as terrifyingly unpredictable as before. I dared not go to sleep for five minutes, and as the long days and interminable nights melded into each other, a dreadful thought began to assail me— that it was not Missie whose mind had become deranged . . . it was mine. I became a hollow-eyed zombie, sleepless and utterly exhausted, but Missie never showed any signs of tiredness and harried me endlessly to play hide-and-seek with her, to flatter her, to comfort her, to fight with her, or to go to bed with her.

I found I had come to hate her.

Twice a day the doctor met me in the garden to give me news of the husband's progress and to inject me with floods of B12 to keep me going. By Saturday evening I could go no further.

"I can't make it through tonight," I told him. "The plane's on time . . . he arrives tomorrow morning. For God's sake give her a jab and put her out so that I can *sleep. . . . I can't go on.*"

He looked at me carefully for a long time. "It's completely illegal," he said, "but OK, I'll do it."

He outlined the plan. I was to leave the front door open, and at nine o'clock exactly he would slip in with a trained nurse, who, he said, would act as a witness, help with the injection, and also stay the night to take care of Missie when she came around. The two of them would hide in the downstairs bathroom; then, on some pretext, I would coax her into the hall, grab her, throw her on the ground, and hold her down while the deed was done.

"It's going to be very rough," he said, "and God knows I hate to do it—but it's the only way."

Missie seemed to sense that something was going to happen. For the first time her eyes lost their wild look; she seemed calm, almost normal and very vulnerable. She followed me wherever I went. Also, for the first time, she talked about her husband. She had not mentioned him once during the whole time I had been with her. "I hope he comes to see me," she said sadly.

It was eerie.

A few minutes before nine o'clock I told her I was hungry and asked her to come help me fix a sandwich. She left her favorite place in front of the television set and put her hand trustingly and childlike in mine. As we passed through the hall into the kitchen, I caught a glimpse through the curtains of the doctor's darkened car at the gate.

We puttered about in the kitchen, and I received another reminder of the premonition that had awakened within my charge. Suddenly Missie said, "You won't let them take me away, will you?"

For a moment I thought she too might have seen the car.

"Who?" I asked.

"Oh!" she said mysteriously. "*They* will be coming for me one day. . . .They want to take me away, but you won't let them, will you?"

"Of course not," I said, loathing every second of the dreadful charade that was unfolding. Slowly I ate my sandwich.

When I judged that sufficient time had elapsed for my co-conspirators to be in position and ready, I took Missie's trusting hand in mine and led her into the hall; a chink of light showed from beneath the bathroom door. Clumsily I spun the poor naked girl around, hooked one leg behind her knees, and flung her to the ground.

After a first startled gasp she fought with incredible ferocity and strength. She didn't scream; she was spitting like a panther, biting, clawing, and kicking. I finally managed to spread-eagle her on the floor and to pinion her arms by kneeling on the elbow joints. I yelled for the doctor.

When she saw two strange forms approaching, one in white uniform and the other bearing a hypodermic syringe, Missie screamed at last, long, piercing notes of pure animal terror.

"They've *come!* They've *come!*"

The nurse held Missie's feet, and between us we controlled her convulsive struggles while the doctor did his work.

It was soon over, and as she began to calm down I avoided her eyes, filled as they were with such blazing hatred at my base betrayal.

Later, when we carried her to bed, her face was as innocent and as peaceful as a baby's.

The nurse cleaned up my many bites and scratches, and the doctor gave me something that would enable me to go to sleep at last. None of us spoke.

At six o'clock the next day, refreshed, but with a leaden conscience and a three-day growth of beard, I drove, on my way to the airport, through the peaceful emptiness of the early-morning streets.

A few kids were already abroad, experimenting with brightly colored bikes, and some early risers in curlers and bedroom slippers were retrieving carelessly delivered Sunday papers from beneath bushes in their front gardens.

I felt as though I had returned from far, far away.

> To gild refined gold, to paint the lily,
> To throw a perfume on the violet,
> To smooth the ice, or add another hue
> Unto the rainbow, or with taper-light
> To seek the beauteous eye of heaven to garnish,
> Is wasteful and ridiculous excess.
>   —WILLIAM SHAKESPEARE

17
Long Shots and Close-Ups

CARY

*I*T is very easy to write about Cary Grant's pedigree as an actor, to enthuse over the way he comported himself as a great star, and to be amazed at the extraordinary composure he displayed on the screen—appearing utterly relaxed and therefore, like a magnet, drawing the eye of the beholder—but it is another thing altogether to try to describe Cary, the private individual, because he was a will-o'-the-wisp.

Enthusiasm was a most important ingredient in Cary's makeup, and it shone out of that side of his character which he presented to his friends; the other side was as mysterious as the dark side of the moon. Cary's enthusiasm made him search for perfection in all things, particularly in the three that meant most to him: filmmaking; physical fitness; and women.

He found it without too much difficulty in the first two categories, becoming a perfectionist in his work and a living monument to bodily health, but in the third group he struck a few snags. He passed rapidly through his marriages to Virginia Cherrill, Barbara Hutton, and Betsy Drake and filled in the lonely gaps between them by falling in and out of love with most of his leading ladies, which, as his output of films was prodigious, underlined the excellence of his physical condition.

"The trick," he said, "is to be relaxed. If you can attain true relaxation, you can make love forever." This was heady advice, but it seemed odd coming from the mouth of one who freely admitted that from the age of twelve when he had run away from school to join an acrobatic troupe, he had been searching for peace within himself. When I say Cary attacked his amours with enthusiasm, I don't mean to conjure up a picture of him in an executioner's outfit, advancing purposefully with a rawhide whip; he was gentle and thoughtful, and they all loved him dearly, but he went headfirst into the affrays, throwing caution to the winds and quite convinced, in his boundless enthusiasm, that each romance was the one for which he had been put into the world. If his disillusionments were many, his defeats were few, and he always, with great gallantry, took the blame when things went wrong, saying that he had been too egocentric to give the union a proper chance.

He showed great resilience when things didn't work out, his recipe being "to stay within the pattern" and to try again with another lady of much the same physical appearance as the last. When he met the earthy Sophia Loren during the shooting of her first Hollywood picture, Cary took unto himself the role of "patron" and taught her carefully how to pick the most rewarding path through the Hollywood jungle. He often proclaimed that while doing this, he had fallen in love with her, but if so, he got over it with typical alacrity when Sophia, not the least ambitious of actresses, suddenly announced that she was marrying her portly producer, Carlo Ponti. Upon receipt of this news Cary allowed no grass to grow under his feet. He "followed the pattern" and was off like a flash in a gypsy caravan with a younger and more voluptuous edition of Sophia—a bouncing lady called Luba, a Yugoslav basketball player.

The first day that Cary, the perfectionist, walked into my house, he went immediately into high gear. He pursed his lips, made clucking noises, and set about straightening the pictures. Through the years to come he made generous efforts to straighten out my private life by warning me of the quirks and peculiarities of various ladies, by giving me complicated advice on how to play a part in a film I was making with him, by telling me which stocks to buy when I could not afford a phone call to a broker, and by promising that he could cure my liking for scotch by hypnotizing me. These offers of help were spontaneous and genuine, and if they did not noticeably improve my shortcomings, they did at least help me perceive that if Cary spent a great deal of his time worrying about himself, he spent much more worrying about others.

His was a restless soul. He changed houses the way most of us changed agents—without a backward glance—and long before computers went into general release, Cary had one in his own brain. A brilliant businessman himself, he was fascinated by the very rich and the ultrasuccessful and was in his element in the company of Howard Hughes, Onassis, Kirkorian, Hearst, and assorted tycoons.

His perfectionist urge with regard to his own body was nothing short of mystical. He invariably looked, moved, and behaved like a man fifteen or twenty years his junior. "I just *think* myself thin—and it happens," he was fond of saying, but he conveniently forgot his frugal eating, his daily workouts, and his appointments with the masseur.

Early one morning at his Palm Springs hideaway (he was passing through his Desert Period at the time), I heard loud commands followed by hideous grunts and splashing. Cary was taking lessons in how to swim the crawl. "Why lessons?" I asked sleepily from my bedroom window. "You swim the crawl beautifully—I've seen you do it for years."

"I want to do it *perfectly,*" he gurgled, and plowed on.

During the same period Cary, who had seldom thrown a leg over a horse, invested in a white stallion and a beautifully cut riding outfit of black Levi's, discreetly decorated with small silver stars, and within an incredibly short space of time he was a Valkyrie, galloping about the dunes with great panache and perfect control.

Anyone as silhouette-conscious as Cary was bound, sooner or later, to go through a health food period, and some of us suffered stoically through his Days of the Carrot. A vast clanking machine was installed in his kitchen, shaped like the mouth of a great white shark.

"Today we'll have nothing but carrot juice," Cary announced, and emptied a couple of sacks of roots into its gaping maw. Fearful throbbings and crunchings followed us into the garden, where we were given a preluncheon cocktail of buttermilk, wheat germ, and molasses. When the sinister sounds died down, we reentered the house to find that the machine had gone berserk and had redecorated the kitchen from top to bottom; walls, windows, ceiling, and linoleum flooring were covered with a fibrous yellow paste.

Cary's exercises in hypnotism were less messy, and he certainly cured himself of smoking by saying over and over for weeks, "Your fingers are yellow, your breath smells, and you only smoke because you are insecure." He also claimed that he had cured a nasty slash on his back collected in a film duel by applying oxygen to the affected area and commanding his lungs to dissolve the useless tissues. This so impressed us that before long we were lying like stranded tuna on his drawing-room carpet, waiting for him to bring us around.

Betsy, Cary's third wife, had a very unattractive experience after visiting him on location in Spain. She booked on a luxury liner to return to America, and when she landed in New York, she was badly in need of therapy to help her forget her trip. The name of her ship had been *Andrea Doria*.

Betsy spent a great deal of time with a Dr. Mortimer Hartman, who gave her a series of treatments which included doses of LSD. Betsy then reported that she was completely released from her haunting memories of the liner settling beneath her feet but said she now had the feeling that it was time she scuttled Cary—which she did. Cary, to whom the unknown was an irresistible challenge, promptly registered himself with Dr. Hartman and spent many weeks contentedly munching LSD, listening to music, and baring his soul. Apparently, it was a most salutary experience, sometimes joyful, sometimes shattering, but he persevered until he could announce to his spellbound friends, who were half envious and half horrified by what he had willingly subjected himself to, that he was a totally new man, cleansed and purged of all inhibitions, with a subconscious which could no longer cause him any problems.

"All actors long to be loved," he said. "That's why we become actors . . . but I don't give a damn anymore. . . . I'm self-sufficient *at last!*"

It seemed to the rest of us a most hazardous trip for Cary to have taken to find out what we could have told him anyway: that he had always been self-sufficient, that he had always been loved, and that he would continue to give a damn about himself—and particularly about others.

George

If Cary Grant was an optimist then George Sanders was the opposite, and he genuinely harbored all the cynicism he so joyfully displayed.

Russian-born George, a giant grizzly of a man, had a face, even in his twenties, which looked as though he had rented it on a long lease and had lived in it so long he didn't want to move out. He was a highly undervalued actor probably because he didn't give a damn whether or not his efforts were appreciated. "I don't ask questions," he said. "I just take their money and use it for things that *really* interest me."

As early as 1937, when we were working on a John Ford picture together, he said, "I will have had enough of this earth by the time I am sixty-five. After that I shall be having my bottom wiped by nurses and being pushed around in a wheelchair. I won't be able to enjoy a woman anymore, so I shall commit suicide."

I don't remember George's ever taking any exercise. He would show up immaculately dressed and watch the rest of us playing tennis or would sit comfortably near the eighteenth green till we finished playing golf and would throw up his hands in horror at any suggestion that he might like to take a walk along the beach.

His reaction to war service was one of instant repulsion, and he never modified it. "The stupidest thing young men can do is to throw away their youth, as Thomas Carlyle said,

'With clenched teeth and hell fire eyes hacking one another's flesh.' They'll never get me to do it." And they never did. "I shall keep ahead of the sheriff," he announced. "Luckily I hold three passports—Russian, American, and British. I shall play one off against the other till they either give up or order me to do something. Then I shall immediately become a Quaker, and if they tell me to drive an ambulance, I shall crash so many learning how to drive that they'll send me home."

George did, however, try to make a tongue-in-cheek contribution to World War II. In 1943 he forwarded to Washington a detailed suggestion for the organization and administration of an infantry battalion equipped with roller skates. He enclosed a graph of gradients and the estimated attack speeds of troops along main roads. To me, in England, around the same time, he sent an envelope "To be forwarded instantly to Winston Churchill." It contained the specification of an attachment to be clamped to the nose cone of RAF bombs. On their way earthward, he claimed, they would sound the German all-clear and the ensuing disaster among those issuing from their shelters would add "a gratifying bonus in casualties."

George suffered bouts of black oppression which his friends dismissed as "another of his Russian moods," but when they were on him, he was inconsolable. He was a loner and would often disappear for days on end into his beautifully equipped workshop; several strange but very clever inventions awaited patents as a result.

Women were fascinated by George, and before Zsa Zsa Gabor decided to become a caricature of her real self, the two of them made a fascinating couple. She enjoyed and encouraged his peculiar outlook on life and his sometimes outrageous utterances; he was fascinated by her very great beauty and her vivacity. No mean hand with an acid quip herself, Zsa Zsa once told me that she and Conrad Hilton, her millionaire ex-husband, "only had one thing in common . . . *his* money."

When Zsa Zsa "left" George, she somehow contrived to stay on in their Bel Air home facing the fifteenth fairway of the Country Club and took in as a houseguest "the great Parisian lover" himself—Porfirio Rubirosa. If this infuriated George, he gave little sign of it, but it certainly awakened him to the very grave financial dangers of the California divorce laws.

"This is no time to behave like a gentleman," said George. "I am a cad and shall react like one."

On a misty evening in late December with the surrounding hills twinkling with half a hundred illuminated Christmas trees, George left his car near the fifteenth green and set off up the fairway. He was accompanied by his lawyer and a man with big black camera.

The lawyer and the photographer carried a ladder. George carried a brick.

The plan was simple. The french windows of the master bedroom, in which George was convinced action sooner or later would be taking place, overlooked the golf course. The french windows opened onto a veranda. Bedroom and veranda were on the first floor—hence the ladder.

Once inside the room, George had every reason to believe he would find his wife in bed with Rubirosa—hence the camera.

But, George reasoned, the french windows might well be locked—hence the brick.

The lawyer, with the caution of his ilk, was worried that police might intercept their cortege and ask embarrassing questions. "Certainly," he said, "there's not a reason on earth why a householder shouldn't enter his house by ladder if he so desires, but a brick could be construed as an offensive weapon. . . . I'm worried about that brick."

George had a brainwave. "I'm bringing my wife a present on Christmas Eve," he said. "So we gift-wrap the brick."

The operation, according to George, went without a hitch. When the signs were that the big double bed above was working overtime, the ladder was placed in position and the assault was mounted, but Zsa Zsa, an unwitting fifth columnist, had forgotten to lock the window, and the brick became redundant.

Zsa Zsa and Rubirosa, their eyes wide with apprehension

and dazzled by flashbulbs, were photographed clutching the sheets to their chins; then, like two plump partridges, they broke from the undergrowth and scuttled for the bathroom.

George and his henchmen waited, but the culprits, in a sudden burst of modesty, refused to come out again because there was only one towel. At last matters were arranged, dressing gowns were permitted, and the whole party descended the stairs in an embarrassed silence. Hesitant farewells were being made when Zsa Zsa, with a flash of great style, said, "Oh, George darling. . . . I almost forgot, I have a gift for you under the tree!"

To which George could not resist replying, "And I have a gift for *you*," and he handed her the brick.

The calmest time of George Sanders' life was during his marriage to Benita, Ronald Colman's beautiful widow.

The most understanding and generous-hearted of women, Benita encouraged George's inventions and eccentric ways, applauded his excellent screen performances, survived the soaring arias and Wagnerian bellowings that blared permanently from his homemade hi-fi, and even invested heavily in his manufacturing company, named Cad Co. The company went down to defeat quixotically trying to make English sausages in Scotland filled with Italian meat.

George was not a man endowed with optimism and hope, so when Benita died, he became daily more cynical and disillusioned, and at the age of sixty-five, he did what he had always promised he would do: He took his own life.

ERNST LUBITSCH

Ernst Lubitsch was a pixie. There were three or four master directors in Hollywood in the thirties and forties, men for whom the biggest stars in the world tripped over each other in their anxiety to be invited to work. Ernst Lubitsch was the master's master. For a big established star to perform for Lubitsch was the sign that a career had reached its zenith, and for a beginner to be cast in a Lubitsch picture was notification that a new career was off to the most promising of starts.

One day in 1936 the "producers' producer" called me in to his office. I had lately been signed by him to a long-term beginners' contract, and I held him in such awe that if he had said, "I have cast you as a performing dog," I would have rushed out and taken barking and hoop-jumping lessons. The great Samuel Goldwyn looked at me unsmilingly out of his small, deepset eyes. "You are a very lucky young man," he said.

I nodded in agreement.

"But you don't know it," he added.

I nodded again.

"I have just loaned you to Ernst Lubitsch for *Bluebeard's Eighth Wife*. Report to Paramount Studios tomorrow. Keep your ears open and your mouth shut, and put yourself in Ernst's hands—they're the best in Hollywood."

Tottering on legs made rubbery by my unbelievable good fortune, I made my way to the office of Reeves Espy, the calm and considerate right hand of the volcanic Mr. Goldwyn.

"This is a real break for you," said Espy. "I've read the script—it's written by Billy Wilder and Charlie Brackett—it's marvelous, and your part is *great!*"

"What is it?" I asked breathlessly.

"Secretary to Mr. Brandon," said Espy.

"Who's Mr. Brandon?"

"Gary Cooper," said Espy, "and you're also in love with his girl."

"Who's his girl?"

"Claudette Colbert—and they both get to beat you up. . . . It's a very sympathetic role."

What a bonanza! An unknown beginner to be directed by Lubitsch, in a script by Wilder and Brackett, and to play with Paramount's two superstars, Gary Cooper and Claudette Colbert, and to be beaten up by both of them!

The next morning, shining like a new pin, I checked in at the Paramount lot, was handed the key to a dressing room and given a script.

"Read it right away, David," advised the casting director, "then about eleven go over to Ernst's office—he wants to meet you and talk to you about wardrobe et cetera."

By eleven o'clock I was in poor shape. The part was indeed

beautifully written, but I was quite convinced that I could never play it.

Lubitsch was a tiny man, with a heavy German accent, straight black hair slicked down, twinkling black eyes, and a cigar out of all proportion to the ensemble. When I walked into his office, he was in shirtsleeves with heavy suspenders supporting his pants. He rose from behind his desk and greeted me with both hands outstretched and a slice of blatantly overdone flattery.

"This is indeed a pleasure." He beamed. "We are so lucky to get you for this part! Now before we sit down," he said, "would you mind dropping your trousers?"

"I beg your pardon?" I said nervously.

Gales of laughter swept over the little man. "Don't worry." He chortled. "I have a very beautiful wife! But I have to see your legs, because your opening scene is on the beach with Claudette. If you have strong legs, there will be no problem, but if you have twigs like mine, we'll have to rework the scene so you can wear slacks."

I dropped my pants, and he pronounced himself satisfied. "Good"—he nodded—"like a Bavarian bullock."

Then he sat me down on a sofa and proceeded to act out all my scenes, giggling and hugging himself as he explained the visual business he was intending to incorporate into them, and the more he gesticulated and pranced about, the more convinced did I become that I did not have the equipment or the training to deliver to him that which he obviously thought was his for the asking.

Finally, sensing that I was holding something back, Lubitsch asked me what was the matter.

"I don't think I can do it, Mr. Lubitsch," I mumbled.

He looked at me, and his eyes shone with merriment. "Do I frighten you?" he asked.

"No, sir," I said, "but I'm terrified of Gary Cooper and Claudette Colbert. . . ."

He jumped up and hooted with laughter.

"Do you know something?" He chortled. "Claudette is frightened of Coop because of his natural acting, and Coop is frightened of Claudette because she's so expert and this is his first comedy, and both of them are scared out of their wits by the small-part players Edward Everett Horton, Franklin Pangborn and Herman Bing, because they are supposed to be scene stealers . . . but d'you know who is the most frightened of all? . . . Me!"

He put his arm around my waist (because he could not reach my shoulders) and led me to the door.

"Everyone will be nervous on the first day," he said, "even the electricians in case they set fire to the studio, but we're all going to be together for many weeks, and I promise you it'll be fun. Now run along to wardrobe and makeup, they have some fittings and tests set up for you. . . . Drop in to see me anytime. . . . We don't start for two weeks—you're a member of the family now!"

I couldn't wait to start.

When Ernst Lubitsch described us as his family, it was no understatement, and we all had complete respect for the father figure. I never once heard him raise his voice, and he loved to be given suggestions, listened patiently to them, and then just as patiently explained why they wouldn't work.

Billy Wilder, the future master director, was constantly on the set, and there was obviously a great rapport between him and Lubitsch: he may even then have set his sights on directing, because he was unfailingly understanding and appreciative with the actors, a nice change from many writers who winced painfully as their golden words fell from the performers' mouths.

Lubitsch took infinite pains with everyone, especially with me, the novice, and for several days before I started work, he ordered me to be on the set so that I could get to know everyone and feel at home.

"I don't know what I'm going to do about Gary." He chuckled. "He's just *too* relaxed!"

Cooper had ambled onto the set in a crumpled flannel suit.

"Just look at him!" said Lubitsch. "It's the first time he's played a comedy, and we had that business-tycoon suit made by Eddie Schmidt, but he still thinks he's a cowhand. Where've you been, Gary?" he asked conversationally.

"I just grabbed me a little shut-eye on that pile of straw back there on Stage Six," drawled the tall man from Montana.

Lubitsch sent for Slim, Cooper's gangling stand-in, and Cracker, his small devoted dresser from Georgia.

"Now you two!" He giggled. "Coop is playing a business tycoon on holiday in Cannes, France, his wardrobe is very elegant, and he has to be stopped going to sleep in it every time he finishes a scene, so get him out of that suit and into pajamas, then have it pressed *again*!"

Gary Cooper was no poseur—he was exactly what he seemed, a charming, slow-talking, gentle country boy who loved animals and open air and avoided problems—but he was also a phenomenal natural actor with spectacular good looks and a great sense of timing. I was fascinated by the way he "thought" on the screen, and during a lull when we were shooting a scene together, I asked him about this.

"You have such great concentration," I said. "How do you do it?"

Coop looked genuinely startled. "Concentration?" he said slowly. "Bullshit! I'm just tryin' to remember what the hell I have to say next!"

My first big scene was indeed on the beach with Claudette Colbert—outside the Carlton Hotel, Cannes (where Brigitte Bardot was later discovered by a photographer, and a naked starlet by Robert Mitchum). It was simulated by dumping a few truckloads of sand inside Stage 4, and gaudy umbrellas above bronzed extras completed the illusion. The scene was a long one, and the comedy content was delicate. Claudette and "Bullock Legs" were in swimsuits, and the sun arcs blazed down from on high. Claudette, the soul of enchanting fun and a most generous performer, did all she could to calm my twittering nerves, but she made things a little difficult for the cameraman because, convinced that it was her best side, she insisted that she be photgraphed only on the left side of her face. Many stars harbored the same beliefs and specified in their contracts which one could be presented to the camera.

Lubitsch perched himself atop a small stepladder at the side of the camera, the inevitable howitzer-type cigar in his mouth. He rehearsed us carefully and finally said, "Let's shoot it!" Very conscious of the fifty or so bronzed extras (all would-be stars), I was about as relaxed as a bulldozer, but

Claudette patted my knee and whispered, "It's going to be great." We started the comedy scene, and I noticed that Lubitsch was crying.

"Cut!" he sobbed helplessly at the end. "That was *wonderful!* You made me laugh so much I nearly choked! . . . Now, just a couple of little suggestions. . . ."

We absorbed them eagerly, and he clambered back up his stepladder. "Action!" he commanded. Again we played the scene, and again Lubitsch wept.

"Wonderful! Wonderful! *How* you made me laugh! . . . Now just a couple of little suggestions. . . ."

We probably played the scene a dozen times, each time our efforts were saluted by paroxysms of mirth from the master director, and each time he managed to blurt out "a couple of little suggestions" before climbing back onto his perch. By the time we had performed the scene to his complete satisfaction we had, of course, like many before us, given performances of "pure Lubitsch," and as Claudette pointed out, "And why not? . . . He's better than any of us!"

JOHN HUSTON

All the directors had their little idiosyncrasies. Lubitsch had his cigar and his stepladder. John Ford sat beneath the camera chewing the corner of a grubby white handkerchief. Michael Curtiz strode about wearing breeches and riding boots and brandishing a fly whisk. William Wyler liked to make anything up to forty takes and then print the first. Otto Preminger seemed to enjoy working in an atmosphere of tension, and generated it by screaming loudly at people. Henry Hathaway objected to chairs on the set for actors—"I'm on *my* feet all day . . . they should be on theirs." W. S. Van Dyke chain-sipped gin out of paper cups, and Bill Seiter, who specialized in comedies, employed a goosing stick on the touchy bottoms of the unsuspecting—a long cane on the end of which was clenched a plaster fist with the second finger rudely extended.

Of the master directors (Ford and Wyler were also on everybody's list) the most relaxed, with his poet's heart and misleading broken boxer's face, was John Huston. "Let's just kick it around, kids," he would say to his actors, and from their first natural and tentative playing and thereafter through many rehearsals, he would build up a scene piece by piece till he was satisfied; then he would invite the cameraman to watch a run-through. "That's it," Huston would say. "Now go ahead and light it." While that was being done, he would wash all problems from his mind by settling down with a box of panatelas and a good book.

I first met John in 1935 when he was a scriptwriter at the Samuel Goldwyn Studios; his father, Walter, a monumental actor, was playing the name part in the film of *Dodsworth,* directed by William Wyler. I was playing a small part in the picture, and John was constantly on the set. In spite of his many great directorial successes there, John never fully settled for the Hollywood way of life and found his ultimate happiness with a home in Southern Ireland, leaping fearlessly over jagged stone walls as Master of the Galway Blazers Fox Hounds. He once made a tentative stab at living in Hollywood and moved into a house near Clark Gable's in the San Fernando Valley. It was a revolutionary structure consisting almost entirely of glass with some necessary beams and supports of redwood. John lived inside this bizarre cage with an extremely beautiful wife and a very ugly monkey. History does not relate where the monkey came from, but John persuaded delicious Evelyn Keyes to join him during a long dinner at Romanoff's Restaurant. They flew that night to Las Vegas to get married after Mike Romanoff had first bustled off to his house and retrieved a wedding ring which had fallen off somebody's finger into his swimming pool. Evelyn was a highly intelligent girl, and for a while great happiness reigned, interrupted admittedly by the gibberings and shrieks of the monkey.

Only those involved can ever know what tensions have pulled apart a marriage, and John maintained a gentlemanly silence when he and Evelyn finally called it quits. Evelyn, too, had nothing but the deepest affection and respect for John, and they remained firm friends. Evelyn enjoyed relating the final scene before they went their separate ways:

EVELYN: John, darling, I'm sorry. One of us has to go. . . . It's the monkey or me.
JOHN: (after long pause) Honey . . . it's you!

During World War II John Huston headed a particularly gallant photographic unit and became a familiar figure among front-line troops at Monte Cassino and other Italian battlefields, puffing away at his panatelas and calmly photographing the moments of maximum danger.

The war over, John returned to the United States and was there when I arrived aboard the *Queen Mary* with 15,000 joyful fighting men, mostly of the 101st Airborne Division. We were welcomed by several bands and a posse of beautiful Powers models, whose cover-girl smiles froze on their faces when the returning warriors released several hundred fully inflated condoms from the boat deck far above their heads. During drinks that evening at Jack and Charlie's, I reconstructed for John's benefit the spectacle of coveys of flying French letters eddying about the clifflike sides of the giant Cunarder, and he was moved to quote the observation of a Parisienne countess of the eighteenth century upon her first view of one of those well-intentioned envelopes: "A battlement against enjoyment, and a fishnet against infection." The conversation having taken such a soldierly turn, I was not surprised to hear John say, "While we've been away, they've opened the greatest whorehouse right here in New York, better than anything in Rome or Paris—what d'you say we go take a look at it?"

I shook my head like a bishop finding a fly button in the collection. "No, thanks—I'm a happily married man these days."

"Oh, come on!" said Huston. "You don't have to *do* anything. . . . Just come and case the joint, then we'll take the madam out for dinner—she's a lot of laughs."

I was hungry, so after John had made a phone call, we set off. The house on Park Avenue had a most imposing façade.

John pressed the bell, and a saucy-looking maid opened the door and took our coats. "Good evening, Mr. Huston." She smiled. "May I get you a drink while you're waiting?" Huston ordered a scotch, and I did the same. The maid served us the drinks in an attractively decorated drawing room, and John pointed casually to a Monet on the wall.

"Of course this is a clip joint on a big scale," he explained. "The madam has the greatest girls in New York, all shapes and colors, and anything goes, but boy, does she charge for it!"

"I'll bet," I said, "but even so—a Monet!"

"Well," said Huston, lighting up one of his smokes, "she has some old guy for herself who collects paintings, and she screws an occasional Impressionist out of the poor bastard—she has a dandy Braque right over her bed . . . it leaves marks on the wall as it swings!"

After a while the madam, very petite, beautifully dressed, and bejeweled, descended the stairs and walked into the room. John rose, kissed her hand, and introduced me.

"I'm so glad you could join us," she said in a charming voice. "John is an old friend, and he's told me so much about you."

"Well," I said, "I don't really want any action tonight, I just came to take a look at the place. . . . Where are the girls . . . all upstairs banging their brains out?"

The madam looked mystified, and Huston, like a canary-swallowing cat, smugly broke the news to me that she was in fact Nin Ryan, the most elegant society hostess in New York City.

John, the director, was famous for being easy and thoughtful with his actors; as a writer he was famous for being easy and thoughtful with his directors, and as an actor (he was an excellent performer when the spirit moved him) he was the soul of discretion in his relationships with one and all. A paragon of all virtues, so it seemed, but when the smoke of his panatelas cleared away, it was invariably found that John had quietly achieved whatever he had been striving for, no matter which hat he had been wearing. He even ended up with Jack Warner of Warner Brothers eating out of his hand.

JACK WARNER

Loud, gregarious, flashy, wisecracking Jack Warner, with his slicked-down hair and carefully plucked pencil-thin mustache, was the prototype of the Hollywood mogul. The son of a cobbler in Lynchburg, Virginia, he and his brothers were delighted when their father diversified by becoming a butcher, and they hacked happily away at the remains of dead animals, "counting," as Jack liked to say, "their thumbs along with the purchases." He freely admitted that he was a frustrated actor, and his after-dinner speeches were so long and so corny that Jack Benny was moved to remark, "Jack would rather tell a bad joke than make a good movie." Jack Warner had early worked off some of his actor urge by using the stage name of Leon Zuardo and singing in vaudeville as a boy soprano, but he listened to the advice of one of his older brothers, who said, "Don't *be* an actor. . . . *Pay* actors—the money is where the customers are."

Later, as head of production, Jack amassed a reputation as the most unbending employer of talent in Hollywood. "I pay 'em—they do what I tell 'em," he said, and conducted through the years epic running battles with most of his stars, including Flynn, Bogart, Bette Davis, and Paul Muni. When Lauren Bacall questioned his ability to handle her career, she was led to the window of his office and invited to contemplate the sprawling, humming, thriving acreage of the studio below. "Would all *that* be there," Warner inquired, "if I didn't know what the fuck I was doing?"

The Warner Brothers Studio buzzed with frustrations, which tended to be ventilated late in the day, and long after shooting had finished, cries of rage, threats of vengeance, and the sounds of rebellion issued from offices, bungalows, and dressing rooms.

Afternoon tea on the set became a popular feature while I was making a picture there with Jane Wyman. Toward the end of the day we made it a point to invite friends from nearby sound stages to drop over and join us at the charming ritual. I handed around little cakes while Jane from a large Rockingham teapot dispensed lethal dry martinis, and our

Warner-contracted guests obtained an extra charge from these clandestine sips, from the knowledge that they were enjoyed on Jack Warner's time.

Jack Warner lived the way a movie mogul was supposed to live: He was a generous host, a big gambler at work and at play, and with supreme confidence he put his money where his mouth was. In his spare time he became a well-known figure in the casinos, harbors, and other playgrounds of the Mediterranean, and entertained at his sumptuous estate in Beverly Hills with splendid abandon, but at his studio, efficiency and closely watched budgets were the watchwords. His writers were encouraged to get up early, read the papers, and then produce screenplays based on what they had read, and his actors were advised to accept the roles they were assigned without argument, to take the money and be grateful.

Many felt that his highly publicized wars with his stars were the outward signs of Jack Warner's unfulfilled inner longings to be a star himself, but one thing was sure: He never practiced discrimination, and he fought with equal gusto against producers, directors, writers, and agents.

CECIL B. DEMILLE

If Jack Warner was the militant mogul, Cecil B. DeMille, the man who "discovered" Hollywood, was the prototype producer-director. Also a onetime actor, he was the possessor of a beautifully modulated speaking voice and a very definite set of principles.

Long after he had become world-famous with his superspectaculars, such as *The Sign of the Cross, Cleopatra, The Crusades, The King of Kings, Samson and Delilah, The Greatest Show on Earth,* and *The Ten Commandments,* he voluntarily gave up, for a principle, a yearly salary of more than $100,000 which he could have continued to collect by paying just $1.

DeMille's epic career at Paramount had started when he persuaded the heads of the studio that they could no longer afford to pay the mountainous salary demanded by the queen of the box office—Mary Pickford (known to an adoring public as America's Sweetheart and to the heads of the studio as the Bank of America's Sweetheart).

"Let her go," DeMille had counseled, "and give the money to me. I'll make big pictures for you with small names, and when the small names get too big, I'll let *them* go."

It worked, and then, in 1936, as a sideline, DeMille, fascinated with radio, became producer of the *Lux Radio Theater*. Every Sunday evening thereafter for the next nine years his pear-shaped tones announced, "Greetings from Hollywood," and 40,000,000 listeners settled back and prepared to enjoy one of the most popular shows on the air.

In order to perform on radio, DeMille had long since joined the American Federation of Radio Artists, but in late 1944, around the time that American soldiers were producing their own superspectacular at the Battle of the Bulge, DeMille was informed by the AFRA that all members of the union were being assessed $1 for a fund to fight an amendment to a California law. DeMille saw the law in question as one which preserved the freedom of workers to decide whether or not they wished to join a union, he refused on principle to be ordered to subscribe toward altering it, and his "nuts" to AFRA shared the headlines with General McAuliffe's famous reply to the German High Command when he was invited to surrender Bastogne.

General McAuliffe won the Battle of Bastogne, but DeMille lost his with AFRA, and the most prestigious producer in radio was prevented from working by his union.

Watching DeMille direct a film crowd was a spectacular in itself. I was one of a thousand extras naked except for a loincloth, and as I was being constantly belabored with special "hurt-proof" whips, I gathered that I was a slave and the film was probably *Cleopatra*. (Extras focusing on the $2.50 they would be paid for their efforts seldom bothered about the titles of the pictures they worked on.) For two days I saw DeMille in the far distance high up on a platform dressed in riding boots, breeches, and an open-neck shirt and watched him issuing his instructions for the shoallike eddying of our vast throng around some pillars. Occasionally, DeMille would seize the loud-hailer and chastise some unfortunate individual among us for some minor lapse. DeMille, with his aristocratic face and fringe of hair at the base of a shining skull, looked like a benevolent bishop, but he did not sound like one. Once he had singled out his whipping boy he would berate him publicly: "Thanks to the inattention of Mr. Kowalski, I must ask you all to do this long and arduous scene once again."

The set was volcanic with discontent during my days under the lash, as we were endlessly harried by the patrician figure on high. We were cheered, however, by a story that passed among us like wildfire. DeMille on a previous production had selected his daily "Mr. Kowalski" from among the thousands and had chased him relentlessly throughout a hot, dusty day; rehearsal after rehearsal had been endured, always "Mr. Kowalski" had been blamed for everything that went wrong. Finally all was prepared. "We will now shoot the scene," came DeMille's voice, "provided Mr. Kowalski is ready."

"Mr. Kowalski," at the end of his tether, threw his $2.50 to the winds, cupped his hands, and bellowed back, "I'm ready when you are, Mr. DeMille."

He was removed.

Later I worked many times for DeMille on the *Lux Radio Theater,* but on those occasions he was always the soul of courtesy, appearing only for the dress rehearsal and the shows themselves, attired invariably in a dark suit and white shirt. After several performances on the show he presented me with a coffee mug with my name on it and singled me out for long lectures about Hollywood's moral and intellectual obligations to the public.

In 1959 DeMille called me and bade me come to his house that afternoon "for tea." I drove downtown intrigued by the invitation, because I had never set eyes on DeMille at a Hollywood function, nor had I ever seen it reported that he had attended one. I was delighted to be afforded this opportunity to glimpse the hideaway of the great man. As I passed through Beverly Hills and Hollywood, my curiosity increased in direct proportion to the smog. From my sun-drenched home on a hillside near the ocean I had looked down with dread upon a yellow-brown stagnant haze hanging over the distant restless city, and by the time I had reached Western Avenue the sun above me was diffused to a brassy glare, my chest felt encased in a lead vest, my eyes were prickling, my nose was dribbling, and even the wheezing birds were walking. I arrived at last at the bottom of a tree-covered hill surrounded on all sides by the sprawling mass of Los Angeles. I passed through a gate, drove up a winding private road, and at the summit came at last upon DeMille's abode. He had lived there all his Hollywood life, and the low, rambling structure set in its considerable acreage seemed peaceful and contented and far removed from the Hollywood he had created.

DeMille's wife, a charming gray-haired lady, met me at the door and led me through a maze of wonderfully cluttered passages and rooms to a final chintzy resting place where De-Mille was reading and where she later dispensed tea and cakes. At last, with the tea things and Mrs. DeMille gone, he told me the reason for my visit, but not before he had launched into another of his dissertations on "Hollywood's obligations to the public."

"I have made seventy films," he said suddenly. "I will make only one more; and you will be in it."

Having just completed six exhausting months making a picture for Mike Todd and knowing of DeMille's predilection for Biblically oriented ventures, I was less than fascinated by the prospect of spending the next year beneath forty pounds of false hair and being yelled at from the middle of a burning bush. He noted my hesitation.

"I am appalled by the violence in the world today," he said, "and I am going to do something about it. I am going to show that there is something else for youth besides street gangs and switch blades."

DeMille rose from his chair and paced the floor with the purposeful resolve of a planner of the Mayflower Caper; then he stopped in front of me.

"I'm going to tell the story of Baden-Powell and the Boy Scouts," he said, "and you will be Baden-Powell."

I think I voiced some mild surprise that such a gentle-sounding subject could have the ingredients for a massive DeMille epic because he spent the rest of the afternoon outlining the action-filled life of the man who had longed to be a poet, who had fought with the British cavalry in India, had developed Scouting as a martial art during service in Matabeleland, had conducted the heroic defense of Mafeking during the South African War, and had then thrown up his medal-encrusted military career to campaign against violence and to dedicate the rest of his life to helping youth. He formed the Boy Scouts and Girl Guides and saw those movements flourish in two-thirds of the countries of the world.

"Imagine!" said DeMille. "The final Jamboree, when the old man is almost eighty, with a hundred thousand youngsters of every race and color from all over the world gathered around him in peace and happiness . . . it will be my last film," he said again, "and my greatest."

It was a tragic loss when DeMille died before he could turn the cameras on his "last and greatest film."

BOBBIE

It will never be known if Utrillo or Van Gogh would have painted better pictures if they had drunk less or if Picasso would have excelled even himself if he had drunk more. Many modern musicians are convinced that they play finer music when high, but when Arthur Rubinstein or Yehudi Menuhin performs, he is stone cold sober. Certainly surgeons, airline pilots, and racing drivers avoid the stuff, but for writers and actors it presents a rather special problem.

How much of Scott Fitzgerald's brilliance and perception was aided by the bottle? How much of John Barrymore's or Spencer Tracy's was dimmed? Certainly, if the actor is not at ease, the audience is restless, so the temptation to relax oneself artificially before or during a performance is very real, and on average, I suppose, actors and writers do expose themselves to the hazards of drink more than most.

During World War I a great entertainer of legendary conviviality named Herbert Mundin volunteered for the Royal Navy and served as a stoker in a minesweeper.

For four years he obeyed regulations, so he ate, slept, and presumably stoked encased in a hideously bulky and uncomfortable cork life jacket, the theory being that there was always a possibility that the ship could hit a mine instead of sweeping it.

Herbert Mundin grew to loathe that life jacket with a passion, but this hatred notwithstanding, for four years, day and night, he was trapped inside it.

On November 11, 1918, in the middle of the North Sea he was called on deck with the rest of the crew, and after triple rum rations had been issued, the Captain announced that the war was over. In the midst of the general excitement, the cheering, the backslapping, and the sobbing, Herbert Mundin quietly looked down at his detested life jacket, his prison for four years; then he left the group and very deliberately undid its canvas straps one by one. Next he slid the loathsome garment over his head and approached the rail, smiling secretly to himself and savoring the delicious moment. Holding it in both hands, with the grip and narrowed eyes of a strangler, he looked it right in the eye. "Fuck *you!*" he said quietly, and flung it into the cold gray northern waters.

The life jacket sank like a rock.

When, a brief twenty-one years later, the Germans came on for their encore and launched World War II on a trembling and ill-prepared world, Robert Newton was near the peak of his career as a London stage actor and was already receiving the most flattering offers from Hollywood. Himself a carouser of some repute, it seemed natural that he would follow in Herbert Mundin's footsteps. He promptly joined the Royal Navy and served as a stoker in a minesweeper. His ship was very possibly the same, the equipment probably was identical, and the regulations certainly were unaltered, so, with the exception of one short respite, Robert Newton for four years wore a life jacket in which he ate, slept, and presumably stoked.

The short respite came in 1942. Submarines and bombers had taken heavy toll of His Majesty's ships and the loss of life had been appalling. Short of good officer material as a result of this tragic attrition, the Admiralty brass was poking around in the most unlikely nooks and crannies, looking for suitable candidates for commission.

Deep in the bowels of his minesweeper, they found Able-bodied Seaman Newton. His nose by now was a threat to the memory of W. C. Fields, and the legend of his intake of bottled goods was firmly established, but these were not the factors that made the brass dispatch him, posthaste, to the King Alfred Training School for Officers at Devonport; the big attraction to them was that he held an excellent degree from Oxford University.

Degree notwithstanding, the mysteries of navigation eluded Bobbie Newton, and he viewed with apprehension his final examination after four months of intensive coaching.

He saw to it that he was suitably relaxed when a stern-faced master-at-arms called out his name, "Abled-bodied Seaman Newton!" Bobbie shuffled forward and found himself on a mock-up ship's bridge. Awaiting him was the selection board, two admirals and a captain. The imitation bridge was fully equipped with a wheel, engine room telegraph, compasses, calipers, binnacles, radars, depth sounders, logbooks, and gadgets for shooting the sun and, when in great difficulty, oneself.

The captain blew down a tube and issued brisk orders to a nonexistent engine room staff, rattled off a lot of information about rhumb lines, GMT nulls, fixes, lorans, and sonars; then he spun the wheel.

"Newton," he said, with something of a flourish, "that is the situation—what is your course?"

Bobbie peered dazedly at the maze of sophisticated hardware, the helpful possibilities of which had largely escaped him during his tuition. The admirals consulted their notes and leaned expectantly forward.

"Well," said Bobbie, trying an engaging smile, "I should hazard a guess . . . that . . . we . . . are . . . heading . . . roughly, er, west?"

"Thank you," said the senior officer present. "Report back to your ship."

Bobbie Newton was a brilliant actor, but in his case the bottle, little by little, took charge. With just the right amount on board he could be fascinating, for he was a highly intelligent, erudite, kindly, and knowledgeable man, but once he had taken the extra one and his Plimsoll line had disappeared below the surface he changed gear and became anything from unpredictable to a downright menace.

Demobilized from the Royal Navy in 1945 and before taking off from a sparkling career as a character actor in Hollywood, he made a film of Noel Coward's *This Happy Breed* and at the same time performed at night in a play in London's West End.

It could have been brought on by overwork or a longing for the play to close so that he could indeed "head west," but one Saturday night at the St. James's Theatre the curtain did not rise. The audience became first restless, then impatient, and finally, from the gallery, the slow handclapping started and spread to the dress circle and the stalls.

At last the middle of the curtain wobbled uncertainly and a pair of shoes appeared beneath it. Sensing an announcement, the audience hushed itself into silence. Unsteady hands pulled the curtain apart just enough to frame the purple countenance of the star.

"Ladies and gentlemen," roared Bobbie Newton, rolling his eyes at every corner of the house, "the reason this curtain has so far not risen it because the stage manager . . . has the fucking impertinence to suggest that I am *pissed.*"

Very shortly after that episode Bobbie was on his way to Hollywood.

He did well, and his work there was greatly admired, but as word of his barhopping and extravagant behavior got around, the bush telegraph between studios signaled a preliminary warning and producers began to ask embarrassing questions about his reliability.

With millions of dollars being spent on production the last thing anyone wanted was to have precious shooting time wasted because of an actor's self-indulgence.

It was dreadfully sad to see such a flowing talent being destroyed, and Bobbie's friends tried hard to stop the rot. He would listen to us with great solemnity and agree with everything we said, and for weeks on end he would keep his promises, but some little bell inside would sooner or later summon him to the bar, and off he'd go again.

The astonishing thing was that though drunk, he could still give great performances, so long as his memory remained unimpaired, but gradually that vital part of the actor's equipment showed signs of stress, and the bush telegraph beat out another set of warnings.

As he became more and more eccentric, assistant directors watched the clock apprehensively every morning to see if he would throw the cameraman into utter disarray by arriving too late to put into the makeup department for urgently needed repairs. During the filming of the Kipling story *Soldiers Three* at MGM he arrived on several occasions just in time for the first shot but still in pajamas.

Throughout the long weeks of shooting on that picture, I dreaded the magic hour of six o'clock because at the close of work Bobbie had accumulated a man-eating thirst, but he hated to drink alone.

"Dear fellow," he would wheedle, "a little light refreshment this evening? . . . A tiny tipple on your way home to the old ball and chain?" I made up a variety of excuses; they were coldly received.

"Getting a little settled in our ways, are we? A little sedentary perhaps? No sense of adventure anymore?"

On the last day of the shooting, Bobbie made it crystal clear that he had no intention of letting me slip away without a "farewell posset."

"I know a little bistro, dear fellow; it's just around the corner—come, let us away."

He shoveled me, protesting, into his car, both of us still wearing the bemedaled khaki drill uniforms, pith helmets, and drooping mustaches of Queen Victoria's army in India.

The car was a 1921 Rolls which he had found in a Burbank junkyard and had renovated at huge expense. The chauffeur in full regalia with the Rolls-Royce cockade on his cap was an ex-stuntman whom Bobbie had befriended when he found him working as a bouncer in a Gardena gambling hall. The "bistro" turned out to be thirty-three miles away in Long Beach. The Rolls had a top speed of about twenty-five miles per hour, and the honest citizens of Southern California blinked in amazement as we rolled sedately through their communities perched up like two visiting generals with the phony chauffeur pinching a big black rubber bulb at the end of a long curling brass horn and coaxing therefrom a mournful upper-class baying.

On arrival at Long Beach, I warned Bobbie for the umpteenth time that I had no money on me.

"My treat, old cock . . . and I'm loaded with the good stuff . . . we'll only stay a few minutes."

We entered Bobbie's "little bistro," and I shuddered. It was a long, dimly lit, evil-smelling bar. There were many customers, some on stools, others playing cards at tables. All were fishermen from the big tuna boats: Russians, Yugoslavs, and Japanese. They looked a little perplexed when they noticed the entrance of two soldiers of the Queen but soon returned to their drinking and playing.

"I knew you'd love it, dear fellow," said my host. "Full of color, don't you think?"

We gave our order to the barman, who prepared it in sulky silence. He was blue-black and would have made Sonny Liston look like a choirboy. The "chauffeur" remained with the car. "Can't have people removing souvenirs from Old Mary, can we?" said Bobbie.

He called for constant refills, and for the first half hour the time passed pleasantly enough, but quite suddenly he interrupted a quiet, sentimental description to me of a hill farm on the Welsh borders to roar at some Yugoslavs the first lines of a lengthy poem by Thomas Lodge:

> Love in my bosome like a bee
>   Doth sucke his sweete:
> Now with his wings he playes with me,
>   Now with his feete. . . !

The Yugoslavs backed away in some alarm, and the barman muttered, "Hey, you—cut that out, willya?"

Bobbie fixed him with a stony eye; then in a conspiratorial aside to me, he delivered a few lines from the Clown in *Antony and Cleopatra:*

Look, you, the worm, is not to be trusted but in the keeping of
wise people; for, indeed, there is no goodness in the worm.

"Wazzat you say, man?" demanded the barman belligerently.

"If you don't like Shakespeare, dear fellow," said Bobbie,
"then I shall give you a taste of Andrew Marvell," and off he
launched into the whole lengthy "Nymph Complaining for
the Death of her Faun":

> The wanton troopers riding by
> Have shot my faun and it will die. . . .

By the time he had finished there was no doubt that Bobbie had lost his audience; he was the recipient of several complicated pieces of advice from the barman and quite a number of Bronx cheers from the tuna boat men. I had a nasty
feeling that things were getting out of hand and said so to
Bobbie. "Let's pay and get the hell out of here."

"On the contrary," said Bobbie firmly, "the greatest joy an
actor can have is to tame a hostile audience and make them
his own. . . . I now propose to do what Laughton has lately
done in a film . . . I shall deliver to this scum the Gettysburg Address."

"Let's deliver everyone a drink first," I pleaded, hoping
thereby to soften the impending blows.

"Good thinking," said Bobbie with enthusiasm, and ordered drinks all around. Then, an incongruous figure in his
creased uniform, he began pacing up and down the bar,
roaring and declaiming, whispering or giving it the full bel-
lows. He went, without a hitch, the whole route from "four-
score and seven years ago" to "that government of the people, by the people, for the people, shall not perish from the
earth."

He did not finish to a standing ovation, it's true, but at least
he came to the end in a respectful hush, a slightly embarrassed hush, perhaps, because by the time he was reveling in
the last rolling sentence, the Russians, the Japanese, and the
Yugoslavs, whether they understood what he was saying or

not, had caught on to the fact that tears were streaming down his face.

"Let's go, Bobbie," I begged.

"Of course, dear fellow . . . do you have any money, dear boy?"

"No," I hissed. "I told you forty times that I haven't."

"Ah!" he said, pressing a forefinger against the side of his nose and rolling his eyes. "We have a tricky situation here."

It was indeed tricky, and the big blue-black barman, with the antennae of his ilk working at full volume, was sidling up the bar in our direction flicking overnonchalantly at the top of it with a dirty napkin.

"Dear boy," said Newton in a ventriloquial whisper between unmoving lips, "nip outside and prepare the getaway car; then call me from the door."

I wandered away, looking vaguely at my watch, and caught a last glimpse of that huge man, arms akimbo, staring straight into Bobbie's face from across the bar. Bobbie was smiling back uneasily.

Outside, the ex-stunt man caught the urgency of the situation and cranked the starting handle. The Rolls stood throbbing like an elderly "wolfhound in the slips," and leaving both doors on the curbside open, I hurried back to the entrance. The tableau had not changed during my absence.

"Bobbie!" I yelled, and keeping a foot in the door, I made ready to flee.

Newton started to back toward me, and I heard him get off his exit line.

"Barman, dear, just put it on my mother's charge account at Sears, Roebuck."

The barman's roars, like those of a wounded stag, we heard for quite a while as we motored peacefully away.

As Bobbie's unreliability increased, so the number of scripts sent to him decreased. This depressed him, and he sought more solace—it was a vicious circle. Living now in Bogart's old house far up on Benedict Canyon, his wife tried loyally and desperately to help him. His friends tried too, but his charm was so great and, when he took only a couple of drinks, his entertainment value was so spectacular that there was always some idiot who would press him to take the fatal third and fourth.

In 1956 before New York's supershowman Mike Todd died when his plane crashed in New Mexico, he realized a long-cherished ambition—he brought to the screen Jules Verne's classic *Around the World in 80 Days*. It was his first and sadly, because Hollywood needed him so badly, his only film. It won the Oscar and became one of the top grossers of all time. A key role was that of Mr. Fix, the detective, and Todd cast Bobbie Newton. Not before some soul-searching, however, because the red-flag warning of Newton's unreliability had been waved, and with Todd's shoestring financial structure, he could ill afford delays in his shooting schedule. He called Newton in and said, "I hear you're a lush."

"An understatement, dear fellow," said Bobbie blithely, and was hired on the spot.

Todd extracted a promise from Newton that he would go on the wagon for the entire four months of his engagement, and Bobbie stuck manfully to his word.

In early autumn on location at Durango, Colorado, Bobbie was in his element. He was a superb fisherman, who "tied" his own flies, and we went fishing every evening after work. With the golden colors of the fall reflected on the mirror surface of the lakes, I saw him bring to gaff countless huge fighting rainbows.

It was becoming cold on those high lakes, so one evening I thoughtlessly put a half bottle of bourbon with my gear. Thoughtlessly, because I had not appreciated how great was Bobbie's struggle to keep away from the stuff.

As I opened it, I caught his eye and quickly slid the bottle back into my tackle bag.

"Dear fellow," said Newton, "that was very kind of you, but please don't worry. First of all, I daren't ask for a little nip because quite apart from having no intention of breaking my word to Todd, my doctor has told me that if I really get at it again, I shall very likely leave the building for good. So please don't feel that I am tempted by the sight of it"—he paused and chuckled—"however, kindly pass me the cork from time to time so I may sniff it. . . . I really do *love* the stuff, dear boy."

Bobbie completed his role in the picture and left the company, looking fitter than I had seen him for a long time. Two weeks later he was called unexpectedly for an added scene. At seven thirty in the morning I was sitting in the makeup room when the passage outside was shaken by a roaring delivery from *King Henry V,* Act IV:

> We few, we happy few, we band of brothers;
> For he to-day that sheds his blood with me
> Shall be my brother. . . .

I was horrified at Bobbie's blotched and puffy face when he lurched into the room.

"Don't chide me, dear fellow," he said. "Please don't chide me." Tears coursed down his cheeks.

Within a very short time Bobbie Newton's doctor's diagnosis was proved tragically correct.

EDDIE

Edmund Goulding was eccentric, but he was also a first-class director. Performers, male and female, loved to work with him because, an actor once himself and unlike Jack Warner, he understood their problems, tiptoed over their egos and, above all, never made light of their built-in insecurities. A highly sensitive man, he was especially sought after by the important actresses and became famous as a "woman's director." He was, however, allergic to this label, and to prove that he was bisexual in his work, at the height of his fame, he took on *Dawn Patrol,* an extremely tough picture with an all-male cast, including Errol Flynn, Basil Rathbone, myself, and other unreliables.

His greatest triumph in the realm of personality handling was *Grand Hotel,* which boasted a potentially explosive cast: first—introverted Garbo, who was genuinely timid with strangers and suffered from acute claustrophobia in public; next—extroverted John Barrymore, who enjoyed nothing so much as blowing apart myths with a whiskey breath and treading heavily on sensibilities; then—Joan Crawford, very entrenched at the studio, very cognizant of her own box-office appeal, and determined to play second fiddle to nobody; and, finally—the ex-female impersonator Wallace Beery whose lovable "aw shucks, ma'am" onscreen personality was in direct contrast with his belligerent, rude, egotistical side which made him easily the most unpopular actor at Metro-Goldwyn-Mayer.

Goulding flattered, badgered, bullied, or cajoled this spiky troup until it was individually and collectively eating out of his hand, and the picture—the biggest of its year—won the Academy Award.

Goulding's wife—the dancer Marjorie Moss—died, and thereafter he lived a rather sad bachelor existence, but he was never without friends, except at the studio, where he had somehow run afoul of studio politics, and for reasons he could never discover, his intangible enemies destroyed him. Irving Thalberg, the head of production, had been his greatest admirer, and Goulding was probably the only person on the lot, L. B. Mayer included, who could walk, unannounced, into the great man's office.

Once he barged in and said, "Irving, I've a brilliant idea for Harlow and Gable!"

"Tell it to me, Eddie," said Thalberg.

When Goulding had finished telling his story and even acting out some of the roles, Thalberg was ecstatic.

"We'll buy it!" he announced, and they settled the terms there and then.

"Let me have a few pages of outline by the end of the week, and we'll decide who to put on the screenplay."

When the end of the week came, Thalberg called and asked for the outline, but Goulding had completely forgotten what his brilliant idea had been. Within a week, however, he retrieved the situation by coming up with another which Thalberg bought.

After Thalberg died, so tragically young, the knives were honed for the outspoken and eccentric Goulding, and he was slowly maneuvered out of his contract and off the lot. He directed spasmodically at other studios, but his heart was at

MGM. The pictures he was given were not up to his old standard, and the trickle of offers finally dried up altogether.

Goulding became deeply depressed, and when he found the depression unbearable, he would seek refuge in the bottle but in a very methodical way. Before he took the first swig, he would call an ex-boxer-chauffeur he knew and tell him for how many days he thought his bender would be therapeutically good for him. Then, secure in the knowledge that he would come to no harm nor, above all, bring harm to others, he would take off.

Goulding died, and his friends were stricken. He was much loved and had passed through the Hollywood jungle dispensing nothing but kindness, thoughtfulness, generosity, and talent with both hands. He had a wild and woolly sense of the ridiculous, and I am convinced that from some private Valhalla he directed his own funeral.

Goulding's sister Ivis called me and said that her brother had left a note saying that he would like me to be one of his pallbearers.

As instructed, I dusted off my dark suit and black tie and drove sorrowfully to a grotesque little slate-roofed church in the middle of several hundred acres of rolling hills which make up Hollywood's much-publicized burial complex, Forest Lawn.

At the door of this gray-stone monstrosity a professionally mournful undertaker's assistant gave me a white carnation, my badge of office, and instructed me to join the other pallbearers already seated in the front pew. The church inside was every bit as grisly and depressing as its name: the Wee Kirk o' the Heather. Seated in it were friends of Goulding, and at the back I noticed several pious-faced members of the very studio hierarchy which had left no stone unturned to ensure that his last years had been so unproductive and frustrating.

As I sat down, I was alarmed at the sight of Goulding's casting of the other pallbearers—alarmed because he had put on quite a lot of weight in his last years, and the people I was now teamed up with were quite evidently not up to the job. My disquiet mounted when I noticed that the open coffin directly in front of us was of the heaviest and thickest black mahogany and its fittings of solid brass. Herbert Marshall was next to me. He had one leg, the other having been blown off during World War I. Next to him was Reginald Gardiner, who had only one serviceable arm; the other had been badly mangled in an appalling headfirst fall down the iron steps of the fire escape outside his apartment down which for some reason best known to himself he had been chasing Hedy Lamarr.

Beyond Gardiner, I spotted the diminutive Al Hall, Mae West's director, who was hardly far enough out of the ground to be sanitary, and the heaviest thing he could lift with any cohesion was a scotch and soda.

Craning forward, I saw beyond Hall a business manager, a man of immense girth with a purple complexion and a concertina of double chins. At the moment in the humidity of that Los Angeles August, he was overflowing out of a tight blue suit, sweating profusely and wheezing loudly.

Just as I registered that we were a potentially unbalanced five in number—four and a half if one remembered Al Hall's specifications—our full complement was made up by the welcome arrival of a gigantic young man of Tarzanesque proportions wearing a light-gray suit and a pink shirt. The raised eyebrows and shaken heads of the original incumbents of the pallbearers' pew betokened the fact that none of us had the faintest idea who he was. Indeed, he seemed to be only a distant friend of the deceased because he leaned forward, peered directly inside the coffin, and said with a loud lisp, "Oh, my *God!* Is that *him* in there? . . . In a goddamn *tux!* How did they put his socks on, for heaven's sake?"

This query caused a certain restlessness among the congregation, but it was instantly stilled by the appearance of the priest, minister, moderator, or high lama of the strange Hollywood cult which professed atheist Goulding had, unbeknownst to his friends, embraced during his last days. This individual appeared before us wearing a sensible business suit beneath a seedy greenish-black gown reminiscent of graduation day. True, the mortarboard was missing, but in its place he sported a wig of flaming red hair. He had eyebrows and a drooping mustache to match.

He stared at us menacingly for a long time. We stared mournfully back. Suddenly, he clapped his hands together. "This is ridiculous," he said sharply. "Come along now. . . . *Perk up!* . . . Why are you all sitting there looking so miserable? . . . Let's see a little smile. . . . Edmund is perfectly happy. . . . What right have you to be so downbeat? . . . Just look at yourselves with all your gloomy faces! Edmund *hates* it!"

We looked at each other uncertainly. He clapped his hands together more loudly. "Perk up," he ordered us. "Everybody *smile!* . . . Let's see those teeth!"

I glanced at the back of the church. The studio brass were sitting there, staring straight ahead with flat, expressionless eyes, but dutifully exposing their expensive, perfectly graded dentures—it looked like a piano shop.

"This guy is *fantastic!*" breathed the young man from Muscle Beach, nudging Al Hall and nearly knocking him off his perch. After a twenty-minute pep talk we dutifully filed with averted eyes past the open coffin and waited outside for matters to be arranged so that we might bear it to the waiting hearse.

In the hot sun, standing before one of the many flaming hibiscus bushes which relieved the gloom of the Wee Kirk o' the Heather, I found myself bathing in the cheerful incandescence of Ginger's red-fringed smile.

"Nice to have you here, Dave," he said. "Hope to see you again, real soon." (An unnerving wish, I thought.)

"I so much enjoyed your talk just now," I said truthfully. "It really did cheer me up. . . . I suppose we all wonder about what happens next, and it's hard to believe that great brains like those of Einstein or Marconi or Sophocles just faded away when their bodies gave up."

"You said it," said Ginger heartily. "It would be such lousy economy, wouldn't it?"

He looked at the back door where a church attendant was nodding conspiratorially.

"It's OK. You boys can fetch Edmund down to the collection bay now."

The motley troop of "boys" returned to the church, and three on each side, we managed to lift our incredibly heavy cargo and struggle with it down the path to the waiting Cadillac hearse. The church attendant followed us and instructed us minutely how to deposit it near the curb at a special angle.

"So's there'll be no slipups this time," he said ominously.

The chauffeur of the hearse pressed a switch on his dashboard, and the glass side rolled back. Then two obscene chromium pincer arms unfolded themselves from the interior and fastened themselves avidly onto each end of the coffin.

The church attendant signaled his satisfaction, another button was pressed, and the coffin in one smooth, silent convulsion was lifted from the ground and rotated slightly so that it fitted perfectly onto a velvet-covered tray which had slithered out from the inside; then, with just a hint of a hydraulic hiss, the whole thing disappeared, and the glass side of the hearse slid back into place.

"Plot seventeen ninety," said the church attendant, briskly nodding down the white road shimmering in the heat, "about three hundred yards. . . . The grave is just over the brow of the hill shaded by those pines and blessed with a beautiful panoramic view of all Hollywood."

The hearse pulled slowly away from the curb, and we stared after it, saying nothing. Bart Marshall broke the silence. "That is one hell of a walk for me," he observed. "Let's get the cars."

"We'll never get Goulding up that hill," said Al Hall. "The thing weighs a ton."

We sorted out our transport problems and arrived at the foot of the pine-covered knoll to find that the coffin had already been electrically ejected from the hearse.

"It's all yours, fellows," said the driver of the hearse, nodding toward the crest and removing his cap and jacket. "This is as far as I go." He winked and waited expectantly for a tip, then drove off rapidly.

"We have to have a little discipline here," said the large unknown in the shocking-pink shirt. "Fall in now, you guys, three on each side—it's gonna be a long haul up there."

Grateful to find we had a leader, we waited a couple of minutes while Bart Marshall made some mysterious adjustments behind the knee of his artificial leg. "Just shifting into 'climb,'" he explained. Then obediently we lined up as directed. The giant young man placed himself in front, followed by Al Hall and Reggie Gardiner on one side, Bart Marshall, the purple business manager, and myself on the other. We grunted and groaned, but finally we hoisted our cargo onto our shoulders and started up the steep incline toward the silhouetted pines. Zigzagging carefully between headstones, we toiled manfully uphill.

The business manager was the first to go. He started quite early on, making the most extraordinary noises—trumpetings and belches in about equal proportions.

"Sorry, fellows, can't make it" he finally spluttered, and producing a large red handkerchief, he staggered out from in front of me and settled himself, fanning and mopping on a grave; his color had changed from purple to sap green.

Although Al Hall, on the other side, with upstretched arms, had so far been making but a token contribution to the fair distribution of the load, trotting beneath the coffin and occasionally making contact with it with his fingertips, he was the next to decide to take time out.

With his black silk suit clinging stickily to his birdlike frame, he treacherously deserted us. "See you on top," he muttered like a mutinous Sherpa, "if I can make it up there." He fell behind.

"Get with it, fellows, *please*," commanded Tarzan. "It's only another twenty yards—we can't let him down now." A strange choice of phrase, I thought as, blinded with sweat, I plodded grimly upward, wondering which would be the next to go: me, with a hangover, Marshall with his leg, or Gardiner with his arm. In any event, about ten yards from the summit, they both went together. Bart's performance had been truly heroic, but he had come to the end of the line. "Sorry, boys, can't go another yard. In fact, I don't think I can even make it down again."

"I'll help you," panted Gardiner, basely grabbing his chance.

"Okay, fellows, let's put it down for a moment," grunted our leader.

Bart and Gardiner collapsed together against a nearby headstone and took off their jackets. Twenty yards away Al Hall was lying facedown in the grass, and far below him, we could see the red dot of the business manager's handkerchief as he rhythmically stirred some movement into the blast furnace air.

"Dave," ordered our leader, "go on up to the top and see what gives."

As I toiled on by myself, I noticed with mounting apprehension that the wind had detached a fair proportion of pine needles from the trees. Brown and dried out, these had formed a carpet which decreased my traction with every step I took toward their parent clump.

Puffing and slipping, I reached the shade of the trees. Twenty yards down the reverse slope below me, I saw the freshly dug grave banked with flowers on the far side and seated on wooden chairs, with their backs luckily toward me, was a small group of relatives. Glancing impatiently at his watch was Ginger. Beside him stood a church attendant, and far below, in the golden heat haze, the whole panoramic view of Hollywood as advertised. The hum of traffic rose.

I returned, skidding on the icelike surface, to find that Marshall and Gardiner had already started down to base camp, but their place had been taken by a refreshed and invigorated Al Hall. I also noticed a smell of spirits when he beat his hands together like a quarterback and said, "OK, you guys, let's go."

I gave Hall a dirty look and made my situation report to Tarzan. He issued commands with commendable clarity.

"We can't get it on our shoulders, so I'll take the top end and you two push at the back. When we get to the top, we'll get those guys from the church to give us a hand."

"It's slippery as hell near the top," I warned.

We struggled upward, and my warning became painfully true: painful for Hall, whose feet suddenly shot away from under him. As he pitched forward, he was all but knocked unconscious when his jaw connected with the top of the coffin.

Gravely unbalanced as a result of this, I pleaded with the leader to rest for a minute and reconsider our strategy.

He was adamant. "We *have* to make it to the top . . . the family's waiting."

"But it's like going up a glacier," I argued. "We should be roped."

"Why don't you two take off your shoes and socks?" mumbled Hall. "You'll be able to grip with your toes."

"That's a disgusting idea," Tarzan said sternly. "Let's go, Dave!"

Sourly I spurned Hall's proffered flask and God alone knew (I choose those words advisedly) how much actual poundage Tarzan and I, with minimal help from Hall, manhandled up those remaining yards, but by the time we reached the top my heart was pounding in my ears, and I was on the point of blacking out.

"We made it!" whispered Tarzan ecstatically. "Try to act unconcerned. Al, you go on down there and speak to the preacher." Hall slithered off on this mission, but luckily he did not get far.

The little group below were unaware of our arrival on the summit above them which was just as well because almost imperceptibly at first the coffin began to slide forward. Transfixed with horror, I had a vision of Goulding in his heavy container happily tobogganing past his own grave, pursued by the remnants of his friends, and with increasing momentum charging down the hill, crossing Hollywood Boulevard and winding up in the bar of the Roosevelt Hotel.

In front the Man from Muscle Beach grabbed wildly at the passing coffin, was caught off-balance, and fell down. Al Hall it was who made up for his past imcompetence and unreliability with a heroic save. He just lay on his back in the path of the oncoming Goulding with his knees bent and the soles of his shoes positioned like buffers at a railway terminal. The impact shunted him several feet and forced a hissed oath from between his clenched teeth, but apart from that, the day was saved in silence and no head was turned in our direction.

A few minutes later, suitably reinforced, we completed a dignified delivery of our much-loved cargo, but I will always remain suspicious of Goulding's casting of his pallbearers.

WINIFRED

Despite the fact that she was permanently teetering on the verge of bankruptcy, Clemence Dane, known to her friends as Winifred, was the richest human being I have ever known.

The normal dread that we mortals harbored—that we would not be able to earn enough to fill our stomachs, to care for our dependents, or to pay for any prescribed drugs we might need—never entered into Winifred's head. If her bills remained unopened, so did the check she earned remain uncashed; she did not regard money as filthy lucre—she just did not have the faintest idea what it was.

I was in a temporary state of financial shock when I met Winifred. I had decided one December evening in the late fifties to take a long walk in the hills behind my heavily mortgaged house, hoping, if not to find a seam of gold where the fire roads had been ruthlessly gouged out of the beautiful lonely landscape, at least to arrive at a possible solution to my problem.

It was bitterly cold, and there was an unheard-of sprinkling of snow on the tips of the surrounding Santa Monica Mountains.

"Sssh!" whispered a voice.

So engrossed had I been in my thoughts that I had failed to notice in the gathering dusk a very large lady in a bush by the roadside, with a finger to her lips.

"Come and help me," she ordered in a calm but authoritative voice. "The poor little darling is so cold it can't fly, and I can't quite reach it."

The large lady was spread-eagled in the branches of a scrub oak, in imminent danger of snapping the branches of that notoriously treacherous growth and cartwheeling to her death several hundred feet below on the canyon floor.

Whatever "it" was became of secondary importance to extricating the large lady from her position of heart-stopping danger. It was a difficult operation because she weighed in the neighborhood of 220 pounds and, despite the extreme cold, was firmly impaled upon the thorny branches in a voluminous garment of black chiffon. She had a lineless face of great beauty and infinite sweetness and was at least seventy years old.

"It's a hummingbird," she explained.

At grave personal risk I managed to extricate the large lady, and then, because she was watching me with eyes filled to the brim with trust and confidence, with lunatic bravery I rescued the semicongealed hummingbird from its perch above the horrifying drop.

"How kind of you," said Winifred. "The little darling has a tummy of cadmium yellow."

We wandered back down the fire road together, she with the tiny honey-eating creature fluttering in her cupped hands as it thawed out and I, like Hernando Cortez when he first set worshipful eyes on Doña Marina, forgetting all my petty problems and impending disasters.

Winifred, a top-class sculptor and painter, was also the author of half a hundred plays, novels, and books of short stories. Hollywood had wooed her, and she had lately arrived with considerable fanfare to work on a screenplay.

Her studio, once the red carpet had been rolled back into mothballs, had allocated her to a small cell in the writers' building, and the producer designate had tried to make her feel at home with an antique Hollywood joke. "Miss Dane," he said, "we need this script in a hurry, so those pencils on your desk I expect to see half as long by tonight. HA! HA! HA!"

If Winifred had been amused, she had given no sign, but she had immediately relinquished her apartment in the Beverly Hills Hotel and moved into a two-room cottage in the trees on the canyonside below my house which had no telephone. The cottage, the property of my neighbor Douglas Fairbanks, Jr., was accessible only by a flight of sixty almost perpendicular wooden steps, hazardous for a mountaineer, but no problem apparently for an old lady with arthritis of the hip, and further protection against interference by her producer designate. Its small front porch was the rallying point for the local rattlesnakes . . . Winifred slept on the porch.

My family adored Winifred, and the children became the recipients of a constant stream of handmade presents. Hjördis and I were introduced to painting by Winifred, and after turning out a steady flow of canvases that looked like the bottom of Lake Erie, we were persuaded by her to convert our living room into a studio.

My wife, a lady of spectacular beauty, became Winifred's favorite model. She also became resigned to the gradual change that overtook her carefully chosen color scheme in the living room thanks to Winifred's habit of catching the sleeves of her flowing garments on the corners of still-wet canvases, sweeping bottles of linseed oil onto the sofa, and sitting heavily on capless tubes of Yellow Ocher and Venetian Red; gray modeling clay was also trodden into the carpet.

One morning I was awakened by a jangling telephone.

"I *have* to paint the sunrise over the mountains," announced Winifred. "Will you be a darling and pick me up at the top of the steps in five minutes and take me up into the hills?"

I did as I was asked because, for some strange reason, however eccentric, one always acceded to Winifred's requests. She was waiting for me at the top of the steps wearing a nightgown overlaid by a Japanese kimono; her still-brown hair, usually worn in a bun, reached to her waist. In one hand was a large wicker basket full of paints and bottles, and in the other, a collapsible easel.

We drove up a winding road in the virgin hills, and as the first silver streaks were appearing in the sky, Winifred indicated her spot. On foot we toiled up a deer track, and at long last she pointed imperiously to a flat, relatively scrub-free space on top of a knoll.

"That will do nicely," she said.

I fixed up her easel and prepared to take my leave.

"What time would you like the car, madame?" I asked facetiously.

"About eleven," she replied, squeezing enormous dollops of paint onto her palette, "and would you be a darling—I badly need a roll of lavatory paper . . . for the brushes," she added, banishing a bizarre spectacle from my imagination.

I was back in about half an hour with her request and

found her utterly engrossed, standing like the figurehead of an ancient sailing ship and attacking her canvas with bold slashes of color. Winifred's pictures were as magnificent as herself and as full of vitality, but her friends had learned forcibly to take her canvases away from her after her first instinctive onslaught because she invariably ruined them later by fiddling.

"Be a darling," she said through a mouthful of brushes, "pop up here a little later on with a thermos of tea and a packet of biscuits."

"Watch out for the rattlers," I said as I turned to go. "The hills are full of them."

"Oh, the little dears," she said, "they won't hurt me—they're my friends."

I made several trips during the morning, keeping Winifred topped up with tea, biscuits, turpentine, and Titanium White, and by midday her large canvas was finished—a glorious impression of the first rays had been preserved with the distant snows of Mount Baldy touched with pure gold and the awakening foreground kept in perfect balance. The colors on the canvas were subtler than those on Winifred herself. As the sun had risen, she had realized the need to protect her head. Making a nest of lavatory paper on the ground, she had tipped into it the paints from her large wicker basket and placed the basket on her head. The hot rays of the sun had melted the residue of paint at the bottom of it, and Winifred looked, when I came to take her home, like an Apache brave. Hair, face, kimono, and nightdress were caked and streaked with Vermilion, Cobalt Blue, Rose Madder, Ivory Black.

"Be a darling," she said, completely unconscious of this blaze of color, "take me home now—I really *must* wash my hands and do some work on that script. They *keep* sending messengers for it."

During her months as our neighbor, Winifred ruined our living room for genealogical time, but she also painted some beautiful pictures and completed some remarkable sculptures. She found time to write many children's stories for my offspring and gave endless pleasure to the rest of us with her outpourings of wit and wisdom, but there is no record with the Screen Writers Guild of her having completed a screen-play.

She left quite suddenly because she missed an immensely crusty mongrel named Ben and a cluttered flat in the middle of London's Covent Garden vegetable market. Soon after she returned there, the market was largely destroyed by fire. The residents evacuated in a hurry, all except Winifred, who stayed to paint the conflagration from her bedroom window. When firemen finally came to force her to leave, they found her rummaging around, looking for a two-gallon can of highly inflammable turpentine.

Her next residence was in a field in the midst of beautiful Sussex woodland. As a grudging concession to her arthritic hip she had allowed the locals to replace its steps with a wooden ramp, and there, writing, sculpting, and painting, surrounded by the birds and little animals from the woods, by her priceless collection of Meissen, Dresden, and Nymphenburg porcelain, and, above all, by her friends, she spent her days—in a gaily painted gypsy caravan. Winifred was not a Hollywood type.

THE ELEVENTH COMMANDMENT (THOU SHALT NOT BE FOUND OUT)

Some people liked L. B. Mayer, many were fond of Samuel Goldwyn, everyone loved Fred Astaire, Tyrone Power, and Clark Gable, but hardly any were devoted to their agents. Actors, writers, and directors all had contracts with them, and all, with varying degrees of resentment, paid them 10 percent of everything they earned.

At the beginning of a career it was virtually impossible to get started—to graduate from the extra ranks, for example—without an agent, because he knew about the pictures that were being planned, and if he was a high-class agent, he had contacts among those who were doing the planning. The giant step was, of course, the first good job, but if that job led to a coveted seven-year contract, the agent who had found it became a financial albatross around the neck and was entitled to 10 percent of the client's earnings for the next seven years without the obligation even to send him a card at Christmastime. The spectrum of agents went from the cheap little flesh peddlers, confident that they had a proprietary right to play grab-ass with their clients among the bit players and dancers, to the big wheels in their receptionist-controlled and beautifully furnished offices, who could walk unannounced into the sanctums of the moguls and there play power politics because of the demand they had generated for their high-priced stable of stars. In between these two extremes was a variety of agents, most of whom worked hard to find and develop talent, but who became resigned to seeing ambitious clients drifting away from them to join the stables of the big wheels with the possibility of a power-assisted boost up the ladder.

Big wheels such as Myron Selznick, Leland Hayward, Harry Eddington, Charlie Feldman, Lew Wasserman, and Bert Allenberg represented the Holy Grail for actors whose principles were apt to melt like butter on a hot stove when the chance of being represented by one of these men presented itself. A particularly unattractive example of this was the behavior of an actor I knew very well. This man was under contract to an excellent, hardworking, clear-thinking, honest, middle-of-the spectrum agent named Phil Gersh. Gersh had been very successful with this actor, and under his guiding hand his client's career had prospered exceedingly. They had been together for some years, and although their contract had only a few more weeks to run, it would be renewed: Neither had any intention of dissolving the association; also, the men had become good friends. The actor, however, like most of his profession, was susceptible to flattery and made uneasy by suggestions that his progress up the ladder could be accelerated by a new approach.

One night, in a house on the crest of Mulholland Drive, with the whole of Los Angeles twinkling like a million stars on one side and with the San Fernando Valley glowing like the Milky Way on the other, the actor was listening with rapt attention to the siren words of one of the big wheels—Bert Allenberg.

Tall, good-looking, charming Bert Allenberg personally guided the fortunes of half a dozen of the biggest stars in Hollywood, and to be one of his handpicked clients was the dream of every actor, the underwriting of a career.

"I'd like to handle you," Allenberg was saying. "I've a whole lot of ideas for you. . . . What d'you say?" The actor took a deep breath; he had visions of being catapulted over the heads of his contemporaries and into the very forefront of the Hollywood galaxy. He thought about the offer all evening and carefully weighed his ambition and greed against his integrity.

"I'll talk to Phil Gersh tomorrow and tell him I'm leaving him," he said to Allenberg as he was saying good-night, and was surprised at how easy it must have been for Judas Iscariot.

The actor liked Phil Gersh very much and wished him no harm, but he was dazzled by the golden gates swinging on their hinges before him. The confrontation between the actor and Phil Gersh was unpleasant for both. The agent listened in amazement as the actor explained that he would not be renewing his contract.

"But why?" asked Gersh.

"Of course, it's nothing personal," said the actor. "It's just that . . . I feel like, er, changing my butcher," he finished lamely. The agent rose to leave.

"You were the first actor I had ever *really* liked . . . ever *really* trusted," he said quietly. "Now I know you are just the same as all the rest. . . . I'll stick with writers and directors from here on in. . . . I'll never handle another."

In his comfortable leather-bound office, Bert Allenberg lolled back in an armchair and listened as the actor recounted the scene. "Gersh'll get over it," he said flatly. Then he broke out the champagne and outlined his plans for the future. "I'm meeting with Darryl and L.B. tomorrow," he said. "I'll have big news for you by Wednesday. Call me first thing in the morning."

The actor slept little on Tuesday, and on Wednesday

morning, in a high state of expectancy, he called his new agent's office. The secretary's voice was muffled. "Mr. Allenberg died last night," she sobbed.

The name of the actor can be found on the next page.

David Niven